Robert Jay Dilger, Editor
University of Redlands

AMERICAN INTERGOVERNMENTAL RELATIONS TODAY

perspectives and controversies

Prentice-Hall, Inc., Englewood Cliffs, NJ 07632

Library of Congress Cataloging in Publication Data
Main entry under title: ·

American intergovernmental relations.

Includes index.
1. Federal government—United States—Addreses,
essays, lectures. I. Dilger, Robert Jay (date)
JK325.A658   1986   321.02'3'0973   85-9332
ISBN 0-13-027624-3

Editorial/production supervision ana
interior design: Shirley Stern
Cover design: Wanda Lubelska
Manufacturing buyer: Barbara Kittle

To Gloria and Anne

Printed in the United States of America

10 9 8 7 6 5 4 3 2 1

ISBN 0-13-027624-3 01

PRENTICE-HALL INTERNATIONAL (UK) LIMITED, *London*
PRENTICE-HALL OF AUSTRALIA PTY. LIMITED, *Sydney*
EDITORA PRENTICE-HALL DO BRASIL, LTDA., *Rio de Janeiro*
PRENTICE-HALL CANADA INC., *Toronto*
PRENTICE-HALL OF INDIA PRIVATE LIMITED, *New Delhi*
PRENTICE-HALL OF JAPAN, INC. *Tokyo*
PRENTICE-HALL OF SOUTHEAST ASIA PTE. LTD., *Singapore*
WHITEHALL BOOKS LIMITED, *Wellington, New Zealand*

CONTENTS

2 The United States Supreme Court and Intergovernmental Relations   by Cynthia Cates Colella **30**

CONTRIBUTORS

Thomas J. Anton is a Professor of Political Science and the Director of the A. Alfred Taubman Center for Public Policy and American Institutions at Brown University. He is the former editor of *Policy Sciences* and is a current editorial board member of *Policy Studies Journal* and *Publius*. His recent books include *Moving Money: An Empirical Analysis of Federal Expenditure Patterns* and *Federal Aid to Detroit*.

David R. Beam is Director of Research for the Naisbitt Group. A former Senior Research Analyst at the U.S. Advisory Commission on Intergovernmental Relations, he has contributed to several major ACIR studies of federal grant and regulatory policies affecting state and local governments, including *Reducing Unemployment: Intergovernmental Dimensions of a National Problem*. He also directed and was a principle author of *Regulatory Federalism: Policy, Process, Impact, and Reform*.

Cynthia Cates Colella is a Senior Research Analyst at the U.S. Advisory Commission on Intergovernmental Relations. She has written extensively on the courts' role in defining intergovernmental relations and has contributed to several major ACIR studies, including *Jails: Intergovernmental Dimensions of a Local Problem, Protecting the Environment: Politics, Pollution, and Federal Policy* and *Public Assistance: The Growth of a Federal Function*.

Timothy J. Conlan is a Senior Research Analyst at the U.S. Advisory Commission on Intergovernmental Relations. He has written widely on the politics of federal aid and intergovernmental regulatory programs. He has contributed to several major ACIR studies, including *The Condition of Contemporary Federalism: Conflicting Theories and Collapsing Constraints* and *The Evolution of a Problematic Partnership: The Feds and Higher Ed*. He also directed and was a principle author of *Transformations in American Politics and Their Implications for Federalism*.

Robert J. Dilger is an Associate Professor of Political Science at the University of Redlands. He has served as a Lincoln Government Fellow at the National League of Cities and as a Research Fellow at the U.S. Advisory Commission on Intergovernmental Relations and the Brookings Institution. He is the author of *The Sunbelt/Snowbelt Controversy: The War Over Federal Funds*.

Daniel J. Elazar is Director of the Center for the Study of Federalism at Temple University, chairman of the International Association of Centers for Federal Studies, and editor of *Publius*. He is president of the Jerusalem Center for Public Affairs, and Senator N. M. Paterson Professor of Intergovernmental Relations at Bar Ilan University. He has written many articles and several books on intergovernmental relations, including *American Federalism: A View from the States, Cities of the Prairie: The Metropolitan Frontier and American Politics,* and *The American Partnership*. He is a recipient of the Donald C. Stone Award for "distinguished contributions to research and scholarship in intergovernmental relations".

Robert B. Lucke is a Research Analyst in the Tax Analysis Division at the Congressional Budget Office. He has also served as a Research Analyst at the U.S. Advisory Commission on Intergovernmental Relations. His research has focused on intergovernmental fiscal policy.

Ronald W. Reagan is President of United States and former Governor of the State of California.

Mavis Mann Reeves is an Associate Professor of Political Science at the University of Maryland. She has authored or co-authored numerous books and articles on intergovernmental relations and state and local government, including *Pragmatic Federalism* and *Controversies of State and Local Political Systems*. She is a recipient of the Donald C. Stone Award for "distinguished contributions to research and scholarship in intergovernmental relations."

Albert J. Richter is a Senior Research Analyst at the U.S. Advisory Commission on Intergovernmental Relations. He has also served as the Associate Commissioner for Policy, Medical Services Administration (Medicaid) in the U.S. Department of Health, Education, and Welfare and as the Research Director for the Citizens League in Minneapolis, Minnesota. He has contributed to several major ACIR studies, including *State and Local Roles in the Federal System*.

Lester M. Salamon is Director of the Center for Governance and Management Research at the Urban Institute. He has also been a Deputy Associate Director of the U.S. Office of Management and Budget and an Associate Professor of Political Science at Duke University. He has authored numerous books and articles concerning policy formation and implementation, including *The Illusion of Presidential Government* and *The Federal Government and the Nonprofit Sector*.

Frank Shafroth is Director of the Office of Federal Relations at the National League of Cities. His research has focused primarily on national tax and budgetary decisions and their implications for cities.

John Shannon is Executive Director of the U.S. Advisory Commission on Intergovernmental Relations and was an Assistant Director of the U.S. Advisory Commission on Intergovernmental Relations, heading the Taxation and Public Finance section of the Commission's staff. He has written numerous articles concerning intergovernmental fiscal relations and has directed and written many major ACIR studies, including *Significant Features of Fiscal Federalism*.

David B. Walker is a Professor of Political Science in the Public Affairs program at the University of Connecticut. He has served as an Assistant Director of the U.S. Advisory Commission on Intergovernmental Relations, heading the Structures and Functions section of the Commission's staff, and as Staff Director of the U.S. Senate Subcommittee on Intergovernmental Relations. He has written numerous books and articles on intergovernmental relations, including *Toward a Functioning Federalism*. He has also directed and written many major ACIR studies. He is a recipient of the Donald C. Stone Award for "distinguished contributions to research and scholarship in intergovernmental relations."

PREFACE

This book's objective is to provide a broad and general understanding of the structure, function, and operation of contemporary American intergovernmental relations, its historical development, and the politically and ideologically charged controversies that surround it. To accomplish this, seventeen essays were selected, each examining a specific aspect of intergovernmental relations. The selections are organized into four parts: *National Institutions in Intergovernmental Relations, State and Local Institutions in Intergovernmental Relations, Federalism in the 1980s*, and *Implementation Problems and the Future of Intergovernmental Relations*. Each part begins with a brief introduction to the topics examined and indicates the major points raised in each of the selections.

Thirteen of the seventeen selections were either published or accepted for publication when they were chosen for inclusion in this collection. Four selections were written exclusively for it. All seventeen are written in clear, concise language and reflect the latest research approach.

In the past, the dominant research approach used by political scientists to study intergovernmental relations emphasized the legal or constitutional relationship between the national and state governments. Courses utilizing this approach were usually titled *American Federalism* and had as their two central objectives the examination of the changing legal configuration of American governance throughout history and the various normative positions taken concerning which governmental level ought to perform what governmental activity. In examining these issues, students were often asked to study the relative advantages and disadvantages of the unitary and federal governmental systems by reading the works of democratic political theorists such as Charles Montesquieu and Alexis Tocqueville. They were also required to examine various American political documents, including the Articles of Confederation and Perpetual Union, the Framers' debates at the Philadelphia Convention of 1787, the *Federalist Papers*, and the actual wording of the United States Constitution, to determine if the Constitution was a compact among the states (the states' rights theory) or a compact among the people (allowing the Supreme Court to determine the extent of national governmental power). Students were then asked, among other things, to examine the Supreme Court's decisions concerning national/state relationships and to determine which governmental level they felt ought to have greater responsibility for policymaking based upon their interpretation of constitutional agreements and their knowledge of democratic political theory.

The question of which governmental level ought to perform what function is still central to the study of intergovernmental relations. President Nixon's and Reagan's efforts to rearrange governmental responsibilities are given ample attention in this collection. The relatively recent growth of governmental responsibilities at all governmental levels and the enhanced national role in financing, setting administrative guidelines, and defining programmatic goals for many programs administered by state and local governments, however, has altered the focus of many intergovernmental scholars. Instead of titling their courses *American Federalism* and concentrating on the normative question of who ought to be doing what, they title their courses *Integovernmental Relations* and focus their attention on evaluating and comparing governmental performance at all levels. With this new focus, intergovernmental scholars are now emphasizing empirical as opposed to philosophical or ideological arguments and, as Deil Wright has indicated, tend to examine ongoing political as well as legal relationships between governmental units and their representatives.[1] This collection reflects this new research approach.

Although this book has been put together with the needs of an undergraduate audience in mind, it can be used as a supplementary text at the graduate level. In addition, intergovernmental scholars will find the selections a rich and useful source of information for their own research efforts and public officials, both elected and nonelected, will find them an invaluable resource for understanding how they fit into the overall governmental system.

I would like to thank David Beam, Cynthia Cates Colella, Timothy Conlan, Mavis Mann Reeves, Albert Richter, and David Walker for making valuable suggestions concerning the book's organization and selection of materials.

I would also like to thank Timothy Conlan for reading and commenting on a draft of "The Expansion and Centralization of American Governmental Functions;" Walter Dean Burnhan, Ballard Campbell, Timothy Conlan, William Riker, and David Walker for reading and commenting on a draft of "American Political Parties and Intergovernmental Relations: An Historical Perspective;" Cynthia Cates Colella and John Shannon for volunteering to update and revise their selections; and Christopher Leman for introducing me to intergovernmental relations while I was in graduate school. Many thanks to the thoughtful reviewers, Dr. Richard D. Willis, University of Iowa; Dr. Peter Bergerson, Southeast Missouri State University; and Professor Richard Chackerian, Florida State University, who lent their time and perceptions to this edition. Finally, I would like to thank Gloria Dilger for reading and commenting on various stages of this project and for her continuing understanding and support.

---

[1] Deil Wright, *Understanding Intergovernmental Relations*, 2nd. ed. (Monterey, CA: Brooks/Cole Publishing Company, 1982), pp. 26–29.

INTRODUCTION

Intergovernmental relations encompasses all the relationships that exist between and among all the various governmental units in a given polity. In the United States, intergovernmental relations refers to the relationships between and among the 82,341 governmental units currently in existence. There are fifty state governments and one national government. There are also 3,041 county governments, 19,076 municipal governments, 16,734 townships, 14,851 school districts, and 28,588 special districts (created for flood control, fire protection, library systems, etc.).[1]

Intergovernmental relations also encompasses the relationships between and among the representatives of these 82,341 governmental units. There are approximately 2.7 million civilian employees of the national government, 3.1 million state government employees, and 7.7 million local government employees.[2] Of course, not all of these public employees have an equal role in governing the nation, but you can readily see that whenever 82,341 governmental units, all in the business of providing program services to the public and staffed by

[1]U.S. Bureau of the Census, *Governmental Organizations*, Vol. I (Washington, DC: U.S. Government Printing Office; 1983), p. vi.

[2]Advisory Commission on Intergovernmental Relations, *Significant Features of Fiscal Federalism*, 1982–83 Edition (Washington, DC: U.S. Government Printing Office, 1984), p. 127.

over 13 million employees, operate under a federal relationship, there are bound to be conflicts and problems of program coordination. Under a unitary system of governance the national or central government holds the supreme power and delegates authority to constituent governments as it sees fit. If a conflict between governmental units arise under such a system, the national government can recall, or threaten to recall, the constituent government's delegated authority and resolve the intergovernmental conflict to its satisfaction. Under a federal system, powers are specifically divided among the national and constituent governments, giving substantial functions to each. If a conflict arises between the national and constituent governments within a federal system, the national government cannot recall the constituent government's authority because that authority has been guaranteed in a previously negotiated legal document. Intergovernmental conflicts in federal systems, therefore, are resolved by the country's courts, negotiated agreements between the governmental units involved, and, in rare instances, by civil war.

The binding legal document that defines the powers and responsibilities of the various governmental units in the United States is the *United States Constitution*. According to James Madison, the *Constitution* created a system of government in the United States that was neither wholly federal nor wholly unitary, but a blend of both. The national government was empowered by the *Supremacy Clause* to take certain actions that superseded states' rights, but it was understood that these actions were limited to the seventeen enumerated powers in Article 1, Section 8, of the Constitution. These powers included, among others, the power to declare war, to run the postal system, to coin money, and to support an army and navy. The eighteenth, and last, enumerated power in Article 1, Section 8, however, opened up the possibility of greater national responsibilities in governance by declaring in rather broad and imprecise language, subject to differing interpretations, that the national government could adopt laws "necessary and proper for carrying into execution the foregoing powers."

Fearing an expansion of national governmental power, the states strengthened their legal position in 1791 by ratifying the Tenth Amendment to the Constitution. It specifically reserved to the states all powers not delegated to the national government. At the time, many believed that the Tenth Amendment guaranteed public policy would be dominated by the states in perpetuity. It soon became obvious, however, that the national government could not conduct its assigned governmental responsibilities without interfering with state prerogatives. Because neither the national nor the state governments could recall or cancel the other's legal authority, they either negotiated an agreement or appealed to the Supreme Court to settle the intergovernmental conflict. Over the years, the Supreme Court has arbitrated hundreds of intergovernmental disputes. Until the New Deal period, the Court usually sided with the states on most of these issues. Since the New Deal period, it has reversed many of its earlier rulings on these issues and has allowed the national government to expand its role in governing the nation.

As you are probably aware, national policymakers' ideas concerning the best course of action on a number of issues are often significantly different than many state and local policymakers' ideas. These differences of opinion sometimes lead to fascinating and dramatic clashes between national, state, and local policymakers. Intergovernmental issues include such explosive topics as racial segregation of schools and the means to address that segregation, affirmative action, environmental standards, and welfare policy. Other less dramatic, but equally important, intergovernmental issues include health, education, labor, and transportation policy.

Even when national, state, and local governmental units and officials reach agreement on such programmatic goals as caring for the elderly and the poor, or rebuilding our cities and infrastructure (dams, roads, bridges, sewers, etc.), they often disagree on the best means of achieving these goals. This book is designed to show you how policymakers attempt to resolve these disagreements within our federal system of governance.

The first five readings offered in Part 1, *National Institutions in Inter-governmental Relations*, provide an indepth understanding of the legal and political developments that have served to define national policymakers' contemporary role in intergovernmental relations. Reading 1, "The Expansion and Centralization of American Governmental Responsibilities," examines the historical development of the national government's now-dominant role in domestic policymaking. The national government currently spends approximately $100 billion a year on over 400 intergovernmental programs. It also sets demanding administrative guidelines and specific eligibility criteria for many of them. In addition, it provides states and localities with over $39 billion in tax credits by exempting state and local taxes and securities from national taxation.[3]

Given the enhanced national role in determining domestic program objectives and administrative procedures, four readings are offered that examine in depth each of the four major national institutions that individually and collectively define the national government's role in intergovernmental relations: the United States Supreme Court, the United States Congress, the presidency, and the political party system.

The first five readings will provide a very good understanding of how the national government operates within the intergovernmental system. Under our federal system, however, states and localities also play an important role in financing, running, and defining domestic public policies. Part 2, *State and*

---

[3]U.S. Office of Management and Budget, *Special Analyses: Budget of the United States Government, FY 1985* (Washington, DC: U.S. Government Printing Office, 1984), pp. H-11, H-12. At the time of this writing, proposals to eliminate the deductibility of state and local taxes and the exemption of interest on state and local bonds in exchange for lower federal marginal tax rates were being given serious consideration by Congress.

Local Institutions in Intergovernmental Relations, is designed to indicate the states' and localities' unique contribution to American goverance. The three readings in Part 2 were chosen in response to the recent rise of national governmental powers and the ongoing debate over which governmental level can do a better job in delivering program services to the public. These readings examine, respectively, recent efforts by many states to modernize their state constitutions so that they are better able to effectively manage a greater share of governmental responsiblities, the structure of local governmental units and their contemporary role in governance, and some of the fiscal pressures faced by states and localities as they try to assume a greater share of governmental responsiblities.

Despite recent improvements in state constitutions, the enhanced professional reputations of state and local administrators, the decline of overt racism in many states, the growing dissatisfaction with the performance of the national government in delivering program services, and President Reagan's efforts to reduce the national government's role in domestic policymaking, there has been only a marginal shift in governmental responsibilities towards the states and localities in recent years. The three readings in Part 3, *Federalism in the 1980s*, examine President Reagan's efforts to reduce national governmental responsibilities and the many political and fiscal obstacles that stand in any president's way who wants to decentralize the intergovernmental system.

By the time you have completed Parts 1, 2, and 3, you will have acquired an acute understanding of how the American intergovernmental system has evolved; of the relative position, priorities, and concerns of national, state, and local governments and their representatives in that system, and of how these differences have been resolved on a systematic level. The five readings in Part 4, *Implementation Problems and the Future of Intergovernmental Relations*, indicate some of the operational difficulties faced by governmental officials in our federal system, or, as a subtitle of one of the leading books on implementation issues put it, "why it's amazing that federal programs work at all."[4]

The five readings in Part 4 reveal that even before state and local governments receive their allocation of a particular program's funds, national political considerations—as well as objective, programmatic needs—have affected the determination as to which constituent governments will receive any funds and what share of the funds each of the chosen governments will receive. After the program's funds arrive at the state or local level, a host of nationally imposed regulations—from environmental impact statements to health and safety standards—slow down and complicate the implementation process, even in those programs supposedly freed from excessive national requirements. Moreover, as Lester Salamon indicates, the national government has increasingly turned to third parties—state and local governments, private companies, and nonprofit

---

[4]Jeffrey L. Pressman and Aaron Wildavsky, *Implementation* 2d ed. (Berkeley, CA: University of California Press, 1979).

groups—to administer many of their programs. While third party administration may help the national government adapt programs to specific state and local needs, it also reduces the national government's ability to coordinate programs across policy areas, to conduct effective oversight, or to assure any significant degree of accountability.

The book concludes with two opposing views of the contemporary intergovernmental system and its future. Thomas Anton argues that the recent rise in national power has not really altered the fundamental concept of federalism and there is no reason to radically restructure contemporary intergovernmental relationships. Daniel Elazar disagrees. He argues that we are no longer a "true" federal system and that we must strengthen state and local roles in governance. He is convinced that, if we continue on our current path, we will lose our sense of community and, perhaps, our political freedom as well.

part one

NATIONAL INSTITUTIONS IN INTERGOVERNMENTAL RELATIONS

The national government has become the dominant governmental entity in the American federal system. It plays a central role in financing, defining programmatic standards, and setting administrative guidelines for many domestic programs. It contributes directly to many program services by providing grants-in-aid, loans, and certain tax incentives to state and local governments and by regulating some activities and not others. It also contributes indirectly through its policies affecting the national economy.

The national government currently spends approximately $100 billion on over 400 grants-in-aid programs. These programs are used by states and localities to alleviate problems caused by natural disasters or other emergencies; to upgrade conditions of the poor and elderly by supplementing their incomes through such programs as *Medicaid* (approximately $21 billion to medically needy persons over age 65, blind, disabled, or members of families with dependent children), *Aid to Families With Dependent Children* (approximately $7 billion to assist eligible needy families with dependent children to meet the cost of the necessities of life), and *Lower Income Housing Assistance* (approximately $6 billion to assist eligible renters pay their rents); and to stimulate economic development by subsidizing selected governmental services through such programs as *Highway Planning and Construction* (approximately $14 billion for building and rehabilitating the Interstate Highway system, primary and secondary roadways, and bridges) and *Community Development Block Grants* ($3.5 billion to upgrade housing and economic opportunities within urban areas).

One of the biggest controversies in intergovernmental relations is over which of the three types of grants-in-aid programs—categorical grants, block grants, or general revenue sharing—is best. These grants are differentiated in three ways:

1. the range of national bureaucrats' funding discretion,
2. the range of discretion exercised by recipients over aided activities, and
3. the type, number, detail, and scope of nationally imposed administrative conditions.[1]

Of the three grant types, categorical grants provide national bureaucrats with the greatest control over who gets funded, the least recipient choice in program service, and the greatest number of nationally imposed administrative conditions, otherwise known as "red tape." Block grants provide national bureaucrats little funding discretion, a middle range of recipient choice concerning program services, and a middle range of nationally imposed administrative conditions. General revenue sharing also denies national bureaucrats funding discretion, but offers recipients a maximum amount of choice concerning program activities and the least number of nationally imposed administrative conditions.

There are four types of categorical grants: project, formula, formula/project, and open-ended reimbursement. All four can only be used for the single program activity that has been predetermined by the national government. For example, if a categorical grant specifies that its funds are to be used for airport construction, the recipient cannot use the funds to build tennis courts.

Project categorical grants are the most used grant mechanism. States and localities receive project grant funding only after applying to the national bureaucracy that administers the program. Funds are then allocated among those states and localities on a competitive basis according to criteria specified by Congress and the discretion of national bureaucrats. Formula categorical grants are automatically distributed to eligible states and localities according to a formula that has been predetermined by national policymakers. The most common criteria used in these formulas are population and per capita income. As you can readily see, formula categorical grants tend to disperse program funding to a large number of recipients while project categorical grants can be targeted to selected recipients. Formula/project categorical grants are allocated among recipient governments according to factors specified by national policymakers. Usually, a formula allocates program funding among the states and territories and then local governments apply to their state's appropriate bureaucracy for funding. Finally, open-

---

[1] Advisory Commission on Intergovernmental Relations, *Categorical Grants: Their Role and Design* (Washington, DC: U.S. Government Printing Office, 1978), pp. 5–9.

ended reimbursement categorical grants reimburse, usually on a percentage basis, states and localities for undertaking certain predetermined activities. Although there are only a few open-ended reimbursement categorical grants, two are very large and have a significant impact on American society: *Aid to Families With Dependent Children* and *Medicaid*.

Block grants are allocated by formula (though some block grants allow national bureaucrats to allocate a small percentage of the program's funds) and provide recipient governments a specified number of functionally related choices for program use. *Community Development Block Grants*, for example, can be used for a number of activities, including urban renewal, model cities, open space, urban beautification, historic site preservation, neighborhood facilities, water and sewer facilities, and economic development projects.

General revenue sharing funds are also allocated among the states, territories, and localities according to a predetermined formula. These funds, however, can be used for whatever purpose the recipients choose, subject only to national laws concerning discrimination, environmental standards, and the like.

As you might suspect, conservatives and state and local elected officials tend to prefer the more flexible block grant and general revenue sharing approaches while liberals, who worry that governors and mayors may allocate the funds to groups or for purposes they do not like, and national bureaucrats prefer the more restrictive categorical grant approach.

The national government also subsidizes state and local governments by excluding state and local taxes and securities, such as industrial development bonds, from national taxation. These tax subsidies are estimated to cost the national government nearly $40 billion in lost revenues every year.[2] In addition, the national government provides states and localities with nearly $1 billion in new guaranteed loans every year. These loans are used to finance housing construction and rehabilitation, land and water resource development, and educational loans. Total outstanding national loans to state and local governments will exceed $26 billion in 1985.[3]

The following five readings provide a good understanding of the national government's contemporary role in the intergovernmental system. The first reading focuses on the growth of national responsibilities and the mechanisms the national government employs to expand its powers. In addition, it examines the key historical events that have shaped the American intergovernmental system.

Readings 2 through 5 examine in great detail the intergovernmental role played by the national government's four major institutions: the United States Supreme Court, the United States Congress, the presidency, and the political party system. Each of these major institutions have had a profound impact on

---

[2]U.S. Office of Management and Budget, *Special Analyses: Budget of the United States Government, FY 1985* (Washington, DC: U.S. Government Printing Office, 1984), pp. H-11, H-12.

[3]Ibid., p. H-36.

intergovernmental relations. Be prepared to discuss which of them you think has had the most prominent role in shaping the intergovernmental system during the past twenty years. Would your answer be different if you were asked which had the most influence fifty or 100 years ago? Which do you think will be most prominent during the next twenty years?

Robert Jay Dilger

1

THE EXPANSION
AND CENTRALIZATION
OF AMERICAN
GOVERNMENTAL FUNCTIONS

When the Framers gathered in Philadelphia during the summer of 1787 to rework the existing constitutional arrangement, the national economy was in a state of depression, the state governments were saddled with large debts left over from the Revolutionary War, the continental dollar was unstable and destined to be a national joke ("not worth a continental"), the navy failed to adequately protect international shipping, and the army could not protect its own arsenal during Shay's rebellion in 1786. Given these deficiencies, the Framers decided to change the entire governmental structure, including the existing intergovernmental relationship. At that time, two intergovernmental systems were used: confederal and unitary. Confederal systems are relatively loose associations of autonomous political entities that enter into a joint agreement, or compact, creating a central government to perform certain agreed-upon functions. The central government does not govern individual citizens directly. Instead, it regulates the constituent governments' activities within the agreed areas, usually defense and interstate commerce. In most confederal systems, each constituent government has an equal vote in the central government's decisions.[1] Unitary systems, on the other

[1]Martin Diamond, "The Ends of Federalism," in *The Federal Polity*, ed. Daniel Elazar (New Brunswick, NJ: Transactions Books, 1974), pp. 130–32; and James MacGregor Burns, J.W. Peltason, and Thomas Cronin, *State and Local Politics*, 3rd ed. (Englewood Cliffs, NJ: Prentice-Hall, 1981), p. 29.

hand, vest all powers in the central goverment. This central government can, if it so chooses, delegate responsibilities to its constituent units, but what it delegates it can also take away.[2]

The American confederal relationship established under the *Articles of Confederation and Perpetual Union* had proven to be unsatisfactory. The Framers, however, could not adopt a unitary system. The states had just won their independence from a nation governed by unitary principles and they were not willing to give up their hard-won political autonomy. So, the Framers invented a new intergovernmental system—called federalism—that was neither a unitary nor a confederal system, but a composition of both.[3]

The following analysis documents the historical evolution of our unique intergovernmental system. At first, governmental responsibilities were relatively distinct and the states were the most important governmental entity in the American federal system. But over the past fifty years, American federalism has undergone enormous change. Governmental responsibilities have grown tremendously and earlier distinctions have blurred. The national government (often erroneously called the federal government) has become involved in many traditional state and local functions, such as education, welfare, and law enforcement. It has also entered into wholly new fields of governmental activity, such as environmental protection, aid to the handicapped, and employment training, stimulating state and local involvement in the process. As a result, the American federal system during the past fifty years has seen more intergovernmental relationships, more intricate patterns of governmental administration, and more problems of planning, coordination, and accountability.[4]

CONSTITUTIONAL AMBIGUITIES

Under a confederal relationship, a central governmental authority cannot be acknowledged as primary, yet, in the *Supremacy Clause* in Article VI of the *United States Constitution*, the Framers clearly indicated that the national government's laws "shall be the supreme Law of the Land, and the Judges in every State shall be bound thereby, any Thing in the Constitution or Laws of any State to the Contrary notwithstanding."[5] The *Supremacy Clause* reflected the unitary theory of governance—in which the best governmental system is viewed as being

---

[2]Burns, Peltason, and Cronin, *State and Local Politics*, pp. 28, 29.

[3]James Madison, "Federalist 39," in *The Federalist Papers*, introd. Clinton Rossiter (New York: New American Library, 1961), p. 246.

[4]Advisory Commission on Intergovernmental Relations, *The Condition of Contemporary Federalism: Conflicting Theories and Collapsing Constraints* (Washington, DC: U.S. Government Printing Office, 1981), pp. 1, 2.

[5]"The Constitution of the United States," in *The Federalist Papers* introd. by Clinton Rossiter (New York: New American Library, 1961), p. 540.

one in which the executive, legislative, and judicial powers are vested in a central authority. Moreover, many have interpreted the *Necessary and Proper Clause* that appeared in Article I, Section 8 as also supporting the unitary theory. This clause indicated that the national government could take any action that was necessary and proper to carry out its assigned duties.[6]

On the other hand, the Framers carefully enumerated the national government's powers in Articles I, II, and III. Also, Madison's notes on the constitutional debate indicate that most of the Framers intended all other governmental powers to be constitutionally reserved to the states—reflecting their commitment to the confederal theory of governance. Moreover, the Tenth Amendment to the *Constitution* reinforced the confederal theory by explicitly guaranteeing that all powers not specifically granted to the national government are reserved to the states or to the people.

This constitutional imprecision created a national paradox. The *Constitution* became sanctified in American folklore while American federalism became a battleground where diverse interests competed for governmental power.[7]

THE STATES' RIGHTS ARGUMENT VS. THE NATIONALIST INTERPRETATION

Because of the aforementioned constitutional ambiguities, two differing interpretations of American federalism have emerged, the states' rights, or compact, theory and the nationalist theory. Each of these theories has important implications for the distribution of powers among the various levels of government and, because each governmental level has historically displayed different approaches to solving societal conflict, for the distribution of goods and services within our society.

Advocates of the states' rights, or compact, interpretation of the *Constitution* have included, among others: Thomas Jefferson, Andrew Jackson, John C. Calhoun, and Roger Taney. In addition, President Ronald Reagan has also indicated his support for the states' rights theory. It argues that the *Constitution* is an intergovernmental compact among the states, and the national government cannot exercise its enumerated powers if in the process of executing those powers it interferes with the powers reserved to the states by the Tenth Amendment.

The extreme view of the states' rights argument was articulated by John C. Calhoun in 1828. At that time, Calhoun was protesting the national government's imposition of high tariffs on imported goods. Calhoun argued that because the national government received its authority from the states when they ratified

[6]Ibid., p. 534.

[7]Advisory Commission on Intergovernmental Relations, *The Condition of Contemporary Federalism*, p. 27.

the *Constitution*, the states had the right to declare any national law null and void within its boundaries.[8]

The Civil War ended the concept of nullification as a viable political alternative, but most Americans still believed that the vast majority of domestic policies were best handled by the state governments. Today, many Americans continue to believe that state and local officials are physically closer to the public than national officials and are, therefore, better able to determine state and local needs, better able to determine the most efficient means of answering those needs, and more accountable to the public for their actions. Those who argue for greater state and local responsibilities also tend to share a philosophical fear of national governmental control. They believe that genuinely democratic government can only flourish in small political communities and that to maximize democratic participation and accountability all governmental functions that lack a compelling rationale for national involvement should be left to the states and localities.[9] It is their contention that powerful central authorities threaten republican liberties.

The nationalist interpretation of the *Constitution* rejects the idea that it is an interstate compact. Instead, it is viewed as a compact among the American people. As a result, the national government receives its authority from the people, not the states, and is free to do whatever is "necessary and proper" to carry out its enumerated powers. Advocates of the nationalist interpretation have included, among others: John Marshall, Henry Clay, Abraham Lincoln, and Franklin Roosevelt. Contemporary nationalists believe that there are certain national goals, such as the achievement of clean air and water, civil rights, and communicable-disease control, that can be best attained through the auspices of the national government. Unlike states' righters, nationalists do not have a philosophical fear of national governmental control. Instead, they advocate the use of those powers to defend republican liberties, especially for minority groups.

DUAL FEDERALISM

At first, American intergovernmental relations closely resembled what one would expect under the states' rights theory. Governmental powers and responsibilities were allocated between the national government and the states, leaving each considerable autonomy within its own areas of jurisdiction—often called dual federalism.[10] As James Madison explained in "Federalist 39":

[8]*Richard Hofstadter, The American Political Tradition* (New York: Vintage Books, 1948), p. 72.

[9]Advisory Commission on Intergovernmental Relations, *The Condition of Contemporary Federalism*, p. 6.

[10]David Beam, Timothy Conlan, and David Walker, "Federalism: The Challenge of Conflicting Theories and Contemporary Practice," in *Political Science: The State of the Discipline*, ed. Ada W. Finifter (Washington, DC: The American Political Science Association, 1983), p. 248.

. . . the proposed government cannot be deemed a national one; since its jurisdiction extends to certain enumerated objects only, and leaves to the several States a residuary and inviolable sovereignty over all other objects.[11]

In Article I, Section 8, the *Constitution* granted the national government seventeen specific powers including the power to coin money and to regulate its value, to establish post offices, to regulate copyright laws, to declare war, to regulate the armed forces, to borrow money, and to lay and collect taxes. To augment the national government's authority in foreign policy, interstate commerce, and certain, specific domestic policies, the *Constitution* prohibited states from entering into treaties, coining money, establishing post offices, or entering into interstate compacts without the consent of Congress. But the states were expected to continue to be the primary instrument of governance in domestic affairs and were granted the concurrent power to lay and collect taxes to fund activities. The Framers believed that the United States Senate, comprised of representatives chosen by the state legislatures, would prevent the national government from infringing upon the states' authority to conduct their own domestic affairs. They also anticipated that the president would veto any congressional bill that infringed upon state prerogatives.

Historically, the doctrine of dual federalism has been used by several Presidents of the United States to justify their vetoes of nationally financed intergovernmental assistance programs, by the United States Supreme Court to restrict both national and state governmental powers, by Southerners to protect slavery, segregation, and the right of secession, and by conservative business interests to avoid governmental regulation.[12] In carrying out their responsibilities, however, the various governmental units in the United States have never operated under a perfect dual federalism relationship. Daniel Elazar and Morton Grodzins have argued that American federalism has always been cooperative. They point out that virtually all the activities of government during the nineteenth century were shared, involving national, state, and local governments. Specifically, they argue that even before the *Constitution* was ratified by the states, the Continental Congress granted nationally owned lands to be sold for the support of public education to states formed out of the Northwest Territory. These land grants, re-authorized in the *Northwest Ordinance of 1787* and supplemented by land grants to all the states in 1787, involved the national government in one of the most local functions of all, public education. More than 2.6 million acres of the national domain were subsequently donated to the states in support of universities and 1.3 million acres for primary and secondary schools. These land grants set a precedent. Many times since the national government has used its superior

---

[11]Madison, "Federalist 39," p. 245.

[12]Daniel J. Elazar, "Federal–State Collaboration in the Nineteenth-Century United States," in *American Federalism in Perspective*, ed. Aaron Wildavsky (Boston: Little, Brown, 1967), pp. 191, 192.

resources to encourage states and localities to pursue national policy objectives.[13] During the nineteenth century the national government also relied on state officials to administer its elections, paid state governments to house some of its prisoners, and allowed state courts to try cases concerning its laws.[14] The national government also joined state and local governments in financing joint stock companies that undertook specific projects—usually involving internal improvements—and provided Army Engineers to assist state officials in surveying and planning their states' internal improvement projects.[15]

Although dual federalism did not exist in the strictest sense and the national and state governments cooperated in several areas, some intergovernmental scholars disagree with Elazar and Grodzins' conclusion that American federalism has always been cooperative.[16] These scholars argue that intergovernmental relationships were very limited in both number and scope during the nineteenth century and that the states were correctly recognized at the time as the dominant governmental entity in American federalism. Specifically, they argue that the states exercised virtual exclusive jurisdiction in most domestic policy areas, including property rights, business organization, family life and social relations, criminal and civil law, law enforcement, elections, civil rights, and conservation. Moreover, in those domestic areas where the national government provided economic assistance the states were provided considerable administrative and programmatic flexibility.[17]

LAND GRANTS

Although intergovernmental scholars still argue over the precise nature of national–state relations during the nineteenth century, they do agree that, with the sole exception of the Civil War, land grants from the national government to the states were the prime molders of nineteenth-century American federalism. The national government gave over 3 million acres to the states to help pay for wagon roads, 4.5 million acres for canal construction, 2.25 million acres for river navigation, and 64 million acres for flood control.[18]

[13]Ibid., pp. 191–221; and Morton Grodzins, *The American System (Chicago: Rand McNally, 1966), pp. 17, 18, 35.*

[14]*Morton Grodzins, "The Federal System,"* in American Government, 5th ed., ed. Peter Woll (Boston: Little, Brown, 1975), p. 144.

[15]Elazar, "Federal–State Collaboration in the Nineteenth-Century United States," p. 196.

[16]Harry N. Scheiber, "Federalism and Legal Process: Historical and Contemporary Analysis of the American System," in *Law & Society Review* 14, no. 3 (Spring 1980): 669–683.

[17]Harry N. Scheiber, *The Condition of American Federalism: An Historian's View,* a study submitted by the Subcommittee on Intergovernmental Relations to the Committee on Government Operations, U.S. Senate, 89th Cong., 2d Sess., 15 October 1966, p. 3.

[18]Grodzins, *The American System,* p. 35.

The most famous land grant during the nineteenth century was authorized by the *Morrill Act*. Adopted in 1862, it provided each existing and future state with 60,000 acres of the national domain, plus an additional 30,000 acres for each of its congressional representatives, to be sold for the "endowment, support, and maintenance of at least one college where the leading subject shall be . . . agriculture and the mechanic arts."[19] States were required to invest the money generated by the sale of the land in approved securities and to use their own funds for construction. They were also required to report all expenditures involving these land grant colleges to Congress on an annual basis. An additional requirement for military instruction was subsequently added.

The *Morrill Act* reflected the temper of its time. The national government needed engineers to help win the Civil War. To meet this national need, it used its superior resources to encourage states to establish these colleges. Because national administrative conditions were relatively few and the grant of land so generous, state government officials could hardly refuse to participate in the program.

GRANTS-IN-AID

The national government has provided cash grants, or grants-in-aid, to the states for the support of the National Guard since 1808.[20] The movement from land grants to grants-in-aid, however, did not gain momentum until the twentieth century. One reason for the shift to cash grants was that much of the national domain had been given to the states by the turn of this century. The new emphasis at that time was land preservation, not exploitation. President Benjamin Harrison, for example, set aside millions of acres of the national domain in 1891 by declaring them forest preserves.

The adoption of the *Hatch Act* in 1887 marked the beginning of the modern grants-in-aid system. It authorized the national government's first annual cash grant to the states in the modern era by providing each state with $15,000 per year to establish agricultural experiment stations. In 1888, an annual grant of $25,000 was appropriated for the care of disabled veterans in state hospitals. States were given $100 per disabled veteran.[21] In 1890, national funding was provided to subsidize resident instruction in the land grant colleges created by the *Morrill Act*, and, in 1894, national funds were provided to subsidize irrigation projects within the states.[22]

[19]Ibid., p. 34.
[20]Ibid., p. 37.
[21]Ibid., pp. 36, 37.
[22]David B. Walker, *Toward a Functioning Federalism* (Cambridge, MA: Winthrop, 1981), p. 61.

By 1902, only the aforementioned four cash grants were in operation, accounting for only $7 million in national expenditures. State and local expenditures, in contrast, were slightly over $1 billion, indicating the extremely limited nature of intergovernmental relations at that time.[23]

An important difference between national land grants and cash grants had emerged even at this early date. National governmental policymakers, particularly congressmen, believed that because grants-in-aid programs were funded out of the national treasury, they had the right (some felt, the obligation) to specify how the funds were to be spent. As a result, the national government began to attach and to enforce an increasing number of administrative conditions to these programs. In 1889, states were required to match the national government's funding for the care of disabled veterans or lose it. In 1890, the Secretary of the Interior was authorized to certify each state's compliance with the *Morrill Act*'s conditions and was also given the authority to withhold payments if those conditions were not being met. In 1895, expenditures authorized by the *Hatch Act* for agricultural experiment stations were conditioned by annual audits. In 1911, expenditures authorized by the *Weeks Act* to subsidize state efforts to prevent forest fires were conditioned by advance approval of state plans for the use of the funds, annual audits and inspections, as well as a state matching requirement.[24]

THE PROGRESSIVE ERA: NATIONAL REGULATORY POWERS
AND THE SIXTEENTH AMENDMENT

Objecting to the monopolistic trusts' corruption of the economic marketplace and the political arena at the turn of this century, the progressives supported the positive use of governmental regulatory powers to restore free enterprise. Although they were generally more active at the state and local levels than at the national level, the progressives were instrumental in persuading Congress to follow President Theodore Roosevelt's lead and exercise more aggressively its constitutional authority to regulate interstate commerce. During the Roosevelt Administration, the national government moved aggressively into regulation of several areas that the states and localities had previously regulated alone. These areas included gambling, food and drugs, prostitution, and an array of additional practices considered socially, medically, or economically harmful to the public.[25] In addition, the Interstate Commerce Commission was revitalized and, during

[23]U.S. Bureau of the Census, *Historical Statistics of the United States: Colonial Times to 1970* (Washington, DC: U.S. Government Printing Office, 1975), p. 1126.

[24]Advisory Commission on Intergovernmental Relations, *Categorical Grants: Their Role and Design* (Washington, DC: U.S. Government Printing Office, 1978), pp. 15, 16.

[25]Advisory Commission on Intergovernmental Relations, *Regulatory Federalism: Policy, Process, Impact, and Reform* (Washington, DC: U.S. Government Printing Office, 1984), p. 27.

the Wilson Administration, the Federal Trade Commission and Federal Reserve Board were established. These national regulatory agencies sustained and enlarged the national government's regulatory powers and, in the process, increased intergovernmental contacts and tensions.

One of the most important years for American intergovernmental relations is 1913. In 1913, the Sixteenth Amendment to the *United States Constitution* legalized the national income tax. Before adoption of the Sixteenth Amendment, the national government was limited to the sale of the public domain, excise taxes, and custom duties (tariffs) for its revenue. When you match these limited revenue resources with the states' rights philosophy that dominated the polity for most of the nineteenth century, it is not surprising that the states and localities' combined expenditures were often twice as large as the national government's expenditures. The income tax, however, provided the national government with an elastic revenue generator, one that grows with the economy. Although, at first, the income tax was not broadly applied and did not generate significant amounts of additional national revenues—in 1915, only $125 million, or 24 percent of the $513 million collected in national taxes was generated by the income tax—some of these additional national funds were shared with the states in the form of intergovernmental grants.[26] Between 1914 and 1921 five new national grants-in-aid programs were established, providing funding for the agricultural extension service, rural roadways, vocational education, the rehabilitation of disabled veterans, and maternal and infant care.[27]

The national government's expanding role in domestic affairs was a matter of great constitutional concern and controversy during the 1920s. In 1923, the Supreme Court addressed the issue of whether the national government's grants-in-aid mechanism infringed upon states' rights under the Tenth Amendment. In *Massachusetts* v. *Mellon*, the Supreme Court sidestepped the broad constitutional controversy involving the national government's implied spending power to promote the general welfare versus the states' protection under the Tenth Amendment. Instead, the Supreme Court ruled that Massachusetts did not have legal standing in its attempt to prevent Andrew Mellon, the Secretary of the Treasury at the time, from spending funds authorized by the *Sheppard–Towner Act* to combat the high mortality rate of mothers and their infants. The Supreme Court ruled that Massachusetts had the option to refuse the funds and, therefore, could not show injury in the case. In *Frothingham* v. *Mellon*, also decided in 1923, the Supreme Court ruled that Mrs. Frothingham also lacked legal standing in her taxpayer challenge to the *Sheppard–Towner Act* because the national government does not earmark specific taxpayer dollars for specific programs, meaning that she could not prove injury because she could not prove that her tax dollars were being spent on this particular program. By indicating the absence of legal

[26]U.S. Bureau of the Census, *Historical Statistics of the United States*, p. 1107.

[27]Advisory Commission on Intergovernmental Relations, *Categorical Grants*, pp. 16, 17.

standing in these cases, the Supreme Court allowed the grants-in-aid mechanism to stand intact.

THE NEW DEAL

When Franklin Roosevelt became President in 1932, the grants-in-aid mechanism and national regulatory powers were accepted, though controversial, parts of public administration. When he left office in 1945, the scope of national regulation and the number and funds committed to nationally financed intergovernmental grants had reached unprecedented levels. By 1942, the Supreme Court had reversed its earlier rulings that had limited national regulatory powers and most observers concluded that those powers were now virtually unlimited (see reading 2 "The Supreme Court and Intergovernmental Relations" for more details). In addition, between 1932 and 1938, sixteen continuing and six emergency relief grants-in-aid programs were enacted to help combat the Great Depression. Although the dollar amount of intergovernmental aid fluctuated during the 1930s because of the temporary nature of the relief programs, as Table 1–1 indicates, national grant-in-aid expenditures grew rapidly under the Roosevelt Administration and shifted functionally from an emphasis on highway construction to social welfare assistance. Also, as Table 1–2 indicates, the national government increased its direct link with the cities. This greater emphasis on direct national–local aid was due, at least in part, to the efforts of the newly formed United States Conference of Mayors (in 1933) and the National League of Cities. They argued that because state legislatures were dominated by rural representatives protected by gerrymandered districts (the Supreme Court did not invoke the one man, one vote principle until 1964), state legislatures allocated the majority of national intergovernmental funds to rural areas. As a result, the mayors lobbied hard for more direct national intergovernmental funds for their cities.

The single most significant legislative enactment of the New Deal period was the *Social Security Act of 1935*. It established grants for old age assistance, aid for the blind, aid to dependent children, unemployment compensation, aid for maternal and child care, aid for crippled children, and child welfare. Although initial expenditures for these programs were modest, they set the precedent for the expansion of national governmental expenditures and involvement in domestic welfare policy.

WORLD WAR II THROUGH 1963

As Table 1–3 indicates, national expenditures skyrocketed during World War II and have remained significantly higher than the combined total of state and local expenditures ever since, even after taking intergovernmental transfers into ac-

TABLE 1–1   National Grants-In-Aid, Expenditures by Function, Selected Years, 1902–1983 (in millions of dollars)

CALENDAR YEAR	TOTAL	TRANSPOR-TATION	EDUCATION	PUBLIC WELFARE	HOUSING AND URBAN DEVELOPMENT	OTHER
1983	$88,539	$8,851	$12,528	$36,282	$5,583	$25,295
1980	90,836	9,457	12,889	28,494	6,093	33,903
1976	69,057	6,243	9,254	17,225	2,820	33,515
1972	33,178	4,741	6,250	13,251	1,981	6,955
1968	17,216	4,313	2,498	7,480	787	2,138
1964	9,969	3,978	479	3,875	564	1,073
1960	6,889	2,999	358	2,612	226	694
1956	3,642	746	208	1,879	125	684
1952	2,393	448	122	1,476	106	241
1948	1,629	334	37	892	69	287
1944	1,009	153	25	506	207	118
1940	2,401	167	24	1,990	37	193
1936	2,318	230	13	2,042	—	33
1932	229	132	11	60	—	26
1925	123	95	8	2	—	18
1920	43	20	5	3	—	15
1912	11	—	3	1	—	7
1902	7	—	1	1	—	5

Sources: U.S. Bureau of the Census, *Governmental Finances in 1982–83* (Washington, DC: U.S. Government Printing Office, 1984), p. 18; Advisory Commission on Intergovernmental Relations, *Periodic Congressional Reassessment of Federal Grants-In-Aid to State and Local Governments* (Washington, DC: U.S. Government Printing Office, 1967), pp. 16–33; Advisory Commission on Intergovernmental Relations, *Significant Features of Fiscal Federalism, 1982–83 Edition* (Washington, DC: U.S. Government Printing Office, 1984), p. 122; and U.S. Bureau of the Census, *Historical Statistics on Governmental Finances and Employment* (Washington, DC: U.S. Government Printing Office, 1969), pp. 37, 38.

count. National grants-in-aid expenditures, however, leveled off at just under $1 billion during the war because the national government concentrated its economic resources on defense and foreign policy concerns. As Table 1–2 indicates, the direct national–local link was significantly curtailed at this time. Moreover, all six emergency relief programs enacted during the New Deal were terminated by the war's conclusion and five war-related grants were discontinued following the war. Nonetheless, twenty-nine intergovernmental programs were in operation in 1945.

TABLE 1–2   National Grants-In-Aid, Intergovernmental Revenue from the National Government to State and Local Governments, Selected Years, 1902–1983 (in millions of dollars)

CALENDAR YEAR	TOTAL	TO STATE GOVERNMENTS	%	TO LOCAL GOVERNMENTS	%
1983	$88,539	$67,384	77%	$21,155	23%
1980	90,836	64,249	71	26,587	29
1976	60,057	51,426	74	17,631	26
1972	31,342	26,791	85	4,551	15
1968	17,182	15,228	88	1,954	12
1964	10,002	9,046	90	956	10
1960	6,974	6,382	92	592	8
1956	3,338	3,027	91	309	9
1952	2,566	2,329	91	237	9
1948	1,861	1,643	88	218	12
1944	954	926	97	28	3
1940	945	667	71	278	30
1936	948	719	76	229	24
1932	232	222	92	10	5
1927	116	107	92	9	8
1922	108	99	92	9	8
1913	12	6	50	6	50
1902	7	3	43	4	57

Note: Yearly total expenditures on Tables 1–1 and 1–2 differ because the Advisory Commission on Intergovernmental Relations defines grants slightly differently than the Bureau of the Census and included national emergency relief program funding administered by state and local agencies.

Sources: U.S. Bureau of the Census, *Governmental Finances in 1982–83* (Washington, DC: U.S. Government Printing Office, 1984), p. 17; U.S. Bureau of the Census, *Government Finances in 1979–80* (Washington, DC: U.S. Government Printing Office, 1981), p. 30; U.S. Bureau of the Census, *Government Finances in 1975–76* (Washington, DC: U.S. Government Printing Office, 1977), p. 20; and U.S. Bureau of the Census, *Historical Statistics of the United States: Colonial Times to 1970*, Part 2 (Washington, DC: U.S. Government Printing Office, 1975), pp. 1129, 1133.

During the Truman Administration (1946–1952), national expenditures continued to outpace state and local expenditures, national grants-in-aid expenditures rose from $894 million to over $2.5 billion (see Table 1–2), and the total number of grants increased to seventy-one (see Table 1–4). During the Eisenhower Administration (1953–1960), all three trends continued. National expenditures remained significantly higher than state and local expenditures, national grants-in-

TABLE 1–3 Total Governmental Expenditures by Level, after Intergovernmental Transfers, Selected Years, 1902–1983 (in billions of dollars)

YEAR	NATIONAL	TOTAL STATE/LOCAL	STATE	LOCAL
1983	$785.7	$564.8	$232.7	$332.1
1980	513.4	355.5	137.8	219.9
1976	323.7	251.2	92.8	158.3
1972	207.2	126.2	65.4	60.8
1968	166.4	116.2	44.3	71.9
1964	115.8	80.5	29.6	50.9
1960	90.2	61.0	22.1	38.8
1956	72.6	43.1	15.1	28.0
1952	68.9	30.8	10.7	20.1
1948	33.8	21.2	7.9	13.3
1944	99.4	10.5	3.3	7.1
1940	9.1	11.2	3.5	7.6
1936	8.2	8.5	2.4	6.1
1932	4.0	8.4	2.0	6.4
1927	3.4	7.8	1.4	6.4
1922	3.6	5.6	1.0	4.5
1913	.9	2.2	.3	1.9
1902	.5	1.1	.1	1.0

Sources: U.S. Bureau of the Census, *Governmental Finances in 1982–83* (Washington, DC: U.S. Government Printing Office, 1984), p. IX; Advisory Commission on Intergovernmental Relations, *Significant Features of Fiscal Federalism, 1982–83 Edition* (Washington, DC: U.S. Government Printing Office, 1984), p. 8; Advisory Commission on Intergovernmental Relations, *Significant Features of Fiscal Federalism, 1976 Edition* (Washington, DC: Government Printing Office, 1977), pp. 7, 11, 15; and U.S. Bureau of the Census, *Historical Statistics of the United States: Colonial Times to 1970,* Part 2 (Washington, DC: U.S. Government Printing Office, 1975), pp. 1123, 1130, 1132.

aid expenditures increased to nearly $7 billion, and sixty-one new grants-in-aid programs were enacted, bringing the total number of nationally financed intergovernmental programs to 132.

The most significant intergovernmental program adopted during the 1950s was the interstate highways program. The national government provided states that established state highway departments with 90 percent of the cost of building the interstate highway system. As a result of the national government's offer, highway assistance nearly doubled as a percentage of total nationally financed intergovernmental grants-in-aid, from 22 percent in 1956 to 42 percent in 1960. Also, the highways program was the main reason intergovernmental expenditures

TABLE 1–4   National Grants-in-Aid, by Type, Selected Years, 1902–1984

CALENDAR YEAR	TOTAL # OF GRANTS	CATEGORICAL GRANTS	BLOCK GRANTS	GENERAL REVENUE SHARING
1984	405	392	12	1
1983	410	398	11	1
1982	441	429	11	1
1981	539	533	5	1
1978	498	492	5	1
1975	448	442	5	1
1968	387	385	2	0
1966	331	330	1	0
1964	181	181	0	0
1962	160	160	0	0
1960	132	132	0	0
1952	71	71	0	0
1945	29	29	0	0
1940	34	34	0	0
1935	32	32	0	0
1930	15	15	0	0
1920	11	11	0	0
1902	4	4	0	0

Sources: Advisory Commission on Intergovernmental Relations, *Federal Grants-In-Aid Programs to State and Local Governments: Grants Funded FY 1984* (Washington, DC: U.S. Government Printing Office, 1985). Advisory Commission on Intergovernmental Relations, *Significant Features of Fiscal Federalism; 1982–83 Edition* (Washington, DC: U.S. Government Printing Office, 1984), p. 120; Advisory Commission on Intergovernmental Relations, *Categorical Grants Their Role and Design* (Washington, DC: Government Printing Office, 1978), pp. 25, 28; and David Walker, *Toward a Functioning Federalism*, (Cambridge, MA: Winthrop, 1981), pp. 61, 62, 79, 81.

increased so much during the 1950s. While the increase in absolute dollars is impressive, it actually only mirrored the national economy's growth. From 1942 through 1958, national intergovernmental grant expenditures represented approximately 1 percent of the gross national product (GNP), and only increased to 1.4 percent of GNP in the 1959–1962 period.[28]

The increased number of intergovernmental grants-in-aid programs and of the nationally imposed administrative conditions attached to them became a source of increasing concern during the late 1940s and 1950s. A number of commissions were formed to study the grants-in-aid system. In 1949, a commission headed by former President Herbert Hoover indicated that grant programs

[28]Advisory Commission on Intergovernmental Relations, *Categorical Grants*, p. 23.

were unrelated, uncoordinated, and developed in a haphazard manner. It recommended the use of block grants.[29] In 1955, on the other hand, the Commission on Intergovernmental Relations headed by Meyer Kestnbaum was much less critical of the growing number of intergovernmental grants. The establishment of the ongoing United States Advisory Commission on Intergovernmental Relations in 1959 to monitor the operation of the American federal system and to recommend improvements marked the "arrival" of intergovernmental relations as a national concern.

According to the Advisory Commission on Intergovernmental Relations, intergovernmental relations in 1960 were still relatively few, narrow, and, in many respects, not very intrusive on state and local prerogatives.[30] Although there were 132 intergovernmental programs in operation, four areas (highways, aid to the aged, aid to dependent children, and employment security) accounted for 75 percent of all national intergovernmental expenditures and those expenditures (nearly $7 billion) represented less than 2 percent of GNP and less than 15 percent of total state–local expenditures. Moreover, all but 8 percent of the grants-in-aid funds were distributed directly to state governments. This significantly eased administrative difficulties. As one of the Advisory Commission on Intergovernmental Relations' reports indicated:

> The system in 1960 clearly was a good example of 'cooperative federalism' in action. . . . Programmatically, there was a sharing of some functions. Administratively, the officials involved at the different levels were not adversaries, they were more like allies. Politically, the decentralization that existed did result from 'independent centers of power.'
> Few, if any, traditional municipal functions and only about half of the states responsibilities were touched in any way by federal grant or other programs.[31]

THE CATEGORICAL EXPLOSION: 1963–1968

During the Johnson Administration (1963–1968), national expenditures continued to increase as did the number of national grants-in-aid programs and the funds committed to them. The most striking departure from the past was the increased number of categorical grants, from 132 in 1960 to 385 in 1968 (see Table 1–4). National expenditures on intergovernmental grants also increased from nearly $7 billion in 1960 to over $18 billion in 1968, with proportionally greater funding

[29]The Commission on the Executive Branch of Government, *Federal–State Relations, A Report to Congress* (Washington, DC: U.S. Government Printing Office, 1949), p. 30.

[30]Advisory Commission on Intergovernmental Relations, *An Agenda for American Federalism: Restoring Confidence and Competence* (Washington, DC: U.S. Government Printing Office, 1981), p. 2.

[31]Ibid.

going to health (symbolized by the adoption of *Medicaid* in 1965), education (symbolized by the adoption of the *Elementary and Secondary Education Act of 1965*), and public welfare (see Table 1–1).

The explosion and continuation of categorical assistance during the 1960s was primarily a reflection of the interests of the new, more liberal Congress that entered office on President Johnson's coattails in 1964. Intergovernmental programs were adopted to combat poverty, disease, illiteracy, racial injustice, crime, substandard housing, and urban decay.[32] Following the Congress' liberal ideology, most of these new grants-in-aid programs were project categorical grants. As a result, the cooperative flavor of intergovernmental relations began to take on a more coercive nature as nationally imposed administrative standards became the norm. Specifically, the 1960s categorical explosion brought six new features to the intergovernmental system. First, the direct national–local link was strengthened as seventy-two new grants bypassed the states entirely.[33] Second, there was an increasing variety of state and local matching requirements, raising serious questions concerning consistency and equity across grant programs. Third, private or third-party federalism emerged as some grants were awarded to non-governmental recipients such as community-action agencies. The most famous example of this was the *Economic Opportunity Act of 1964*, which subsequently funded approximately 850 community-action organizations that operated beyond the effective control of state and local government officials.[34] Fourth, the proliferation of programs created an information gap because potential recipients could not keep up with all the new programs and the procedures required to apply for them. This, in turn, led to grantsmanship problems where some recipients were able to secure funds because they were better able to wade through the "red tape," not because they had greater demonstrable need. Fifth, to cope with enhanced intergovernmental interactions, the national government set up four new systems of regional offices to assist in the processing and advertising of national grants-in-aid programs. Unfortunately, these new systems hindered each specific program's implementation as many state and local officials were forced to deal with national administrators in as many as ten different cities. Finally, the seven public interest groups (PIGs)—Council of State Governments; National Governor's Association; National Conference of State Legislatures; National

[32]Claude E. Barfield, *Rethinking Federalism* (Washington, DC: American Enterprise Institute, 1981), p. 15.

[33]Although the number of direct national–local grants-in-aid programs increased dramatically during the Johnson Administration, as Table 1–2 indicates, they still accounted for only 10–12 percent of total nationally financed intergovernmental assistance during the late 1960s. The largest increase in direct national–local intergovernmental assistance followed the adoption of the general revenue sharing program in 1972. Since the mid 1970s, approximately 25 percent of total national intergovernmental expenditures have been of the direct national–local type.

[34]Barfield, *Rethinking Federalism*, p. 16.

Association of Counties; National League of Cities; U.S. Conference of Mayors; and the International City Management Association—all began to lobby national officials for increased intergovernmental assistance coupled with reductions in administrative conditions.[35]

According to James Sundquist, before 1960 the typical national grant-in-aid program was intended to assist state and local governments in accomplishing their own objectives. Aid was typically allocated by formulas designed to provide assistance to nearly every governmental jurisdiction in the nation, was awarded on a 50–50 matching basis, and nationally mandated administrative requirements were flexible. During the 1960s, national grants-in-aid programs increasingly sought to move state and local governments into new areas or more aggressively into existing ones, particularly environmental protection, education, public assistance, and urban renewal. To encourage states and localities to move in the desired direction, the national government made recipient matching requirements low, but at the expense of greater administrative oversight and grants allocated on a competitive basis.[36]

While national grants-in-aid programs encouraged states and localities to comply with national objectives, national regulatory agencies increasingly forced the states to comply. The most significant new regulatory law enacted during this period was the *Civil Rights Act of 1964*. It prohibited discrimination in any program receiving national assistance. In the past, the national government had regulated industries, such as railroads and meat packers, and standards, such as weight and measures. The *Civil Rights Act* was a new departure. Its purpose was to regulate the social behavior of the American public and the actions of the states and localities in that regard.[37]

Symptomatic of growing state and local complaints concerning the national government's new role in intergovernmental relations was Terry Sanford's 1967 book, *Storm Over The States*. Sanford complained that the 1960s' categorical grants-in-aid explosion had undermined the governor's ability to govern their states effectively. Most of these new programs, he argued, were awarded by national bureaucrats to localities without the governors' input or advance knowledge despite the fact that they are held accountable by the voters for the states' welfare. He likened the new intergovernmental relationship to a picket fence with each picket representing a vertical alliance among like-minded bureaucrats within each specific programmatic area at the national, state, and local levels. He argued that if program coordination and effective delivery of services was

[35]Advisory Commission on Intergovernmental Relations, *Categorical Grants*, pp. 27, 28.

[36]James Sundquist, *Making Federalism Work* (Washington, DC: The Brookings Institution, 1969), p. 3.

[37]Theodore H. White, *America in Search of Itself* (New York: Harper & Row Pub., 1982), p. 108.

the objective, national intergovernmental policymakers had to show a greater sensitivity to the needs and administrative abilities of elected officials at the state and local levels of government, especially the governors.[38]

THE FIRST NEW FEDERALISM: 1969–1975

President Richard Nixon shared Sanford's concern that the role of state and local elected officials in intergovernmental relations had become too weak and that the system lacked coordination. He was convinced that the best way to improve the delivery of program service was to sort out and rearrange governmental responsibilities among the three levels of government. His essential criticism of the Democrats' New Frontier and Great Society programs was that they created too much dispersal of responsibility and authority.[39]

On August 8, 1969, President Nixon announced his New Federalism proposals on nationwide, prime-time television. He asked Congress for legislation nationalizing the financing, programmatic standards, and administrative responsibility of four intergovernmental income-maintenance programs that transferred national cash benefits directly to individuals: *Aid to Families With Dependent Children, Supplemental Security Income* (cash benefits for poverty-striken elderly), *Social Security Disability Insurance*, and *Medicaid*. He also sought legislation to decentralize the programmatic standards and administrative responsibilities, through the use of block grants and general revenue sharing, of a number of programs that provided services directly to localities. He argued that such programs occurred in areas where conditions and needs varied considerably and local discretion was especially important. Grant areas to be decentralized included education, social services for the poor, law enforcement, and job training (see reading 3, "The Presidency and Intergovernmental Relations," for more details).

The congressional response to Nixon's proposals was mixed. Both *Supplemental Security Income* and *Social Security Disability Insurance* were nationalized, but *Medicaid* and *Aid to Families With Dependent Children* were not. President Nixon had also asked Congress to add six new block grants (he called them special revenue-sharing programs) to the two enacted during the Johnson Administration (*Partnership for Health Act* and *Omnibus Crime Control and Safe Streets Act*). Specifically, he asked for block grants for community development, education, employment and job training, law enforcement, social

---

[38]Terry Sanford, *Storm over the States* (New York: McGraw-Hill, 1967).

[39]Richard P. Nathan, *The Plot That Failed: Nixon and the Administrative Presidency* (New York: John Wiley, 1975), p. 18.

services, and transportation. Collectively, these six block grants were to replace 129 existing categorical grants, reflecting Nixon's long-range goal of reducing both the number of and proportion of intergovernmental funds committed to categorical grants.

Three block grants were subsequently adopted by Congress: in 1973, the *Comprehensive Employment and Training Act* (CETA) consolidated seventeen employment and training categorical grants; in 1974, the *Community Development Block Grant* program consolidated six community-development categorical grants; and, also in 1974, the *Social Services Block Grant* consolidated three social services categorical grants. As Tables 1–4 and 1–5 indicate, however, the number of categorical grants continued to increase and the proportion of intergovernmental funds committed to categorical grants remained very high.

The "crowning" achievement of Nixon's New Federalism was the enactment of the *State and Local Fiscal Assistance Act of 1972*. This law created the general revenue-sharing program where intergovernmental funds are allocated among the states and localities by a predetermined (and very complex) formula on an unconditioned basis. Nixon had hoped that the general revenue-sharing program's funds would replace existing categorical grants funding and, in the process, reduce governmental red tape, improve program efficiency by bypassing national administrators, increase state and local officeholders' control over intergovernmental grants, and reduce overall national expenditures. Congress, however, refused to reduce categorical aid and, instead, significantly increased the proposed budget of the general revenue-sharing program to $6 billion and added it to existing intergovernmental expenditures. As Table 1–5 indicates, intergovernmental expenditures jumped from $18.6 billion to $43.3 billion during the Nixon Administration. Most of this increase was due to the persistence of a Democratic Congress committed to the continuation and expansion of most of the New Frontier and Great Society programs and to the natural growth of entitlements once the eligible populations began to take advantage of the program's available benefits.

Frustrated in the legislative arena, President Nixon issued several executive orders designed to improve intergovernmental program coordination (see reading 3, "The Presidency and Intergovernmental Relations," for greater detail). His efforts, however, met with limited success. His two most significant administrative efforts, the formation of ten Federal Regional Councils and the Office of Mangement and Budget's circular A-95, were criticized by many state and local officials for causing additional and costly delays in program implementation.[40] OMB A-95 was revoked by President Reagan on April 30, 1983, and the Federal Regional Council's effectiveness is still a matter of great controversy.

[40]Rochelle Stanfield, "Federal Regional Councils—Can Carter Make Them Work?" *National Journal* (18 June 1977), p. 950.

TABLE 1-5 National Grants-in-Aid, Expenditure by Type Selected Years, 1968–1985 (in billions of dollars)

CALENDAR YEAR	Amount				Percentage		
	TOTAL	CATEGORICAL GRANTS	BLOCK GRANTS	GENERAL PURPOSE GRANTS*	CATEGORICAL GRANTS	BLOCK GRANTS	GENERAL PURPOSE GRANTS
1985e	$102.1	$82.1	$13.2	$6.8	80.3%	12.9%	6.7%
1984e	98.7	78.8	13.1	6.8	79.8	13.3	6.9
1983	92.0	73.6	12.9	6.5	79.1	13.9	7.0
1982	88.6	70.2	11.9	6.5	79.6	13.0	7.4
1981	91.4	72.5	10.3	6.8	82.2	10.6	7.2
1980	91.3	72.5	10.3	8.5	79.3	11.3	9.4
1978	77.8	56.7	11.5	9.6	72.9	14.8	12.3
1976	58.9	45.7	6.1	7.1	77.5	10.4	12.1
1974	43.3	35.4	1.1	6.7	81.8	2.6	15.6
1972	34.3	31.0	2.8	.5	90.2	8.3	1.5
1968	18.6	18.2	.1	.3	98.0	.1	1.9

e—estimated

*General Purpose Grants include general revenue sharing, payments to the District of Columbia, the five territories, Bureau of Land Management, the Forest Service, and several other broad-based programs.

Sources: U.S Office of Management and Budget, *Special Analyses: Budget of the United States Government, FY 1985* (Washington, DC: U.S. Government Printing Office, 1984), p. H-19: Idem, *Special Analyses: Budget of the United States Government, FY 1984* (Washington, DC: U.S. Government Printing Office, 1983), p. H-20 Idem: *Special Analyses: Budget of the United States Government, FY 1978* (Washington, DC: U.S. Government Printing Office, 1977), p. 276; and Advisory Commission on Intergovernmental Relations, *Categorical Grants: Their Role and Design* (Washington, D.C. U.S. Government Printing Office, 1978), p. 32.

THE MID-1970s

There were no dramatic changes in the intergovernmental grants-in-aid system under the Ford or Carter Administrations except for the massive growth of public-employment programs, which were adopted to combat the frequent downswings in the national economy at the time. Several block grants were proposed during the 1975–1979 period, but none were enacted. The number of intergovernmental programs continued to increase, from 448 in 1975 to 498 in 1978, as did intergovernmental expenditures, from \$43.3 billion in 1974 to \$77.8 billion in 1978. Much of this increase in intergovernmental expenditures, however, was attributed to maintaining program service at existing levels because of the high inflation rates of the late 1970s.[41]

One of the most significant developments in intergovernmental relations during the 1970s was the tremendous increase in the number and scope of nationally imposed intergovernmental regulations. One study identified 1,036 national mandates on local governments as a condition of receiving national grants-in-aid,[42] and the Advisory Commission on Intergovernmental Relations recently observed that:

> During the 1960s and 1970s, state and local governments for the first time were brought under extensive federal regulatory controls. . . . Over this period, national controls have been adopted affecting public functions and services ranging from automobile inspection, animal preservation and college athletics to waste treatment and waste disposal. In field after field, the power to set standards and determine methods of compliance has shifted from the states and localities to Washington.[43]

National regulations became so pervasive that matters once left to the judgment of private individuals, localities, or states were routinely raised as national issues and brought to the courts for adjudication.[44] Increasingly, the Supreme Court preempted private and governmental decisions by ruling on such issues as racial desegregation, affirmative action, busing, abortion, and law enforcement.

Another significant intergovernmental development during the 1970s was the increased volume of tax-exempt bonds that were issued by state and local governments to finance traditional public purposes such as hospitals, highways, sewers, and transit facilities as well as private economic development projects and home mortgages. Led by sharp increases for private economic development

[41]George F. Hale and Marian Lief Palley, *The Politics of Federal Grants* (Washington, DC: Congressional Quarterly Press, 1981), p. 14.

[42]Catherine Lovell et al., *Federal and State Mandating on Local Governments: An Exploration of Issues and Impacts*, report to the National Science Foundation, University of California/Riverside, June 20, 1979, p. 32.

[43]Advisory Commission on Intergovernmental Relations, *Regulatory Federalism*, p. 246.

[44]Theodore H. White, *America in Search of Itself*, p. 123.

and home mortgage bonds, total tax-exempt bond volume increased from approximately $18 billion in 1970 to $55 billion in 1975, topped $87 billion in 1982, and has been rising ever since. The Congressional Budget Office has estimated that these bonds are currently costing the national government approximately $26 billion in lost tax receipts.[45]

The recent increases in the volume of tax-exempt bonds has led to several concerns. First, states and localities may be using the bonds to obtain economic subsidies from the national government that they could not obtain through the traditional means of grants-in-aid. Second, these bonds represent a significant erosion of the national tax base and contribute to the national debt. Third, public bonds disrupt the private bond market as private investors wait to see if they can secure the subsidied, lower interest rates of the municipal bond market. Finally, some economists argue that, in many cases, direct subsidies are less expensive and a more efficient funding alternative because bonds involve substantial administrative expenses, including fees provided to bondholders, issuers, underwriters, and attorneys.[46]

THE SECOND NEW FEDERALISM

When Ronald Reagan became President in 1981, he announced that one of his highest priorities was to decentralize the intergovernmental grants-in-aid system.[47] The former governor shared President Nixon's concern that state and local elected officials no longer played a strong enough role in the intergovernmental system. He adopted Nixon's New Federalism theme and announced, in a major address before a Joint Session of Congress on February 18, 1981, his intention to transfer national domestic policymaking authority in several areas to the states. He asked Congress for legislation to consolidate eighty-four existing categorical grants into six new block grants and asked for signifcant funding reductions for a number of income maintenance categorical grants, including

[45]Alice M. Rivlin, statement before the House Committee on Ways and Means, *Trends in Municipal Financing and the Use of Tax-Exempt Bonds to Finance Private Activities*, 98th Cong., 1st Sess., 15 June 1983, pp. 52, 53.

[46]Ibid., p. 50; and John E. Chapoton, statement before the House Committee on Ways and Means, *Trends in Municipal Financing and the Use of Tax-Exempt Bonds to Finance Private Activities*, 98th Cong., 1st Sess., 15 June 1983, p. 37. Congress imposed state per capita volume caps on state and municipal bonds in 1984 and, at the time of this writing, is considering several tax reform proposals that would significantly reduce the value of tax exempt bonds to investors.

[47]At that time, there were 533 categorical grants, 5 block grants, and one general revenue sharing program. Fourteen intergovernmental grants had estimated obligations exceeding $2 billion, cumulatively accounting for 76 percent of all intergovernmental grant funding. The five programs with the largest annual obligations were: *Lower Income Housing Assistance*, $20 billion; *Medicaid*, $12.6 billion; *Highway Construction*, $8.4 billion; *Comprehensive Employment and Training*, $8.2 billion; and *Aid to Families With Dependent Children*, $7 billion.

housing (rental) assistance, food stamps, *Medicaid*, and job training (CETA). President Reagan argued that:

> We know, of course, that the categorical grant programs burden local and state governments with a mass of Federal regulations and Federal paperwork.
>
> Ineffective targeting, wasteful administration—all can be eliminated by shifting the resources and decision-making authority to local and State government. This will also consolidate programs which are scattered throughout the Federal bureaucracy, bringing government closer to the people and saving $23.9 billion over the next five years.
>
> In the health and social services area alone the plan we are proposing will substantially reduce the need for 465 pages of law, 1,400 pages of regulations, 5,000 Federal employees who presently administer 7,600 separate grants in about 25,000 separate locations. Over 7 million man and woman hours of work by state and local officials are required to fill out government forms.[48]

The legislative battle over the President's 1981 block grant proposals, his even more dramatic "swap" proposal in 1982, and his "mega-block" grant proposals in 1983 are discussed in detail in Part 3, *Federalism in the 1980s*, and in reading 3, "The Presidency and Intergovernmental Relations." The following excerpts from President Reagan's State of the Union Address delivered on January 26, 1982, provide his rationale for altering the intergovernmental grants-in-aid system. First, he indicated that it promoted a lack of governmental accountability by confusing the public:

> Our citizens feel they have lost control of even the most basic decisions made about the essential services of government, such as schools, welfare, roads, and even garbage collection. And they are right. A maze of interlocking jurisdictions and levels of government confronts average citizens in trying to solve even the simplist of problems. They do not know where to turn for answers, who to hold accountable, who to praise, who to blame, who to vote for or against.[49]

Second, he indicated that the cause of this lack of accountability was the proliferation of categorical grants:

> . . . The main reason for this [lack of accountability] is the overpowering growth of Federal grants-in-aid programs during the past two decades.
>
> In 1960, the Federal government had 132 categorical grant programs,

---

[48]*Weekly Compilation of Presidential Documents* 17, no. 8 (23 February 1981): 133.
[49]*Weekly Compilation of Presidential Documents* 18, no. 4 (1 February 1982): 79.

costing $7 billion. When I took office, there were approximately 500, costing nearly a hundred billion dollars—thirteen programs for energy, thirty-six for pollution control, sixty-six for social services, ninety for education. And here in Congress, it takes at least 166 committees just to try to keep track of them.[50]

Third, with such a great number of separate, independent programs in operation, he argued that there was bound to be a lot of waste, fraud, and poor delivery of program service because it was impossible to effectively engage in administrative oversight:

> You and I know that neither the President nor Congress can properly oversee this jungle of grants-in-aid, indeed, the growth of these grants has led to the distortion in the vital functions of government. As one Democratic Governor put it recently: 'The National Government should be worrying about arms control, not potholes.'[51]

In a related action, President Reagan has also moved to reduce the number and scope of national regulatory actions on states and localities. In 1981, he created a *Presidential Task Force on Regulatory Relief* and named his vice-president, George Bush, to head it. The *Task Force* subsequently recommended a number of changes in regulatory policy that were implemented, including a relaxation of reporting requirements concerning the school lunch program, streamlining of the grants appeal process within the Environmental Protection Agency, and reduction of housing assistance planning requirements.[52]

President Reagan's comments and actions underscore the dramatic expansion and centralization of governmental responsibilities that has taken place in the United States since the New Deal. His comments do not, however, indicate the many arguments made by those who oppose his efforts to decentralize the intergovernmental system. First, the President's opponents point out that the national government's fiscal capacity far exceeds the fiscal capacity of the individual states and localities. Although state revenues have increased as they have moved away from dependence on inelastic property taxes and toward greater reliance on the more elastic sales and income taxes, the national government's use of the income tax to generate the bulk of its funds puts it in the logical position to finance many programs that many states, particularly the poorer ones, cannot afford. Second, many programs have benefits that "spillover" to citizens of neighboring cities or states, such as wastewater treatment plants where the main beneficiaries of cleaner water often live downstream from the source of

[50]Ibid., pp. 79, 80.

[51]Ibid., p. 80.

[52]U.S. Office of Management and Budget, *Special Analyses: Budget of the United States Government, FY 1985* (Washington, DC: U.S. Government Printing Office, 1984), pp. H-20, H-21.

the pollution and certain highways that carry high volumes of intrastate traffic that benefit both in-state and out-of-state residents. Many economists have suggested that since state and local residents do not receive all or a majority of the benefits of such programs, they are naturally reluctant to fund them. The national government, on the other hand, recognizing the spillover benefits, is more likely to fund these programs.[53] Third, many national officials and interest groups distrust the intentions, performance, and, in some cases, the competence of certain state and local officials. Fourth, many argue that there are certain national goals, such as equal civil rights for all citizens, clean air, and clean water, that can be best accomplished by the national government's use of the administratively restrictive categorical grant mechanisms.

CONCLUSION

Since the formation of the American republic, politicians and interested groups have recognized that intergovernmental relations defined who would make the key decisions concerning the financing, programmatic standards, and administration of government domestic policy. They also knew that those decisions directly affected the allocation of goods and services within American society. Indeed, we fought a civil war over the "proper" intergovernmental relationship.

Given the profound growth of governmental responsibilities in the domestic sector over the past fifty years, intergovernmental relations has become an even more important and controversial area than ever before. Although we are not likely to have another civil war over intergovernmental relations, it does define the parameters of domestic policy and, as such, has a significant influence upon the relative status of various groups within American society and, indirectly, our status as a world economic power as well. With the stakes so high, you can readily understand why politicians and interest groups are so interested in intergovernmental relations and battle so hard to protect and enhance the relationship that they believe will most benefit their constituencies.

As the subsequent readings will indicate, intergovernmental scholars, like politicians and interest groups, disagree over what constitutes the best intergovernmental relationship. Indeed, there is even disagreement concerning the nature of the current system. One fact is clear, however. There has been a tremendous growth and centralization of governmental responsibilities since the New Deal, making the national government the dominant political entity in American federalism today.

[53]Advisory Commission on Intergovernmental Relations, *Categorical Grants*, pp. 50, 51.

Cynthia Cates Colella

2

THE UNITED STATES SUPREME COURT AND INTERGOVERNMENTAL RELATIONS

In 1787, James Madison wrote that the proposed Constitution of the United States was "neither wholly federal nor wholly national."[1] Rather, it was a hybrid—the product, to a certain extent, of political expediency, pragmatism, and convention bargaining.

The document claimed to be the "supreme law of the land"[2] was ratified as such, and rapidly gained a near reverential acceptance among the nation's citizens. The product of foresight, the Constitution was both flexible and timeless. The product of bargaining among a variety of political ideologies and sectional rivalries, it necessarily lacked specificity. Thus, those questions over which there existed the least fundamental agreement became the least precise components of the Constitution and foremost among such questions was the nature of the Union itself.

---

[1]"Federalist 39," in *The Federalist Papers*, introd. Clinton Rossiter (New York: New American Library, 1961), p. 246. All references are to this edition.

[2]*United States Constitution*, Art. VI.

Revised version of "Breakdown of Constitutional Constraints: Interpretative Variations from the First Constitutional Revolution to the 'Fourth'," in *The Condition of Contemporary Federalism: Conflicting Theories and Collapsing Constraints* (Washington, DC: U.S. Government Printing Office, 1981), pp. 27–110. Reprinted with permission of the U.S. Advisory Commission on Intergovernmental Relations.

THE CREATION OF FEDERALISM AND UNION:
CONVENTION POLITICS AND COMPROMISE

Because of the practical necessity of creating a real document to serve as the foundation of a real government, the ideological and political predilections of the Convention delegates were forced from the high plane of philosophic debate and into real politik dominated by bargaining and even a little stylistic obscurantism. Of the bargains, certainly the most renowned was the Great Compromise.

In large part, the Great Compromise created the "neither wholly federal nor wholly national" character of the Constitution. A settlement between the highly nationalistic Virginia Plan and the New Jersey Plan, which proposed little more than a strengthening of the Articles of Confederation, the compromise (otherwise known as the Connecticut Compromise) is generally credited with saving the Convention. Thus, the federal character of the Constitution (supported by the Anti-Federalists and a number of small state interests) was supposedly ensured by equal state representation in the upper house of Congress while the national character (supported by the Federalists and a number of large state interests) was ostensibly guaranteed by proportional representation in the lower house.

Article I, Section 8: The Mouse That Roared

If this representative scheme proved to be relatively unimportant in succeeding years, the intent of the delegates regarding the powers of Congress, was historically more troublesome. In particular, several clauses are worth noting.

Article I, Section 8 of the new Constitution set forth Congressional and, thus, national powers. By virtue of such a listing, the central national government was considered one of enumerated powers, most of which were limited in scope and quite unambiguous in meaning. However, two powers—added to the Constitution precisely because their exclusion from the Articles of Confederation had badly impaired the position of the Continental Congress—later were to be the sources of intense debate and increasing national power.

Under the Articles of Confederation, Congress was not allowed to levy taxes, an obvious reaction to colonial experience with Britain. Instead, it was forced to rely on state appropriations, a situation which Alexander Hamilton described as ". . . afford[ing] ample cause of mortification to ourselves, and triumph to our enemies."[3] Certainly, in this instance, the New York statesman was espousing common wisdom, for the old system of taxation was, at least, inefficient, at most, delibilitating. Accordingly, the Constitution empowered Congress "To lay and collect taxes, duties, imposts, and excises. . . ."[4] Because

---

[3]Madison, "Federalist 30," in *Federalist Papers*, p. 189.
[4]*United States Constitution*, Art. I, Sec. 8.

the major prevailing concern was that a national system of taxation might be pre-emptive, Hamilton assured the readers of the *Federalist* Papers that taxation "is manifestly a concurrent and coequal authority in the United States and in the individual states. There is plainly no expression in the granting clause which makes the power exclusive in the Union."[5]

More important in succeeding years, however, would be court interpretations of direct versus indirect taxes and their Constitutionally specified means of apportionment. Hence, Article I, Sections 2 and 9 state that *direct* taxes (early on defined as land taxes and capitations) were to "be apportioned among the several states . . . according to their respective numbers. . . ."[6] In the late nineteenth century, a series of conservative court decisions (generally considered to be the product of faulty interpretation and unsound reasoning) would interpret direct taxation in such a way as to thwart the collection of a federal income tax and, contrary to judicial intentions, would eventually force a Constitutional amendment, the legal circumvention of prior judicial obstruction.

Like taxation, the Congressional power to regulate commerce was born of reaction to the chaos produced by its absence under the Articles of Confederation. "Failure to delegate to the Confederation the power to regulate interstate commerce led to disastrous 'economic wars' among the various states, and made a national commercial policy impossible."[7] That situation, in turn, made the commerce clause one of the more popular provisions in the Constitution or, at least, according to Madison, ". . . a new power . . . that seems to be an addition which few oppose and from which no apprehensions are entertained."[8] After 1787, however, what seemed clear to James Madison became successively murkier. Even more than the power to tax, the commerce clause became a Constitutional source of confusion, a phrase subject to multiple interpretations, and the vehicle through which judges would make economic policy and define the parameters of federal and state regulatory powers. In contradiction to the "Father of the Constitution," it became a power from which many apprehensions were entertained.

In addition to listing the specific functions of Congress. Article I, Section 8 contained two clauses which generalized or gave legislative scope to the enumerated powers. Thus, the first clause of Section 8 reads, "The Congress shall have power to lay and collect taxes, duties, imposts and excises, to pay the debts and *provide for* the common defence and *general welfare* of the United States. . . ."[9] Coming directly before the list of Congressional powers, this

[5] Madison, "Federalist 32," in *Federalist Papers*, p. 199.

[6] *United States Constitution*, Art. I, Sec. 2.

[7] Alfred H. Kelly and Winfred A. Harbison, *The American Constitution: It's Origins and Development*, 5th ed. (New York: W.W. Norton & Co., Inc., 1976), p. 99.

[8] Madison, "Federalist 45," in *Federalist Papers*, p. 293.

[9] *United States Constitution*, Art. I, Sec. 8 (emphasis added).

phrase was meant as an umbrella generalization encompassing the ensuing power. Yet, the term, ''general welfare,'' was viewed by some as being too vague and, perhaps, as yielding to Congress powers which were unenumerated and unintended. Such contentions were dismissed as inconsequential by Madison who seemed to view the phrase merely as a useful literary device.[10] Indeed, he viewed the enumerated powers and ''the common defence and general welfare'' as the specific and general sides of the same coin. Latterday readers of the Constitution would not be as certain.

The final clause of Section 8, ''the coefficient clause,'' elicited even more criticism than the general welfare clause. In order to give legislative scope to the powers immediately proceeding, the Framers gave Congress the power ''To *make all laws which shall be necessary and proper* for carrying into execution the foregoing powers, and all other powers vested by this Constitution in the government of the United States or in any other department or office thereof.''[11] Needless to say, Constitutional critics claimed that this clause gave the national government vast and even dangerous powers since necessity and propriety were not defined. Nor, it appears, did Madison adequately explain the meaning or limits of necessary and proper. Instead, he sidestepped the issue by listing the pitfalls of deleting or changing the phrase—to the ''Father of the Constitution,'' necessary and proper meant necessary and proper.[12]

Reserved Powers under the Tenth Amendment

Throughout the ratification debates, Constitutional proponents had promised the creation of a bill of rights in exchange for adoption in several states. This promise was realized in the form of the first ten amendments submitted in 1789 and ratified by 1791.[13] Until 1868, the first nine amendments did not directly pertain to federal–state relations or to the states: thus, they will be discussed in a later section. However, the Tenth Amendment to the Constitution sought to acknowledge the powers of the states:

> The powers not delegated to the United States by the Constitution, nor prohibited by it to the states, are reserved to the states respectively, or to the people.[14]

Obviously, this was less a clarification of powers than, as Chief Justice Harlan Stone described it 152 years later, an attempt ''to allay fears that the new national

---

[10]Madison, ''Federalist 41,'' in *Federalist Papers*, p. 263.

[11]*United States Constitution*, Art I, Sec. 8 (emphasis added).

[12]Madison, ''Federalist 44,'' in *Federalist Papers*, pp. 280–88.

[13]In all, twelve amendments were submitted to the states but only ten were ratified.

[14]*United States Constitution*, Amendment X.

government might seek to exercise powers not granted, and that the states might not be able to exercise fully their reserved powers.''[15]

Yet, the fact that Stone needed to address the Amendment so many years after its adoption is testament to its interpretive flexibility. To some, the Amendment implies state sovereignty; to others, the implication is clearly one of national supremacy.

A further interpretive dilemma was caused by the absence of a single adverb. At the time of the Amendment's drafting, states' rights advocates sought to have the modifier, "expressly" inserted into the language. Under this scheme, the Amendment would have read, "The powers not *expressly* delegated. . . ." According to constitutional scholars Alfred H. Kelly and Winfred A. Harbison, "[t]his move was blocked by Madison and other moderates as well as the nationalists all of whom believed that in any effective government 'powers must necessarily be admitted by implication.' ''[16] Although the Framers had specifically deleted the term "expressly," it refused to die quietly. In years to come, it would contribute to Constitutional confusion, foster bitter debate, and find its way into Supreme Court decisions designed to deny the Constitutionality of certain Congressional actions.

JOHN MARSHALL AND THE NATIONAL JUDICIARY

Few Americans, if asked to identify the greatest and most influential Chief Justice, would hesitate to answer, "John Marshall." Presiding over the Supreme Court for a record 34 years, Marshall shaped its character, ensured it of its high prestige, and so defined its role as to make it a coequal branch of government. In his own time, he was often opposed by powerful adversaries, but he was, nonetheless, always respected. At the very least, he created a national judiciary; at the very most, he began the process of expanding the scope of legitimate national actions.

Establishing the Judiciary's Right to Review

Though certainly not his most significant case from the standpoint of federalism and national powers, John Marshall's decision in *Marbury* v. *Madison* (1803)[17] was a landmark for the functional independence of the national judiciary. Among the most politically astute of his contemporaries, Marshall imbued his court with potentially vast powers, while managing to temporarily mollify his rivals, President Jefferson and Secretary of State Madison. Thus, he refused to

---

[15]*United States* v. *Darby*, 312 U.S. 100 (1941).

[16]Kelly and Harbison, *The American Constitution*, p. 165.

[17]*Marbury* v. *Madison*, 1 Cranch 137 (1803).

issue a Writ of Mandamus on behalf of the plaintiff, William Marbury, to Secretary James Madison on the grounds that Section 13 of the *Judiciary Act of 1789*, which allowed the Court to issue such writs to officials, was unconstitutional.

Although *Marbury* v. *Madison* marked the first time the Court had declared an act of Congress unconstitutional and had definitively affirmed its right to do so, its impact (like so many other "Constitutional landmarks") was muted for years to come. Marshall's decision to rule in favor of his political opponents and his failure to declare any other act of Congress unconstitutional throughout the remainder of his Chief Justiceship, gave the case far more potential than immediate importance. The lack of immediacy was, no doubt, fortuitous (allowing the Chief Justice a great deal of latitude among his "enemies"), the potential would be realized repeatedly.

Power by Implication: "Let the End Be Legitimate"

In 1819, Marshall made his most important contribution to federalism and Constitutional construction. In *McCulloch* v. *Maryland* (1819),[18] the Chief Justice expounded in Hamiltonian breadth on the scope of federal powers and national supremacy. No narrow constructionist, Marshall viewed the Constitution as flexible, providing the national legislature with unspecified means to carrying out its Constitutional duties. Marshall's interpretation in *McCulloch* v. *Maryland* of the necessary and proper clause of the Constitution was one of the most, if not the most, significant Constitutional statements of all time. It vastly expanded the potential realm of the national government within the federal system and denied the existence of strict limitations on the Congressional role. The decision is worth quoting at length:

> . . . [T]here is no phrase in the [Constitution] which . . . requires that everything granted shall be expressly and minutely described. . . .
>
> . . . [T]he Constitution of the United States has not left the right of Congress to employ the necessary means, for the execution of the powers conferred on government, to general reasoning. To its enumerated powers is added, that of making "all laws which shall be necessary and proper, for carrying into execution the foregoing powers, and all other powers vested by this Constitution, in the government of the United States. . . .
>
> . . . We admit, as we all must admit, that the powers of government are limited, and that its limits are not to be transcended. But we think the sound construction of the Constitution must allow to the national legislature that discretion, with respect to the means by which the powers it confers

[18]*McCulloch* v. *Maryland*, 4 Wheaton 316 (1819). The case involved the State of Maryland's right (which Marshall asserted it did not possess) to tax the Bank of the United States.

are to be carried into execution, which shall enable the body to perform the high duties assigned to it, in the manner most beneficial to the people. Let the end be legitimate, let it be within the scope of the Constitution, and all means which are appropriate, which are plainly adapted to that end, which are not prohibited, but consist with the letter and spirit of the Constitution, are Constitutional. . . .[19]

Having established the doctrine of implied national powers, Marshall went on to powerfully and clearly state the principles of national supremacy:

. . . [T]he Constitution and the laws made in pursuance thereof are supreme . . . they control the constitution and the laws of the respective states, and cannot be controlled by them. From this, which may be almost termed an axiom, other propositions are deduced as corollaries. . . . These are; first, that a power to create implies a power to preserve, second, the power to destroy, if wielded by a different hand, is hostile to, and incompatible with these powers to create and preserve; third, that where this repugnancy exists, that the authority which is supreme must control, not yield to that over which it is supreme. . . .

. . . *[T]he states have no power, by taxation or otherwise, to retard, impede, burden, or in any manner control, the operations of the Constitutional laws enacted by Congress to carry into execution the powers vested in the general government.* This, we think, the unavoidable consequence of that supremacy which the Constitution has declared. . . .[20]

The Commerce Power: "Something More"

Five years after its McCulloch decision, the Court gained the opportunity to consider the implications of the interstate commerce clause. In the case of *Gibbons* v. *Ogden* (1824),[21] Marshall was compelled to address four crucial questions of significant breadth. First, what is commerce? Ogden's counsel and a great deal of prevailing opinion had reduced it to its lowest common denominator, traffic. But Marshall rejoined,

. . . Commerce, undoubtedly, is traffic, but it is something more; it is intercourse. It describes the commercial intercourse between nations, and parts of nations, in all its branches, and is regulated by prescribing rules for carrying on that intercourse. . . .[22]

[19]Ibid.

[20]Ibid. (emphasis added).

[21]*Gibbons* v. *Ogden*, 9 Wheaton 1 (1824). The case involved New York State's grant of an exclusive license to Ogden to navigate the state's waters by steamboat. Gibbons had obtained a license to operate steamboats between New York and New Jersey under an act approved by Congress. Ogden sought to enjoin Gibbons from further operation. The New York courts ruled for Ogden and Gibbons appealed to the Supreme Court.

[22]Ibid.

Second, to what extent did the power of Congress to regulate commerce reach? Ogden and states' rights advocates demanded that it was confined to the external boundaries of any given state. Marshall, however, countered that,

> . . . The word "among" means intermingled with. A thing which is among others, is intermingled with them. Commerce among the states, cannot stop at the external boundary line of each state, but may be introduced into the interior. . . .[23]

Third, should the Constitution in general be construed narrowly or broadly? The feeling outside the Court (now increasingly coming under attack) held that the Constitution was subject to precise and narrow construction. The Chief Justice left no doubt as to his opinion on this sensitive subject:

> Powerful and ingenious minds, taking as postulates that the powers expressly granted to the government of the Union, are to be contracted by construction into the narrowest possible compass, and that the original powers of the states are retained, if any possible construction will retain them, may, by a course of well-digested but refined and metaphysical reasoning founded on these premises, explain away the Constitution or our country, and leave it a magnificent structure indeed, to look at, but totally unfit for use. . . .[24]

In contrast to the judicial intrepidation and clarity which had characterized his answers to the foregoing questions, Marshall was apparently unable to adequately address the question of concurrent powers over commerce. Thus, he strongly stated that the Congressional power was complete but failed to say whether it was preemptive:

> . . . what is this power?
>
> It is the power to regulate: that is, to prescribe the rule by which commerce is to be governed. This power, like all others vested in Congress, is complete in itself, may be exercised to its utmost extent, and acknowledges no limitations other than are prescribed in the Constitution. . . .[25]

Marshall's decision not to address concurrency or exclusivity did little to rob *Gibbons* v. *Ogden* of its extreme historical Constitutional significance. Moreover, in this instance, the facts and parties to the case contributed to its acceptance and, probably, to its eventual widespread and longterm importance. By 1824, nearly every word that John Marshall uttered was coming under attack.

[23]Ibid.
[24]Ibid.
[25]Ibid.

Certainly, the political and popular tides were increasingly turning toward narrow Constitutional construction and states' rights—the polar opposites of Marshall's broad construction and nationalism. Thus, by all rights, the Court's broad interpretation of the national commerce power should have met with extreme anti-national sentiment and resistance. Circumstances, however, made it one of Marshall's most popular decisions. His ruling against Aaron Ogden's steamboat monopoly met with acclaim and apparently overshadowed the broader implications.

ROGER TANEY AND THE DUALITY OF THE COMMERCE POWER

In 1851, more than a quarter of a century after John Marshall sidestepped the issue of concurrent powers, his successor, Roger Taney, issued his court's most famous commerce power decision. In *Cooley* v. *Board of Wardens of the Port of Philadelphia*,[26] Taney applied what has come to be known as the doctrine of "selective exclusiveness" in asserting a limited sphere of commercial concurrency:

> . . . The grant of commercial power to Congress does not contain any terms which expressly exclude the states from exercising an authority over its subject matter. If they are excluded, it must be because the nature of the power, thus granted to Congress, requires that a similar authority should not exist in the states. . . . [T]he mere grant of such power to Congress, did not imply a prohibition on the states to exercise the same power. . . . [I]t is not the mere existence of such a power, but its exercise by Congress, which make it incompatible with the exercise of the same power by the states. . . .
>
> Now, the power to regulate commerce, embraces a vast field, containing not only many, but exceedingly various subjects, quite unlike in their nature; some imperatively demanding a single uniform rule, operating equally on the commerce of the United States in every port; and some, like the subject now in question, as imperatively demanding that diversity, which alone can meet the local necessites of navigation.
>
> [T]he nature of this subject is such, that until Congress should find it necessary to exert its power, it should be left to the legislation of the states. . . .[27]

To many who associate dual federalism and states' rights with the Taney Court, a reading of *Cooley* may come as something of a surprise. Indeed, the court admitted that concurrent commerce powers did exist but not universally, and, in fact, one could infer that a specific Congressional decision to regulate

---

[26]*Cooley* v. *Board of Wardens of the Port of Philadelphia*, 12 Howard 299 (1851).
[27]Ibid.

in this area would preempt state authority. Certainly, the Court did nothing to alter the broad interpretation of the national commerce power which Marshall had articulated twenty-seven years earlier, though it did attempt to maintain some measure of jurisdictional balance.

WAR BETWEEN THE STATES:
THE GREAT CRISIS IN AMERICAN FEDERALISM

By the 1840s, the Court's moderate seed of dual federalism would increasingly be offset by a national duality of far more extreme and tragic consequence. Obscured by the enlarged franchise and "commonizing" of government which Jacksonian Democracy had wrought, sectional antagonisms simmered below the surface—steadily worsening rather than abating as westward expansion and territorial acquisition extended the arena of hostility.

In the second third of the nineteenth Century, the basic source of sectional conflict remained economic. But, where the discrete economic issue of the first third of the century bore the wholly economic and comparatively innocuous trappings of a tariff, the issue surfacing in the second third bore noneconomic implications as well—implications of the most profoundly moral, human, and emotional nature. Of course, the result of these massive conflicts was the great American tragedy known as the Civil War.

The ultimate Union victory in the Civil War acted as the official solution to the three great paradoxical dichotomies which had plagued the American federal system since its inception. Officially (though, in reality, not without much post-war struggle), northern triumph established the nature of the Union, the nature of American democracy, and the nature of the economy.

First, from an obviously Constitutional perspective, the most important result of the Civil War was the resolution of the nature of the Union. The long struggle between national supremacy and state sovereignty was militarily resolved in favor of national supremacy. Four years after the War's end, in *Texas* v. *White*,[28] Chief Justice Salmon P. Chase gave judicial sanction to national supremacy:

> The union of the states never was a purely artificial and arbitrary relation . . . [T]he Constitution was ordained "to form a more perfect Union." It is difficult to convey the idea of indissoluble unity more clearly than by these words. What can be indissoluble if a perpetual Union, made more perfect, is not? . . . The Constitution, in all its provisions, looks to an indestructible Union, composed of indestructible states.[29]

[28]*Texas* v. *White*, 7 Wallace 700 (1869).
[29]Ibid.

Second, the Civil War ended the enslavement of black people in a nation which guaranteed to "all men . . . life, liberty, and the pursuit of happiness." Certainly, slavery was the great visible issue over which the War was fought. It was an American paradox, so immense in its moral and economic implications that it produced insoluble political polarization. Thus, according to Robert Dahl:

> Whether any republic could have arrived at a peaceful solution to any issue as monumental as slavery had become in the United States, no one can say with confidence. What we do know—what no American can forget—is that the American political system was unequal to the task of negotiating a peaceful settlement of the problem of slavery. Violence was substituted for politics.[30]

Through violence, a Constitution which has been repeatedly interpreted as safeguarding the institution of slavery, was significantly altered so that henceforth it barred that institution. Through violence, the Constitution now guaranteed national and state citizenship to "all persons born or naturalized in the United States."[31] The ultimate violence of human subjugation, then, was itself answered with violence. The manifest paradox of American democracy was solved—resolution of the subtle paradox, of course, would take more time.

Third, the War resulted in the triumph of commercialism over agrarianism, serving as America's violent introduction to the industrial revolution. With Union victory, Hamiltonian commercial expansion would prevail over Jeffersonian agricultural parochialism; northern capitalism over southern feudalism:

> Unimpeded by the political opposition of the southern slavocracy, the Republican coalition of north and west carried through a program of comprehensive changes that insured the expansion of industry, commerce, and free farming . . . Instead of the policies of economic laissez faire that the slavocracy had demanded (side by side with a rigid and meticulous governmental intervention to protect slavery), the Republicans substituted the doctrine that the federal government would provide assistance for business, industry, and farming: the protective tariff, homestead, land subsidies for agricultural colleges, transcontinental railways and other internal improvements, national banks. When the defeated south came back into the Union, it had to accept the comprehensive alteration in government policy and economic institutions that the historian Charles A. Beard was later to name the Second American Revolution.[32]

---

[30]Robert A. Dahl, *Pluralist Democracy in the United States: Conflict and Consent* (Chicago: Rand McNally, 1967), p. 302.

[31]*United States Constitution*, Amendment XIV, Sec. 1.

[32]Dahl, *Pluralist Democracy in the United States*, pp. 318–19.

In resolving the three paradoxes, the Civil War—that great and horrible maelstrom of American federalism and Constitutionalism—made the United States what many twentieth-century Americans assume it always had been a democratic, capitalist nation.[33]

The Fourteenth Amendment
and the Second Constitutional Revolution

The second "American Revolution"that was the Civil War was Constitutionally acknowledged by ways of the Fourteenth Amendment, particularly its first section:

> All persons born or naturalized in the United States, and subject to the jurisdiction thereof, are citizens of the United States and of the state wherein they reside. No state shall make or enforce any law which shall abridge the privileges or immunities of the citizens of the United States; nor shall any state deprive any person of life, liberty, or property, without due process of law; nor deny to any person within its jurisdication the equal protection of the laws.[34]

Indeed, "the Great Fourteenth Amendment" has itself been called a "revolution." First, and most readily apparent, it signaled a "revolutionary" change in federalism for it made "national citizenship primary and state citizenship derivative therefrom."[35] Second, through Court decisions, it institutionalized dual federalism, "the theory that the reserved powers of the states must be considered in determining the extent of the powers delegated to Congress. . . ."[36] The theory of state sovereignty was thus increasingly replaced with a judicial coupling of national supremacy and states rights. Third, and less obvious from the beginning, it "revolutionized" due process of law, elevating it from a procedural safeguard to a substantive Constitutional guarantee. Finally, in the years to come, the Amendment would be instrumental in "revolutionizing" the role of the Supreme Court, affording that body the opportunity to shape the economic policy of the nation and the states.

---

[33]Samuel Beer presents an elegant alternative means of examining and organizing the nation's pre-Civil War history. According to his typology, it was characterized by porkbarrel politics, decentralizing intergovernmental relations, and state's rights federalism. See Samuel Beer, "The Modernization of American Federalism," *Publius* 1, no. 3 (Fall 1973): 57–63.

[34]*United States Constitituon*, Amendment XIV, Section 1.

[35]Edward S. Corwin, *The Constitution and What It Means Today*, 12th ed. (Princeton, NJ: Princeton University Press, 1958), p. 248.

[36]Walter Hartwell Bennett, *American Theories of Federalism* (Birmingham, AL: University of Alabama Press, 1964), p. 201.

DUAL FEDERALISM
AND THE REGULATORY "NO-MAN'S LAND"

The great industrial growth of the late nineteenth and early twentieth centuries did not confine itself neatly within the borders of the several states. Railroads carried people and cargo across the nation and the "captains of industry" readily created "interstate trusts." It was an era that saw small entrepreneurs locked out of the "competitive" process and the public locked into the stranglehold of rampant industrial expansion. The states were helpless to control the transnational arrogance of the "robber barons" and, by the turn of the century, the Court had badly curtailed even their internal controls. By the 1880s, it was becoming increasingly clear that only Congress could act to abate all the ill-effects of America's industrial revolution. It alone possessed a powerful Constitutional tool in the interstate commerce clause and it remained only to find a systematic and legally acceptable means of employing that tool. The Congressional answer was the *Interstate Commerce Act of 1887*. In view of recent events, little debate seemed necessary and little, apparently, occurred.

The *Interstate Commerce Act* averred that common carrier rates should be just and reasonable. Rebates and rate discrimination between persons or places were delcared illegal. Long–short haul discrimination was forbidden. Pooling and traffic agreements were outlawed. Finally, the new law created a five-member Interstate Commerce Commission (ICC).

The ICC was significant for a number of reasons. First, the Commission was authorized to administer this completely overt manifestation of the Congressional interstate commerce power. Second, to that purpose, it was given the power "to hear complaints, to inquire into books and accounts of railroads, to hold hearings . . . to compel attendance of witnesses . . . [and] to issue cease-and-desist orders against any carrier found to be violating the provisions of the law."[37] Third, the ICC was wholly unique at the time because it was the first federal commission to be given what appeared to be quasi-legislative, quasi-administrative, and quasi-judicial powers. It appeared, that is, to cut through the normal "separation of powers" at the federal level as well as to place federal regulations where, until recently, only state regulations had existed..

All of this gave the Commission a substantial amount of potential power to bring order to an increasingly chaotic situation. This potential, unfortunately, was not soon to be realized.

The problem was two-fold. In the first place, the Court—as it had done with state regulations—was attempting to shore up its own laissez faire economic doctrine by ruling against some of the clear statutory authority of the ICC. Thus, in *Interstate Commerce Commission* v. *Brimson*,[38] the Court stated that

---

[37]Kelly and Harbison, *The American Constitution*, p. 518.
[38]154 U.S. 447 (1894).

> [a] quasi-judicial agency cannot be granted by Congress the power to compel testimony or to make a final determination of private rights. Such an agency cannot be invested with authority to punish for contempt by fine or imprisonment. The proper procedure is for the agency to place the witness before a federal court. The courts support the valid findings of quasi-judicial agencies and issue enforceable orders.[39]

Obviously, the *Brimson* ruling drastically curtailed the hearing capacity of the ICC, one of its most important statutory functions.

In the second place, and in some fairness to the Court, the enabling legislation may have assumed too much but said too little. That is, certain capabilities essential to the effectiveness of the ICC were not actually stated in the *Interstate Commerce Act*. This was glaringly true of the Commission's power to fix rates. And when the ICC attempted to do just that, the Court made clear "that the grant of such a power is never to be implied."[40]

By the turn of the century, the Commission, courtesy of the Supreme Court, had become little more than a glorified public information agency. For the time being, control of interstate commerce was a sham, existing (or rather, "nonexisting") in that Constitutional "no-man's land." Lest it feel lonely, however, it was soon to be joined there by government antitrust activities.

In 1890, responding to blatantly monopolistic activities on the part of some of the nation's leading industries, Congress enacted the *Sherman Antitrust Act*:

> Naturally the Constitutional basis for the act was the interstate commerce clause. It declared every contract or combination or conspiracy in restraint of interstate or foreign trade or commerce to be illegal. It also declared it illegal to monpolize or attempt to monopolize any part of interstate or foreign commerce. Violation of the act was made a punishable offense. The act lay on the statute book for several years without serious ruffling of its page.[41]

The several years were five. In 1895, the federal government brought suit against the American Sugar Refining Company in an attempt to dissolve its near-monopolistic holdings—in this case, "near"-monopolistic meant 94 percent of the U.S. sugar refining capacity.[42] The government claimed that this resulted in a restraint of interstate commerce, unnaturally high prices, and a restriction of

---

[39]Paul C. Bartholomew, *Governmental Organization, Powers, and Procedure*, Vol. 1 of *American Constitutional Law*, 2nd ed. (Totowa, NJ: Littlefield, Adams, 1978), p. 242.

[40]*Interstate Commerce Commission* v. *Cincinnati, New Orleans, and Texas Pacific Railway Company*, 167 U.S. 479 (1897).

[41]Andrew C. McLaughlin, *A Constitutional History of the United States* (New York: D. Appleton–Century, 1935), pp. 777–78.

[42]*United States* v. *E.C. Knight Company*, 156 U.S. 1 (1895).

trade. However, the Court ruled against the government. In so doing, it fell back upon the narrowest possible definition of commerce, declaring that "commerce succeeds to manufacture, and is not a part of it."[43]

Thus, although the Court admitted the sugar trust to be a monopoly restraining free manufacture, it declared that it was not on this account illegal for manufacturing was not commerce. Further, if this unregulable manufacturing trust did restrain commerce, it was an "indirect" restraint and, therefore, presumably, legally benign. Again, the Supreme Court—bastion of laissez faire economic purity—had turned dual federalism upside-down. Again, it had created a Constitutional "no-man's land" in which no one could act to protect the public, small business, and, increasingly, the economy itself.

THE PROGRESSIVE INTERLUDE: NATIONAL POLICE REGULATORY, SPENDING, AND TAXING POWERS

In 1901, President McKinley was assassinated and his Vice-President succeeded to the high office. A liberal nationalist, Theodore Roosevelt obviously was not aligned with the conservative limbo typified by the Court. He considered himself progressive and intended to use the federal government in general and the Presidency in particular to further his objectives. Thus would begin a twenty-year period in which, for the most part, judicial laissez faire economics lay dormant. To be sure, it was merely a period of latency, but a latency long enough to allow a significant coup in federalism. The "third revolution" did not occur until the era of the second Roosevelt, but the planting of its seeds were begun by the first.

Creating a Federal Police Power

One would search endlessly and in vain for the "police clause" in the United States Constitution. If the founders possessed legal vision, they were neither social nor economic prophets. Thus, they failed to foresee the beginning of urbanization, the crushing floods of immigrants, or the problems of an era two centuries removed. They failed to foresee the merchandizing of putrid meat from the great packing houses of the Midwest—they failed, for that matter, to foresee even the packing houses. Nor did they possess the prescience to conjure up visions of widespread, sophisticated international trafficking in prostitutes. Finally, the mostly gentlemen farmers who framed the Constitution did not envision small children laboring sixty hours a week and more in industrial sweatshops. In short, national police problems in times of peace were simply unanticipated. Police problems were local in their narrowest definition; state problems in their broadest.

[43]Ibid.

The first Congressional attempt to police or regulate the public morals occurred in the area of gambling. The opening wedge was an 1895 act which declared illegal the interstate shipment of lottery tickets. Needless-to-say, "interstate" was, in this case, the significant variable, and what was the shipment of tickets but commerce in its most obvious form, traffic?

The Supreme Court did not gain an opportunity to comment upon the Congressional policing of gambling for eight years. When it did, in *Champion* v. *Ames*,[44] it was asked by those opposed to the law to judge the case on two counts; first, that lottery tickets had no "real or substantial value in themselves, and therefore [were] not subjects of commerce;"[45] and second, that Congress could not use the commerce power at any rate in a prohibitory form—that is to eliminate entirely a certain activity.

In a rather tentative, case-specific, but nonetheless progovernment decision, the Court rejected both arguments.

As had so often been the case in the past, the Court proceeded with caution, seemingly aware of the potential functional applicability of *Champion* v. *Ames*. Indeed, the case did open the way for increasing and more significant use of the commerce power as a federal policing device. Yet, first, Congress was to invent another Constitutional means to the same approximate end, for as John Marshall had once taught the nation, "the power to tax involves the power to destroy. . . . "

The Case of Oleomargarine

In the year before the lottery case came to the Court, Congress took action to limit the sale of artificially colored oleomargarine. The law was largely the result of intense lobbying from the nation's dairy producers—margarine obviously cut into their markets—but it was also predicated upon a valid social concern: margarine producers were passing their product off as real butter. Unlike the lottery law, however, Congress here looked beyond its power to regulate interstate commerce. Instead, it levied a prohibitory (ten cents per pound) tax upon colored margarine, while requiring a benign one-quarter cent per pound on color-free margarine. The intent was exceedingly clear and the case was before the Court in near-record time.[46]

Again, the Court favored the government and therefore denied the two major contentions of the litigant: (1) that Congress could only tax for the purpose of raising revenues and not "to suppress the manufacture of the taxed article;"[47] and (2) that "the power to regulate the manufacture and sale of oleomargarine

[44]*188 U.S. 321 (1903)*.

[45]Ibid.

[46]Kelly and Harbison, *The American Constitution*, p. 555.

[47]*McGray* v. *United States*, 195 U.S. 27 (1904).

[was] solely reserved to the several states. . . ."[48] The judicial blessing apparently given, the Congressional "police power" moved full speed ahead with passage in succeeding years of the *Pure Food and Drug Act*, the *Meat Inspection Act*, and the *White Slave Trade* (or *Mann*) *Act*. Moreover, in dramatic reversals of judicial policies promulgated just twenty years previously, the Court sanctioned aggressive federal regulatory efforts in the areas of antitrust and interstate commerce.[49]

"To . . . Provide for the General Welfare": The Birth of the Federal Grant-in-aid

Unlike the police power, federal grants to the states were not unique to the "progressive interlude" of the early twentieth century. Certainly, land grants had not been at all unusual and financial grants too had been in existence—if not prominently, at least consistently since the 1880s.[50] However, the first of the modern grants (those which, in years to come, would greatly increase the federal role) was developed in the *Weeks Act of 1911*. By the *Weeks Act*, Congress authorized the Secretary of Agriculture "to cooperate with any state or group of states, when requested to do so, in the protection from fire of the forested watersheds of the navigable streams. . . ."[51]

In practice, the *Weeks Act* was hardly an earth-shaking example of intergovernmentalization—total appropriations amounted to only $200,000. Yet, it was prototypical. Thus, three years later, Congress enacted the *Smith-Lever Act* and if the *Weeks Act* was a conditional prototype, *Smith-Lever* set a financial pattern. Establishing the Agricultural Extension Service, the act allocated millions of dollars in its first years of operation—paltry sums by current standards but colossal by those of the 1910s. Moreover, within the next seven years, subsequent grants-in-aid included highway construction funds (the Congressional response to the automobile), appropriations for vocational education, public health allocations, and maternity care grants. By 1925, grants-in-aid totaled about $93 million.[52]

Constitutional authority for this spurt of Congressional spending activity derived from the general welfare clause in Article I, Section 8. Accordingly, Congress was entitled ". . . To . . . provide for the . . . general welfare of the United States. . . ."[53]

[48]Ibid.

[49]See *Northern Securities Co.* v. *United States*, 193 U.S. 197 (1904), *Swift and Co.* v. *United States*, 196 U.S. 375 (1905); and *Houston, East and West Texas Railroad Co.* v. *United States*, 234 U.S. 342 (1914).

[50]Morton Grodzins, *The American System* (Chicago: Rand McNally, 1966), p. 36.

[51]Ibid.

[52]Ibid.

[53]*United States Constitution*, Art. 1, Sec. 8.

In 1923, the State of Massachusetts brought suit against the Secretary of the Treasury, Andrew Mellon, claiming that the maternity care grants offered by the *Sheppard-Towner Act of 1921* were unconstitutional.[54] Rather than rule directly on the merits of the grants, the Court dismissed the case on the grounds that it lacked jurisdiction. Nonetheless, Justice Sutherland, opining for a unanimous Court, indicated his acceptance of this form of Congressional spending. Such grants, he claimed, were not coercive instruments and "probably it would be sufficient to point out that the powers of the state are not invavded, since the statute imposes no obligation, but simply extends an option which the state is free to accept or reject."[55] Though they would experience little growth in the next several years, grants-in-aid were here to stay.

The Income Tax Amendment

Harry N. Scheiber has described the Constitutional period 1890 to 1933 as, overall, an era of "centralizing federalism."[56] It is a characterization—particularly as it pertains to the first two decades of the twentieth century—with which few would argue. A new police power, a revitalized regulatory function, and the growth of conditional grants-in-aid had tilted the scales of "dual federalism" toward the center. Yet, one single event, more than any of the others, contributed to this trend: the *piece de resistance* of the Progressive movement, the Sixteenth Amendment, which reads:

> The Congress shall have the power to lay and collect taxes on incomes, from whatever source derived, without apportionment among the several states, and without regard to any census or enumeration.

As clear and concise as any portion of the Constitution, the Sixteenth Amendment offered the federal government a vast and ever-expanding source of revenue. Truly, the power to tax opened the way for the power to spend. The great centralizing mechanism had been added: the dispersal of its product would centralize even further.

The Seventeenth Amendment:
Repeal of the Great Compromise

The reader will recall that Madison's "neither wholly federal nor wholly national" description of the Constitution had been given its most overt expression in the make-up of Congress. Hence, the Great Compromise of the Constitutional

---

[54]*Massachusetts* v. *Mellon* (*Frothingham* v. *Mellon*), 262 U.S. 447 (1923).

[55]Ibid.

[56]Harry N. Scheiber, "American Federalism and the Diffusion of Power: Historical and Contemporary Perspectives," *The University of Toledo Law Review*, 9, no. 4 (Summer 1978): 640–43.

Convention required that members of the House of Representatives be popularly and proportionately elected (theoretically making that body representative of the people), while the Senate (two members per state) was to be chosen by the respective state legislatures (theoretically making that body representative of the states).

In practice, the compromiser's plan had never quite materialized in the ideal manner. Instead, because of population trends, the House, historically, tended to represent northern, more densely populated parts of the country and the Senate, the South. In a sense, then, the result had been sectional, rather than state representation. However, because Senators were chosen by the state legislatures they were, to a certain extent, creatures of those legislatures and thus the selection method "merely succeeded in converting the elections to state legislatures into indirect senatorial elections."[57] A more sophisticated population saw the anomaly and that insight, coupled with the widespread belief that state legislatures were less than trustworthy seats of great statesmanship, led to the drive—begun as early as 1828—for the Seventeenth Amendment.

Ratified just three months after the Sixteenth Amendment, the Seventeenth Amendment to the Constitution states that, "The Senate of the United States shall be . . . elected by the people thereof. . . ." The effect of the Amendment has been the subject of some debate. While some contend that it has had very little effect on the course of American federalism, others contend that, in fact, the Amendment required a formal repudiation of the state-centered theory of federalism—that it constituted the first successful drive to democratize the federal government. Certainly, inasmuch as it divorced the choice of Senators from the more overt politics of state legislatures, it created a less state-beholden Senate. Directly elected Senators have been far less willing to act as spokespersons for their respective states—in a governmental, not a constituency sense—than their predecessors.[58] Finally, of course, the Amendment was symbolic of an era—an era of national feeling ostensibly to be expressed by a national legislature.

JUDICIAL REACTION IN THE 1920s:
THE REBIRTH OF DUAL FEDERALISM

The first two decades of the twentieth century had witnessed an unprecedented growth in the powers and functions of the federal government. The congressional powers to tax and to regulate interstate commerce were transformed not only into effective means of economic regulation but into a theretofore unheard of

[57]Dahl, *Pluralist Democracy in the United States*, p. 48.

[58]Advisory Commission on Intergovernmental Relations, *Citizen Participation in the American Federal System* (Washington, DC: U.S. Government Printing Office, 1979), pp. 50, 51.

federal police power. To these accumulated powers was added a great potential revenue source, the income tax, and with the power to efficiently tax would come the power to spend—directly and through the states, with "strings attached."

Those years had seen the growth and development of the modern dynamic Presidency—a Presidency of some formal powers but, more important, of vast informal powers. Congress also had begun its modern metamorphosis—creating strong commissions to which it could delegate its own Constitutional authority. And, the Court had changed—becoming more flexible, more accepting of Congressional action, less bound to economic dogmatism. The lone dissents of John Marshall Harlan had been transformed into leading opinions written by the same Mr. Justice Harlan.

Late in the period, the nation entered its first major international conflict, World War I; and, with the War over, the national progressive mood had changed. The Court, too, had changed responding to what previously seemed to be discarded Constitutional theories and economic doctrines and a new twist as well— the "red scare." The so-called liberal bloc, once regularly able to sustain a majority, was whittled down to the point where it merely whispered in the dissents of Justice Holmes, for himself and Justices Brandeis and Stone.

In short, the nation and most of its major institutions had entered upon a period of reaction, spawned by the rapid movement of previous decades, the fear of alien thoughts and ideas, and the ascendancy of business and the entrepreneurial ethic.

Like its prototype thirty years before, the Court of the 1920s created a void in regulatory policy. Again, it preempted the actions of both state and federal governments. Again, in the name of dual federalism, public initiatives were frustrated. But lest the picture be painted too simply, all was not as it had been in the 1890s. For the two decades before 1920, powerful precedents had been established. The powers to tax and spend, to regulate the economy, and to police may have been relegated to a state of relative dormancy through individual judicial decisions, but they had not been consistently nor definitively overruled. Such functions could be revived and strengthened as a result of changing economic conditions, societal outlooks, or judicial tendency. In 1929, the nation was on the verge of experiencing a radical change in the first two variables and though the third would resist it would ultimately have no choice but to change itself. At the close of the "Roaring Twenties"—the age of "normalcy" and reaction—the nation teetered on the brink of great economic upheaval and the "third Constitutional revolution."[59]

---

[59]Unfortunately, space does not permit a thorough assessment of this period. For some of the more notable Court decisions of the decade see: *Hammer* v. *Dagenhart*, 247 U.S. 251 (1918); *Bailey* v. *Drexel Furniture Co.*, 259 U.S. 20 (1922); *Truax* v. *Corrigan*, 257 U.S. 312 (1921); and *Adkins* v. *Children's Hospital*, 261 U.S. 525 (1923).

ORIGINS OF MODERN AMERICAN FEDERALISM

In the year 1929, the age of normalcy came to an abrupt end. Symbolized by a devastating failure of the stock market, the nation entered the age of the Great Depression, an economic cataclysm which would endure for more than a decade. In its inception, the Depression was typified by uncertainty at the very least and by outright panic at the very most. Its life cycle was one which alternately witnessed the greatest of public despair or its opposite, extreme hope. Finally, at its end, the nation was embroiled in the second of the world wars.

By the end of the Depression, the American governmental system was transformed. Whether or not conscious of its plunge into modernity, the nation had modified its view of economy, realigned itself politically, and amended its attitudes on poverty and unemployment. Yet, the Constitution stood practically if not formally transformed. When the clouds of depression lifted, the remaining Constitutional constraints to the growth of the central government had been eroded. The character of American federalism was thenceforth forever changed.

MANAGING THE ECONOMY: FROM NIRA TO AAA

Sector One: Business

The Great Depression of the 1930s was the catastrophic culmination of a major malfunctioning in the economic system of the capitalist world, a failure which temporary relief measures would do little to correct. To the nation's radicals, this was both an anticipated and desired phenomenon. Yet, few Americans were willing to "throw in the towel" on the existing system, preferring instead to correct the defects which had so disrupted their lives. Free enterprise would be retained but at the cost of its own management. The question remained, however, "what constituted a 'managed' economy?"

In the Spring of 1933, while still in the midst of its "Congressional honeymoon," the Roosevelt Administration asked for and received the Tennessee Valley Authority (TVA), "the most imaginative in conception and one of the most successful [New Deal programs] in operation."[60] Representing a quantum-leap in what constituted the proper sphere of government activity,

> The TVA would build multipurpose dams which would serve as reservoirs to control floods and at the same time generate cheap, abundant hydroelectric power. Its power operations were designed to serve as a "yardstick" to measure what would be reasonable rates for a power company to charge.

[60]Paul K. Conkin, *The New Deal*, 2nd ed. (Arlington Heights, IL: AHM Publishing, 1975), p. 46.

> The Authority, which would be a public corporation with the powers of government but the flexibility of a private corporation, would manufacture fertilizer, dig a 650-mile navigation channel from Knoxville to Paducah, engage in soil conservation and reforestation, and. . . . co-operate with state and local agencies in social experiments.[61]

Having succeeded in gaining regionally and functionally limited management, the Administration next eyed the broader arena.

The *National Industrial Recovery Act* (NIRA) of 1933 was the symbolic centerpiece of the early New Deal. An omnibus bill, the NIRA created a massive Public Works Administration (PWA) under long-time Roosevelt cohort, Harold Ickes. More important, however, the legislation brought into being the National Recovery Administration (NRA), the purpose of which was to promulgate "code agreements" with the nation's major industries.

As originally conceived by "braintruster," Rexford Tugwell, the notion of a managed economy under an agency such as the NRA would probably have frightened off any potential supporters, for when Tugwell said "managed" he meant "managed." However, the sort of regimentation and centralized planning which Tugwell proposed had little appeal for the typically practical Roosevelt. Hence, the President's version of NRA offered "a little for everyone."[62]

> Business got government authorization to draft code agreements exempt from antitrust laws; the planners won their demand for government licensing of business; and labor received Section 7(a), modeled on War Labor Board practices, which guaranteed the right to collective bargaining and stipulated that the codes should set minimum wages and maximum hours.[63]

Yet, if everyone got something, initially at least, it was corporate America which got the most. Allowed to write its own regulations, in the beginning, the business world dominated even the code enforcement mechanisms, a veritable bonanza which allowed open price collusion at the same time that it permitted many corporations to evade "the labor codes (bargaining rights, wage-hour protection, prevention of child labor) required by Section 7(a) . . . either by establishing company unions or by deliberate refusals to recognize legitimate unions."[64] For all but a few crusty old nonconformists the business community found precious little to complain about being "managed." Nonetheless, business soon began to grow restless under the codes and regulations. By 1935, NRA's days were numbered.

---

[61]William E. Leuchtenburg, *Franklin D. Roosevelt and the New Deal* (New York: Harper & Row, Pub., 1963), p. 57.

[62]Ibid.

[63]Ibid.

[64]Conkin, *The New Deal*, p. 33.

Section Two: Agriculture

Among those hardest hit by the Great Depression were the nation's farmers. Plagued by an economic crisis which deflated their dollars and left them unable to sell their crops profitably, many were additionally scourged by the heavens themselves as cruelly unremitting dust storms and drought ravaged the mid- and southwest. To the dustbowl farmer of the 1930s, deciding who was his worst enemy, nature or banker, was a difficult choice indeed.

Thus, in 1933, threatened by a nationwide farm strike, Roosevelt and Congress decided to speed through pending agricultural legislation. The resulting *Agricultural Adjustment Act* (AAA) horrified conservatives with its price-setting provisions, subsidies, land retirement program, and its promise of government payments at parity in exchange for decreased production. Beleaguered farmers, however, considered it a godsend. Yet, like the *National Industrial Recovery Act*, the bolder and more effective *Agricultural Adjustment Act* had powerful enemies—enemies in a position to cripple the fledgling law. And, like the NIRA, the AAA's swan song would follow swiftly upon the footsteps of its overture.

DUAL FEDERALISM'S "LAST HURRAH"

Beginning in January of 1935, the Supreme Court of the United States made up its collective mind to substantially crush the New Deal. Working incrementally through the first five months of that year, the Court picked away at or hinted its displeasure with the NIRA, portions of the AAA, and the *Railroad Retirement Act of 1934*, until on "Black Monday," May 27, 1935, those decisions came to an ominous crescendo. On that day, the Supreme court reached out to quell the New Deal through a singularly humble instrument: the Schechter brothers and their "sick chickens."

The case of *Schechter Poultry Corporation* v. *United States*[65] rocked the Roosevelt Administration to its foundations. At issue was the NRA's live-poultry code for the New York metropolitan area poultry industry. The code regulated wages, hours, production, and marketing in the area and as a result, the local Schechter brothers were accused by the federal government of selling "unfit chickens."[66] When the Schechters decided to fight back, the end of the NIRA—Roosevelt's centerpiece legislation—was clearly in sight. Chief Justice Hughes delivered the Court's shattering opinion:

> The Constitution established a national government with powers deemed to be adequate, as they have proved to be both in war and peace, but these

[65] 295 U.S. 495 (1935).

[66] Stanley I. Kutler ed. *The Supreme Court and the Constitution*, 2d ed. (New York: W.W. Norton, 1977), p. 373.

powers of the national government are limited by the Constitutional grants. Those who act under these grants are not at liberty to transcend the imposed limits because they believe that more or different power is necessary. Such assertions of extra-Constitutional authority were anticipated and precluded by the explicit terms of the Tenth Amendment. . . .

[W]here the effect of intrastate transactions upon interstate commerce is merely indirect, such transactions remain within the domain of state power. If the commerce clause were construed to reach all enterprises and transactions which could be said to have an indirect effect upon interstate commerce, the federal authority would embrace practically all the activities of the people and the authority of the state over its domestic concerns would exist only by sufferance of the federal government. . . .

It is not the province of the Court to consider the economic advantages or disadvantages of such a centralized system. It is sufficient to say that the federal Constitution does not provide it. . . . [T]he authority of the federal government may not be pushed to such an extreme as to destroy the distinction, which the commerce clause itself establishes, between "commerce among the several states" and the internal concerns of a state. . . .[67]

The NIRA was dead, the victim of dual federalism and a narrow interpretation of the commerce clause. The broader implications of *Schechter* were aptly summed up by a *London Daily Express* headline: "AMERICA STUNNED; ROOSEVELT'S TWO YEARS' WORK KILLED IN TWENTY MINUTES."[68]

The Court, however, was not finished with the New Deal. In 1936, it ruled that "little NRAs" aimed at specific industries were also unconstitutional.[69] In addition, although the *Agricultural Adjustment Act* lacked the unconstitutional regulatory codes of the NIRA and, instead, offered cooperating farmers payment to reduce production, the Court ruled in 1936 that it too was unconstitutional because it infringed on the reserved rights of the states to regulate and control agricultural production.[70]

TOWARD A CONSTITUTIONAL REVOLUTION: ROOSEVELT, THE SECOND NEW DEAL, AND A "SWITCH IN TIME"

On August 14, 1935, President Roosevelt signed into law one of the most (if not the most) important and profoundly consequential pieces of American legislation ever conceived, the *Social Security Act*. With a stroke of his pen Roosevelt increased the size and scope of the federal role a thousandfold, for thus had the

[67]*Schechter Poultry Corporation* v. *United States*, 295 U.S. 495 (1935).

[68]Leuchtenburg, *Franklin D. Roosevelt and the New Deal*, p. 145.

[69]*Carter* v. *Carter Coal Co.*, 298 U.S. 238 (1936).

[70]*United States* v. *Butler*, 207 U.S. 1 (1936).

central government permanently and massively entered the realm of old age insurance, unemployment insurance, categorical cash assistance (or welfare), and social and health services. In addition, the "second" New Deal, launched in 1935, included the *National Labor Relations Act* which threw the weight of government behind the right to bargain collectively; the *Wealth Tax Act* which added to the increasingly substantial federal taxing power; the *Public Utilities Holding Act* which expanded the powers of the Securities and Exchange Commission; and the *Banking Act* which further centralized the banking system.

Throughout the turbulent summer of 1935, one question must have plagued Roosevelt more than any other, "Would the Court approve?"

Executive Versus Judiciary:
The Court Battle of 1937

Stung by the defeats of his major first New Deal legislation, early in 1937 Roosevelt decided that the same fate would not befall the laws of his second New Deal, particularly the *National Labor Relations* and *Social Security Acts*. His "enemy" was evident and he [decided] to fight it on Congressional turf. His weapon was the Court Bill of 1937.

Whether Roosevelt really expected anyone to believe that the Court Bill was a genuine reform, needed in the long-run for the efficacy of government, is open to question, but if in fact he did hold such expectations, he was to be sorely disappointed. At any rate, the President claimed that the Court system was inefficient, partially due to "the question of aged or infirm judges. . . ."[71] Hence, his proposed court reform

> . . . recommended that when a federal judge who had served at least ten years waited more than six months after his seventieth birthday to resign or retire, the President might add a new judge to the bench. He could appoint as many but no more than six new justices to the Supreme Court and 44 new judges to the lower federal tribunals.[72]

Obviously, what Roosevelt was suggesting was, "court packing," and the very fact that this ploy was so obvious brought down the wrath not only of conservatives, Republicans, and die-hard Roosevelt haters, but of many of his long time supporters as well. Despite initial cries of indignation, however, the President persisted—in fact, seemed obsessed—with the Court legislation. To its end, he wasted an entire session of Congress; angered or insulted many groups whose support he badly needed; made himself appear vulnerable for, perhaps, the first

---

[71]Public Papers, VI, pp. 51–66, cited in Leuchtenburg, *Franklin D. Roosevelt and the New Deal*, p. 233.
[72]Ibid.

time in his Presidency; strengthened the position of the anti-New Dealers; and destroyed the tenuous unity of his own party.[73] What, if any, positive effect all this produced is uncertain, but in the Spring of 1937, the Court did indeed begin to change.

Like 1789 and 1865, 1937 was a banner Constitutional year, for between April and May the legal foundation of America began a metamorphosis, the effects of which have persisted to this day. Hence, in April, the Court handed down its much heralded decision upholding the *National Labor Relations Act,*[74] declaring that:

> Although activities may be intrastate in character when separately considered, if they have such a close and substantial relation to interstate commerce that their control is essential or appropriate to protect that commerce from burdens and obstructions, Congress cannot be denied the power to exercise the control. . . .[75]

On May 25, 1937, the Court considered the Constitutionality of the *Social Security Act* in two companion cases: *Steward Machine Company* v. *Davis*[76] (regarding the Constitutionality of the unemployment insurance tax) and *Helvering, Welch, and the Edison Electric Illuminating Company* v. *Davis*[77] (regarding the Constitutionality of the old age social security tax). In both cases, the use of taxes to provide for so broad a definition of the general welfare was contested and in both cases, the Court upheld that new, massive use:

> The excise is not void as involving the coercion of the states in contravention of the Tenth Amendment or of restrictions implicit in our federal form of government. . . .[78]
> When money is spent to promote the general welfare, the concept of welfare or the opposite is shaped by Congress, not by the states. So the concept be not arbitrary, the locality must yield.[79]

The meaning of the general welfare clause had been changed dramatically; judicial restraints [were] lifted. The remaining constraints on the commerce power would soon be swept away also.

---

[73]See Conkin, *The New Deal*, pp. 88–92; and Leuchtenburg, *Franklin D. Roosevelt and the New Deal*, pp. 231–39.

[74]*National Labor Relations Board* v. *Jones and Laughlin Steel Corporation*, 301 U.S. 1 (1937).

[75]Ibid.

[76]301 U.S. 548 (1937).

[77]301 U.S. 619 (1937).

[78]301 U.S. 548 (1937).

[79]301 U.S. 619 (1937).

In 1938, Congress passed the *Fair Labor Standards Act*. By almost any analysis the act could hardly have been considered a strong piece of legislation, so watered down had it become by the time of its passage. Yet, significantly, the law established a national minimum wage and prohibited the shipment in interstate commerce of goods produced by child labor. Even more significantly, in 1941, a new "Roosevelt Court," drawing heavily upon John Marshall's decision in *Gibbons* v. *Ogden* held the law Constitutional:

> The power of Congress over interstate commerce is not confined to the regulation of commerce among the states. It extends to those activities intrastate which so affect interstate commerce or the exercise of the power of Congress as to make regulation of them appropriate means to the attainment of a legitimate end, the exercise of the granted power of Congress to regulate interstate commerce. . . .
>
> Our conclusion is unaffected by the Tenth Amendment. . . . The amendment states but a truism that all is retained which; has not been surrendered. There is nothing in the history of its adoption to suggest that it was more than declaratory of the relationship between the national and state governments as it had been established by the Constitution before the amendment or that its purpose was other than to allay fears that the new national government might seek to exercise powers not granted, and that the states might not be able to exercise fully their reserved powers.[80]

Obviously, *United States* v. *Darby Lumber Company* was a monumental Supreme Court decision for, in effect, it laid official waste to what for years had been interpreted as the Constitutional centerpiece of dual federalism, the Tenth Amendment.

In 1942, "the judicial reinterpretation of the national government's economic regulatory power was completed. In scope and effect that power was now virtually unlimited."[81] At issue in *Wickard* v. *Filburn* was the *Agricultural Adjustment Act of 1938* and its consequent fixing of acreage quotas—even when excesses were to be consumed by the individual farm family itself.[82] Certainly, this constituted the most *intra* of intrastate consumption. Yet, the Court now recognized no bounds to Congressional power over commerce:

> . . . even if appellee's activity be local and though it may not be regarded as commerce, it may still, whatever its nature, be reached by Congress if it exerts a substantial economic effect on interstate commerce, and this irrespective of whether such effect is what might at some earlier time have been defined as "direct" or "indirect." . . .[83]

[80]*United States* v. *Darby Lumber Co.*, 312 U.S. 100 (1941).

[81]Robert S. Hirschfield, *The Constitution and the Court: The Development of Basic Law through Judicial Interpretation* (New York: Random House, 1962), p. 60.

[82]317 U.S. 111 (1942).

[83]*Wickard* v. *Filburn*, 317 U.S. 111 (1942).

Wickard v. *Filburn* served as the judicial finale to the New Deal, a finale which was to be repeated time and again by the Court. How far the Court had come in relatively few short years from disallowing nearly all Congressional attempts at economic regulation to giving Congress free reign, for the Court— once economic watchdog of the nation—now stated that in this area, "we have nothing to do." Where Congress chose to act in economic and regulatory matters, it would thenceforth be Constitutionally—if not politically—absolute, and as the Court asserted in 1946, the commerce power is "as broad as the economic needs of the nation."[84]

ACQUIESCENCE AND ACTIVISM: JUDICIAL SCHIZOPHRENIA AND THE "FOURTH CONSTITUTIONAL REVOLUTION"

Constitutional development did not end with the New Deal. Rather what did end was a long held judicial notion that the federal government was somehow strictly limited as to the sphere and scope of its undertakings. Hence, as early as 1946, Carl Brent Swisher could assert that "in a sense, what has happened is that the Supreme Court has gotten out of the way of Congress."[85] Indeed, the New Deal left in its wake a legacy of judicial passivity vis-a-vis Congress—a passivity that has largely persisted to form half of the character of the modern Court.

Yet, that the whole character is somewhat schizophrenic is evidenced by the active—and more widely noted—other half, for overall in the past three decades the Court has been a policy leader in advancing racial justice, securing civil liberties, developing criminal procedures, and reforming political processes. The Court, thus, has variously displayed the dichotomous traits of acquiescence on the one hand and activism on the other.

The following noted quotation from a 1963 opinion is illustrative of how fully the Court's vision of its role—at least in relation to the legislature—has changed since 1937:

> We have returned to the original proposition that the Courts do not substitute their social and economic beliefs for the judgement of legislative bodies, who are elected to pass laws.[86]

Moreover, this attitudinal conversion has been accompanied by an even more significant Congressional metamorphosis transforming the Congress from a group of individuals acting as a relatively constrained collectivity, to what, in the past

---

[84]*American Power and Light* v. *Securities and Exchange Commission*, 392 U.S. 90 (1946), cited in Kutler, *The Supreme Court and the Constitution*, p. 406.

[85]Carl Brent Swisher, *The Growth of Constitutional Power in the United States* (Chicago: University of Chicago Press, 1946), pp. 43, 44.

[86]*Ferguson* v. *Skrupa*, 372 U.S. 726, 730 (1963).

twenty years has become, practically, a mere architectural resting place for a loose body of individual activist policy entrepreneurs—albeit somewhat constrained in the past few austerity years. The combined effect of these two transformations—in concert, of course, with other systemic changes—in turn has altered the face of American federalism, the meaning of national supremacy, and the extent of national purpose.

NATIONAL SUPREMACY AND THE POWER TO SUPERSEDE

Since 1937, when the Supreme Court "got out of the way of the Congress," much of the expansion of the federal government has been accomplished through the highly elastic Congressional power to regulate commerce and through extension of the Bill of Rights to the states through the Fourteenth Amendment. Largely uninhibited by judicial taboo, these powers have allowed Congress to increase substantially both the breadth and depth of national functions and goals.

There being, presumably, a finite number of actions or items which may be subject to legislation and fifty-one major legislatures in the United States, at least some functional overlap is bound to occur. As previous sections have detailed, this problem of concurrent powers has been a major Constitutional dilemma since the founding of the Republic. In retrospect, though the debate was often more scurrilous and vocal than today, for the first one and one–half centuries of the nation's existence, the dilemma was comparatively mild—the number of laws enacted by any of the legislatures, especially Congress, were relatively few. However, in the past thirty years, encouraged by the widespread acceptance of active government, the opportunities for overlap and conflict have increased tremendously. In such cases, the law of one legislative body may supersede or preempt those of the others and, though hardly imagined by the founders for the breadth of its authority, Article VI of the Constitution, containing the National Supremacy Clause, has determined whose laws shall preempt and whose shall be preempted.

Though Congress has long been in the business of preempting state laws which conflict with national objectives, the body of supersessive legislation enacted since the mid-1960s has been multiplying at a rate that has begun to alarm many observers. Moreover, a relatively recent congressional innovation— also based on the commerce power and supremacy clause—has been afforded widespread judicial blessing. Hence, "partial preemption":

> . . . is preemption with a twist. Unlike traditional preemption statutes, preemption in these cases is only *partial*. While federal laws establish basic policies, administrative responsibility may be delegated to the states

and localities, provided that they meet certain nationally determined standards.[87]

Examples of federal laws with partial preemption mechanisms include the *Clean Air Act* and the *Federal Water Pollution Control Act*.

The spate of relatively recent preemptory activity has prompted a great deal of concern over the modern meaning and significance of the Tenth Amendment, that addition to the Constitution which the New Deal Court asserted to be "but a truism." And, by and large, the contemporary Court has treated it as just that. However, on June 24, 1976, the Supreme Court handed down a decision which at least was surprising and at most seemed to disrupt long established policy toward the commerce power and the "reserved powers" of the states. At issue in *National League of Cities* v. *Usery*[88] were the 1974 amendments to the *Fair Labor Standards Act of 1938* (FLSA). The amendments extended the minimum wage and maximum hour provisions of the act to most state and local employees. Given the fairly deferential attitude which both the Warren and Burger Courts had exhibited toward Congress, there was little reason to believe that the amendments would be questioned. Moreover, in 1968, the Court had upheld extension of the FLSA wage and hour provisions to state hospital and school employees in *Maryland* v. *Wirtz*.[89] Yet, strong precedent notwithstanding, Justice Rehnquist, speaking for a narrow majority (5–4) revived an interpretation of the commerce clause and Tenth Amendment thought to have been judicially buried almost forty years before. Very briefly, in *NLC*, the Court held that:

> Congress may not exercise its power to regulate commerce so as to force directly upon the states its choices as to how essential decisions regarding the conduct of integral governmental functions are to be made.[90]

That ruling was later refined by means of a fairly stringent three-pronged test, each portion of which a jurisdiction's claim must meet in order for it to invalidate Congressional legislation:

> First, there must be showing that the challenged statute regulates the "States as States;"
>
> second, the federal regulation must address matters that are indisputably "attributes of state sovereignty;" and

[87] Advisory Commission on Intergovernmental Relations, *Regulatory Federalism: Policy, Process, Impact, and Reform* (Washington, DC: U.S. Government Printing Office, 1984), p. 9.

[88] 426 U.S. 833 (1976).

[89] 392 U.S. 183 (1968).

[90] *National League of Cities* v. *Usery*, 426 U.S. 833 (1976).

third, it must be apparent that the States' compliance with the federal law would directly impair their ability "to structure integral operations in areas of traditional functions."[91]

The difficulty of meeting all three requirements was nowhere more apparent than in 1983's most prominent *NLC*-based case.

In *Equal Employment Opportunity Commission (EEOC)* v. *Wyoming*[92] the Court considered a challenge to the 1974 amendments to the *Age Discrimination in Employment Act* (ADEA). Those amendments expanded the definition of "employer" to include state and local governments. Accordingly, it became unlawful for states or their political subdivisions to discriminate against employees or potential employees between the ages of forty and seventy solely on the basis of age, except in instances where age is a "bona fide occupational qualification."[93] For all practical purposes, then, a decision to retire a state or local employee prior to age seventy must be made on an individualized case-by-case basis.

In a 5–4 decision requiring four separate opinions, the Court ruled that "the extension of [ADEA] to cover state and local governments is a valid exercise of Congress' powers under the Commerce Clause . . . and is not precluded by virtue of external constraints imposed on Congress' commerce powers by the Tenth Amendment." Conceding that the management of state parks (the function at issue in the case) "is clearly a traditional state function" and that ADEA does indeed "regulate States as States," the Court nonetheless based its decision on a finding that the state failed to demonstrate that the law would directly impair its ability to structure integral operations. Indeed, the Court hinged its decision on the *degree of federal intrusiveness* as opposed to the simple *fact of intrusiveness*.[94]

Hence, it is doubtful that *NLC* v. *Usery*, as currently construed, has set an immutable precedent reviving old interpretations of the Tenth Amendment and repudiating the totality of the congressional commerce power. And even if that were the case, Congress may achieve virtually the same ends through other means. It is to the most powerful of these methods that we shall now turn.

THE CONDITIONAL SPENDING POWER: COMING AT NATIONAL PURPOSE THROUGH THE BACKDOOR

Over the past two decades, if there has been a single phenomenon which has worked to permute practical intergovernmental relations and erode the concept

---

[91]*Hodel* v. *Virginia Surface Mining and Reclamation Association*, 452 U.S. 264 (1981).
[92]51 LW 4219 (1983).
[93]Ibid.
[94]Ibid. Note: the *Usery* case was overturned in *Garcia* v. *San Antonio* on February 19, 1985.

of federalism, it has been the dramatic expansion in the number, scope, and purpose of federal grants–in–aid.

The now popular and increasingly catch-all term "mandate" has nowhere been applied more frequently than in relation to grant–in–aid conditions. Thus, inasmuch as a mandate is synonymous with an order, the casual observer could arrive at the conclusion that a federal grant condition allows about as much discretion to those it potentially touches as a Hitlerian diktat. Indeed, the frequency and level of complaints from states and localities as well as a growing army of sympathizers in the federal government and academia attest to a widespread perception that such grant-related mandates have a virtual stranglehold on state and local grant recipients. The contractually based notion that compliance is voluntary ("if you don't like the rule, don't take the money") is, within the context of fiscal realities, considered by many antiquated, if not absurd.

However, if the political attitude toward grants and their attendant strings has changed (or at least become considerably more vocal) in recent years, the legal groundrules have remained practically unaltered since 1923. Hence, although in the intervening years grants have become pervasive and their conditions complex, the judicial conception of fiscal and political free-will remains unaffected, as excerpts from these recent decisions indicate:

> The State, by entering into this venture, *voluntarily submitted itself* to federal law. It entered with its eyes open, having more than adequate warning of the controversial nature of the project and of the applicable laws. [*San Antonio Conservation Society* v. *Texas Highway Department* (1971)]
>
> Neither States nor their political subdivisions are compelled to participate in the grand federal scheme created by the Act and thereby receive money. The particpation is *purely at their option.* [*Macon* v. *Marshall* (1977)]
>
> It must be remembered that this act is *not compulsory* on the State. . . .[It] gives to the States an option to enact such legislation and in order to induce that enactment, offers financial assistance. [*North Carolina* v. *Califano* (1977)]

The courts, then, have viewed grant agreements—conditions and all—as completely voluntary mechanisms for disbursing federal funds and, indeed, one can make a very good case for this "caveat emptor" approach, in spite of the often onerous nature of such agreements. Thus, in his seminal statement on the matter, Justice Cardozo offered an eminently practical line of reasoning:

> [To] hold that motive or temptation is equivalent to coercion is to plunge the law into endless difficulties. The outcome of such a doctrine is the acceptance of a philosophical determinism by which choice becomes impossible. Till now the law has been guided by a robust common sense which

assumes the freedom of will as a working hypothesis in the solution of its problems.[95]

Yet, not every Constitutional expert would agree with those sitting on the bench. For instance, Professor A.E. Dick Howard has called such reasoning "simplistic." He argues that it makes constitutional limitations on Congress' power illusory by permitting Congress to do indirectly what it cannot do directly.[96] Moreover, as Richard Cappalli points out, there is an after-the-fact component to the grant agreement where the United States can unilaterally, by either statute or regulation, modify the terms of the relationship during the term of the grant.[97] Thus, under certain circumstances, the federal government may change the rules of the game after the grantee has already bought into the "contract"—often an extraordinary investment.

Crosscutting Requirements and Crossover Sanctions

Grant conditions come in a number of forms—the most common being relatively innocuous, program-specific requirements. However, the past twenty years have witnessed the development and increasing use of conditional techniques—specifically, the crosscutting requirement and the crossover sanction—which, practically speaking, are quite different from their program-specific counterparts. Yet, despite practical differences, the courts have upheld both of these mechanisms as perfectly valid exercises of the spending power.

The modern prototype of crosscutting requirements is Title VI of the *Civil Rights Act of 1964*. Once established in connection with civil rights—a social policy of unquestionable necessity, constitutionally grounded in the Fifth Amendment prohibition against federal financing of governments of other entities that discriminate—the crosscutting device encountered little legal difficulty. While other such requirements—including those copied almost word-for-word from Title VI—have not received the same judicial hands-off treatment as the civil rights statute, the crosscutting device itself has been left constitutionally unscathed, despite the fact that generally applicable requirements may "not [be] reasonably related to achieving the purposes of the spending programs to which they are attached."[98] Thus, although such conditions have added a third dimension to the legality of grant requirements—the federal government may "prevent

---

[95]*Steward Machine Co.* v. *Davis*, 301 U.S. 548 at 590 (1937).

[96]A.E. Dick Howard, "Judicial Federalism: The States and the Supreme Court," in *American Federalism: A New Partnership for the Republic*, ed. Robert C. Hawkins (San Francisco: Institute for Contemporary Studies, 1982), p. 220.

[97]Richard B. Cappalli, *Rights and Remedies under Federal Grants* (Washington, DC: Bureau of National Affairs, Inc., 1979), pp. 177, 178.

[98]"The Federal Conditional Spending Power: A Search for Limits," *Northwestern University Law Review* 70, no. 2 (May–June 1975): 309.

the use of federal funds for purposes contrary to general government policies''— they are, in the greater legal scheme of things, just conditions.[99]

So, too, the crossover sanction is a perfectly legitimate conditional device, albeit a device with a unique twist—failure to comply with program requirements may endanger continued funding of other, distinct programs. It is just that feature which Lewis Kaden finds not only unique, but assails as being the most objectionable of all conditional techniques in terms of restricting state sovereignty.[100] Yet, in response to a Montgomery County, MD challenge to the *National Health Planning Act,* a district court declared that:

> The act imposes no civil or criminal penalties on such states or their officials. While the withholding of federal funds in some instances may resemble the imposition of civil or criminal penalties and while economic pressure may threaten such havoc to a state's well-being as to cause the federal legislation to cross the line which divides inducement from coercion, that line is not crossed in this case. Nor does the act displace local initiative with federal directives. The act mandates essentially a cooperative venture among the federal government and state and local authorities.[101]

Similarly, a North Carolina decision, affirmed by the Supreme Court, upheld the same act despite the fact that it conflicted with North Carolina's Constitution.[102]

More recently, the District of Columbia Court of Appeals upheld a provision of the *Social Security Act* which conditions state receipt of *Medicaid* funds upon the states' ''passing-through'' Congressionally approved cost of living increases to Supplemental Security Income recipients. In the case of *Oklahoma* v. *Schweiker*[103] states argued that the ''pass-through'' provision constituted an unconstitutional exercise of the spending power and a violation of the Tenth Amendment because the condition was completely unrelated to the Medicaid program. Speaking for the court, however, Judge Mikva dismissed state argumentation, ruling that:

> The contention that the pass-through provision is unconstitutional because there is no relationship between a state's supplementary payments and the Medicaid program is overly simplistic. . . .
> . . . Congress' . . . ability to impose conditions on the receipt of federal funds is . . . unquestioned. Although there may be some limit to the terms

[99]Ibid.

[100]Lewis B. Kaden, "Politics, Money, and State Sovereignty: The Judicial Role," *Columbia Law Review* 79 (1979): 881–883.

[101]*Montgomery County* v. *Califano*, 449 F. Supp. 1230 at 1247 (D. Md. 1978).

[102]*North Carolina* v. *Califano*, 445 F. Supp. 532 (E.D.N.C. 1977). aff'd 435 U.S. 962, 985 Ct. 1597 (1978).

[103]49 LW 2822 (D.C. Cir. June 18, 1981).

Congress may impose, this court has been unable to uncover any instance in which a court has invalidated a funding condition.[104]

Pennhurst: Sui Generis Ruling or Judicial Forecast?

The legitimacy of Congress' power to legislate under the Spending Power thus rests on whether the State voluntarily and knowingly accepts the terms of the "contract." . . . Accordingly, if Congress intends to impose a condition on the grant of federal money, it must do so unambiguously.[105]

In its 1980–81 Term, the Supreme Court considered a challenge to conditions at a Pennsylvania state institution for the mentally retarded. The challenge was based in part on the *Developmentally Disabled Assistance and Bill of Rights Act of 1975*—specifically the "bill of rights" component. The Court's response, capsulized in the quotation above, noted that the "bill of rights"—worded in terms of legislative "findings"—represented, at most, a Congressional preference and, in the absence of language specifically saying so, could not be construed as a condition of aid. Congress was thus admonished for its tendency to favor statutory obscurity. Moreover, the decision in *Pennhurst State School and Hospital* v. *Halderman* could potentially set "the stage for attacks on administrative implementation of grant strings—through regulations, guidelines, etc.—on the ground that the agency has imposed duties beyond those in the relevant statute itself."[106]

Two additional statements made by the Court in *Pennhurst* may— though *won't necessarily*—have a profound affect on future judicial grant rulings. Justice Rehnquist's majority opinion warned that:

Though Congress' power to legislate under the Spending Power is broad, it does not include surprising participating States with post-acceptance or 'retrocactive' conditions.[107]

While it is unclear what would constitute a "retroactive" condition, it is at least conceivable that this approach could call into question enactment of new crosscutting conditions which apply to existing programs.

Adding even more to the ominous tone taken by the Court in *Pennhurst* was a footnoted suggestion that "[t]here are limits on the power of Congress to

---

[104]Ibid.

[105]*Pennhurst State School and Hospital* v. *Halderman*, 451 U.S. 1 (1981). The Spending Power refers to the federal government's right to spend funds to provide for the general welfare of the United States.

[106]George D. Brown, "Grant Law and Grant Reform: The Role of the Courts in Federal Financial Assistance Programs," *Intergovernmental Perspective* 7, no. 4 (Fall 1981): 8.

[107]451 U.S. 1 (1981).

impose conditions on the States pursuant to its Spending Power."[108] Thereafter, among other cases, the majority cited *National League of Cities* v. *Usery*. Whether or not this may be taken as an intimation that the Court will, in the future, be disposed to "fill up the empty *NLC* vessel" is impossible to know—a footnote does not a strong precedent make. "Still," according to Professor George Brown, "Supreme Court footnotes are often harbingers of things to come; and this particular statement may force lower courts to take more seriously challenges to grant conditions based on state sovereignty grounds."[109]

THE NEW JUDICIARY AND CIVIL RIGHTS

If the Warren and Burger Courts have been notable for their acquiescence to Congressional preemption and mandating, they have been far more notable for their activism in creating a legal framework for racial justice. Beginning with the *Brown* decision in 1954, which denounced the "separate but equal" dictum of *Plessy* v. *Ferguson*, the Court has, with only a few exceptions over the past thirty years, constructed a judicial stream espousing as its goal equality and integration. Hence, in the realm of integration, the Court, despite encountering massive state and local resistance in the South, tenaciously pursued a policy of desegregation, based upon application of the due process and equal protection clauses of the Fourteenth Amendment. Moreover, in enacting Title VI of the *Civil Rights Act of 1964*, Congress bolstered its case by using the spending power to ensure against discrimination by recipients of federal grants.

During the same period, the Warren Court and Congress also attacked the problems of voting rights and housing discrimination as well as discrimination in property rentals and sales. The Burger Court's civil rights rulings, while somewhat more inconstant than those of the Warren Court, have sustained, at least generally, the decisions of its predecessor and, in a few instances, have gone even farther. Thus, in ordering the first major busing effort,[110] the Burger Court exhibited its willingness to go beyond the Warren Court in the area of desegregation and its *Fullilove* affirmative action decision has been described by some as the greatest civil rights decision since *Brown*.[111] Yet, oddly, less than three months before the *Fullilove* decision, the Burger Court overturned a District Court ruling that the city of Mobile, Alabama's at-large electoral system invidiously discriminated against blacks in violation of the Fifteenth Amendment and the equal protection clause of the Fourteenth Amendment.[112] Needless to

---

[108]Ibid.

[109]Brown, "Grant Law and Grant Reform," p. 8.

[110]*Swann* v. *Charlotte-Mecklenburg Board of Education*, 402 U.S. 1 (1971).

[111]Fullilove v. *Klutznick*, Docket No. 78-1007, July 2, 1980.

[112]*City of Mobile, Alabama, et al* v. *Bolden, et al*. Docket No. 77-1844, April 22, 1980.

say, such apparent flip-flops invite varying interpretations. Critics have accused the Burger Court of vacillating and, thus, bringing uncertainty to that area of Constitutional rights which can least afford such judicial fluctuation. While few would accuse the current Court of turning its back on civil rights, some charge that it has unduly confused the issue.

Proponents of the Burger Court, on the other hand, claim that other factors have entered into the Court's civil rights decisions—factors against which the Court had to weigh its role as protector of minority rights. Hence, in the *Mobile* case, the Court claimed that the city's at-large electoral system was not purposively constructed to discriminate against blacks, that such districts do not depart from the principle of apportionment on the basis of population, and that so long as a local electoral process adheres to the "one man, one vote" rule, it is not within the purview of the Court to interfere with local practice. Such an opinion, say Court proponents, does not imply an insensitivity to minority rights and the federal principle. Whether the area of civil rights allows for such "weighing" will, undoubtedly, be a critical subject of debate for some time to come.

In recent history perhaps no civil rights statute has provoked as much intergovernmental tension as the ancient *Civil Rights Act of 1871*—specifically, 42 U.S.C. Section 1983 which reads:

> Every person who, under color of any statute, ordinance, regulation, custom, or usage, of any state or territory, subjects, or causes to be subjected, any citizen of the United States or other person within the jurisdiction thereof to the deprivation of any rights, privileges, or immunities secured by the Constitution or laws, shall be liable to the party injured in an action at law, suit in equity, or other proper proceeding for redress.

Rarely used for the first ninety years of its existence, a series of Court decisions beginning in 1961 and greatly accelerating throughout the late 1970s and early 1980s:

1. expanded the scope of the phrase "under color of state [law]" to include actions by authorities not necessarily acting according to official state policy;
2. declared that municipalities could be liable as "persons" under Section 1983;
3. averred that municipalities could not employ a "good faith defense" in order to invoke qualified immunity from Section 1983 claims;
4. extended the scope of legal rights, the deprivation of which could trigger a Section 1983 action, beyond constitutional rights to include rights created by federal statutory laws; and
5. sanctioned the availability of punitive damages under the Act—even in cases where the deprivation of rights is caused by official indifference as opposed to malicious intent.[113]

[113]*Monrove* v. *Pape*, 365 U.S. 167 (1961); *Monell* v. *Department of Social Services*, 436 U.S. 658 (1978); *Owens* v. *City of Independence*, 455 U.S. 622 (1980); *Maine* v. *Thiboutout*, 448 U.S. 1 (1980); and *Smith* v. *Wade*, 51 LW 4407 (1983).

According to a 1980 survey undertaken by the National Institute of Municipal Law Officers (NIMLO), if damages were collected for all civil rights claims then pending against municipalities, the dollar cost to local treasuries would be an estimated $4.1 billion.[114] According to some observers, however, the indirect effects of continued litigation under the law are more troublesome than the potential direct effects:

> Because [the Court's] decision will inject constant consideration of Section 1983 liability into local decisionmaking, it may restrict the independence of local governments and their ability to respond to the needs of their communities. . . . If officials must look over their shoulders at strict municipal liability for unknowable Constitutional deprivations, the resulting degree of governmental paralysis will be little different from that caused by personal liability.[115]

THE NEW JUDICIARY AND CIVIL LIBERTIES

Over the past thirty years, the Supreme Court has engendered a revolution in First Amendment freedom at least comparable to the revolution effected in civil rights. This extension of civil liberties has enveloped the rights of political dissent, unhindered speech, an unfettered press, and personal privacy.

The first hints of the new and expansive judicial attitude toward civil liberties became evident in the 1950s and 1960s in a series of rulings regarding the Communist Party. Such decisions struck heavy blows at restrictive McCarthy-era controls on party members and other so-called subversives at both the national and state levels.

Political dissent and the right to articulate such dissent came once more to the Court's attention during the Vietnam War. In these cases, the tendency of the Court was to distinquish between actual speech and action. Hence, it held a law which punished the casting of verbal aspersions on the American flag unconstitutional, but upheld a local ordinance which outlawed the burning of draft cards.[116]

In 1976, the Burger Court moved beyond the realm of alleged subversion and political dissent into the question of political patronage as a potential infringement upon First Amendment rights. Thus, in the case of *Elrod* v. *Burns*,[117] a Court plurality held that the Constitutional rights of some noncivil service employ-

---

[114]*Brief Amicus Curiae of the National Institute of Municipal Law Officers in Support of Petitioners, City of Newport, et al.*, in the Supreme Court of the United States, October Term, 1980, *The City of Newport, Rhode Island et al., v. Fact Concerts, Inc., et al.*, No. 80-396.

[115]Dissenting opinion in *Owen* v. *City of Independence*, 455 U.S. 622 (1980).

[116]*United States* v. *O'Brien*, 391 U.S. 367 (1968).

[117]965 U.S. 2673 (1976).

ees were violated when they were fired for Republican Party affiliation in Democratic Cook County, Illinois. Four years later, in *Branti* v. *Finkel,*[118] the Court reaffirmed the *Elrod* decision.

All of the free speech/association cases noted above presented the Court with grave questions of political freedoms under the First Amendment. Equally complicated questions of First Amendment rights were raised in the 1960s and 1970s in a series of pornography cases. For its part, the Burger Court has seen fit to offer somewhat more leeway to individual communities in determining their own moral standards than did the Warren Court. While a local community may not be able to ban pornography outright, under Burger Court dicta, it may at least regulate certain aspects of pornographic businesses within its boundaries.[119]

Freedom of the press cases generally have dealt with one of four issues: prior restraint, press access (particularly with regard to court trials), the right to withhold information regarding news sources, and libel. Of particular interest here has been the Court's "nationalization of the law of libel."[120]

With few exceptions, throughout most of American history, libel has been considered either a matter for state statutes or for state courts to determine based on common law. However, beginning in 1964, the Warren Court took steps to bring libel under the umbrella of the Constitution. In *New York Times* v. *Sullivan,*[121] the Court enunciated the so-called "New York Times formula." Thus, in a unanimous decision, the Supreme Court held that a public official could not recover damages for a defamatory falsehood unless it is proved that the statement was made with "actual malice."[122] Moreover, the Court subsequently extended libel immunity to cases involving such diverse public figures as a football coach, a retired army officer, and even a family whose privacy allegedly had been invaded.

Although the Burger Court refused, in 1974, to go so far as to extend libel immunity to stories concerning any peripherally public figure, it nonetheless has articulated very broad rules which all but free responsible publishers and reporters from successful libel suits.

In no area did the activism of the Warren Court meet with more widespread and sustained hostility than its reform of criminal procedure. Employing the Fourteenth Amendment, the Court began in the early 1960s to apply Fourth, Fifth, and Sixth Amendment guarantees to state and local police departments and courts and in doing so ran squarely into claims that it was hamstringing officers of the law, being soft on criminals and hard on innocent victims, intruding

[118]Docket No. 78-1654, March 31, 1980.
[119]*Paris Adult Theater I* v. *Slayton*, 413 U.S. 49 (1973).
[120]Kelly and Harbison, *The American Constitution*, p. 958.
[121]367 U.S. 254 (1964).
[122]Ibid.

on local prerogatives, and encouraging ubiquitous criminality. Specifically, the Warren Court applied the Fourth Amendment's "exclusionary rule"—which ordained as inadmissable trial evidence obtained through illegal (warrantless or without "probable cause") search and seizure—to the states,[123] required them to provide defense attorneys to indigent defendants in criminal cases,[124] and, in *Miranda* v. *Arizona*,[125] applied the Fifth Amendment's prohibition against self-incrimination to them by requiring that the accused be adequately and effectively appraised of his or her rights.

If any area of law recently has witnessed a departure in the Warren Court philosophy from that of the Burger Court, it has been the field of criminal procedure. Hence, in a series of 1983/84 Term cases, the Court began relaxing the exclusionary rule for the first time in seventy years, creating a "good faith" exception to its strictures.[126] In the same Term, the Court announced a "public safety" exception to *Miranda*'s prohibition against self-incrimination.[127] Moreover, in previous Terms, the Court moved to restrict somewhat the use by state prisoners of habeas corpus petitions.[128]

THE NEW JUDICIARY AND EQUITY

While civil rights constitutes a very distinctive and discrete category of equity concerns, other grave matters coming before the Court have also revolved around questions of equity. Among these, the most notable have been those involving legislative apportionment.

Though in the long-run less controversial than the Court's civil rights and criminal procedures decisions, Chief Justice Warren regarded the reapportionment cases as the most important decisions of the decade and a half in which he presided over the Court.[129] Indeed, in many states the apportionment of state legislatures and Congressional delegations was nothing short of scandalous. Yet, until 1962 the Court had fallen back on an 1849 doctrine which held that certain problems were inherently "political problems" and, therefore, "beyond [the Court's] appropriate sphere of action."[130]

---

[123]*Mapp* v. *Ohio* 367 U.S., 643 (1961).

[124]*Gideon* v. *Wainwright*, 372 U.S. 335 (1963).

[125]*Miranda* v. *Arizona*, 483 U.S. 436 (1966).

[126]*U.S.* v. *Leon*, 52 LW 5155 (1984); *Massachusetts* v. *Sheppard*, 52 LW 5177 (1984); and *Segura* v. *United States*, 52 LW 5128.

[127]*New York* v. *Quarles*, 52 LW 4790 (1984).

[128]*Rose* v. *Lundy*, 50 LW 4272 (1982); and *Engle* v. *Issac*, 50 LW 4376 (1982).

[129]Archibald Cox, *The Role of the Supreme Court in American Government* (New York: Oxford University Press, 1976), p. 68.

[130]*Luther* v. *Borden*, 7 Howard 1 (1849).

In 1962, however, the Court found in *Baker* v. *Carr*—a case concerning Tennessee's apportionment of its general assembly—that apportionment was a legitimate judicial question. In 1963, the Court overturned Georgia's county "unit rule" which effectively discriminated against the state's most populous counties and, in 1964, in *Westberry* v. *Sanders*, the Court enunciated its famous "one man, one vote" principle in nullifying Georgia's method of congressional apportionment. Finally, in *Reynolds* v. *Sims*, also decided in 1964, the Court elaborated on its "one man, one vote" principle by ruling that major population disparities within state legislative districts were unconstitutional.[131]

As might be expected, the Burger Court has been less expansive in its equity decisions than its predecessor. For example, it has allowed slightly larger disparities in the size of electoral districts than did the Warren Court. In *Brown* v. *Thompson* (1983), the Burger Court let stand a Wyoming apportionment scheme in which the voters of one small county were effectively given more than two and one-half times the voting strength of the state's average citizen on the basis that the policy was representative of "consistent and nondiscriminatory application of a legitimate state policy."

Reapportionment/voting cases (and, of course, the civil rights cases) have not been the only equity issues with which the Court has had to grapple. Indeed, "[t]he successful accomplishment of [the reapportionment] reforms by Constitutional litigation led other groups to invoke the Equal Protection Clause in an effort to obtain by adjudication what they could not win in the political arena."[132] The majority of these cases fell upon the Burger Court.

One such category of equal protection cases encompassed state residency requirements of various sorts. In such cases, the Court held prior residency unconstitutional as it applied to welfare payments, some voting requirements, and free hospital care and Constitutional as it applied to less lengthy voting requirements and tuition differentials between in-state and out-of-state student at state universities.[133]

CONCLUSION

In the area of equity, as in those of civil rights, civil liberties, and criminal procedure, the Burger Court, apparently, has attempted to weigh individual rights against the rights of the states in a federal system. Indeed, in one way or another, the Supreme Court has been grappling with this dilemma for almost 200 years. Yet, in its treatment of the dilemma, the Burger court often has tended to appear

[131]*Baker* v. *Carr*, 369 U.S. 186 (1962); *Westberry* v. *Sanders*, 376 U.S. 1 (1964); and *Reynolds* v. *Sims*, 377 U.S. 533 (1964).

[132]Cox, *The Role of the Supreme Court in American Government*, p. 69.

[133]*Shapiro* v. *Thompson*, 394 U.S. 618 (1969); *Dunn* v. *Blumstein*, 405 U.S. 330 (1972); *Memorial Hospital* v. *Maricopa County*, 415 U.S. 250 (1974); *Starns* v. *Malkerson*, 326 F. Supp. 234 affirmed, 401 U.S. 985 (1971).

inconsistent, if not incomprehensible, on both counts. Clearly, all concerned—analysts, casual observers, the ever-increasing army of litigants, even the Court itself—are confused. Nor is it immediately apparent whether this confusion is the symptom of a wrenching Constitutional transition, a genuine attempt to balance the protection of individual rights with the traditional institutional relationships such as federalism, the legal manifestation of an overloaded society, or merely the product of faulty judicial logic.

Of course, any given judicial philosophy or the lack thereof, particularly regarding the federal system, is a fleeting thing. As Woodrow Wilson asserted more than seventy-five years ago:

> The question of the relation of the states to the federal government is the cardinal question of our Constitutional system. It cannot be settled by the opinion of one generation, because it is a question of growth, and each successive stage of our political and economic development gives it a new aspect, makes it a new question.[134]

Or perhaps, as former Chief Justice Charles Evans Hughes put it:

> We are under a Constitution, but the Constitution is what the judges say it is . . .[135]

---

[134]Woodrow Wilson, *Constitutional Government in the United States* (New York: Columbia University Press, 1908), p. 173.

[135]Charles Evans Hughes, quoted in Corwin, *The Constitution and What It Means Today*, p. xv.

Albert J. Richter

3

THE PRESIDENT
AND INTERGOVERNMENTAL
RELATIONS

The American presidency has been involved in intergovernmental relations from the time the office was established in 1789. Yet that involvement was minimal until the 1930s when, under the leadership of Franklin D. Roosevelt, the national government was thrust into a leading role in the nation's domestic affairs. The programs of the New Deal brought a dramatic centralization of power in fields previously occupied exclusively or largely by the states.

Presidential involvement in federalism issues took on a new dimension in the 1960s, when federal grants-in-aid expanded greatly in number, scope, and complexity, becoming the dominant mechanism of federal–state–local relations. Since that time, the president's role in intergovernmental relations essentially has depended on his view of the desired sharing of responsibilities among the federal, state, and local governments, and on his concern about the impact of federal grants and, in the past decade or so, of federal regulations, upon that relationship. It has depended further on his ability and willingness to dedicate personal and political resources to pursuing his intergovernmental goals in the face of the many other demands on his time and attention.

THE FIRST 144 YEARS: 1789–1933

From the earliest days of the Republic, presidents have cultivated state support in advancing their national programs and policies, preeminently through state governors. In 1807, for example, Thomas Jefferson sought the cooperation of the governor of Massachusetts in making his *Embargo Act* policy work,[1] and during the Civil War, Lincoln maintained close touch with the "loyal" governors of the northern states. In 1907, President Theodore Roosevelt invited the governors of the states to a White House conference to solicit their support in promoting his conservation programs. This event had special significance in that it led the governors to set up an annual Governors' Conference, which evolved into the permanent body now known as the National Governors' Association.[2]

Presidential relations with the states were not always sweetness and light, of course. Witness Lincoln's jousting with the governors of the Confederate states and Jackson's dispute with South Carolina (and most specifically, Senator John C. Calhoun) over that state's attempt to declare the protective tariff null and void. Moreover, when governors saw federal actions as unconstitutional encroachments on powers reserved to the states, they usually were among the leading objectors and resisters.[3]

Early in this century Woodrow Wilson recognized the importance of federal–state relations when he wrote that "[t]he question of the relation of the States to the federal government is the cardinal question of our constitutional system."[4] Although the eight years of his presidency saw the initial enactment of pioneering grants-in-aid for the Agricultural Extension Service (1914), highways (1916), and vocational education programs (1917), however, they registered little further impact on intergovernmental relations.

Generally, then, presidential involvement in national–state relations was a random and occasional phenomenon in the nation's first century and a half. It did not assume anything near its present proportions until the coming of the New Deal in the Depression days of the 1930s, when a sea change occurred in federal–state–local relations.

FROM THE NEW DEAL TO THE GREAT SOCIETY

In the "depression decade," the federal government moved aggressively into welfare and economic security areas that historically had been the province of the states and localities but which they now were uanble to handle because of shrunken resources and burgeoning demands created by the collapse of the

[1]For Jefferson's views on federalism, see James C. Bradford, "Thomas Jefferson and Federalism," *The Administration of the New Federalism: Objectives and Issues* (Washington, DC: U.S. Government Printing Office, 1973), pp. 112–14.

[2]Joseph E. Kallenbach, *The American Chief Executive: The Presidency and the Governorship* (New York: Harper & Row Pub., 1966), p. 522.

[3]W. Brooke Graves, *American Intergovernmental Relations* (New York: Charles Scribner's Sons, 1964), p. 178.

[4]Woodrow Wilson, *Constitutional Government in the United States* (New York: Columbia University Press, 1961), paperback ed., p. 173.

national economy. The principal instrument of federal involvement was the grant-in-aid, which then, as now, carried with it administrative supervision by the federal government to see that national purposes were being carried out by state and local recipients.

> During 1933–35 alone, new intergovernmental programs were established for distribution of surplus farm products to the needy, free school lunches, child welfare, maternal and children's health, and crippled children's serv-ices, old-age assistance, aid to dependent children, aid to the blind, general health services, emergency highway expenditures, and emergency work relief, and aid in support of general local-government costs, general relief, and administration of Social Security insurance. Between 1935 and 1938, Congress added new programs for fish and wildlife conservation, public housing, emergency road and bridge construction, and venereal disease and tuberculosis control.
>
> Measured in terms of cash expended for Federal grants to State and local government, the New Deal programs dwarfed anything that had been un-dertaken before.[5]

The New Deal brought other basic changes in intergovernmental relations. The emergency relief agencies broke new ground by making grants-in-aid directly to localities, bypassing the states. Other programs cut across the traditional political jurisdictions by creating special district governments or by establishing multistate regional offices. The massive flow of federal funds caused a skewing of state and local government financing as legislators tended to allocate revenues to programs that commanded matching federal funds. And the growing impor-tance of intergovernmental programs tended to fractionalize responsibility and power between and among the several levels of government.[6]

One of the earliest evidences of presidential concern about these and other impacts of federal programs on states and localities came when President Franklin D. Roosevelt named White House personnel to attempt to coordinate such pro-grams.[7] But the first concerted effort to establish institutions to help the president focus on intergovernmental relations stemmed from the broader problems of dealing with the president's overall managerial responsibilities. Concern for this problem resulted in establishing the first Commission on the Organization of the Executive Branch (Hoover Commission) in 1949. Among the many management issues it identified was the "fragmentation" of federal assistance programs. The Commission urged a strengthening of the president's administrative authority

---

[5]Harry N. Scheiber, *The Condition of American Federalism: An Historian's View*, a study submitted by the Subcommittee on Intergovernmental Relations to the Committee on Government Operations, U.S. Senate, 89th Cong., 2nd Sess., 15 October 1966, pp. 8–9.

[6]Ibid., pp. 10–11.

[7]Graves, *American Intergovernmental Relations*, p. 886.

and the reorganization of governmental departments and agencies by major purpose. Although the number and scope of intergovernmental programs was small by today's standards, the Commission criticized the "fragmentation" of federal assistance programs and recommended creation of a continuing agency on federal–state relationships.

Further action, however, awaited the inauguration of President Dwight D. Eisenhower, who came into office with a definite attitude favoring strong state partners in the federal system. In one of his 1952 campaign speeches he declared:

> I want to see maintained the constitutional relationship between the Federal and State governments. My oath of office [as President] would demand that. My convictions would require it.
>
> . . . if the States lose their meaning, our entire system of government loses its meaning. And the next step is the rise of the centralized national state in which the seeds of autocracy can take root and grow.[8]

And in a message to Congress in early 1953, he stated that

> Our social rights are a most important part of our heritage and must be guarded and defended with all of our strength. I firmly believe that the primary way of accomplishing this is to recommend the creation of a commission to study the means of achieving a sounder relationship between Federal, State, and local governments.[9]

Congress responded by creating the temporary Commission on Intergovernmental Relations, directing it to examine the role of the national government in relation to the states and their political subdivisions. It became known as the Kestnbaum Commission after its second chairman, Meyer Kestnbaum. The Commission issued its report in June 1955 with an extensive list of recommendations, including a proposal that concerted attention be given to interlevel relationships. To this end, it recommended a special assistant in the Executive Office of the President to serve with a small staff as the president's aide and adviser on state and local relationships. The staff aide would be the coordinating center of administration policies on interlevel relationships. In addition, the Commission urged intensification of Bureau of the Budget (BOB) activity, particularly on the fiscal aspects of intergovernmental relations, and creation of an Advisory Board on Intergovernmental Relations.[10]

President Eisenhower responded to the recommendation by naming a Deputy Assistant for Intergovernmental Relations. Significantly, each succeeding

---

[8]Cited in Graves, *American Intergovernmental Relations*, p. 892.

[9]Cited in Commission on Intergovernmental Relations, *A Report to the President for Transmittal to the Congress* (Washington, DC: U.S. Government Printing Office, 1955), p. v.

[10]Ibid., pp. 87–88.

president has designated one or more staff members to be primarily responsible for intergovernmental relations. Although they have differed in regard to their other duties and their relationship to the rest of the Executive Office, three common threads pervade the roles played by these presidential advisers on intergovernmental matters. First, their chief function has been to maintain close contacts with state and local government interest groups. Second, they have played essentially a political role, dealing with issues of policies, politics and management. Third, their influence, impact, and effectiveness have varied extensively.[11]

Partially in response to another one of the Kestnbaum Commission's recommendations, and partially as a follow-up to its own field hearings on the federal aid system, the House Subcommittee on Intergovernmental Relations held hearings in 1959 on the proposal to create a permanent national, nonpartisan Advisory Commission on Intergovernmental Relations (ACIR) to study and make recommendations for improving the operation of the federal system. A bill to establish such a body was introduced the same year and passed both houses and was signed by the President in September 1959.

The president has a number of responsibilities with regard to ACIR: he appoints twenty of the twenty-six members (the other six being named by the Senate and the House), he names the chairman, and receives, along with the Congress, the Commission's annual report. The Commission's budget is also subject to review and approval by the U.S. Office of Management and Budget and is included in the president's budget, which is submitted annually to Congress.

The final significant action taken by President Eisenhower concerning intergovernmental relations began with his appearance before the National Governors' Conference in June 1957. Here he suggested that the Conference join with his Administration to form a committee to designate which functions performed by the national government the states would be willing to take over and to recommend federal and state revenue adjustments to enable the states to fund these functions. The Conference endorsed the proposal and the Joint Federal–State Action Committee, composed of 10 governors and seven top-ranking federal officials, was organized. The committee met several times and in December 1957 recommended that the states assume full responsibility for the federally aided programs of vocational education and waste-treatment plant construction in exchange for the federal government's relinquishing a portion of its tax on local telephone service. In May 1958, the President sent draft legislation to Congress to implement the committee's recommendations. No Congressional action was taken, however, chiefly because about twenty states would have been financially disadvantaged by the transfer proposal, even though it would have resulted in a net loss of more than $50 million a year to the federal government.[12]

[11]Deil S. Wright, *Understanding Intergovernmental Relations*, 2nd ed. (Monterey, CA: Brooks/Cole, 1982), p. 137.

[12]Delphis C. Goldberg, "Intergovernmental Relations: From the Legislative Perspective," *The Annals* (November 1974), pp. 56–57.

THE GREAT SOCIETY AND CREATIVE FEDERALISM

The 1,000 day administration of President John Kennedy was marked by relatively little focus on intergovernmental relations as such. A member of his staff (former Congressman Brooks Hays) served as intergovernmental liaison on federal–state–local relations, but the President's attention was directed more at foreign relations and, on the domestic scene, toward stimulating the economy and addressing longstanding social issues, primarily civil rights.[13] Many of the domestic initiatives that were to succeed in the rush of legislative activity in the successor Johnson Administration, however, had their gestation in the Kennedy Administration, including the controversial community-action program and other elements of President Johnson's War on Poverty.

A key feature of Johnson's plans for a *Great Society* was *Creative Federalism*, defined as the cooperation of state and city, business and labor, and private institutions and private enterprise.[14] It was characterized mainly by an explosive growth in the use of grants-in-aid, particularly project (discretionary) grants. By one count, the total number of grants grew from 160 in 1962 to 379 in 1967, with project grants increasing from 107 to 280. Administratively, this growth was complicated by the attachment of numerous and detailed conditions for use of the grants. Planning requirements, for example, accompanied sixty-one of the new grant programs enacted between 1961 and 1966. In addition, the preference for project over formula grants increased the diversity of activities supported by federal funds and expanded autonomy and discretion of federal program administrators. Moreover, direct federal linkages with localities increased dramatically (especially fostered by some seventy new grant programs that permitted direct disbursement to substate units, shortcircuiting the established federal–state–local channel), further complicating intergovernmental administrative and program relationships.[15]

It was no surprise, then, that the fiscal and administrative aspects of grant-in-aid programs became a central concern of federal–state–local relations and of the president's involvement therein. As one observer commented later:

> . . . the executive branch is confronted with the reality that the grant-in-aid is in the forefront and is the "warp and woof" of day-to-day intergovernmental relationships which must be performed if the system is to work at all. The grant structure is where IGR becomes an operating reality and where the battle is joined.[16]

[13]Erwin C. Hargrove, *The Power of the Modern Presidency* (Philadelphia: Temple University Press, 1974), p. 210.

[14]Congressional Quarterly, *Congress and the Nation*, vol. II (Washington, DC: Congressional Quarterly, Inc. 1965–68), p. 650.

[15]David B. Walker, *Toward a Functioning Federalism* (Cambridge, MA: Winthrop, 1981), p. 102.

[16]Thomas Graves, "The New Federalism," *The Annals* (November 1974), p. 42.

In response to the rising chorus of complaints about the administrative confusion and complexities caused by proliferating grant programs, President Johnson undertook a number of initiatives. He inaugurated a new procedure for federal officals to consult with state and local officials before issuing new federal regulations (BOB Circular A-85), and dispatched teams of top-level political and administraive officials—the "Flying Feds"—to meet and confer with state and local leaders about funding, coordination, and other intergovernmental problems arising from administration of the grant programs. He also directed the Bureau of the Budget to initiate a comprehensive program for reforming grant administration, which included possible consolidations of categorical grants, reviewing federal field office structure to make it more responsive to local needs and more effective in coordinating federal programs at the point of service delivery, and issuing BOB management directives on such subjects as uniform administrative requirements, cost principles, and uniform auditing procedures. Moreover, the President launched the Community Action, Model Cities, and Appalachian Regional Commission programs which, among other things, aimed to induce improved coordination of services at the point of delivery. He also gave his support to Congressional passage of the *Intergovernmental Cooperation Act of 1968*, which addressed a number of problems in federal–state–local administrative relations. These included controlling the impact of federal grant programs on orderly physical development by requiring that all federal aid for development purposes be consistent with state, local, and regional planning.[17]

All these measures of the Johnson presidency were basically efforts to improve administration, to strengthen informational contacts, and to reduce intergovernmental frictions within the existing distribution of power and functional responsibilities between the national government on one hand and the states and localities on the other. Unlike his Republican successors, President Johnson had no intention to effect a basic decentralization or devolution of power. On the contrary, he fully intended to use the national government as the major engine driving the Great Society programs. In the final analysis, however, fulfillment of those good intentions was to suffer from the President's increasing absorption in the Vietnam War and its domestic reverberations.

NIXON'S "NEW FEDERALISM"

When Richard Nixon succeeded to the presidency, it became apparent that his interest in intergovernmental relations extended well beyond a preoccupation with easing friction points in grant administration. He committed himself to the concept of "New Federalism," which he defined as

---

[17]Donald H. Haider, *When Governments Come to Washington* (New York: Free Press, 1974), chap. 3.

A cooperative venture among governments at all levels . . . in which power, funds, and authority are channeled increasingly to those governments which are closest to the people.[18]

The thrust of Nixon's New Federalism, according to one knowledgeable observer, was anticentralization, anticategorical, and anti-administrative confusion, but it also embraced on the positive side:

. . . greater decentralization within the federal departments to their field units; a devolution of more power and greater discretion to recipient units; a streamlining of the service delivery system generally; a definite preferring of general governments and their elected officials; and some sorting out of some servicing responsibilities by government levels.[19]

Some *decentralization* was effected by reorganizing the administrative field structure into ten standardized regions and establishing common headquarters cities and a federal regional council for each region. Key departmental representatives served on the councils, which performed an interdepartmental coordinative and an intergovernmental liaison role. General revenue sharing (GRS) and special revenue sharing were the instruments of *devolution.*[20] GRS was enacted in 1972, strengthening the discretion of states and general purpose local units by enabling them to use federal funds for a wide range of purposes. None of the President's six special revenue proposals were adopted, yet they laid the groundwork for two later block grants, which also vested more discretion in recipients than in categorical grants. *Streamlining* the grant delivery system was accomplished by standardizing and simplifying administrative procedures and requirements and establishing a procedure for jointly funding state, areawide, and local grant application projects. *Preference* for generalists and general governments was expressed in the eligibility provisions of general revenue sharing and the new block grants, which excluded special districts and favored elected officials of general purpose units.

The New Federalism had a three-part approach to achieving some *sorting out* of functions. First, the special revenue sharing measures proposed giving state and local recipients most of the decisionmaking authority in the six functional areas covered. Second, the unsuccessful but innovative *Family Assistance Program* would have replaced a patchwork of separate welfare programs, which

---

[18]Richard M. Nixon, *The New Federalism: An Address and Statement by the President,* Address to the Nation, August 8, 1969.

[19]Walker, *Toward a Functioning Federalism*, p. 105.

[20]General revenue sharing funds are distributed by formula with few or no limits on the purposes for which they may be spent and few if any restrictions on the procedures by which they may be spent. Special revenue sharing funds are similar to GRS except that their use is limited to a single purpose, such as law enforcement or urban development. See Haider, *When Governments Come to Washington*, pp. 258–59.

varied extensively from state to state, with a national system covering all low-income families with children. Finally, the *Supplementary Security Income* program (SSI) was a federal takeover of the financing of the adult public assistance categories—an effective sifting out of functions.[21]

President Nixon made several other organizational changes to promote his intergovernmental goals. During his first months in office, he created a Council for Urban Affairs to develop and implement a coordinated national urban policy. He also established an Office on Intergovernmental Relations under the vice-president to provide a link with the nation's governors, legislators, mayors, and county officials.

Another key Nixon action affecting intergovernmental relations was transformation of the Bureau of the Budget into the Office of Management and Budget (OMB) and creation of a Domestic Council composed of cabinet members and other high-ranking domestic affairs officials. Modeled upon the National Security Council, the Domestic Council was commissioned to provide policy leadership—determining what government would do, leaving to OMB responsibility for how and how well objectives were achieved.

In the last years of the Nixon (and Ford) Administrations, the Advisory Commission on Intergovernmental Relations, in a comprehensive review of the federal grant system, addressed the issue of the president's machinery for handling his intergovernmental responsibilities. Conceding that individual presidents should have flexibility to organize their central staff agencies as they wish, the Commission urged that:

> A high-ranking assistant for intergovernmental affairs be appointed to monitor and evaluate for the President the various intergovernmental relations activities performed on a governmentwide basis:
>
> Organization, staffing, and internal operating procedures of the Office of Management and Budget be thoroughly reviewed and evaluated;
>
> The performance of the Domestic Council, or its successor, in identifying domestic problems and developing general domestic policies be improved; and
>
> Federal regional councils be strengthened through improved communications with state and local officials, increased support by OMB and the Under-Secretaries Group, decentralization of authority (where feasible), and designation as federal clearinghouses for OMB Circular A-95.[22]

Presidents Carter and Reagan assigned intergovernmental liaison to an office in the White House, but retrogression rather than progress has been the record on the other three proposals.

---

[21]Walker, *Toward a Functioning Federalism*, pp. 105-6.

[22]Advisory Commission on Intergovernmental Relations, *Improving Federal Grants Management* (Washingaton, DC: U.S. Government Printing Office, 1977), pp. 269–70.

CARTER'S "NEW PARTNERSHIP"

President Jimmy Carter's pre-inaugural approach to intergovernmental relations was a meld, in many respects, of the Creative Federalism of Lyndon Johnson and the New Federalism of Richard Nixon. Reflecting the former, Carter emphasized federal/state/local/private sector partnerships, a heavy urban/city focus, a wide range of expanded and new intergovernmental programs, direct federal–local grants bypassing state governments, greater targeting of federal grant programs, and strong national leadership. He borrowed from the Nixon approach in curbing the growth of categorical grants by grant consolidations, in devolving authority to states and localities, and in overhauling the executive branch for intergovernmental and other management reasons.

Carter replaced Nixon's Domestic Council with an assistant for domestic affairs and policy. He appointed a senior aide to serve as secretary to the Cabinet and Assistant for Intergovernmental Affairs and directed all executive agency heads to provide for a consultative process with state and local officials in developing federal policy. That was followed by a "concentrated attack on red tape and confusion in the Federal grant-in-aid system." This included simplifying planning, application, and reporting requirments, advance funding for more programs, stepped-up audit activity, and improvement of administrative regulations. On the last item, in 1978 Carter issued an executive order aimed at improving regulatory procedures so as to make them less burdensome on the economy, individuals, public and private organizations, or state and local governments.[23]

One of the most important intergovernmental initiatives during the Carter presidendy was a conscious effort to develop an urban policy, designed to encourage states to redirect their resources to support urban areas more effectively and equitably and to encourage localities to streamline and better coordinate their activities. The plan was to launch a dozen new program initiatives and reorient and revise over 150 existing programs. Little was accomplished legislatively, but some success was achieved administratively. The impact of federal programs on urban areas was improved by revising grant formulas so as to target funds to urban centers, by intensifying intra- and interagency coordination, and by streamlining administrative processes and procedures. A number of other steps were taken, including initiating analysis of the impact of proposed programs and policies on local communities, and creating the Interagency Coordinating Council to coordinate program impacts on urban areas. The lack of legislative success with the original formulation of an urban policy led to its later being revised to

---

[23]Advisory Commission on Intergovernmental Relations "Federal Initiatives and Impacts," *Intergovernmental Perspective* (Winter 1978), p. 10–11.

target federal progams more specifically to distressed communities, both urban and rural.[24]

The Administration's regulatory reform program also saw modification during Carter's four-year tenure. The 1978 Executive Order concerning regulatory procedures was renewed in 1979, requiring agencies to analyze the consequences of all major new regulations and to ensure that compliance costs, paperwork, and other burdens were minimized. In addition, the Regulatory Analysis Review Group was created to oversee federal agency compliance with the executive order. The Regulatory Council, consisting of the heads of thirty-five regulatory agencies, dealt with conflicting or overlapping regulations and developed a semiannual calendar of all proposed major regulations.[25]

From the overall record of the Carter Administration, David B. Walker inferred five underlying intergovernmental tenets that capture the thrust of Carter's intergovernmental policies:

> Categorical grants are the preferred intergovernmental transfer mechanism.
>
> Reogranizational and procedural reforms, if properly implemented, are the appropriate approaches to improving the grant delivery system, and the regulatory process.
>
> The existing general revenue sharing and block grant programs should be continued, but major new mergers and consolidations are either unnecessary or politically unwise.
>
> The national government must have direct access to those local jurisdictions who provide a vital membership in the "New Partnership."
>
> Fiscal circumstances dictate a gradually reduced federal fiscal role in intergovernmental programs, but this need not include any reduction in the number or variety of assistance programs nor require any curbs on federal government's regulatory thrusts in the grant-in-aid area.[26]

Viewed in total, the Carter Administration did not score great successes on the intergovernmental relations front, partly, perhaps, because it tried to do too many things.

REAGAN'S "NEW FEDERALISM"

As Ronald Reagan took over the Presidency, it was clear from his previous record and campaign speeches that intergovernmental relations would be emphasized in his administration. In his speech accepting the Republican Party's nomination for president in 1980, he said:

[24]Advisory Commission on Intergovernmental Relations, "In Washington: Not Many Answers," *Intergovernmental Perspective* (Winter 1979), p. 33; see also Wright, *Understanding Intergovernmental Relations*, pp. 139–40.

[25]Michael Mitchell, "National Events in 1979: The New Austerity Takes Hold," *Intergovernmental Perspective* (Spring 1980), p. 11.

[26]Walker, *Toward a Functioning Federalism*, p. 123.

Everything that can be run more effectively by state and local governments we shall turn over to state and local governments along with the funding sources to pay for them. We are going to put an end to the money merry-go-round where our money becomes Washington's money to be spent by states and cities only if they spend it exactly the way the federal bureaucrats tell them to.[27]

In the inaugural address, he declared his intention "to curb the size and influence of the federal establishment and to demand recognition of the distinction between the powers granted to the federal government and those reserved to the states or to the people."[28] Patently, he intended to do more than work on improving grants management, the principal emphasis of much of the presidential effort of the preceding twenty years. Yet streamlining and simplifying the grant system was still an important part of his intergovernmental agenda.

The first Reagan year—1981—disclosed the shape of the Reagan "New Federalism" program. He proposed, and the Congress enacted through the *Omnibus Budget Reconciliation Act of 1981*, significant modifications in the grant system. The uninterrupted growth in volume of grants was halted and the number actually was reduced. Through the enactment of nine block grants, replacing seventy-seven categoricals, greater discretion was shifted to the states. With the block grants went a 25 percent reduction in funding, justified by the need to reduce the federal budget deficit. It also was expected that grant administration would be more economical because of the greater administrative flexibility given the states and the removal of unnecessary performance requirements. Further shrinking of the grant system was effected by outright deletion of some sixty-two programs.

The Administration continued the decentralizing emphasis in its implementation of the block grant legislation, taking a hands-off approach to assure the states of having the full scope of discretion latent in the block grant concept. Federal implementing regulations stressed simplicity and flexibility and emphasized accountability at the recipient level.

Another major objective of the first year of Reagan federalism was regulatory relief. While the primary beneficiary was the private sector, states and localities were also to be relieved of the growing burden of excessive regulations. The President created a Presidential Task Force on Regulatory Relief headed by Vice President George Bush to review existing regulations and revise or delete them on the basis of a rigorous cost–benefit analysis.

In 1982, President Reagan took the second major step in his move to reduce the size of the federal government and shift power to the states. Condemning the existing "maze of interlocking jurisdictions and levels of government"

[27]Ronald Reagan, *Acceptance Speech*, Republican National Convention, Detroit, MI, 17 July 1980.

and the "jungle of grants-in-aid," he proposed restructuring the intergovernmental system in a "single bold stroke."[29] First, he proposed a $20 billion "swap" in which the federal government would return to the states full responsibility for funding Aid to Families with Dependent Children (AFDC) and food stamps in return for federal assumption of state contributions to medical assistance for the poor (Medicaid). Second, he proposed a temporary $28 billion trust fund to replace about forty federal programs "turned back" to the states in the fields of human services, community development, and transportation. The fund would come from certain earmarked federal taxes but would be phased out gradually and states would have the option of replacing the federal taxes with some of their own or of allowing the programs to expire.[30]

This federalism initiative had a mixed reception. Many governors and state legislators favored the notion of sorting-out functions, and their representatives spent much of 1982 negotiating with the Administration on an acceptable proposal. Reactions from other quarters—Congress, local governments, affected interest groups and the media—were less supportive. Many local officials were concerned about reduced federal aid and the severing of direct fedral–local ties. The federal role in public assistance also stirred controversy. Influencing the general reaction were the worsening economic and budgetary conditions. As a result, the swap proposal did not get off the ground in 1982.[31] Although efforts were made in 1983 to keep the negotiations going, they were similarly unproductive.

Other elements of President Reagan's federalism program had mixed results in 1982. He proposed ten more block grants but only two were enacted: the *Job Training Partnership Act*, actually a major revision of the existing *Comprehensive Employment and Training Act* (CETA) block grant, and the *Urban Mass Transportation Capital and Operating Assistance* block grant. On the urban policy front—which had been a central focus of the Carter federalism program—Reagan, consistent with the thrust of his block grant initiatives, indicated a preference for phasing out most direct urban aid programs, returning to the basic federal–state relationship that characterized the original federal grants-in-aid. Overall, the Administration deemphasized the federal role in cities, and put most of its hope in proposed enterprise zones, a program to involve the private sector in creating jobs and stimulating local economies.[32]

On the regulatory front in 1982, the Presidential Task Force made major modifications in thirteen of twenty-seven intergovernmental regulations, yielding an estimated savings for state and local governments of $4–$6 billion in one-time

---

[29]Timothy J. Conlan and David B. Walker, "Reagan's New Federalism: Design, Debate and Discord," *Intergovernmental Perspective* (Winter 1983), p. 6.

[30]*Weekly Compilation of Presidential Documents*, 29 January 1982, p. 80.

[31]Conlan and Walker, "Reagan's New Federalism," pp. 7–13; also see Richard S. Williamson, "The 1982 New Federalism Negotiations," *Publius* (Spring 1983), p. 36.

[32]Conlan and Walker, "Reagan's New Federalism," pp. 13–18.

expenses and \$2 billion more in annually recurring costs. The modifications included withdrawing proposed regulations requiring bilingual education and related services for students whose primary language is not English; revising rules to permit local authorities more discretion in providing access to mass transit for the handicapped; and changing rules implementing the *Davis–Bacon Act* governing determination of prevailing wage rates in federally aided construction projects. Some local government interests were uneasy about regulatory actions, however, feeling that disagreements among private sector and local government interests were too frequently resolved in favor of the former.[33]

In 1983, the Administration concluded early that the chances were slim of reaching a consensus on the "big swap" of 1982: the proposal for the federal government to assume certain functional responsibilities from the states in exchange for the states taking over some functions from the federal government. This central element of the New Federalism was placed on a back burner. However, in his State of the Union Message, Reagan declared his intention to continue his efforts to remold the federal system. His major proposal was to consolidate thirty-four categoricals into four mega-block grants.[34] This proposal generated little state and local support, however, and was soon dropped from the legislative agenda.

The Presidential Task Force on Regulatory Reform closed up shop in 1983, but the Administration continued this reform drive through other means. It maintained the general posture of granting the states wide latitude in implementing block grants, delegating to the states much of the monitoring function, and decentralizing other responsibilities through executive orders, and administrative circulars. Some observers felt that overall, the deregulatory effort had been partially successful in devolving authority back to the states and in cutting administrative burdens. However, a comprehensive approach to intergovernmental regulatory reform was still missing. In 1983, even more than in 1982, the Administration's federalism initiative suffered from the President's preoccupation with higher priority economic and foreign policy concerns.

THE PRESIDENTIAL INFLUENCE ON INTERGOVERNMENTAL RELATIONS

Since the 1930s, and particularly since the early 1960s, the American presidency has been significantly involved in intergovernmental relations, although such involvement has varied in intensity and direction from one chief executive to another. Presidential involvement is inevitable considering that the president is the only elective official with a national constitutency and hence the natural focal

---

[33]Ibid., pp. 19–20.
[34]*Weekly Compilation of Presidential Documents*, 25 February 1983, pp. 301–4.

point for intergovernmental questions. Yet, as is evident from this brief sketch of recent history, the record of presidential attention to and achievement in intergovernmental relations has been mixed.

Deil Wright has identified a number of reasons presidents have not been more effective in this area. Heading the list is the amount of time a president can give to intergovernmental issues. Other reasons are:

> The weakness of party support, affecting the president's ability to deal with Congress and with state and local governments;
>
> The political strength and strategic access of grant-related interest groups within the "triple alliance" (that is, the "iron triangle" formed by federal program specialists, Congressional committees, and special interst groups);
>
> The comparatively modest political payoffs and price accruing from most IGR accomplishments; and
>
> The unexciting administrative and managerial features of intergovernmental relations.[35]

Time—the president's allocation of priorities among all the demands on his office—undoubtedly is the most important factor conditioning his attention to intergovernmental matters. As Wright says:

> Time is a primary reason why a president can have only limited impact on IGR (intergovernmental relations) matters. Foreign affairs and domestic economic policies command prime time on the president's decisionmaking agenda. Policies on domestic programs, of which IGR issues are a subset, tend to be relegated to a lesser status. As it was aptly expressed: "The domestic policy arena is one to which all recent Presidents have devoted limited attention, while within it, new legislation—not program operations—has been the most significant concern."[36]

Thomas E. Cronin provides further insights into the issue of presidential priorities:

> Presidents concentrate on those areas in which they feel they can make the greatest impact, in which the approval of interest groups and the public can be most easily rallied. Getting involved in domestic policy is costly both financially and politically. Moreover, newly elected presidents find that budgets are virtually fixed for the next year and a half and that in domestic matters they are very dependent on Congress, specialized bureaucracies, professions, and state and local officialdom. Is it surprising, then, that the implementation of domestic policy has become the orphan of presidential attention? Is it possible presidents rationalize that they must

[35]Wright, *Understanding Intergovernmental Relations*, pp. 145–46.
[36]Ibid., p. 145.

concern themselves with foreign and macroeconomic policy as they lose heart with the complicated, hard-to-affect, divisive domestic problems?[37]

In one sense, presidential time for intergovernmental matters may be the one factor least subject to control by the president, as Lyndon Johnson found when his attention and energies were focused almost totally on the Vietnam War, taking the steam out of the Great Society and Creative Federalism programs. Yet in another sense, time may be the factor most subject to alteration by the president, since it depends to a considerable extent upon his federalism goals and how they fit in with the other objectives in his overall program. When a president's intergovernmental initiatives are linked to broad political policy goals (rather than mere management/public administration objectives) they are likely to command greater presidential attention.

One observer, for example, suggests that President Nixon pushed general revenue sharing and other aspects of his New Federalism as hard as he did in part because by decentralizing responsibilities to states and localities he would cut down the strength of the entrenched federal bureaucracy. Nixon viewed the bureaucracy, composed mainly of holdover civil servants from prior Democratic liberal administrations, as a major obstacle to achievement of his domestic goals.[38]

Most recently, President Reagan's intergovernmental goals were high on his domestic agenda even before he took office. As a consequence he invested considerable time, as well as political capital, in promoting New Federalism proposals in his first two years. In the first year he succeeded in scoring a substantial victory with passage of the *Omnibus Budget Reconciliation Act*, creating some nine new block grants. These efforts, and the Administration's subsequent policies to implement the block grants, clearly moved in the direction of his declared objective of decentralizing and devolving program authority to the states and localities.

Yet this accomplishment, and later efforts, were not achieved without reference to other goals in the President's total agenda. It seems clear, for example, that the Administration's advocacy of block grants was due in part at least to the fact that block grants promoted another prime objective of the Administration: reduction in the cost of federal grants, since the block grant programs were funded at a level of about 25 percent below the level of the categorical grants they replaced. Similarly, some observers have noted that when the intergovernmental goals of strengthening state and local responsibility came into conflict with other Reagan Administration objectives, the intergovernmental goals had to yield. Such was the case with several proposals for transferring regulatory

---

[37]Thomas E. Cronin, *The State of the Presidency*, 2d ed. (Boston: Little, Brown, 1980), p. 150.

[38]Leonard Robins, "The Plot That Succeeded: The New Federalism As Policy Realignment," *Presidential Studies Quarterly* (Winter 1980), p. 103; see also Richard P. Nathan, *The Plot That Failed: Nixon and the Administrative Presidency* (New York: John Wiley, 1975) pp. 82–84.

powers to the states. These proposals were rejected at the behest of private industry groups in the regulated industries. It seems that the Administration placed greater value in favoring the private sector over the public sector than it did in furthering decentralization of regulatory authority to the states.[39]

Regardless of how future presidents order their domestic priorities, intergovernmental relations will continue to be vastly more important than they were prior to the 1930s. A Special Panel of the National Academy of Public Administration identified the President's role as "Pivot of the Federal System" as one of the four new roles that increased the burdens on the president enormously in recent years. "The results are a need for continuous interactions among the three levels of government and vastly increased presidential responsibilities and influence."[40]

[39]Timothy J. Conlan, "Federalism and Competing Values in the Reagan Administration," a paper prepared for delivery at the 1984 Annual Meeting of the American Political Science Association, The Washington Hilton, August 30–September 2, 1984.

[40]*A Presidency for the 1980s: A Report by a Panel of the National Academy of Public Administration*, November 1980, pp. 8–9. (The other three new roles are: economic policy coordinator, social policy advocate, and crisis manager.)

Timothy J. Conlan

4

CONGRESS
AND THE CONTEMPORARY
INTERGOVERNMENTAL
SYSTEM

Major new developments in intergovernmental relations are commonly associated with bold presidential initiatives. The New Deal, the Great Society, and two versions of New Federalism each came to symbolize not only presidential leadership but distinctive eras of changing federal relationships with states and localities. Yet, despite the obvious importance of such initiatives, it can be argued that in recent years—and especially during the 1970s—Congress has been the chief architect of the intergovernmental system, albeit in its own incremental and often quiet way. Even earlier, when Congress often posed the major obstacle to the expansion of federal involvement into nontraditional fields of activity, congressional conservatism helped shape the system by encouraging the use of grants-in-aid as the preeminent instrument of federal involvement, rather than the seemingly simple approach of direct federal administration. In later years, a reformed and far more activist Congress itself became the leading incubator of new federal programs, conceiving and creating many of the federal grant and regulatory statutes in operation today. At the same time, Congress has often been the principal defender of the many intergovernmental programs it helped establish— resisting a series of Presidential efforts to consolidate grants-in-aid, to streamline intergovernmental management, and to redistribute functional responsibilities in the federal system.

In short, Congress has played a critical role in shaping the contemporary intergovernmental system. Although that role has evolved enormously over time—and is likely to change further in the decade ahead—it continues to be of central importance to understanding the federal government's role in the federal system.

THE EVOLVING CONGRESSIONAL ROLE
IN INTERGOVERNMENTAL RELATIONS:
FROM OBSTACLE COURSE TO POLICY COURSE

For twenty-five years following the New Deal, Congress was commonly viewed as a graveyard for proposals to involve the federal government in new domestic program areas. This view stemmed partly from Congress' historic role as a representative body for territorial and parochial interests. Not only were most members of Congress said to share a "provincial" outlook, "oriented toward local needs and small-town ways of thought," but the "conservative coalition" of Southern Democrats and right-wing Republicans often formed a working majority in the Congress, especially in the House of Representatives.[1] Such members were generally anxious to protect their states' traditional spheres of responsibility from federal encroachment.

This sort of opposition was reinforced by structural characteristics of Congress that could be used by conservatives to frustrate new legislative initiatives, even those with majority support. A system of largely autonomous committees (often dominated by entrenched Southern conservatives), like the House Rules Committee, the use of seniority for distributing authority, and the filibuster tradition in the Senate all served as multiple veto points which promoted a tendency toward the politics of stalemate. Such factors, often reinforced by the actitivies of affected "veto groups," were responsible for obstructing the enactment of major programmatic initiatives from national health insurance to general aid for education.[2]

This is not to say that no significant intergovernmental programs were enacted in the post World War II era. By one count, the number of separately authorized federal grants increased from fifty-two in 1950 to 132 in 1960.[3] However, most of these enactments were small and limited or they owed their existence to a narrow range of special circumstances. For example, major initia-

---

[1]Samuel Huntington, "Congressional Responses to the Twentieth Century," in David B. Truman, ed., *The Congress and America's Future*, 2d ed. (Englewood Cliffs, NJ: Prentice-Hall, 1973), p. 17.

[2]See, for example, Frank J. Munger and Richard F. Fenno, *National Politics and Federal Aid to Education* (Syracuse, NY: Syracuse University Press, 1962).

[3]David B. Walker, *Toward a Functioning Federalism* (Cambridge, MA: Winthrop, 1981), pp. 7, 81, 174.

tives like the interstate highway program and the *National Defense Education Act* were backed strongly by the president, addressed some widely perceived policy crises, and were tied in some way to traditional federal responsibilities. Lesser initiatives, if adopted at all, were generally modest in nature and were viewed as incremental adjustments to existing policies. Even under these circumstances most new programs were subjected to a difficult and protracted period of legislative consideration.

Having endured this legislative gauntlet, successful enactments like the *Air Pollution Control Act of 1955* and the *Area Redevelopment Act of 1961* were carefully tailored to congressional concerns and were respectful of state and local prerogatives. Grant monies were spread broadly across congressional districts.[4] Provisions that threatened to upset established patterns of racial segregation and inequality in the South or to disturb the disproportionate influence of rural interests in many states were invariably diluted or dropped. Despite such modifications, however, the typical pattern remained one of defeat and frustration for major legislative initiatives, prompting scholars as recently as 1964 to characterize congressional politics in terms like "deadlock of democracy" and the "obstacle course on Capitol Hill."[5]

CONGRESS AS INNOVATOR, 1966–1980

Even as such works were being written, this cautious congressional approach to policymaking was breaking down. Beginning incrementally in the late 1950s and early 1960s, this transformation was aided by such actions as the slow diffusion of power in the Senate and the enlargement of the House Rules Committee in 1961. Most critical, however, was the Democratic landslide in the 1964 election, which increased the number of liberal and moderate Democrats in Congress to such an extent that the traditional obstacles of the legislative process were overwhelmed and a legislative outpouring of new federal programs ensued.

The flood of legislation between 1964 and 1966 was followed by new patterns of congressional behavior. Surprisingly, perhaps, Congress did not return to the politics of stalemate—even after the 1966 election sharply reduced the Democratic majority in Congress and the president's attention was increasingly diverted to budgetary and foreign policy matters. Rather, individual members of Congress assumed the role of principal policy innovators in the political system and continued to press for the enactment and expansion of new or existing federal

[4]Phillip Monypenny, "Federal Grants-in-Aid to State Governments: A Political Analysis," *National Tax Journal* 13, no. 1 (March 1960).

[5]See James McGregor Burns, *The Deadlock of Democracy* (Englewood Cliffs, NJ: Prentice-Hall, 1963); and Robert Bendiner, *Obstacle Course on Capitol Hill* (New York: McGraw-Hill, 1964).

programs. As the ACIR concluded after a comprehensive analysis of policy initiatives in this period: "Congress . . . among all the actors and forces contributing to government growth, has loomed the largest in the sphere of policy initiation."[6]

Thus, simply in the area of federal aid, the number of new federal grant programs increased by 160 programs between 1966 and 1980—from 379 to 539.[7] Liberal Democrats in Congress took the lead in establishing many of these programs, but this pattern of increased activism was not confined solely to Democrats. Programs like those providing funds for water and sewer facilities and "special impact" jobs in poverty areas owed their creation in large part to the efforts of Republicans in Congress. Moreover, Republican support in congressional roll call votes for measures to increase federal activity and spending grew enormoulsy between 1960 and 1968. For each of these nine years, *Congressional Quarterly* compiled a "Federal Role Index" score for all members of Congress, based upon their votes for a selected number of significant policy proposals each year. Although Democrats, on average, consistently scored higher on this index than Republicans, Republican scores nearly doubled during this period (see Figure 4–1). In fact, party differences on these matters were reduced so greatly that *Congressional Quarterly* ceased compiling this index in 1969 (see Figure 4–2).

These changes in Congressional behavior were strongly reinforced by the Great Society itself. As the number of federal aid programs tripled during the Kennedy–Johnson years, and federal domestic spending grew from $39 to $99 billion,[8] the number of new interest groups created or located in Washington expanded accordingly. By some estimates, the number of interest groups with Washington offices doubled during the 1960s and 1970s, often in direct response to increased government or foundation funding.[9] Universities and colleges were among the many organizations that found it desirable to keep closer tabs on burgeoning federal activities. During the 1960s, thirteen associations concerned with higher education opened offices in the nation's capital and sixteen established programs to help draw grant funds to their member campuses.[10]

[6]Advisory Commission on Intergovernmental Relations, *An Agenda for American Federalism: Restoring Confidence and Competence* (Washington, DC: U.S. Goverment Printing Office, 1981), p. 10.

[7]Advisory Commission on Intergovernmental Relations, *Significant Features of Fiscal Federalism, 1982–83 Edition* (Washington, DC: U.S. Government Printing Office, 1984), p. 120.

[8]Ibid.

[9]Kay Lehman Scholzman and John T. Tierney, "More of the Same: Washington Pressure Group Activity in a Decade of Change," *The Journal of Politics* 45 (May 1982): 356; and Jack L. Walker, "The Origins and Maintenance of Interest Groups in America," *American Political Science Review* 77 (June 1983): 397–402.

[10]Lauriston King, *The Washington Lobbyists for Higher Education* (Lexington, MA: Heath, 1975), p. 112.

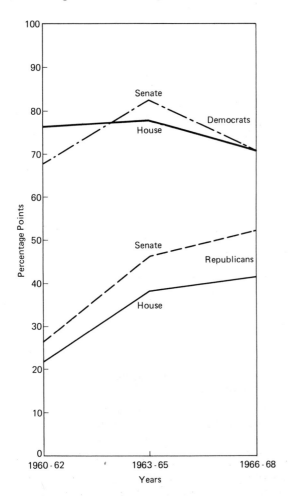

Figure 4–1   Average Republican and Democratic Support Scores for a Growing Federal Role, 1960–1968

Sources: *Congressional Quarterly Almanac*, 1960–1968; and Advisory Commission on Intergovernmental Relations, *The Condition of Contemporary Federalism: Conflicting Theories and Collapsing Constraints* (Washington, DC: U.S. Government Printing Office, 1981), p. 125.

Once established in the nation's capital, groups representing the beneficiaries and providers of new services lobbied Congress to expand their programs' resources and to enact new legislation to meet additional needs.[11] Indeed,

[11]Lawrence Brown, *New Policies, New Politics* (Washington, DC: The Brookings Institution, 1983), pp. 39–46.

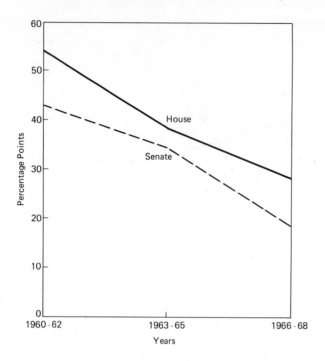

Figure 4–2   Percentage Point Differences between Average Republican and Democratic Scores on Federal Role Index, 1960–1968

Sources: *Congressional Quarterly Almanac*, 1960–1968; and Advisory Commission on Intergovernmental Relations, *The Condition of Contemporary Federalism: Conflicting Theories and Collapsing Constraints* (Washington, DC: U.S. Government Printing Office, 1981), p. 125.

the frequent development of close working relationships between interest groups, Congressional committees, and relevant executive agencies gave rise to a new and widely accepted model of politics which saw policy making dominated by so-called "subgovernments" or "iron triangles" in each policy field. In the simplest form of this model, all three elements tend to join hands in protecting their favorite programs and in boosting federal expenditures and new activities from which all can benefit: interest groups gain additional federal resources to serve their ends; congressional specialists aid their constituents and demonstrate their concern about politically significant issues; and bureaucrats serve their professional goals and enlarge their realms. As former Johnson aide Douglass Cater described this process in the late 1960s:

> Coagulations of power cut across the formal branches of government and incorporate participants, highly effective participants, outside of govern-

ment. There was, in fact, a tendency toward sub-governments in Washington. Key operatives in the executive branch, key committee heads or subcommittee heads in Congress, and key participants outside . . . of government were working, in arrangements of their own to exercise power over vast areas of government.[12]

Such policy communities, whether tightly organized or loosely structured in more porous "issue networks," were a natural outgrowth of governmental specialization and regularized interactions.[13] Nevertheless, their existence demonstrated the political institutionalization of governmental activism, as program specialists organized to nurture their new programs and to address their ancillary needs.

The growth of congressional policy activism resulted also from longer term changes in the political environment. No institution in American government has been more deeply affected than Congress by the decline of political party influence in American politics.[14] In the past, many—perhaps most—members of Congress came from safe, one-party districts. They could count on loyalty of party voters at the polls, in election after election, and they relied upon the efforts and resources of the party apparatus during campaigns. Indeed, in areas with particularly strong party organizations, members were sometimes viewed as virtual ambassadors for the local political "machine."[15]

This predictable electoral environment changed significantly as the parties' influence diminished. Even members whose districts appeared statistically safe frequently began running scared, fearful of increasing volatility in the electorate.[16] Ticket splitting and independent political attitudes became common throughout the electorate. In addition, most of the remaining, highly stable political organizations had disappeared from American cities by the late 1960s. Competing political institutions grew in influence and began assuming traditional party functions: television began to dominate political communications and voter contact; primaries broadened and cemented their role in party nominations; and by

[12]Quoted in Thomas E. Cronin, *The State of the Presidency* (Boston: Little, Brown, 1975), p. 94; see also Douglass Cater, *Power in Washington* (New York: Random House, 1964).

[13]See Hugh Heclo, "Issue Networks and the Executive Establishment," in Anthony King, ed., *The New American Political System* (Washington, DC: American Enterprise Institution, 1978).

[14]The dimensions of party decline are aptly described in Everett Carll Ladd with Charles Hadley, *Transformations of the American Party System*, (New York: W.W. Norton & Co., Inc. 1975); and William J. Crotty and Gary C. Jacobson, *American Parties in Decline* (Boston: Little, Brown, 1980).

[15]Gary Jacobson, *The Politics of Congressional Elections* (Boston: Little, Brown, 1983), p. 19.

[16]Steven Roberts, "Congressmen and Their Districts: Free Agents in Fear of the Future," in Dennis Hale, ed., *The United States Congress* (Chestnut Hill, MA: Boston College, 1982); and Richard F. Fenno, Jr., *Home Style: House Members in Their Districts* (Boston: Little, Brown, 1978), pp. 10, 11.

the 1970s political action committees had greatly expanded their role in election finance.[17]

As Leo Snowiss discovered in this classic analysis of Cook County politics, congressional candidates operating in this kind of unpredictable, weak party environment tend to engage in a very different style of electoral politics—one that focuses on mobilizing issue-oriented volunteers, responding more assiduously to interest groups, and cultivating media and personality politics to establish voter contact. "The non-hierarchic, highly permiable [party] structure," Snowiss observed, "compelled . . . candidates for Congress to rely upon personal initiative and personal resources. The system tends to foster extreme sensitivity to the character of the primary electorate, which candidates must scrupulously cultivate."[18]

With more and more members of Congress forced to build independent, ad hoc political coalitions, the role of policy entrepreneur became increasingly popular.[19] Initiating new programs and related legislative activities proved to be useful both for strengthening alliances with politically helpful interest groups and for appealing to individual constituents. The activities of former Representative John Brademas [D-IN] are a case in point. Brademas utilized his position on the House Education and Labor Committee to "mobilize the education community" on behalf of his difficult 1968 reelection bid.[20] Later, he authored and helped enact the *Environmental Education Act of 1970* in order to demonstrate his commitment to a highly popular issue. As two of his former staff assistants have written:

> Brademas [D-IN] felt very strongly that Congress can and should play a significant role as initiator and creator of public policy. . . . [T]he Environmental Education Act was his baby; he authored it, he felt responsible for it. . . . [T]he environmental response was becoming a burning and timely political issue in late 1969. . . . This bill gave Brademas a perfect opportunity to move into the environmental area, and such opportunities would be limited for members of the Education Committee.[21]

[17]Advisory Commission on Intergovernmental Relations, *Transformations in American Politics and Their Implications for Federalism* (Washington, DC: U.S. Government Printing Office, 1985).

[18]Leo Snowiss, "Congressional Recruitment and Representation," *American Political Science Review* 60 (1966): 632.

[19]Nelson W. Polsby, "Goodbye to the Inner Club," in Nelson Polsby, ed., *Congressional Behavior* (New York: Random House, 1971), p. 110.

[20]Jack H. Schuster, "An 'Education Congressman' Fights for Survival," in Allan Sindler, ed., *Policy and Politics in America* (Boston: Little, Brown, 1973), p. 200.

[21]Dennis Brezina and Allan Overmeyer, *Congress in Action: The Environmental Education Act* (New York: Free Press, 1974), p. 26.

Similar cases of policy entrepreneurship abound in the legislative annals of the 1960s and 1970s.[22]

Another factor contributing to the rise of congressional policy activism was the congressional reform movement that swept through Congress in the early 1970s. Through a series of reform initiatives, the role of congressional committee chairmen was substantially reduced in the House of Representatives, and power was distributed far more broadly to other members. For example, between 1964 and 1975, the number of House subcommittees was enlarged from 105 to 139, and the powers of subcommittee chairmen were enhanced, thus allowing many more congressmen to assume a significant role in the policy process.[23] This process, combined with the retirement of conservative Democratic chairmen, placed many more activist northern Democrats in positions of influence within the chamber. At the same time, committee chairmen were subjected to tighter controls by the party majority in the Democratic caucus. Finally, all members— from both chambers—benefitted from the massive expansion of personal legislative staffs and the enhancement of the information support agencies of Congress.[24] Thus, greatly increased numbers of legislators enjoyed the resources necessary to implement their activist tendencies, while the powers of those committee chairmen who had traditionally worked to limit such activity were sharply reduced.

As a result of all these factors, the locus of federal policy initiatives had shifted significantly toward Congress, in marked distinction from the past. As Gary Orfield put it:

> When the subtitles of the policy process are sorted out and the strands of influence unwoven, it is evident that Congress is a major source of domestic policy, and often the dominant source in government.[25]

CONGRESS AND THE STRUCTURE OF FEDERAL PROGRAMS

As in earlier years, Congress in the post-1965 period not only affected the number of new intergovernmental programs enacted, it significantly influenced their

[22]See, for example, David Price, *Who Makes the Laws?* (Cambridge, MA: Schenkman, 1972); Roger Davidson, *The Politics of Comprehensive Manpower Legislation* (Baltimore, MD: Johns Hopkins University Press, 1972); and Lawrence Gladieux and Thomas Wolanin, *Congress and the Colleges* (Lexington, MA: Heath, 1976).

[23]Lawrence Dodd and Bruce Oppenheimer, "The House in Transition," in Dodd and Oppenheimer, eds., *Congress Reconsidered* (New York: Praeger, 1977), p. 33.

[24]Samuel Patterson, "The Semi-Sovereign Congress," in Anthony King, ed., *The New American Political System* (Washington, DC: American Enterprise Institution, 1978) p. 165.

[25]Gary Orfield, *Congressional Power: Congress and Social Change* (New York: Harcourt Brace Jovanovich, Inc., 1975), p. 257.

structure and design as well. In particular, Congress continued to demonstrate a strong preference for narrowly defined categorical grants and to resist efforts at carefully targeting federal programs to neediest areas and individuals. As fiscal constraints on the federal budget mounted in the 1970s, it also demonstrated a strong proclivity to adopt new federal regulatory programs.

Congressional support for categorical grants was evident in the large numbers (366) that were adopted in the 1960s and 1970s. There were numerous reasons for this preference. First, as David Mayhew has pointed out, categorical grants can be a useful congressional tool for building electoral support. Because they provide "particularized benefits" to discrete congressional constituencies, they enable legislators to claim political credit for tangible benefits delivered to their districts. Thus, Mayhew compared them to a form of modern porkbarrel politics:

> Across policy areas generally, the programmatic mainstay of congressmen is the categorical grant. In fact the categorical grant is for modern Democratic Congresses what rivers and harbors and the tariff were for pre-New Deal Republican Congresses. It supplies goods in small manipulable packets.[26]

The narrowly defined structure of categorical grants can also be helpful in the coalition building process. To begin with, they can be carefully tailored to emphasize only program goals with broad congressional support—avoiding related policy issues that many members may find objectionable. At the same time, these attractive programs can be easily grouped into omnibus bills, combining the pet projects of many different members into one popular package. This process of logrolling through omnibus legislation was especially prevalent during the 1970s.[27] Finally, categorical grants proved attractive to Congress because they permit strict congressional oversight and control over the use of federal funds.[28]

Although categorical grants provided an appealing programmatic focus, the activist Congress retained its traditional lack of enthusiasm for geographically targeting federal spending. Especially in the largest grants, nearly every member of Congress has sought to assure that at least some program funds are spent in his or her own district. This process was clearly evident in two of the most controversial and highly visible programs of the periods—the *Demonstration Cities and Metropolitan Development Act of 1966* (Model Cities) and the *Public*

[26]David Mayhew, *Congress: The Electoral Connection* (New Haven, CT: Yale University Press, 1974), p. 129.

[27]Thomas Wolanin, "Congress, Information, and Policy Making for Post Secondary Education," *Policy Studies Journal* 4 (Summer 1976): 387.

[28]See Morris Fiorina, *Congress: Keystonne of the Washington Establishment* (New Haven, CT: Yale University Press, 1977).

Works Employment Act of 1976. Under the former, Congress more than doubled the number of cities eligible for grants, increasing the president's proposal from 66 to 150. Under the latter, congressional activists initiated and enacted over President Ford's veto a multibillion dollar program of construction grants, pollution control assistance, and "countercyclical" aid to cities.[29] Nevertheless, the widespread use of project grants in most major programs of the sixties helped keep the excessive diffusion of funds in check, since such funds are awarded by bureaucrats who are shielded from some of the intense constituency pressures on members of Congress.[30] In the 1970s, however, the increased reliance on large formula grants, which permit Congressmen to determine the allocation of program funds directly, increased the pressures for spreading federal funds even further. Moreover, the growing use of computerized simulations of alternative formulas also heightened the salience of distribution issues, allowing individual congressmen to determine precisely the impact of different formula allocations on their own districts.

A third, often overlooked, policy development in the late 1960s and 1970s was the enormous expansion that took place in intergovernmental regulation. By one count, thirty-four major regulatory statutes were adopted between 1964 and 1980, each directly or indirectly regulating state and local governments in new and intrusive ways. Moreover, such regulatory statutes were supplemented by hundreds of specific administrative rules and requirements.[31]

Although they imposed unprecedented regulatory burdens on states and localities, such programs were attractive to Congress for several reasons. Most important, perhaps, was the clear and simple moral appeal of many regulatory program objectives. Although their specific statutory provisions and methods of implementation often imposed major unforeseen costs—and may actually have hampered the attainment of certain policy objectives—the broad acceptance of such basic goals as promoting civil rights and protecting the environment frequently made regulatory measures aimed at meeting such ends virtually irresistable to Congress. As Edward Koch, the current New York mayor but a former Representative, now recalls:

> I do not for a moment claim immunity from the mandate fever of the 1970s. As a member of Congress, I voted for many [mandates]. . . . The bills I voted for in Washington came to the House floor in a form that

---

[29] Advisory Commission on Intergovernmental Relations, *Reducing Unemployment: Intergovernmental Dimensions of a National Problem* (Washington, DC: U.S. Government Printing Office, 1982), pp. 95, 96; and R. Douglas Arnold, *Congress and the Bureaucracy* (New Haven, CT: Yale University Press, 1979), pp. 166–68.

[30] R. Douglas Arnold, "The Local Roots of Domestic Policy," in Thomas Mann and Norman Ornstein, eds., *The New Congress* (Washington, DC: American Enterprise Institution, 1981), pp. 250–86.

[31] Advisory Commission on Intergovernmental Relations, *Regulatory Federalism: Policy, Process, Impact, and Reform* (Washington, DC: U.S. Government Printing Office, 1984), pp. 19–24.

compelled approval. After all, who can vote against clear air and water, or better access and education for the handicapped?[32]

Moreover, as fiscal constraints on federal spending grew in the 1970s, intergovernmental regulation became increasingly popular as a means of permitting continued congressional activism while displacing most of the costs onto state and local governments. As one former official in the Johnson Administration has observed:

> Congressmen see themselves as having been elected to legislate. Confronted with a problem and a showing that other levels of government are "defaulting," their strong tendency is to pass a law. [In the 1960s], money was Washington's antidote for problems. Now, the new fiscal realities mean that Congress provides fewer dollars. Still determined to legislate against problems, Congress uses sticks instead of carrots.[33]

The *Education for all Handicapped Children Act* was a case in point. This 1975 law required local school districts to provide a "free and appropriate education" to all physically and mentally handicapped children and to prepare special educational plans for each child. Although federal contributions for implementing the act were initially anticipated to be 40 percent of the total cost of the program, Congress never appropriated funds amounting to more than 12 percent of the program's sizable costs.[34]

Largely as a result of the above factors, initiating intergovernmental regulations appealed to many legislative entrepreneurs in Congress. In several instances, the broad appeal of regulatory objectives greatly simplified the task of coalition building and permitted just one or a few congressmen to shepherd a major regulatory provision through Congress—sometimes even circumventing committee consideration. For example, section 504 of the *Rehabilitation Act of 1973*, which is designed to protect handicapped persons from discrimination in federal programs, was enacted largely through the efforts of a single congressman, Representative Charles Vanick (D-OH). Because of its obviously humane purpose, the provision was adopted by Congress "without one day of congressional hearings, not one word was mentioned in the Senate Committee Report, not one word was spoken about it on the floor when the original bill passed, and there was no explanation in the statement of . . . the House–Senate conference."[35]

[32]Edward Koch, "The Mandate Millstone," *The Public Interest* (Fall 1980), p. 44.

[33]Samuel Halperin, "Federal Takeover, State Default, Or a Family Problem?," in Samuel Halperin, ed., *Federalism at the Crossroads: Improving Educational Policymaking* (Washington, DC: Institute for Educational Leadership, 1976), pp. 2,3.

[34]Erwin Levine and Elizabeth Wexler, *PL 94–142: An Act of Congress* (New York: Macmillan, 1981), p. 189.

[35]Martin La Vor, *Section 504 of the Vocational Rehabilitation Act*, Memorandum to All Minority Members, House Committee on Education and Labor, June 14, 1979 (unpublished), p. 1.

Yet the provision spawned hundreds of pages of specific rules from the various agencies charged with implementing it and imposed tens of billions of dollars of new expenses on state and local governments. Because Congress responded to the regulation largely on a symbolic level and failed to consider alternative methods of achieving this goal, its implications were understood by only a handful of lobbyists and staff members. As Vanik himself admitted after its enactment, Congress "never had any concept that it would involve such tremendous costs."[36] Although many other regulatory programs adopted in recent years have been subjected to far more extensive debate and analysis by Congress, interest groups, and the media, several other major rules were adopted through a similar process of symbolic coalition building, with the principal debate about how best to achieve these goals following rather than preceding their enactment.[37]

CONGRESS AND FEDERAL AID REFORM IN THE 1960s AND 1970s

The mounting programmatic activism of the federal government was bound to arouse a political response from those concerned about its consequences. In particular, the growing reliance by state and local governments on federal aid and the administrative problems stemming from the proliferation of categorical grants—each with its own unique and sometimes conflicting requirements—gave rise to repeated calls for reform. Three broad types of proposals were advanced:

> incremental management reforms intended to improve coordination among existing programs;
>
> grant consolidation, which folds related programs into a single broad block grant to reduce paperwork requirements and to provide much wider flexibility in using federal funds; and
>
> General Revenue Sharing, which provides federal aid with almost no strings attached.

Through one approach or another—and frequently a combination of all three— grant reform stood at the top of the intergovernmental agenda throughout much of the late 1960s and early 1970s. Even though new federal aid and regulatory programs continued to mount during this period (a development that, in retrospect, may have been the principal story of this era), public and professional attention on intergovernmental issues focused mainly on questions of reform.

[36]Quoted in Timothy Clark, "Access for the Handicapped," *National Journal* (21 October 1978), p. 1673.

[37]See for example, Andrew Fishel and Janice Pottker, *National Politics and Sex Discrimination* (Lexington, MA: Heath, 1977), p. 132; Steven Lewis Yaffee, *Prohibitive Policy: Implementing the Endangered Species Act* (Cambridge, MA: MIT Press, 1982), p. 57; and Timothy Conlan and Steven Abrams, "Federal Intergovernmental Regulation: Symbolic Politics in the New Congress," *Intergovernmental Perspective* 7 (Summer 1981).

Largely because of their broad administrative responsibilities, presidents were among the first to begin advocating substantial federal aid reforms. Presidents Truman and Eisenhower each proposed that federal welfare and public health programs be consolidated into block grants, but such proposals generally did not receive broad support until the mid 1960s.[38] Then, in the aftermath of the Great Society, state and local government officials began complaining loudly about the pattern of conflict, controversy, and complexity resulting from the onrush of new programs, and they began to make grant reform a major intergovernmental priority. They were joined in this effort by many in the public administration community and by those in the federal government who had broadly defined intergovernmental responsibilities, including the Budget Bureau, the General Accounting Office, the Advisory Commission on Intergovernmental Relations, and members and staff of the intergovernmental affairs subcommittees of Congress.

Responding to this situation, President Johnson recommended and obtained enactment of the *Partnership for Health Act of 1966*, which consolidated nine public health programs into the first true block grant. The Johnson Administration subsequently launched a series of additional reform initiatives designed to enhance the coordination of federal aid programs and to promote intergovernmental consultation. Budget Bureau officials were also seriously considering plans for enacting additional large scale block grants when the Administration left office in 1969.[39]

The reform agenda expanded even further under Presidents Nixon and Ford. In his first year in office, President Nixon proposed establishing a program of general revenue sharing, a major consolidation of job training programs, and a host of new managerial initiatives. Two years later, dissatisfied with the lack of legislative progress on these proposals and disappointed with the results of other incremental reforms, Nixon recommended consolidating 129 categorical grants into six sweeping "special revenue sharing" block grant programs. President Ford, and to a lesser extent President Carter, followed with additional grant reform initiatives.

Despite this record of strong presidential support, most of these initiatives failed to gather significant backing in Congress. The block grant initiatives are a case in point. Out of approximately twenty major block grants proposed between 1947 and 1980, only five were ever enacted. For reasons already discussed, Congress has tended strongly to prefer categorical grants to block grants or no strings revenue sharing. Backed by interest groups and program professionals eager to protect existing funding sources, it has tended to resist program consolidation efforts.

[38]Selma Mushkin, "Barriers to a System of Federal Grants-in-Aid," *National Tax Journal* 13 (1960): 193–218.

[39]For more details, see Timothy J. Conlan, "The Politics of Federal Block Grants: From Nixon to Reagan," *Political Science Quarterly* 99 (Summer 1984): 248–52.

The reactions of members of Congress and affected interest groups to three of President Nixon's special revenue sharing proposals—designed to consolidate programs in transportation, education and rural development—illustrate the nature of this opposition by program beneficiaries and sponsors. In transportation, for example, the president of the American Trucking Association expressed "revulsion" at portions of the Transportation Revenue Sharing plan, calling it "a large scale raid on the federal Highway Trust fund."[40] Republicans in both the House and Senate refused even to introduce the administration's transportation bill, so hearings were never held on it in either chamber. Undersecretary of Transportation James Boggs observed: "Our categorical programs are nearer and dearer to Congressmen's hearts than any other. They are the porkiest of the pork."[41]

Similarly, before the Rural Development Revenue Sharing proposal was even sent to Capitol Hill, portions of the plan came under vigorous attack from leading Republicans like Senate Minority Leader Hugh Scott (PA) and Senator John Sherman Cooper (KY), ranking member of the Senate Public Works Committe. They opposed its provisions for consolidating (and effectively eliminating) the Appalachian Regional Commission, which provided funds to their states. Supporters of the Agricultural Extension Service mobilized to thwart consolidation of their program as well. Consequently, rural revenue sharing was hardly even considered by the House Agriculture Committee, while a costly version of a rural block grant advanced by Senate Democrats was ultimately rejected by the Congress.

The Nixon Administration's education revenue sharing proposal fared little better. The liberal chairman of the House Education and Labor Committee complained that special revenue sharing allowed little federal control over education funds and likened it to "throwing money down ratholes."[42] Education interest groups, and even some Republicans, echoed this reaction and helped block its enactment.

Overall, this pattern of failure was consistent with the conventional wisdom concerning block grant politics—clients and beneficiaries of categorical programs actively opposed grant consolidation as a threat to their established interest, reinforced by protective credit-claiming program sponsors in Congress. Interestingly, this pattern of subsystem politics was only modestly different in two fields where block grants were enacted—community development and job training. In these cases, however, important interest groups and policy professionals tended to support the block grant concept. The nation's mayors formed the principal clientele of community development programs, for example, and were staunch

[40]Quoted in Jonathan Cottin, "Wide-Ranging Interests Oppose Administration's Proposals," *National Journal* (10 April 1971), p. 773.

[41]Quoted in Timothy Clark, et al., "Drive to Return Power to Local Governments Faces Hill Struggle over Control of Programs," *National Journal* (16 December 1972), p. 1930.

[42]Representative Carl Perkins, quoted in Karen DeWitt, "Administration Revenue Sharing Plan Unlikely to Get Passing Grade from Congress," *National Journal* (24 March 1973), p. 418.

advocates of block grants in this field. Although some members of Congress—especially Senate liberals—did strive to protect the individual programs they had sponsored, many members of key congressional committees (from both sides of the aisle) shared in the professional consensus that consolidation would improve policy performance in these two fields.

As enacted, both the job training and community development block grants shared important common features. Both featured increased levels of federal spending, mainly to reduce differences between fiscal winners and losers under the new program structures. Both also favored local governments over states, and both retained significant federal oversight and control. Politically, however, both programs could be viewed as policy specific reforms, whose design and passage depended largely on the particular alignment of interests and attitudes in each policy arena.

An equally unique pattern of politics was evident in the enactment of General Revenue Sharing (GRS) in 1972. Like CETA and CDBG, the general revenue sharing concept enjoyed strong support from both the President and state and local government officials, but the latter were far more united in this instance. The "public interest groups" representing states and localities fought bitterly over how program authority and funds should be divided in the block grants, but they overcame these differences on GRS and developed a unified position. Their heavy lobbying of Congress on this issue symbolized a major change in state and local governmental influence on federal policy. Having lost many of their old avenues of influence through the traditionally decentralized political parties,[43] governors, mayors and county officials followed the well-worn path of other interest groups and established a significant full-time lobbying presence in Washington.[44]

Thanks in large part to their "intense and massive activity," General Revenue Sharing was supported by a unique congressional coalition.[45] As expected, a sizeable majority of Republicans supported the President on revenue sharing in the crucial House vote, but, more interestingly, they were joined by a majority of liberal northern Democrats who were being lobbied by the big city mayors.[46] Opposition was led by highly conservative Republicans and by the "categorical phalanx," the chairmen of the standing House committees and subcommittees, who voted overwhelmingly against the bill.[47] They viewed the

[43]Lewis B. Kane, "Politics, Money, and State Sovereignty: The Judicial Role," *Columbia Law Review* 79 (1979): 866–67; and Robert Huckshorn and John Bibby, "State Parties in an Era of Political Change," in Joel Fleishman, ed., *The Future of American Political Parties* (Englewood Cliffs, NJ: Prentice-Hall, 1982), pp. 91–92.

[44]Donald H. Haider, *When Governments Come to Washington* (New York: Free Press, 1974).

[45]Samuel H. Beer, "The Adoption of General Revenue Sharing: A Case Study of Public Sector Politics," *Public Policy* 24 (Spring 1976): 190.

[46]*Ibid.*, pp. 175, 188.

[47]*Ibid.*, pp. 177, 186.

legislation as fiscally irresponsible and as an attack on the powers and prerogatives of congressional committees to determine how federal funds should be expended. Their defeat marked the high water mark of the intergovernmental lobby's influence in Congress.

CONGRESS AND THE INTERGOVERNMENTAL SYSTEM IN THE 1980s: CONTINUITY OR CHANGE?

The history of the past thirty years of Congress' role in intergovernmental relations has been marked by major changes, and it is entirely possible that new incentives and constraints in the political environment of Congress may promote a continuing evolution in Congress' role as the 1980s proceed. Although it is highly unlikely that Congress will return to the oligarchical stagnation of the 1950s, the patterns of active congressional involvement in intergovernmental relations developed in the 1960s and 1970s may be substantially transformed.

Significant shifts in congressional behavior certainly appeared to be developing early in the Reagan Administration. Most notable was the dramatic enactment of the *Omnibus Budget Reconciliation Act of 1981*, which made potentially sweeping changes in federal intergovernmental policy. Specifically, the *Reconciliation Act* consolidated seventy-seven categorical programs into nine new or substantially revised block grants, and it terminated sixty-two others. Spending on most education, training, and social service programs was reduced by approximately 25 percent, and the subsequent enactment of large reductions in federal personal and corporate income taxes contributed to growing federal deficits and the strong possibility of further spending cuts in ensuing years.[48]

Equally important, these actions appeared to signal the development of new patterns of intergovernmental policymaking. In establishing the new block grants, for example, many of the political techniques used to overcome congressional opposition to earlier block grants were altered or ignored. Instead of raising federal spending to attract support, the new block grants cut spending substantially. Instead of granting federal funds directly to more numerous and, in many cases, politically influential local governments, the new block grants sent funds almost entirely to the states. Finally, instead of attempting to focus on those policy areas with pre-existing professional support for block grants, the new block grants affected nearly every area of federal domestic social policy.

Given this record, it is hardly surprising that the *Reconciliation Act* was not the product of ordinary subsystem politics in Congress. Indeed, the president's proposed block grants initially were almost gutted as they wound their way

---

[48]For more details on the intergovernmental dimensions of this act, see David Walker, Albert Richter, and Cynthia Colella, "The First Ten Months: Grant-in-Aid, Regulatory and Other Changes," *Intergovernmental Perspecitve* 8 (Winter 1982): 5–22.

through the individual committees and subcommittees of the Congress. During this process, several of the most visible and significant of the affected categoricals were saved from consolidation.[49] Ultimately, however, the politics of incremental, policy specific grant reform were overshadowed by a majoritarian form of politics based on strong presidential leadership. By successfully devising tactics that transformed the fundamental legislative question from "does each specific program change make sense to policy supporters and specialists?" to "do you support the economic recovery plan of a highly popular president?" the Reagan Administration was able to construct a partisan conservative phalanx that rolled comprehensive legislation through the Congress in one fell swoop.[50] Momentarily, at least, the Administration appeared to lay the basis for a new pattern of grant reform politics.

Apart from brilliant tactics, this outcome may have mirrored longer range changes in American politics. The impact of overall party decline on congressional behavior has already been examined. Beginning in the mid 1970s, however, state and national political parties—especially the Republicans—began a process of institutional and financial rebuilding. Although this rebuilding process is unlikely to return the parties to their former preeminence in the political system, it is clear that the parties are now engaged in a process of organizational development and adaptation, not simply decline.[51] Specifically, the Republican National Committee (RNC) and its congressional affiliates have actively recruited promising candidates for congressional office, staged national training seminars in campaign techniques, provided candidates with polling and consultant services, and distributed substantial campaign contributions.[52] Moreover, the party's success in direct mail fundraising enabled the National Republican Congressional and Senatorial Campaign Committees to raise $78.8 million for the 1980 campaign (as of September 1981), 10 times more than the $7.8 million raised by their Democratic counterparts.[53] Finally, the RNC has assumed a leadership role in helping to modernize and enhance state and local party operations. Although it has lagged considerably behind in many of these activities, the Democratic party has sought to emulate these party-building efforts.

[49]See Conlan, "The Politics of Federal Block Grants," pp. 260–64.

[50]Robert Fulton, "Federal Budget Making in 1981: A Watershed in Federal Domestic Policy," *New England Journal of Human Services* (Fall 1981), p. 29.

[51]M. Margaret Conway, "Republican Political Party Nationalization, Campaign Activities, and Their Implications for the Party System," *Publius* 13 (Winter 1983); and James L. Gibson, et al., "Assessing Party Organizational Strength," *American Journal of Political Science* 27 (May 1983).

[52]Thomas Mann and Norman Ornstein, "1980: A Republican Revival in Congress?" *Public Opinion* (October/November 1980), pp. 16–20.

[53]Gary Jacobson, "Congressional Campaign Finance and the Revival of the Republican Party," in Dennis Hale, ed., *The United States Congress* (Chestnut Hill, MA: Boston College, 1982), p. 319.

The potential dividends of such activities were first evident in 1978, when the Republicans succeeded in defeating several prominent Senate Democrats. The effects were even more visible in 1980, when the Republicans gained twelve new seats in the Senate and thirty-three in the House. These developments, combined with the President's popularity and the initial exuberance of a party long out of power, sparked a "striking gain in solidarity" among Republicans in Congress, especially in the Democratically controlled House. On the first budget resolution in 1981, House Republicans voted 190–0 in favor of the President's budget cuts. Six weeks later, they voted 188–2 in favor of the budget cuts and block grants contained in the *Reconciliation Act*. Finally, they voted 190–1 in favor of the President's tax cut bill.[54] It was this highly unusual degree of partisan loyalty—more than any other single factor—that contributed to the President's legislative victories in 1981.

Despite such early successes, the extent and long-term impact of party renewal remains to be seen. The fact that the Reagan Administration's legislative program has had far less success in Congress since 1981 suggests that short-term political factors were of primary importance in determining those early outcomes. Since that time, for example, President Reagan has proposed creating twenty-three additional block grants but succeeded in enacting only one. Moreover, many moderate Republicans sought openly to distance themselves from the President's other policy proposals after 1981, which may signal a return to "politics as usual" in many fields of intergovernmental policy.

More likely, it appears that Congress will face an evolving mixture of both old and new political incentives in the years ahead. On the one hand, continued congressional policy activism may be sharply restricted by new and highly salient fiscal constraints. One of the most significant legacies of President Reagan's initial legislative victories has been the institutionalization of deep deficits in the federal budget. The resulting austerity may not only place a lasting damper on federal program initiatives, it may seriously jeopardize existing federal aid programs which are relatively vulnerable. In short, the era of prolific policy entrepreneurship may be drawing to a close.

On the other hand, even in era of severe fiscal constraints, congressional activism may continue to find modes of expression. This is particularly true in the relatively "cost free" sphere of regulation. Although the pace of new regulatory enactments appears to have slowed in recent years, it has by no means been halted entirely, as indicated by recent legislation overturning state bans on double trailer trucks and establishing a national minimum drinking age.[55] Thus far, the

---

[54] *1981 Congressional Quarterly Almanac* (Washington, DC: Congressional Quarterly, 1982), pp. 5c, 10c.

[55] See Timothy J. Conlan, "Federalism and Competing Values in the Reagan Administration," *Publius* (forthcoming).

Reagan Administration's deregulation initiative has failed to remove major regulatory programs from the statute books, and even conservatives have shown a marked tendency to favor new requirements in some areas of policy. Hence, it remains to be seen whether intergovernmental regulations will continue to mount, albeit more slowly, or whether they may lose their political moorings if the river of federal aid begins to dry up.

In short, the 1980s pose uncertainties for the congressional role in intergovernmental relations. Powerful continuities remain: Congress' proclivity to spread federal funds remains intact; many of the political incentives favoring policy entrepreneurship remain strong; most policy subsystems persist, though some have been weakened by program cuts and administrative changes; and public opinion remains divided between concerns about "big government" and support for many specific federal programs. On the other hand, Congress will likely confront growing fiscal constraints during the 1980s; the role of parties in the political system continues to evolve; and a restless search for new solutions to public problems appears evident among conservatives and liberals alike. Despite such uncertainties, however, one thing remains certain. Congress will continue to exert an important influence over the shape of intergovernmental relations, both now and in the future.

Robert Jay Dilger

5

AMERICAN
POLITICAL PARTIES
AND INTERGOVERNMENTAL
RELATIONS
An Historical Perspective

The *United States Constitution* included several legal safeguards for the federal system that were designed to prevent the national government from encroaching upon the authority of state governments. Not only was the national government divided into three "separate but equal" branches subject to various "checks and balances," but as James Madison argued in *Federalist* 45 and 46, national governmental powers were delegated, few, and defined while those left to states were "numerous and indefinite."[1] Moreover, Madison argued that in the electoral arena, both popular political sentiment and formal electoral procedures would incline national officeholders to respect state prerogatives:

> Without the intervention of the State legislatures the President of the United States cannot be elected at all. They must in all cases have a great share in his appointment, and will, perhaps in most cases, of themselves determine it. The Senate will be elected absolutely and exclusively by the State legislatures. Even the House of Representatives, though drawn immediately

An earlier version of this article appeared in Advisory Commission on Intergovernmental Relations, *Transformations in American Politics and Their Implications for Federalism* (Washington, DC: U.S. Government Printing Office, 1985). Portions reprinted with permission.

[1]James Madison, "Federalist 45," in *The Federalist Papers*, introd. Clinton Rossiter (New York: New American Library, 1961), p. 293.

from the people, will be chosen very much under the influence of that class of men whose influence over the people obtains for themselves an election into the State legislatures.[2]

Because of these electoral links, Madison maintained that "a local spirit will infallibly prevail . . . in the members of Congress."[3]

The Framers thus believed that the electoral system established by the *Constitution* would impose a powerful decentralizing influence on intergovernmental relations. They did not foresee, however, that the electoral system would undergo significant changes in later years: the direct election of Senators, the popular selection of presidential electors, and the extension of suffrage. Yet, as late as the 1960s, many scholars believed that Madison's initial expectations about the decentralizing impact of American political institutions remained correct. This reflected yet another change in the electoral system wholly unexpected by the Framers: the development of American political parties. Morton Grodzins and William Riker, for example, argued that the highly decentralized, nondisciplined nature of American parties was largely responsible for preserving major state and local roles in the federal system. Because city and county party organizations controlled or strongly influenced most congressional nominations, they argued that the party system powerfully reinforced the distinctly localistic orientation of Congress and bolstered its members' natural attentiveness to their local constituencies. Although presidents have a national constituency and, in their view, were much more likely to support centralizing legislation, the president's inability to control congressional nominations helped produce a nondisciplined party system that allowed Congress to resist centralizing tendencies and to assure that important responsibilities remained with states and localities.[4] Grodzins argued that the greatest threat to state and local roles in governance was the prospect of a centralized party system that imposed party discipline upon Congress.[5]

This nondisciplined party thesis seemed to fit the intergovernmental reality of the 1950s and early 1960s fairly well. It was reinforced by several other political factors that also contributed to governmental decentralization. The popular belief in the superiority of local governance and in a limited governmental role in private affairs overall has been shared by many officeholders throughout American history. Moreover, the separation of powers at the national level,

---

[2]Ibid., p. 291.

[3]Madison, "Federalist 46," in *The Federalist Papers*, p. 296.

[4]Morton Grodzins, *The American System* (Chicago: Rand McNally, 1966), pp. 254–60; William H. Riker, *Federalism: Origin, Operation, Significance* (Boston: Little, Brown, 1964), pp. 91–101; also see David Truman, "Federalism and the Party System," in *American Federalism in Perspective*, ed. Aaron Wildavsky (Boston: Little, Brown, 1967), pp. 81–109.

[5]Grodzins, *The American System*, pp. 288, 289.

combined with strong sectional differences expressed in Congress, also served historically to frustrate national initiatives.

On the other hand, the party decentralization thesis underestimated the extent to which American political parties have served as agents of centralization in certain eras. Following the Civil War, for example, the new and highly ideological Republican party not only helped to obtain the abolition of slavery but instituted "an ingrained program of positive federal involvement in the fields of banking and currency, transportation, the tariff, and land grants to small landholders."[6] Similarly, in the wake of the Democrats' nationalizing initiatives during the New Deal, E.E. Schattschneider argued that political parties made possible a strong, plebiscitary presidency which served to weaken federalism by fostering strong national governmental action.[7]

The conflicting role played by parties in both advancing and obstructing centralization in the federal system is highlighted by events during the 1960s. Large Democratic majorities in Congress, fueled by the belief that state and local governments were unable or could not be trusted to exercise their governmental functions responsibly without central governmental supervision, enacted legislation that transformed the national role.[8] Over two hundred new, intergovernmental programs were launched at the national level in fields such as education, health, public welfare, and environmental protection: all areas previously considered to be primarily under state and local jurisdiction.

Importantly, this centralization of governmental responsibilities did not end with the erosion of Democratic majorities in 1966 and the election two years later of a Republican president committed to governmental decentralization. A steady stream of new grant and regulatory programs was enacted over the following decade. At the same time, scholars started to advance the concept that the party system had begun to seriously erode. Although the initial failure of the decentralized party system to halt the Great Society suggests that the decentralized, nondisciplined party theory is incomplete, the subsequent erosion of the party system may help explain the continued enactment of further national initiatives and the development of new patterns of national politics.

The following analysis examines carefully the role of American political parties in influencing the nature of American intergovernmental relations over time. It presents an historical analysis of the development of American intergovernmental relations and the American party system and suggests that the

---

[6]Walter Dean Burnham, "Party Systems and the Political Process," in *The American Party Systems*, ed. William Nisbet Chambers and Walter Dean Burnham (New York: Oxford University Press, 1967), p. 296.

[7]E.E. Schattschneider, *Party Government* (New York: Holt, Rinehart & Winston, 1942), p. 53.

[8]Daniel J. Elazar, "The New Federalism: Can the States Be Trusted?" *The Public Interest* 35 (Spring 1974): 89–102.

decentralized party structure has served as a restraint on national action throughout much of American history, but it was just one factor in a much broader political context that produced periods of both centralization and decentralization.

THE RISE AND DECLINE OF THE FIRST AMERICAN PARTIES: 1776–1828

During the 1770s and 1780s, nationally organized political parties as we know them today did not exist anywhere in the world. In the United States, politics was dominated by shifting, personalized factions within the various state legislatures. Policy decisions lacked the relative order and continuity characteristic of modern party politics. The continually shifting character of factional politics was confusing and contributed, along with the physical difficulty of getting to polling places, to very low voting participation levels.[9]

There were a number of impediments at this time to the development of modern, national parties. America had few elective or administrative offices to fill and little patronage to stimulate party growth. Most of the leading citizens of the nation viewed parties as "evil" and publicly voiced their opinions against party development. In 1787, James Madison warned the nation against "the violence of [party] faction" in the *Federalist Papers* and, as late as 1797, George Washington decried "the baneful effects of the spirit of party generally" in his Farewell Address to the nation. Moreover, the economic and social dissimilarities of the states made it difficult to reach the national policy agreements necessary for party growth.

At the outset, there was no national electorate to mobilize because the members of Congress under the Articles of Confederation and Perpetual Union were selected by the state legislatures. Most citizens had little knowledge of or contact with citizens from other states and many lacked a sense of national "identity." The final and perhaps the most significant factor inhibiting the development of national political parties at this time was the continuance of deference politics. Most people expected politics to be handled by the "better sort," not the "common folk."[10] As a result, candidates "stood" or presented themselves for public office; they did not run, reducing the need for a party organization to assist office seekers in their effort to gain elective office.

Nevertheless, one of the essential prerequisites for party development was already in place. Suffrage was relatively open to most adult, white males despite property and religious qualifications. While exact figures were not kept, it has

[9]William Nisbet Chambers, "Party Development and the American Mainstream," in *The American Party Systems*, ed., Chambers and Burnham (New York: Oxford University Press, 1967) p. 47.

[10]Paul Goodman, "The First American Party System," in *The American Party Systems*, ed. Chambers and Burnham, (New York: Oxford University Press, 1967). p. 87.

been estimated that at least 50 percent, and more probably 75 percent, of the adult, white male population could meet suffrage requirements. Emulating British practice, however, the few elective offices available were routinely filled through personal "connections" and politics was generally limited to a few notable families in each of the colonies.[11]

The *United States Constitution* was a major catalyst to party development. By establishing the popularly elected House of Representatives, the *Constitution*: (1) created the necessary preconditions through which a national electorate could be mobilized, (2) provided additional opportunities for patronage that could be used for party development, and, most importantly, (3) created a new, national political arena where differences over national policy provided the impetus for national officeholders to extend the political battle to the public. The pace of modern party development, however, was slow. The national government was still a remote entity lacking any significant direct effect on most Americans' daily lives. Also, the pace of party development was heavily influenced by the slow growth of adult suffrage and the limited power of individual voters at elections.[12]

The man most responsible for the issue polarization that led to the development of the first nationally organized American parties during the 1790s was Alexander Hamilton. George Washington denounced partisan politics and gave the task of organizing congressional support for the Administration's policies to Hamilton. These policies included the formation of a national bank, assumption of state debts, expansion of the armed force, imposition of an excise tax on whiskey and a protective tariff on manufactured goods, and establishment of a foreign policy supportive of Great Britain.

To gather support for these programs, Hamilton built the Federalist "party" by actively interacting with members of Congress and corresponding with many of his wartime associates, business acquaintances, and others of the social and economic elite who were major or potential beneficiaries of the Administration's policies. The purpose of this correspondence was to garner support for sympathetic candidates running for the House of Representatives and to help elect state legislators who would choose Senators and presidential electors supportive of Federalist views. To enhance communications between himself and his party, Hamilton helped raise funds in 1789 to enable John Fenno to establish the *Gazette of the United States*, which subsequently became the Federalist's semi-official newspaper.

Hamilton was successful in his effort to push the Administration's program through Congress but at the cost of uniting the opposition. By the end of Washington's first term, James Madison had organized the "Anti-Federalists"

[11]William Nisbet Chambers, *Political Parties in a New Nation* (New York: Oxford University Press, 1963), pp. 2–4.

[12]Frank J. Sorauf, *Party Politics in America*, 4th ed. (Boston: Little, Brown, 1980), pp. 18, 19.

in Congress into the Republican "party." Emulating Hamilton's efforts, Madison established correspondence with various state and local notables in an effort to elect congressional candidates and state legislators whose views coincided with the Republican "ideology" and supported the establishment of Philip Freneau's *National Gazette* in 1791 to facilitate communication within the party and to inform the voters of the party's policy positions. These early "parties," however, were more like stable coalitions than highly defined and durable national parties.[13]

The Republicans opposed the Federalist's foreign policies, which were generally supportive of improved relations with England at the expense of relations with France, and their activist stance in domestic affairs. While the Republican party included those who objected only to the distribution of benefits under Federalist policies and not to the use of national power per se, most Republicans supported the party's professed opposition to governmental activism and endorsed states' rights as the best means of promoting economic equality and the interests of agriculture. The Republicans' opposition to an activist government established a pattern that would repeat itself throughout American history: one of the major parties has generally been supportive of increased national activism while the other has generally opposed significant expansion of the national role.

Republican party leaders were convinced that most eligible voters shared their states' rights views and worked to increase voter participation by creating a national party organization to contest the presidential election of 1800. The Republicans went much further than the Federalists in creating a national party organization because they were out of office and needed extralegal machinery to help them organize. The Federalists, in contrast, considered themselves a government, not a party.[14] By working to increase voter turnout, the Republicans helped to break down the deferential notion that political activity was only for the upper class.

The Republican party's organizational efforts paid off in 1800. In the five states that selected their presidential electors by popular vote, eligible voter turnout soared to an unprecedented 38 percent, helping the Republicans capture the presidency as well as a majority of the seats in the House of Representatives (66 of 106) and the Senate (18 of 32). It was the first democratic transfer of power in modern times and was made possible largely because the Federalists failed to develop an organization comparable to that of the Republicans.[15]

The Republican organization continued to expand under President Jefferson's leadership and it also began to employ some modern party tactics. Although

---

[13]Ronald P. Formisano, "Federalists and Republicans: Parties, Yes — System, No," in *The Evolution of American Electoral Systems*, ed. Paul Kleppner (Westport, CT: Greenwood Press, 1981), p. 35.

[14]Ibid., p. 38.

[15]Chambers, *Political Parties in a New Nation*, p. 155; and M.J. Heale, *The Making of American Politcs* (New York: Longman, 1977), p. 85.

Andrew Jackson has been credited with introducing the patronage system, Jefferson removed about the same proportion of national officeholders as did Jackson and for the same reasons: to reward party workers and to strengthen the party organization. In several states, the Republicans abandoned the highly centralized state legislative caucus for making party nominations in favor of the more modern, popularly based county convention system. With improvements in wagon roads, the Republicans held the first state nominating conventions in Delaware and New Jersey. At the national level, however, there was no movement to adopt a national nominating convention, and the Republicans continued to select presidential nominees by the congressional caucus. Ironically, the "elitist" Federalist party held the first national nominating convention in 1808, but only eight of sixteen states were represented. Moreover, the Federalists' convention was closed to the public and the delegates were not popularly elected.

Although substantial progress was made in constructing the essential elements of modern political parties, the first party system was somewhat incomplete and short-lived. Following the second war with Great Britain, a one-party multifactional system emerged. By 1815, the Federalist party had collapsed in all but New England, depriving the Republican party of its main source of vitality—a competitive presidential contest. With the presidency assured, the Republican's state and local organizational efforts atrophied. Also, the lack of significant Federalist opposition in Congress led to the party's split into several competing factions. The extent of this factionalism was evidenced by the failure of the Republican congressional caucus in 1824 to prevent three Republicans—John Quincy Adams, Andrew Jackson, and Henry Clay—from challenging the party's presidential nominee, William Crawford, for the presidency. During the subsequent campaign, Crawford suffered a paralytic stroke and finished fourth in the four man race.

In addition to helping develop a foundation for party politics, the rise of the first Republican party had important consequences for intergovernmental relations. Under the pressure of war, the Republicans did adopt several policies which ran counter to the party's laissez-faire philosophy, including the continuation of the Bank of the United States, the annexation of Louisiana, and the Embargo of 1807. The electoral reforms sponsored by the Republicans, however, ultimately served to slow the further growth of the national government's powers. The Republicans, as the party of the "common man," encouraged the movement begun in the frontier states to have governors and presidential electors popularly elected. The Republican party supported these changes because most voters were yeoman farmers who were sympathetic to the party's laissez faire, states' rights philosophy. This development, made possible by the collapse of the Federalists in 1815, had long-term implications. It not only helped to elect Republicans, but also helped to institutionalize an electoral system responsive to popularly held laissez faire values that continued to influence governmental policy long after the Jeffersonian Republicans had ceased to exist.

Another factor which served to restrict national action during the era of the first party system was the constitutionally imposed link betwen the United States Senate and the state legislatures. As Madison predicted in *Federalist* 45, the Senate's selection by the state legislatures served to preserve state prerogatives. State legislatures at this time routinely provided written instructions to their Senators concerning specific bills. While state legislatures could not recall recalcitrant Senators, the Jeffersonian Republicans' religious adherence to the doctrine of instructions and the state legislature's option to refuse reelection to any offending Senator helped keep most Senators accountable to state officials and their policy preferences during this period.[16]

THE RISE OF THE SECOND PARTY SYSTEM: 1824–1854

The presidential election of 1824 was the starting point in the development of the nation's second party system which was much more competitive, decentralized, and egalitarian than the first. Since no candidate received a majority of the electoral college vote, the election was decided by the House of Representatives from among the top three electoral vote getters. The House chose Adams over Jackson and Clay even though Jackson had received the greatest number of popular votes. Denied the presidency by "King Caucus," Jackson decided to bypass the existing congressionally centered party structure and build his own party at the grassroots level.

Jackson believed that this strategy would put him in the White House because his states' rights, antinational bank, low tariff views were Jeffersonian in origin and popular with the "common man" and because the rules under which politics were conducted had changed to the point where such voters could determine the outcome of the presidential contest. Not only had suffrage been extended to practically all white males at this time, but presidential electors were now popularly elected in twenty-three of the twenty-four states. Although eligible voter turnout for the presidential election of 1824 was only twenty-seven percent, Jackson was convinced that with the proper organizational effort participation could be dramatically increased and his election assured.

With the help of Martin Van Buren and other professional party organizers, Jackson built the new Democratic party from the bottom up, creating the framework for the emergence of the first modern, decentralized political party. While party affiliations at this time were highly personalized, with voters thinking more in terms of the "Jackson" or "Adams" parties, state and local Democratic organizations picked their own officers, used the convention system to nominate their own state and local candidates, took independent stands on issues, and raised their own funds without interference from national party leaders.

[16]William Riker, "The Senate and American Federalism," *American Political Science Review* 49 (June 1955): 457.

As Jackson had anticipated, his party's organizational efforts helped push eligible voter turnout to new heights in 1828. Fifty-eight percent of the eligible electorate voted in the presidential contest and the popular vote jumped from 356,036 in 1824 to 1,155,350 in 1828.[17] The increased turnout was sufficient to defeat Adams as Jackson carried New York and most of the Southern and Western states.

During the Jackson Administration, a number of changes in the political environment reinforced the decentralized foundations of the emerging two-party system. The Framers' view of political parties as illegitimate expressions of corrupt self-interest began to give way to an acceptance of parties as legitimate vehicles for conflict resolution.[18] Moreover, the basic outlines of modern party machinery appeared. The decentralized convention system replaced the centralized congressional caucus for nominating presidential candidates (though this was not firmly established until 1839 when the Whigs also adopted the practice). The convention system also replaced legislative and elite caucuses for nominating state and local candidates in most areas of the country. Finally, Jackson firmly established "rotation-in-office" as standard administrative practice—making party loyalty a prerequisite for getting a government job—in order to build a durable party organization.

Reflecting the new popular dimension of the presidency, the short-lived National Republican party used a national convention in 1831 to nominate Henry Clay for president. Jackson's landslide victory over Clay in 1832, however, brought an end to the National Republicans, and opposition to Jackson was left to the successor Whig party.

The Whigs emulated Jackson's state and local organizational efforts and ushered in a new period in the organization of presidential politics. Presidential and vice-presidential nominations were now regularly contested at party conventions and national party platforms were debated and ratified there.[19] In addition, partisan conflict attained a new degree of legitimacy; voter turnout, especially at the presidential level, increased; stable partisan identifications became prevalent among voters; and the two parties became competitive in every state except South Carolina.[20] Moreover, state party organizations became organizationally complex, well staffed, and hierarchically structured[21]

---

[17]Sorauf, *Party Politics in America*, p. 19.

[18]William G. Shade, "Political Pluralism and Party Development: The Creation of a Modern Party System, 1815–1852," in *The Evolution of American Electoral Systems*, ed. Kleppner (Westport, CT: Greenwood Press, 1981), p. 79.

[19]Ibid., p. 81.

[20]Ibid., p. 84.

[21]Richard P. McCormick, "Political Development and the Second Party System," in *The American Party Systems*, ed. Chambers and Burnham (New York: Oxford University Press, 1967), pp. 105, 106.

Not only were parties well organized and active during the 1840s and early 1850s but the public seemed to be caught up in a partisan frenzy. Voter participation levels often reached eighty percent of the eligible electorate.[22]

Despite the massive changes in party organization that took place during this period, the national government's responsibilities remained modest. The absence of any menacing foreign policy issues (unlike the earlier period), the resolution of boundary disputes with Canada by diplomacy, and the brief duration of the war with Mexico were all indirect factors countering activism in Washington. Even more important were the difficulties of constructing durable nationwide policy alliances in a country segmented by state and regional economies and rent by major cultural, denominational, and racial differences among the regions and states.

The most important factor limiting the national role prior to the Civil War, however, was the overwhelming belief among the general populace and most of its elected leaders in states' rights and a limited governmental role at all levels.[23] These popular beliefs were reflected in the actions and platforms of the major parties of the era, and even some of the minor parties could not escape them. The Democratic Party, sensitive to the South's preccupation with the slavery issue, endorsed the states' rights view in every one of its national platforms during this period.[24] Reflecting the temper of the times, even the National Republican and Whig parties left the states considerable leeway in policymaking. Consesequently, efforts in Congress to allocate national funds to states for internal improvements or other purposes were consistently rejected throughout the pre-Civil War period.

Lacking a strong unifying national perspective, the parties consisted of a decentralized collection of autonomous state-based factions that individually sought to get economic subsidies from the national government but lacked sufficient commonalities to agree on very many strong national actions.[25] Pennsylvania and New York, for example, had already invested a great deal of their own funds on state canals and highways and opposed providing national funds to other states that had not undertaken similar efforts. The states of both the Atlantic and Gulf coasts also opposed significant national expenditures in internal improvements because they were already blessed with "magnificent systems of river transportation" and correctly judged that most internal improvement projects would be targeted to states outside their region—principally to those in the West.[26]

[22]Ibid., p. 107.

[23]Louis Hartz, *The Liberal Tradition in America* (New York: Harcourt, Brace & World, Inc., 1955).

[24]Richard C. Bain, *Convention Decisions and Voting Records* (Washington, DC: The Brookings Institution, 1960), p. 24.

[25]Samuel H. Beer, "The Modernization of American Federalism," *Publius* 1, no. 3 (Fall 1973): 58–62.

[26]Wilfred E. Binkley, *American Political Parties*, 3rd ed. (New York: Knopf, 1959), pp. 135, 136.

In those rare instances when a congressional coalition was able to adopt such a measure, a presidential veto was usually forthcoming.[27] Andrew Jackson, for example, vetoed legislation in 1833 that would have distributed the proceeds of public land sales to the states because he felt the legislation was an infringement on states' rights. In 1854, President Franklin Pierce even vetoed legislation that would have provided funds to the states for the care of the indigent insane. One exception to this pattern, the distribution of the federal surplus in 1837, took place only after Congress agreed to consider it a loan, subject to recall if necessary.

The limited scope of the national government prior to the Civil War is readily seen when examining national governmental expenditures. From 1789 to 1860, the national government spent a total of $1.7 billion, with the largest single year expenditure of $74 million coming in 1858. Not only were the national government's expenditures small, but relative expenditures grew very slowly during the first seventy years of the Republic. In 1800, national governmental expenditures per capita were $2 and sixty years later the figure was still the same.[28] It is not surprising, then, that intergovernmental cash transfers were extremely limited during this period. Up until 1869, only $42 million was granted by the national government to the states and localities, and two-thirds of this total came in the 1837 distribution of the national surplus.[29]

Given the constitutional doubts and political difficulties concerning the use of national revenue for state purposes, collaborative intergovernmental relations during the pre-Civil War era were dominated by the land grant. Millions of acres of the public domain were given to the states to help finance public education, wagon roads, canals, flood control, and river navigation projects.[30] The overwhelming belief in the superiority of the states' and localities' governing ability was reflected in the lack of conditions that the national government placed on the land grants. While broad purposes were designated for the use of the proceeds of land sales, the states were given almost total freedom to do with them as they wished.

Despite the limited role of the national government during the pre-Civil War period, there were some who feared that the advent of modern party organization in the 1830s could create the conditions conducive to a more powerful national role in governance. The most prominent spokesman of this view was

[27]David B. Walker, *Toward a Functioning Federalism* (Cambridge, MA: Winthrop, 1981), p. 52.

[28]Everett Carll Ladd, Jr., *American Political Parties: Social Change and Political Response* (New York: W.W. Norton & Co., Inc., 1970), p. 73.

[29]Paul B. Trescott, "The U.S. Government and National Income, 1790–1900," in National Bureau of Economic Research, *Trends in the American Economy in the 19th Century* (Princeton, NJ: Princeton University Press, 1960), pp. 337–61; cited in the U.S. Congress, Senate Committee on Government Operations, *The Condition of American Federalism: An Historian's View*, by Harry N. Scheiber, Committee Print (Washington, DC: U.S. Government Printing Office, 1966), p. 23.

[30]Grodzins, *The American System*, pp. 36, 37.

[31]Shade, "Political Pluralism and Party Development," p. 93.

John C. Calhoun. The function of political parties, he pointed out, extended beyond electoral politics to the organization and control of legislative bodies. Until 1828, there was little relationship between congressional and presidential elections and congressional voting behavior reflected high cohesion within, but not between, state delegations.[31] Parties, however, threatened to increase voting cohesion between state congressional coalitions by requiring adherence to the party's national platform. Calhoun feared that a determined political majority (especially the manufacturing interests of the more populous North) could enlist the party system as a vehicle to override the constitutional system of checks and balances and use the national government's powers to inflict a majority "tyranny" over the South.[32]

Calhoun's fear that congressional voting would become increasingly partisan was realized during the 1840s. His fear that a monolithic party would centralize governmental powers, however, was checked during the 1840s and 1850s because the Democratic and Whig parties had developed deep "roots" in an electorate that was generally opposed to a centralization of governmental powers. Moreover, the two parties were so evenly matched within Congress that it was often difficult to achieve consensus on national initiatives. Indeed, out of electoral necessity the two parties avoided acting on most controversial issues that could have resulted in national initiatives—slavery, of course, being the prime example.[33]

THE THIRD PARTY ERA: 1860–1896

Neither the Whigs nor the Democrats could cope with the sectional antagonism brought on by the *Kansas–Nebraska Act of 1854*. The Whigs collapsed completely and the Democrats were split into northern and southern factions. The Democrats' frustrations were compounded by their national convention's rule requiring a two-thirds vote for securing the presidential nomination. This provision provided Southern Democrats with a veto over the party's presidential nominees and produced two "doughface" Democratic nominees and presidents (Pierce and Buchanan).

In 1860, the Republicans captured the presidency in a four-way contest largely because the Democratic factions could not agree on a candidate. The Democrats' northern faction backed Stephen Douglas while the Democrats' southern wing backed John Breckinridge. A hastily resurrected Whig coalition, the

---

[32]C. Gordon Post, "Introduction" to *A Disquisition on Government and Selections from the Discourse*, by John C. Calhoun (New York: Bobbs-Merrill, 1953), p. xv.

[33]McCormick, "Political Development and the Second Party System," p. 112. See also William H. Riker, *Liberalism against Populism* (San Francisco: W. H. Freeman and Company, 1982), chap. 9, for an examination of the Whigs' development of the antislavery position to attain office and their subsequent avoidance of action on slavery once they won office.

Constitutional Union Party, was the only real opposition to Breckinridge in the southern and border states.

Following the South's secession, the Republican party found itself in firm control of every major public policymaking body in the North. They not only held large majorities in the House of Representatives and the Senate but also controlled for two years every state legislature and governorship in the North. Also, President Lincoln was able to make five appointments to the Supreme Court, more than enough to assure that the Court would not obstruct the party's actions.[34]

While there was considerable friction between Lincoln and the Republican Congress concerning the conduct of the War, the Republican party nevertheless was presented a unique opportunity for domestic policymaking. The opportunity was not squandered. Composed of a heterogeneous collection of manufacturers and their employees seeking tariff protection, farmers in search of homestead legislation, and abolitionists out to end slavery, the Republican party adopted a higher tariff, enacted a homestead law, ended slavery, provided large land grants for higher education and railroads, and established a new department of agriculture.[35] In reviewing the actions of the Republican party during the Civil War period, Walter Dean Burnham wrote that the "Republican party was genuinely, if unusually, a policymaking party."[36]

To ensure that these national laws were implemented expeditiously and to solidify the allegiance of loyal Northern Democrats, President Lincoln followed Jackson's principle of rotation-in-office and "purged" the national bureaucracy.[37] Patronage was dispersed to both Republican party workers and loyal Democrats. Lincoln's Republican supporters even discarded their party label during the course of the Civil War and, with the loyal Democrats, called themselves the Union Party—forcing the "regular" Democrats in the North who did not join the Union Party to appear to be opposed to the Union.[38]

During the War, Lincoln undertook several extraordinary actions that overrode state prerogatives. He unilaterally called forth the state militias, asked for volunteers, and enlarged the armed forces even though the recruitment of the militia had traditionally been a power of the states' governors. His suspension of the writ of habeas corpus superseded state laws. State and War Department provost-marshalls, operating independently of the states' judicial systems, arrested thousands suspected of disloyal activities.[39] In 1861, he even dispersed

---

[34]Morton Keller, *Affairs of State* (Cambridge, MA: Harvard University Press, 1977), p. 18.

[35]Martin Shefter, "Party, Bureaucracy, and Political Change in the United States," in *Political Parties: Development and Decay* (Beverly Hills, CA: Sage Publications, Inc., 1978), p. 225.

[36]Burnham, "Party Systems and the Political Processes," p. 296.

[37]Shefter, "Party, Bureaucracy, and Political Change in the United States," p. 225.

[38]Binkley, *American Political Parties*, p. 239.

[39]Eric L. McKitrick, "Party Politics and the Union and Confederate War Efforts," in *The American Party Systems*, ed. Chambers and Burnham (New York: Oxford University Press, 1967), pp. 138, 139.

the Maryland legislature and arrested some of its members suspected of disloyal activities.

Lincoln was successful in these endeavors largely because of the war-time sense of emergency and the Republican (and subsequently the Union) party's strength in the North. In 1861, every northern governor was a Republican and politically committed to the positive measures necessary to preserve the Union. Also, Lincoln usd his influence on the patronage and government procurement processes to reward those governors who were cooperative. Moreover, the War Department controlled which states' soldiers would be furloughed on election day, and Lincoln made certain that Republican soldiers were given preference.[40]

Following the War, the ideal of an active, interventionist national government was carried on by the Radical Republicans in their successful battle with Andrew Johnson for control over Reconstruction. While moderate Republicans did limit the degree of the national government's control over the South, the commitment of the Radical Republicans moved the Republican party to adopt Reconstruction policies that went far beyond most expectations.[41]

Nevertheless, the continued expansion of national governmental powers subsided with the end of the national emergency, and measures advocated in the late 1860s and early 1870s were frustrated by a combination of factors. The $2.7 billion national debt left over from the Civil War presented a considerable fiscal obstacle to extending the national sphere of influence.[42] The death of Thaddeus Stevens, the leader of the Radical Republicans in the House of Representatives, created a void in assertive congressional leadership. The number of Democrats in Congress increased dramatically as the passion of war receded, an industrial depression took place, and many Northerners who shared the Democrats' commitment to localism and limited government began to vote Democratic once again. In 1874, the Democratic resurgence was evidenced by the party's capture of a majority of the seats in the House of Representatives, and in the disputed 1876 presidential election their candidate received a majority of the popular vote and nearly won the presidency. Following that contest, Southern Democratic congressional delegations returned to Capitol Hill and a twenty year period of relatively even interparty competition at the national level was launched.

The return of Southern Democrats to Congress had a profound effect on the third party system and on intergovernmental relations. From 1876 to 1892, the partisan linkages between voter and candidate, and officeholder and party

---

[40]Ibid.

[41]Keller, *Affairs of State*, pp. 61–62.

[42]U.S. Bureau of the Census, *Historical Statistics of the United States: Colonial Times to 1970*, Part 2 (Washington, DC: U.S. Government Printing Office, 1975), p. 118.

leaders were stronger than in any other corresponding era. Party became the most important correlate of legislative behavior at all levels of government.[43]

Because the parties were so evenly matched—with Democrats leading in the South and border states, Republicans leading in the Northeast and most of the western states, and certain key states competitive—the parties' national platform and the heightened degree of party discipline served as a powerful restraint against further national initiatives. Electoral and policy cleavages were frozen along sectional fault lines, preventing the parties from accommodating intersectional, cross-ethnic, and class demands. Although the national government during this period did advance distributive policies such as inducements to business growth—by providing favorable tariff rates, land grants, and settling strikes by force—the decentralized and sectionalized parties could not enact policies to accommodate the centralization ethos pursued by corporate executives.[44] As a result, the states continued to exercise the primary responsibility for domestic policymaking and the state legislatures remained the focal points for domestic initiatives.[45]

Changes in the nature of state party organizations in each of the nation's three major regions (Northeast–Midwest, South, and West) also served to restrict the further growth of national responsibilities at this time. In the Northeast–Midwest, these changes were strongly influenced by major socioeconomic shifts which accompanied that region's rapid industrialization. By 1880, more than three-quarters of the New England and Mid-Atlantic states' workforce was employed in nonagricultural pursuits.[46] Along with rapid industrialization came rapid urbanization and massive immigration. The cities' factories needed laborers and when the nation's workforce could not meet the demand, immigrants from Europe did. In the short span of a single lifetime, the nation's overall economy was transformed from a relatively segmented, mercantile, agrarian economy with small cottage industries to an economy of national scale dominated by industrial giants.

The cities' emergence, the expansion of the industrial working class, the dramatic increase in the foreign-born population established conditions conducive to the proliferation of urban political machines in the Northeast and Midwest. While the influence of urban machines and the bosses who ran them can be easily overstated, the nature of the region's party leadership did change. Many of the "independent" middle class clergymen, journalists, and lawyers who had

---

[43]Paul Kleppner, "Partisanship and Ethnoreligious Conflict: The Third Electoral System, 1853–1892," in *The Evolution of American Electoral Systems*, ed. Kleppner (Westport, CT: Greenwood Press, 1981), p. 139.

[44]Ibid., p. 140.

[45]Ballard C. Campbell, *Representative Democracy* (Cambridge, MA: Harvard University Press, 1980), p. 54.

[46]Ladd, *American Political Parties: Social Change and Political Response*, p. 130.

held important leadership positions within the parties were replaced by urban bosses or their representatives. As James Bryce observed at the time, most of the urban bosses were foreign-born, from lower socioeconomic backgrounds than the previous leaders, and more interested in securing patronage than in advancing any particular ideological view.[47]

Party leaders' efforts to control the flow of patronage in the Northeast–Midwest tended to exert a decentralizing influence on intergovernmental relations because the key to gaining that control was the United States Senate. Under the first and second party systems, control over both national and state patronage was held by the state legislatures. At that time, state legislatures controlled state patronage through their own legislative capabilities and national patronage through their influence over their state's United States Senators. Under the third party system, however, changes in the manner of selecting United States Senators freed many members from electoral dependence on state legislators and provided them with substantial control over both national and state patronage.

Prior to the 1850s, Senators usually campaigned for their seats after the state legislature was elected; they canvassed the legislators, not the voters. This contributed to the Senate's subservient relationship to the state legislatures under the first and second party systems and helps to explain the frequent use of instructions. During the 1850s, however, some state's Senatorial candidates began to campaign before the state legislatures were elected, urging voters to elect state legislative candidates pledged to their candidacy. The most famous example of this was the Lincoln/Douglas contest for the Illinois' Senate seat in 1858. By the 1870s, nearly all Senate campaigns were conducted in this fashion, with the contest often deciding the composition of the state legislature.[48]

Because of the Senate's new influence over the composition of the various state legislatures, Senators during the latter part of the third party system era had an unprecedented opportunity to influence the allocation of both national and state patronage. As a result, local political interests throughout the country became increasingly interested in the outcome of Senatorial campaigns. By the 1880s, most of the Northeast–Midwest's Senators were either state bosses who viewed the Senate as a vehicle to maintain their preeminent position in their state's party organization or hand-picked representatives of state or local party leaders.[49]

The urban political machines were interested in the presidential contest for the same reason they were interested in Senatorial contests—jobs. In return for the machines' support in the nomination and general election campaigns, presidential candidates throughout this period promised to abide by the unwritten rule

[47]James Bryce, *The American Commonwealth*, Vol. II (New York: Macmillan, 1911), p. 119.

[48]Riker, "The Senate and American Federalism," p. 463.

[49]Moisei Ostrogorski, *Democracy and the Organization of Political Parties*, Vol. II (1902; reprinted, New York: Haskell House Publishers, 1970), p. 543. One of the most noted examples of this was the crucial role of Senator Roscoe Conkling in New York.

concerning "senatorial courtesy": the right of each state's Senators to control the patronage of the national government within that state's borders. To oppose their own party's desire for patronage was politically foolish for any president. Not only did the machines play an influential role in the national nominating conventions and in getting out the vote in the general election, they also had the power to wreck presidential legislative initiatives through their influence with their Senate delegations.

The urban machines also enjoyed great influence over the voting behavior of their city's Representatives in the House. They often controlled the congressional nomination process through local party conventions and in many districts possessed the political resources necessary for victory in the general election.[50] Indeed, some seats in the House of Representatives were often rotated among party stalwarts. This contributed to the high degree of membership turnover (between 30 percent and 60 percent at every election) and the relative absence of career members in the House of Representatives during the nineteenth century.[51]

This high turnover and lack of member continuity, coupled with frequent alteration of party control, made power extremely fluid within the House. Moreover, while Senators and Representatives were usually allowed to vote as they wished on most issues—written instructions from northeastern and midwestern state legislatures became the exception rather than the rule—state and local party leaders did not hesitate to use their influence on their congressional delegations to maintain their control over patronage or to protect the interests of their financial supporters.[52] Even in the wake of the public uproar following the assassination of President James Garfield by a frustrated office seeker, party leaders were able to convince Congress to exempt over 80 percent of national governmental employees from the civil service provisions of the *Pendleton Act of 1883*.

State and local party leaders were also generally opposed to any measures that would either centralize the party structure or strengthen the national government. The political logic of this defense of American federalism's traditional concept of a strong state role in governance was aptly provided by E.E. Schattschneider over forty years ago:

> . . . Generally the bosses are not interested in public affairs; they read no books, have vague ideas on public business, and are indifferent to conflicts of policy as far as personal prejudice is concerned.

[50]Ibid., p. 544.

[51]H. Douglas Price, "The Congressional Career Then and Now," in *Congressional Behavior*, ed. Nelson W. Polsby (New York: Random House, 1971), pp. 16–18; and Nelson W. Polsby, "The Institutionalization of the U.S. House of Representatives," *American Political Science Review* 62, no. 1 (March 1968): 146.

[52]Ostrogorski, *Democracy and the Organization of Political Parties*, p. 557.

The central–local conflict within the parties does not grow out of irreconcilable differences between central and local party leaders over public policy. It arises out of the fact that a national leadership strong enough to control party majorities in Congress would also be strong enough to cut off the flow of patronage to the local bosses.[53]

Outside the northeastern and midwestern urban states, different patterns of political organization prevailed but with a similar localistic result. A solidly one-party Democratic system dedicated to the preservation of white supremacy gradually emerged in the eleven states of the Old Confederacy and, to a lesser extent, in the five border states. Like the northeastern and midwestern urban machines, the South's urban and rural party organizations had a keen interest in who became their states' United States Senator. Unlike northern party leaders, southern party leaders not only wanted to control patronage but had an overriding concern with muting the practical effects of the Fourteenth and Fifteenth Amendments through such devices as the poll tax, literacy tests, and racially segregated schools. Many of the South's national officials, therefore, were committed to a decentralized governmental system both as a means of preserving their influence over patronage and as a means of controlling racial relations within their states.

The strength of the South and border states in the Democratic Party (providing 70 percent of the electoral vote needed for a presidential victory), along with the pivotal role of New York and Ohio and the two-thirds vote nominating requirement, meant that Democratic presidential candidates and congressional leaders were required to balance the interests of a heterogeneous coalition in ways that neither expanded national authority in various areas (civil rights, tariff, immigration) nor denied the Jacksonian concept of the presidency (power to veto, appoint, and remove). With the Republicans, the delicate balance between the emerging eastern business and western agrarian interests generated a similar balancing act, with the former gradually winning out, along with their national policy of assisting themselves and adhering to laissez faire for all others.

Accordingly, the new leaders of the Republican and Democratic parties lacked the ideological zeal of their predecessors. One of the first indications of the moderating influence of this new generation of state and local political leaders on the national parties was the Republican party's nomination of Ulysses S. Grant for the presidency in 1868 over the party's more radical candidates.[54]

Left out of all this—in part because of the small popular and electoral votes involved—were the western states. Here a steady rhythm of political revolt against the standpattism of both major parties occurred. From the 1870s through most of the 1890s, third-party movements erupted in this area (Greenbackers in the 1870s, Farmers' Alliance in the 1880s, and the Populists, with a southern

[53]Schattschneider, *Party Government, p. 137.*

[54]Kenneth M. Stampp, *The Era of Reconstruction, 1865–1877* (New York: Knopf, 1965), p. 187.

wing, in the 1890s). All sought corrective national action against the abuses they found in the conservative, capitalistic, eastern-dominated party system they were rebelling against. The last such political force—the Populists—took over the Democratic party in the mid-nineties and in the process launched a new political era: a heavily Republican one.

A REPUBLICAN ERA: 1896–1932

With Bryan's nomination by both the Populists and the Democrats in 1896, a new party era emerged. The Republicans became for a third of a century the clear majority party, one-partyism became the rule in many states, especially in the Northeast and Great Lakes states—with the desertion of Cleveland Democrats—and the "solid" South, where the advent of the "white primary" made it more monolithically Democratic than ever.

Due to the problems stemming from the lack of party competition in many states and to widespread dissatisfaction with political corruption, both parties were influenced by a twenty year reform surge during this period. The Progressive movement emerged from the convergence of two independent reform movements: the remnant of the Democratic–Populist agrarian reform crusade of the 1890s and the middle class/urban-based reform movement of the early 1900s, which affected both the Democratic and Republican parties. Each reform group viewed the alliance between big business and party officials as the antithesis of good government, but for different reasons.

The rural reform efforts to sever the ties between government and big business were fueled by economic and regional self-interests. Based in the agricultural areas of the South and West, these reformers considered the alliance of party bosses and big business as counter to their economic interests and to democratic government. These populist Democrats viewed the Republican party's national advocacy of a stable money supply based on the gold standard and a protective tariff as proof that that party was a "puppet" of the trusts. The electoral realignment of 1896, however, made the Republican party dominant in national politics, preventing the populists from achieving many of their legislative goals at the national level, though they did support Theodore Roosevelt's reform initiatives. As a result, the populists concentrated their reform efforts within those states and localities where they were strongest, chiefly in the mountain and southwestern states.

Progressive Republicans were committed to the use of governmental powers to manage equitably an increasingly complicated and interdependent society. Led by members of the newly formed professional communities in education, finance, engineering, and law, these mostly middle class Republicans were generally supportive of most of the party's national policies but objected to the trusts' corruption of the economic marketplace and of the political arena. They were strong advocates of free enterprise and supported the positive use of governmental regulatory powers to address imbalances within the marketplace. Locally, they were particularly concerned about local transit companies and municipal utilties that were able to charge exorbitant fees because of their political connections.[55]

The progressive Republicans' efforts to sever the ties between the party bosses and the trusts were motivated not only by distinct policy differences with party leaders but by middle class moral dictates as well. In their view, political parties were too parochial and geographically limited to respond to the needs of an interdependent and industrial society. Moreover, they felt that political parties violated several moral codes: party patronage violated the code of selecting personnel on objective qualifications; bossism violated the code that votes should be based on individual appraisal of the qualifications of candidates; and bribery, "honest graft," and "protection" for crimes violated the law and social morals.[56]

Although both the rural and the urban wings of these reform movements had a national agenda, they were most concerned with state and local issues where most governmental action still remained concentrated. They emphasized the reform of state and local political and governmental processes as means to dethrone the party bosses and restore "power to the people." Foremost on the reform agenda were electoral reforms transferring power over policymaking from the "corrupt" legislators to the public. These reforms included the initiative, referendum, and recall, the direct election of Senators, and the use of direct primaries to nominate candidates for office. To further curb the power of party bosses, the progressives advocated civil service systems and nonpartisan elections at the municipal level. To promote effective government, they advocated consolidation of local governments, the city commission and city manager form of local governance, and unified executive budget systems.[57] While all of these reforms fall under the heading of progressive reforms, the westerners tended to focus more on the electoral group, while the urban wing placed greater emphasis on the governmental effectiveness and accountability initiatives.

Because party bosses were often staunch opponents of an expanded national role in governance, the progressives' efforts to destroy the party organizations presented the possibility of new, centralizing orientations in intergovernmental relations. The direct election of Senators, for example, eliminated an important institutional link between the national government and the state legislatures—an institutional link Madison viewed as crucial to the maintenance of a strong and

---

[55]James L. Sundquist, *Dynamics of the Party System* (Washington, DC: The Brookings Institution, 1973), p. 156.

[56]Robert K. Merton, "The Latent Functions of the Machine," in *Urban Bosses, Machines, and Progressive Reformers*, ed. with an introduction by Bruce M. Stave (Lexington, MA: Heath, 1972), p. 27.

[57]Sundquist, *Dynamics of the Party System*, p. 158.

viable federalism. Moreover, the progressives also supported a variety of national regulatory and social initiatives.

In the short run, however, the electoral reforms adopted during this period only marginally weakened the political machines and had no immediate, significant impact on American intergovernmental relations. The direct primary was supposed to shatter the party organization's control over candidate nominations, but the party machines usually were able to deliver a large enough block of votes in these primaries to control the nomination process anyway.[58] The direct election of Senators, mandated by the Seventeenth Amendment, was supposed to free that institution from the control of the political machines and the "trusts." Again the machines' ability to deliver the vote helped them maintain influence in the Senate.

The Australian (or secret) ballot was supposed to end vote-buying by preventing party workers from knowing if the vote had been delivered as promised. The secret ballot, however, did little to alter the reasons why many citizens were willing to "sell" their votes in the first place. Political machines remained influential in many areas of the country because they provided important services to the voters:

> Food-baskets and jobs, legal and extra-legal advice, setting to rights minor scrapes with the law, helping the bright poor boy to a political scholarship in a local college, looking after the bereaved—the whole range of crises when a feller needs a friend, and, above all, a friend who knows the score and who can do something about it—all these find the ever-helpful precinct captain available in the pinch.[59]

The resilience of local political machines during the Progressive Era maintained the influence of party leaders over national policymakers, though popular and new interest group access was enhanced where machines were weak. In the South, the primary was converted into a device for assuring one-party, Democratic rule and white supremacy. This continued the party system's localizing influence on national politics which, in combination with the popular values of localism and continued laissez faire, presented powerful obstacles to various national initiatives.

Despite these obstacles, the progressives were able to gain enough support in both parties to extend the national government's police powers. National laws were enacted during the Roosevelt Administration regulating the hours of labor, methods and time of wage payments, employer liability, and factory conditions. During the Wilson Administration, various regulatory agencies were established

---

[58]V.O. Key, Jr., *Politics, Parties, and Pressure Groups*, 5th ed. (New York: Thomas Y. Crowell, 1964), p. 376.

[59]Merton, "The Latent Functions of the Machine," p. 31.

such as the Federal Reserve System (1913), the Federal Trade Commission (1914), and the Federal Power Commission (1920). While the overall impact of these laws was comparatively modest, they established precedents for later expansion of national regulatory powers.[60]

The adoption of the Sixteenth Amendment to the *Constitution* in 1913 provided the national government the potential fiscal clout to undertake additional responsibilities in governance, and World War I provided the first opportunity to tap it. With the end of land grants, the cash grant with its more restrictive administrative conditions also began to be used, but modestly. National intergovernmental expenditures in 1927 amounted to only $123 million out of a total national budget of $3.5 billion. State and local expenditures, in contrast, were $7.8 billion in 1927.[61]

THE NEW DEAL: AN HISTORIC TURNING POINT

The New Deal was an historic turning point in the development of intergovernmental relations and ultimately had important consequences for political parties. Prior to the 1930s, state and local governments dominated most areas of domestic policy, particularly education, highway construction, and public welfare, and had far more tangible impact on most citizens' lives than did the national government. During the 1920s, for example, state and local governments accounted for 74 percent of public spending and 67 percent of taxes.[62] The Great Depression, however, placed a tremendous strain on state and local governments. Already in debt from deficit spending during the 1920s, states and localities were faced with sharply rising welfare costs at a time when tax revenues were falling with equal speed. President Roosevelt responded to the national financial emergency by embarking on the broadest intervention in economic affairs that the country had ever seen.

The national government's new responsibilities were evidenced by the rising level of national expenditures relative to those of the states and localities. In 1932, state and local governments outspent the national government by a 2-to-1 margin ($8.4 billion to $4.2 billion). By 1934, the states and localities' margin had been cut to $1.9 billion ($7.8 billion to $5.9 billion) and, by 1936, the national government had assumed fiscal preeminence, outspending states and localities by $0.6 billion ($8.5 billion to $9.1 billion).[63] This was the first time

[60]Ladd, *American Political Parties: Social Change and Political Response*, pp. 180, 181.

[61]U.S. Bureau of the Census, *Historical Statistics of the United States: Colonial Times to 1970*, pp. 1124, 1126.

[62]James T. Patterson, *The New Deal and the States* (Princeton, NJ: Princeton University Press, 1969), p. 4.

[63]U.S. Bureau of the Census, *Historical Statistics of the United States: Colonial Times to 1970*, pp. 1124, 1127.

the national government had outspent the states and localities in the absence of war. From 1937 through 1940, national governmental expenditures remained approximately equal to the combined expenditures of the states and localities.

The increased size of the national government's budget during the 1930s was accompanied by a steady growth in the number of intergovernmental cash grants and a marked increase in funds committed to them. Intergovernmental outlays jumped from $193 million in 1933 to $1.8 billion in 1934, $2.3 billion in 1936, and peaked at $2.9 billion in 1939. This figure was not reached again until the 1950s.[64] The number of intergovernmental grant programs also increased dramatically. In 1930, there were only fifteen programs in operation. By 1938, the number of intergovernmntal programs had increased to thirty-seven.[65]

The first New Deal programs to alter intergovernmental relationships were the emergency relief programs administered by the Federal Emergency Relief Administration (FERA). Headed by Harry Hopkins, FERA was authorized to distribute $500 million to the states in 1933—$250 million in matching grants which required states to contribute $3 for every $1 of national funds and $250 million in discretionary grants to meet emergency state needs. By 1936, FERA had distributed over $3 billion for relief purposes. While centralizing the source of relief funding, public welfare administration remained at the state level and nationally imposed administrative conditions were flexible. In many ways, the national relief programs seemed to fit the "cooperative federalism" label that was affixed to grants-in-aid programs adopted during the New Deal period. Where state or local program implementation was considered unsatisfactory, however, the national government retained the right to either nationalize program administration, as was done in Kentucky and Ohio, or to cut off national funding altogether, as was done to Colorado.[66]

In 1935, a new intergovernmental program was adopted which permanently altered the nature of American federalism: the *Social Security Act of 1935*. It established the foundation for the emergence of a significant and permanent national role in social welfare policy and further institutionalized cooperative federalism. Specifically, it not only created a national program of old-age assistance but also launched a series of intergovernmental programs requiring state matching funds: aid to the blind, aid to dependent children, aid to crippled children, child welfare, and unemployment insurance.

There were a number of interrelated factors that accounted for the dramatic increase in the national government's responsibilities during the 1930s. The rigid belief in the values of governmental localism and laissez faire was permanently

[64]Harry N. Scheiber, *The Condition of American Federalism: An Historian's View*, a study submitted by the Subcommittee on Intergovernmental Relations to the Committee on Government Operations, U.S. Senate, 89th Cong., 2nd Sess., October 15, 1966, p. 9.

[65]Advisory Commission on Intergovernmental Relations, *Categorical Grants: Their Role and Design* (Washington, DC: U.S. Government Printing Office, 1978), p. 18.

[66]Patterson, *The New Deal and the States*, pp. 50–73.

altered by the Depression's severity. The failure of the old ways of doing things made the public receptive to change. Most importantly, the leaders of the new governing party were supportive of the expansion of national powers. While President Roosevelt stressed the temporary nature of most of his new national programs, he repeatedly argued that government could play a positive role in bettering people's lives.[67]

Many local Democratic political machines, which had previously used their influence in the selection of national officeholders to restrict the growth of national powers, now supported New Deal activism because it promised to provide needed fiscal relief to their cities and unprecedented levels of national patronage that they could use to bolster their organizatons.[68] In addition, the mayors of the nation's cities lobbied Washington for increased intergovernmental asistance. Moreover, the fragmentation of power normally associated with the national government was temporarily superseded by the Democratic landslides in 1932, 1934, and 1936. Finally, in the wake of Roosevelt's threat to pack the Supreme Court in 1937, the Court subsequently upheld the constitutionality of the *National Labor Relations Act* and the *Social Security Act*, clearing a wide legal path for continued national regulation of the economy.

The New Deal thus reflected, and in turn helped to reinforce, dramatic changes in the American party system. It marked the end of the Republican dominated third party system that was launched in 1856 and the beginning of the Democratic dominated fourth party system.

The elections of 1932, 1934, and 1936 were part of a massive electoral realignment. The arrival of a whole new generation of voters, including many women, the defection of progressive Republicans, and the concomitant gains in the industrial centers of the Northeast and Midwest moved the Democratic party into the majority. The Democrats' New Deal coalition (southern whites, northern working class whites, Catholics, Jews, and later, blacks) dominated presidential elections until the 1960s and continues to strongly influence congressional elections today.

Following the elections of 1932–1936, sectional, racial, and religious antagonisms that had dominated party politics and frustrated national initiatives throughout American history were dampened by new national coalitions with significant class overtones. This enabled the Democratic party to establish itself as the working-class party in a broad, national sense and was largely responsible for much of the Democrat's legislative success during the 1930s and later.[69]

[67]Advisory Commission on Intergovernmental Relations, *The Condition of Contemporary Federalism: Conflicting Theories and Collapsing Constraints* (Washington, DC: U.S. Government Printing Office, 1981), pp. 114–17.

[68]Schattschneider, *Party Government*, p. 168.

[69]Everett Carll Ladd with Charles Hadley, *Transformations of the American Party System* (New York: W.W. Norton & Co., Inc., 1975), p. 66.

The conservative coalition's emergence in Congress following the 1938 mid-term elections had several long-term consequences for intergovernmental relations. Composed of conservative southern Democrats and Republicans, this coalition, throughout the remainder of this era and into the next, prevented enactment of many national initiatives and caused many of the initiatives that were adopted to be of an incremental and modest nature. It also contributed to the declining influence of party bosses by eliminating party access to large numbers of patronage positions created by the New Deal. In 1939, the conservative coalition was instrumental in the passage of an amendment to the *Social Security Act* that required state and county agencies managing programs under the *Act* to establish personnel standards on a merit basis or lose their funding. The coalition's objective was to weaken northern, Democratic machines that used New Deal patronage to maintain their influence with the voters. In 1940, the urban machines were further weakened as the limitations on political activity mandated by the *Hatch Act* on national governmental employees were extended to the state and local employees of any agency receiving financial backing from the national government.[70]

THE WAR YEARS AND BEYOND: 1940–1960

The advent of World War II and the national preoccupation with defense temporarily stalled the growth of intergovernmental grants. From 1940 through 1946, annual intergovernmental outlays to states and localities fell to just under $1 billion and the number of intergovernmental programs was reduced to twenty-nine by 1946.[71] Of long-term significance to intergovernmental relations, however, was the dramatic increase at this time in the size of the national government relative to states and localities, as measured by governmental expenditures, and the concurrent and unprecedented reliance on corporate and individual income taxes to fund this new, national government establishment.

In 1940, the national government was outspent by the states and localities ($10 billion to $11.2 billion). By 1942, the national government was spending three times as much as the states and localities ($35.5 billion to $10.9 billion) and nearly ten times as much in 1944 ($100.5 billion to $10.5 billion). While national expenditures did fall to $35.5 billion in 1948 and did not reach the $100 billion level again until 1961, the national government's expenditures remained significantly higher than pre-World War II levels.[72]

[70]Key, *Politics, Parties, and Pressure Groups*, p. 358.

[71]Walker, *Toward a Functioning Federalism*, p. 79; and U.S. Bureau of the Census, *Historical Statistics of the United States: Colonial Times to 1970*, Part 2, p. 1125.

[72]U.S. Bureau of the Census, *Historical Statistics of the United States: Colonial Times to 1970*, Part 2, pp. 1123, 1127.

The national government's reliance on the income tax to fund the war effort and its continued use of the income tax after the War assured it of an "elastic" revenue source for the future. The intergovernmental consequences of this were great. As the national government's revenues grew with the economy during the 1950s and 1960s, national policymakers confronted an unprecedented opportunity to increase both domestic- and defense-related expenditures without raising taxes and to share some of the incoming revenue with states and localities in the form of intergovernmental grants-in-aid.

Most of the increase in the national government's expenditures during the 1940s and 1950s was for defense. During the 1930s, national expenditures totaled approximately $61 billion. Of that amount, only $9.8 billion, or 16 percent was spent on defense. During the 1950s, total national expenditures jumped to approximately $684 billion—more than ten times the 1930s figure—and $354 billion, or 52 percent of it, went to defense.[73]

While defense expenditures accounted for most of the growth in national governmental expenditures during the 1950s, domestic expenditures increased more than 600 percent over the ten-year total for the 1930s (from approximately $51 billion to $330 billion). This increase had broad political support. The typical survivor of the Depression and World War II had experienced several economic upheavals and sought economic security. In individual terms, the typical American sought protection against personal catastrophes such as sickness, unemployment, and dependence in old age. In a collective sense, Americans sought protection against another failure of the economic system. To achieve these goals, Americans increasingly looked to the national government. The national welfare state provided some additional personal protection and its intervention in economic affairs through its use of fiscal, monetary, and regulatory powers provided some increased insurance against another systemic economic failure.[74]

These developments were of historic significance. Politically, however, the growth of national expenditures and responsibilities in the domestic sector was tempered during the 1950s by the nondisciplined nature of the party system and by congressional rules that augmented efforts to protect the status quo. Conservative Democrats in Congress were free to join conservative Republicans on the floor of the House or in the Senate chamber to oppose legislation which would centralize governmental functions. Moreover, prior to the Supreme Court's 1964 "one man—one vote" decisions in *Westberry* v. *Sanders* and *Reynolds* v. *Sims*, requiring the states to apportion their state legislative and congressional districts on the basis of equal populations, the number of conservative congressmen representing rural constituencies in the House had been inflated by at least twenty seats.[75]

[73]Ibid., p. 1114.
[74]Ladd, *American Political Parties: Social Change and Political Response*, pp. 246, 247.
[75]Richard Bolling, *House Out of Order* (New York: Dutton, 1966), p. 26.

More often than not, however, the conservative coalition did not have to form in either the House or the Senate to defeat centralizing legislation during the 1950s. The seniority system had elevated a disproportionate number of conservative Southerners from one-party rural districts and states to committee chairmanships in both institutions, and they used their considerable influence over the legislative process thoughout this period to either defeat or water down any legislative proposals that would significantly augment national responsibilities. In addition, in those rare circumstances when bills authorizing new national initiatives or grants did emerge from committees, such bills still had to pass through the House Rules Committee. From 1937 through 1961, when the Rules Committee was enlarged, it was controlled by a bipartisan conservative coalition that generally opposed a national role in any area but agriculture and defense.[76]

In the past, the organizational rules and procedures within Congress had played a secondary role in fostering a decentralized governmental system. Rules and procedures were elevated in importance during the 1950s partly because constitutional contraints on congressional action had been vastly diminished by the courts during the New Deal and partly because political parties in most areas of the country were beginning to suffer from the combined effects of rising affluence, changing demographic patterns, the gradual corrosive impact of progressive reforms, and the rise of the welfare state. Although state and local officials remained important actors in presidential nominations, a number of very powerful local party organizations still operated in some cities, and party identification retained a strong grip on the populace at large, parties in many areas no longer served a central role in congressional elections and many state and local party organizations had begun to serve primarily as holding companies for contending politicians rather than as independent sources of political influence.[77]

THE CHANGING NATURE OF PARTY AND FEDERALISM

The vast expansion in the scale and intrusiveness of intergovernmental relations during the 1960s coincided with a rapid decline in state and local party organizations' influence in the electoral process. Although the parties were still major factors in many areas, particularly presidential nominations, by the mid-1960s most national officeholders campaigned for office independent of the party apparatus. They developed their own funds, managed their own campaigns, and built their own coalitions among the voters.

At the same time that national officeholders broke away from the normally decentralizing influence of party organizations, economic and technological

[76]Ibid., p. 81.

[77]James MacGregor Burns, *The Deadlock of Democracy* (Englewood Cliffs, NJ: Prentice-Hall, 1963), pp. 236, 237.

changes fostered a new receptivity among the electorate for national governmental activism. As Everett Carll Ladd has observed, the typical American family's income immediately following World War II provided only a small margin over basic subsistence costs. The American economy, however, grew at a phenomenal rate during the 1950s. Examining several economic indices, Ladd concluded that the economic growth of the 1950s had important implications for American politics, removing most American families from subsistence-type concerns and placing new issues on the political agenda.[78] Affluence promoted a new generation of political activists who were not only interested in nonmaterialistic issues such as civil rights, the environment, hunger, abortion, and busing, but had the leisure and inclination to participate in the political process.

This movement was evident in the new forms of political organizations such as reform clubs that were dominated by issue activists of both the left and the right. These activists served to further undermine the old party organizations and helped launch several reforms during the late 1960s and 1970s that further weakened the party's influence in the electoral process. This was particularly evidenced at the presidential level where there was an increased reliance on primaries in the presidential nomination process, new rules were implemented governing presidential caucuses, and campaign financing was enacted.

Technological advances also weakened the parties' role in the electoral process. Political communication has historically rested with the parties but shifted to the national media, especially television, during the 1970s. Television not only stressed candidates and issues rather than parties, it also contributed to the displacement of party professionals at all levels in the electoral process as media and polling consultants gained prominence.[79]

Freed from the party's normally decentralizing influence, congressmen increasingly began to act as independent policy entrepreneurs. As David Mayhew has argued, by supplying goods in small manipulable packets and providing opportunities for interference in the bureaucracy's funding decisions on behalf of their constituencies, congressmen at this time became particularly attracted to the categorical grant mechanism as a means of enhancing their election prospects.[80] Moreover, the proliferation of categorical assistance led to the proliferation of nationally organized and oriented interest groups dedicated to the preservation and further expansion of these programs.[81] These interest groups sought

[78]Ladd, *American Political Parties: Social Change and Political Response*, p. 245.

[79]Jeanne Jordan Kirkpatrick, *Dismantling the Parties: Reflections on Party Reform and Party Decomposition* (Washington, DC: American Enterprise Institute, 1978), p. 11.

[80]David R. Mayhew, *Congress: The Electoral Connection* (New Haven, CT: Yale University Press, 1974), p. 129. See also Morris P. Fiorina, *Congress: Keystone of the Washington Establishment* (New Haven, CT: Yale University Press, 1977).

[81]Advisory Commission on Intergovernmental Relations, *An Agenda for American Federalism: Restoring Confidence and Competence* (Washington, DC: U.S. Government Printing Office, 1981), pp. 14–16.

recognition and enhancement of their narrow functional or ideological concerns and opposed grant consolidation and decentralization as threats to their program's funding levels. The result was the noted growth in the number and strength of "iron triangles" in Congress where clientele interest groups forged electoral alliances with subcommittee members and programmatic alliances with national bureaucrats.

CONCLUSIONS

A number of factors that served to strengthen the role of state and local governments in the federal system began to weaken during the 1960s, making current efforts to decentralize intergovernmental relations more difficult. The public continues to value individual initiative, private enterprise, and limited, localized government yet, at the same time, has grown accustomed to the national government's enlarged role. Although there may be widespread disillusionment with the overall drift of public policy, there is overwhelming support for many specific national programs.[82] The potentially decentralizing influence of party bosses has all but disappeared from the halls of Congress. In addition, decentralizing, but racist, electoral practices in the South have been outlawed. Thus, electoral processes for national officeholders from all regions are no longer entirely dominated by local organizations and activists. In many areas, nationally organized and oriented interest groups have forged powerful alliances with Congress and, for the most part, continue to foster national governmental activism. Moreover, sectional differences in Congress which so often frustrated national action in the past have been eroded to a certain extent, though not eliminated.[83]

During the 1950s, the decentralized, nondisciplined nature of the party system served to strengthen the political power of the conservative coalition and, as a result, fostered a continued decentralized federal system within the New Deal legacy. In recent years, however, the nondisciplined nature of the party system has often served to promote rather than obstruct national activism, as it has been the executive branch, not the legislative, that has attempted to foster governmental decentralization. This reversal in institutional roles has come about, at least in part, because the party system no longer strongly links Congress with state and local party leaders or elected officials.

[82]Advisory Commission on Intergovernmental Relations, *The Condition of Contemporary Federalism*, p. 116.

[83]Robert Jay Dilger, *The Sunbelt/Snowbelt Controversy: The War over Federal Funds* (New York: New York University Press, 1982).

part two

STATE AND LOCAL INSTITUTIONS IN INTERGOVERNMENTAL RELATIONS

States and localities play a crucial role in domestic governance. Not only do they administer most of the national government's domestic programs but they also spend a great deal of money on domestic programs of their own. In addition, the states have a collective intergovernmental budget just as large as the national government's and provide 50 percent of the financing for elementary and secondary education, 39 percent for public welfare, 48 percent for highways, and 48 percent for health and hospitals. Localities provide 42 percent of the financing for elementary and secondary education, 5 percent for welfare, 28 percent for highways, and 45 percent for health and hospitals.[1] Moreover, although the national government has spent more money than all the states and localities combined in every year since World War II, when expenditures for defense, social security, interest on the debt, and intergovernmental grants-in-aid are excluded from the national government's total, the states spend nearly as much and the localities spend more than the national government on domestic programs. For example, in 1983 the national government (excluding the above items) spent

---

[1]Advisory Commission on Intergovernmental Relations, *Significant Features of Fiscal Federalism, 1982–83 Edition* (Washington, DC: U.S. Government Printing Office, 1984), pp. 19–22; and U.S. Bureau of the Census, *Government Finances in 1982–83* (Washington, DC: U.S. Government Printing Office, 1984), p. IX.

$257 billion, the states $232 billion, and localities $332 billion after intergovernmental transfers. The states and localities also employ more people than the national government. Since the mid 1970s, the national government has had approximately 2.7 million civilian employees in any given year, the states 3 million employees, and the localities 7.7 million employees.[2]

The debate over which of the three governmental levels—national, state, or local—ought to have the greatest governmental responsibilities has been at the center of political controversy since the founding of the republic. Like their elected representatives, the public's opinion on this subject is divided but has recently shifted in favor of the states and localities. In a recent national Gallup poll, 65 percent of the respondents indicated that they believed that governmental power should be concentrated at the state and local levels, 16 percent indicated that the national and state/local levels should have about the same power, and only 12 percent indicated that governmental power should be concentrated at the national level. In addition, 67 percent of the respondents indicated that the states and localities were best at understanding the needs of the people, 9 percent indicated that the three levels were about the same, and only 15 percent indicated that the national government was best.[3] Moreover, in another recent national poll, only 24 percent of the respondents indicated that they believed they got the most for their money from the national government, while 27 percent said they got the most for their money from their state government and 35 percent said their local government.[4]

The following three readings are designed to provide you with a rudimentary understanding of state and local roles in intergovernmental relations. The first reading documents the states' recent efforts to "modernize" their constitutions. Try to determine whether or not you think the states are really able (or willing) to assume a greater role in domestic governance. The second reading summarizes the findings concerning local governments that were reached by Albert Richter in a larger study on state and local roles in the federal system.[5] It examines the five types of local governments and provides the basic outlines of what they do. Do you think that we have too many different types of governments? Are local governments too fragmented to govern effectively? Finally, the third reading examines the recent fiscal pressures felt by state and local officials and suggests that we may be entering a new era where fiscal constraints will increasingly determine governmental responsibilities. After reading it, try to determine

[2]Ibid., pp. 8, 10, 127.

[3]Parris N. Glendening and Mavis Mann Reeves, *Pragmatic Federalism*, 2d ed. (Pacific Palisades, CA: Palisades Publishers, 1984), p. 99.

[4]Advisory Commission on Intergovernmental Relations, *News Release*, 1 July 1984, Washington, DC.

[5]Advisory Commission on Intergovernmental Relations, *State and Local Roles in the Federal System* (Washington, DC: U.S. Government Printing Office, 1982), chaps. 1,2,4.

whether the states and localities, even if able and willing, can afford to assume a greater role in domestic governance. At the same time, consider whether governments at all levels are currently spending too much or too little on governmental services and if the current division of revenue resources (for example, income, sales, and property taxes) is appropriate.

Mavis Mann Reeves

6

LOOK AGAIN
AT STATE CAPACITY
The Old Gray Mare
Ain't What She Used to Be

Are the fifty American states the "old gray mares" of a technological age?

This question expresses an appropriate concern when we consider the adoption of President Reagan's proposal to turn over many national programs to the states under the banner of New Federalism. The reputations of the states as "also-rans," way back in the field when it came to dealing with public problems, continues to color the debate. The fact that their performance during the decades from the Great Depression through the Vietnam War merited few cheers has added to the difficulties of making reasoned judgments as to state capability at the present time.

Before the debate proceeds further, current information is needed so that judgments can reflect the states today rather than states in the past. And the judgments that are made should emanate from examinations of capacities of all states. Assessments should not rest on the basis of "best-" or "worst-case" syndromes. Neither should isolated incidents of stellar performance or gross ineptitude provide the principal date for evaluation as they often have in the past.

Unfortunately, there are no firm standards against which to judge, no finish line that a state can cross to be termed "capable." There are, nonetheless, some generally accepted reforms that practitioners and scholars have proposed over the years that can be used as rough measures. Examined in the light of these reforms, state governments have undergone a largely unnoticed transformation in the past quarter-century. Perhaps because of a piecemeal and incremental progress, even the textbooks on state government have failed to recognize the magnitude. One by one and little by little, all the states have upgraded their institutions and improved their processes during this period. Not all states have changed to the same degree; nevertheless, all have participated in the remodeling. This is not to say that model states have emerged. So many facets of structure and operations have been redesigned, however, that "the old gray mare, she ain't what she used to be" as far as state governments are concerned. Following is a brief summary of major developments.[1]

STATE CONSTITUTIONS

No aspect of state government has been more severely criticized than state constitutions. Condemned as antiquated, too long and detailed, poorly organized, difficult to amend, and more concerned with restricting state action than facilitating problem solution, constitutions have been under attack in all states for most of this century. As early as 1921, for example, the Natonal Municipal League designed its first Model State Constitution and then continued its advocacy of revision over the years. Yet, in 1955, the Kestnbaum Commission, studying the return of activities performed at the national level to the states, still could condemn these fundamental documents, writing:

> . . . many State constitutions restrict the scope, effectiveness, and adaptability of State and local action. These self-imposed limitations make it difficult for many States to perform all of the services their citizens require, and consequently have frequently been the underlying cause of State and municipal pleas for federal assistance.[2]

And in 1967, former North Carolina Governor Terry Sanford, while defending the states, classed state constitutions as "drag anchors" on state progress.

States took these criticisms to heart and engaged in almost frenzied activity in regard to constitutional revision in the twenty-five years since the Kestnbaum Commission reported. Albert L. Sturm, writing in 1977, pointed to offical activity

---

Originally appeared in the *American Journal of Public Administration* 16 (1982): 74–89. Reprinted with permission.

[1]Data for this article are drawn from the author's research for the Advisory Commission on Intergovernmental Relations. Interpretations are those of the author and not necessarily those of the Commission. Appreciation goes to David B. Walker, Albert J. Richter, and other ACIR staff members for their assistance.

[2]Commission on Intergovernmental Relations, *A Report to the President for Transmittal to Congress* (Washington, DC: U.S. Government Printing Office, 1955), p. 37.

to modernize state constitutions in more than four-fifths of the states since mid-century.[3] Not all of it was successful; nonetheless, eleven states adopted new constitutions. This figure does not include Alaska, still using its original document of 1956.[4] In addition, significant piecemeal revision, often involving entire articles and major reforms, occurred in other states. Among the changes were the deletion of obsolete passages and unnecessary details; better organization; more reasonable amending processes; and a greater orientation to fundamental principles. Six out of ten of the revised documents are shorter, and eleven states with older charters eliminated considerable detail by piecemeal amendment. Yet, more than half of the existing documents are longer as a consequence of continued amendment.[5]

Equally, if not more important, states broadened somewhat the powers of state and local governments to deal with the problems facing them. Legislative options for raising revenue, for example, were enhanced as provisions restricting income taxation were deleted in more states. Advances in this connection were counterbalanced in a few states, however, by the imposition of taxing or spending limits.

By most standards the recent developments in state constitutions have been positive. In general, state charters are shorter, better written, modernized, less restrictive, more basic in content, and have more reasonable amending processes. Most have created improved governmental structures. As Richard H. Leach concluded after examining constitutional change from 1959 to 1976, "There are not many constitutional horrors left."[6] Other constitutional scholars also point to improvements.[7]

STATE LEGISLATURES

It has long been popular to criticize state legislatures, and such criticism often has been merited. For many years, however, efforts have been underway to reform these institutions and 1982 finds them more representative, more professional, more open, and more efficient than they were twenty-five years ago.

---

[3]Albert L. Sturm, "State Constitutions and Constitutional Revision, 1976–77," *Book of the States, 1978–1979* (Lexington, KY: Council of State Governments, 1978), p. 203.

[4]For a running account of state constitutional revision, see Sturm's annual article in the January issues of the *National Civic Review*.

[5]*Book of the States, 1980–81*, (Lexington, KY: Council of State Governments, 1980), p. 19.

[6]Richard H. Leach, "A Quiet Revolution: 1933–1976," *Book of the States, 1975–76* (Lexington, KY: Council of State Governments, 1975), p. 25.

[7]See for example, Sturm, p. 162; and Elmer E. Cornwell, Jr., Jay S. Goodman, and Wayne R. Swanson, *State Constitutional Conventions: The Politics of the Revision Process in Seven States* (New York: Praeger, 1975), p. 158.

Largely as a result of court reapportionment decisions, legislatures are substantially more representative geographically than formerly, and they now are undergoing regular reapportionment, painful though it may be. Legislatures also reflect their constituencies better in other ways. Women and minorities now constitute a larger proportion of the membership, although a wide gap remains. Black membership increased from 168 in 1970 to 307 in 1979, while the seats held by women after the 1980 election amounted to almost four times what they were in 1951.[8] Occupationally, the number of lawyers, traditionally the dominant occupational group, declined from 26 percent in 1966 to 20 percent in 1979.[9]

The many individuals and groups involved in proposing legislative reforms have recommended a variety of other changes. Most are remarkably similar, however, and have been summarized by Alan Rosenthal as being directed at: (1) elimination of constitutional restrictions on legislative authority; (2) increase in the frequency and length of legislative sessions; (3) reduction in the size of legislative bodies; (4) higher compensation and related benefits for members; (5) adoption of more rigorous standards of conduct; (6) adequate office space and facilities for both committees and individual members; (7) improvement in legislative operations; (8) reductions in the number of standing committees and elimination of their overlapping jurisdiction; (9) improvement in committee procedures; and (10) adequate legislative staffing.[10]

State legislatures have made significant efforts to comply with these recommendations. Despite a conspicuous failure to reduce, and in a few states contain, the size of houses of representatives, states improved both legislative structure and procedures and let more sunshine into legislative activities. Thirty-seven, including California where the legislature meets continuously, now have annual sessions as compared to ten in 1951. Moreover, sixteen no longer restrict the length of legislative sessions, and the number of legislative days has increased. Additional states now allow legislative calls for special sessions, and more than two-thirds can expand the agenda for special sessions as well.[11] Formerly, in many states only the governor had authority to call special sessions and to control the subject matter of the deliberations.

In the past, the large number of legislative committees made it difficult for a legislator to attend all meetings and to contribute effectively. During the quarter-century, thirty-nine states reduced the number of house committees and

---

[8]Figures for blacks from the Joint Center for Political Studies, Wasington, DC; 1951 figures for women from W. Brooke Graves, *American State Government*, 4th ed. (Lexington, MA: Heath, 1953), p. 207; 1979 figures for women from Insurance Information Institute as reported in "Women, Educators Gain Ground in Statehouses," *U.S. News and World Report*, 17 December 1979, p. 74.

[9]Insurance Information Survey, ibid.

[10]Alan Rosenthal, "The Scope of Legislative Reform," in *Strengthening the States: Essays on Legislative Reform*, ed. Donald Herzberg and Alan Rosenthal (Garden City, NY: Doubleday; Anchor Books, 1972), pp. 3–4.

[11]*Book of the States, 1980–81*, pp. 104–5. Much of the legislative data is from this source and the 1964–65 edition.

forty-two decreased the number in their senates while a handful added to the list. The proliferation of subcommittees in some states may have diluted the effects of committee consolidation somewhat. In any event, members now serve on fewer committees and, presumably, can give more attention to the ones with which they are involved.

Other changes in regard to committee operations include requirements in all states that committee meetings be open to the public, except in a few specified instances; the adoption of uniform rules of procedure for committees in two-thirds of the states; and the stipulation in an overwhelming majority of the states that committees must give advance notice of their meetings. Moreover, additional "sunshine" penetrated committee rooms as some legislatures required recorded proceedings and votes and publication of committee reports.[12]

Although there is little evidence of reduction in the staggering number of bills introduced—178,000 in the 1979–80 sessions—a few states limit the number of bills any member may introduce, and thirty-five states set deadlines for bill introduction. Forty-three also allow prefiling of proposed legislation. Both of the latter arrangements lubricate the orderly flow of work through the legislature and facilitate careful consideration of proposals.

A major advance has been improved legislative staffing. All states now have legislative refrence libraries, bill analysis and legal research, fiscal review and analysis, and policy review and analysis assistance. Significant improvements also have been made in staffing for committees and for individual members. Four-fifths of the states employ professional (as well as clerical) staff for committees in both houses. In addition, only three states fail to provide staffing for individual members.[13]

States have enhanced legislative professionalism by providing office space for individual members. Twenty-six states now furnish offices for senators and eighteen for house members. Some others provide for shared space.

As for compensation, direct pay has increased dramatically in current dollars. When adjusted for inflation, however, only a moderate rise can be detected. Legislators fared better as far as fringe benefits are concerned. Many now may participate in public health and life insurance programs and pension plans, opportunities only recently afforded state lawmakers. In addition, there is greater likelihood of reimbursement for out-of-pocket expenses related to legislative work.

A major development has been the move to enact conflict of interest legislation affecting legislators. All but nine states have special laws regarding financial disclosure and conflict of interest. It is difficult to assess the effectiveness

---

[12]Donovan Peeters, "State Legislative History Resources: A Survey of the 50 States" (Annapolis: General Assembly of Maryland, Department of Legislative Reference, September 22, 1981).

[13]Lucinda S. Simon, *A Legislator's Guide to Staffing Patterns* (Denver, CO: The National Conference of State Legislatures, 1979).

of such provisions, but, at least, they indicate a concern for the problem, raise consciousness, and make detection easier. All states require lobbyists to register.[14]

Along with their structural and procedural changes, state legislatures have demonstrated a penchant to assert their authority to a greater degree than was the case in the recent past. Forty of them have taken over the auditing function and a number have moved to appropriate federal grant-in-aid funds[15] and to enact "sunset" legislation to ensure greater oversight of administrative agencies.[16]

All in all, the picture is one of marked reform of state legislatures, although there are still laggards as in almost every area. The extent to which the reforms have affected the quality of the legislative product is difficult to determine, however, because of variations in state needs and resources, and the demands on state governments, along with the enormous quantity of legislation enacted.

GOVERNORS

Suggestions for improving gubernatorial capacity have focused on tenure, appointive powers, control over budget preparation and submission, veto authority, adequate professional staffing, and compensation. In general, governors have advanced in these areas. The title of Larry Sabato's book, *Goodbye to Goodtime Charlie: The American Governor Transformed*,[17] speaks to what has been happening in governors' offices.

In regard to tenure, reformers recommended that in order to operate effectively, governors should be elected for four-year terms and be eligible for immediate reelection. When the governor serves for only two years or is limited to one four-year term, programs requiring a substantial time period for accomplishment cannot be effectuated. Additionally, a governor's influence over the legislature and the administration is diluted by prohibitions on reelection. During the last quarter-century, gubernatorial tenure rose markedly. Only four states now elect governors for two-year terms compared to 19 in 1955. Moreover, in contrast to the seventeen states that limited their governors to one term in 1955, five states do today. The number of states with two-term limitations rose

[14]*Book of the States, 1980–81*, pp. 140–41.

[15]William Pound, "The State Legislatures," *Book of the States, 1980–81*, p. 82. For a discussion of state legislative appropriation of federal funds, see James E. Skok, "Federal Funds and State Legislatures: Executive–Legislative Conflict in State Government," *Public Administration Review* 40 (November/December 1980): 561–67. This issue of *PAR* includes a symposium on legislative administration.

[16]Advisory Commission on Intergovernmental Relations, "State Legislative Oversight of Federal Funds: An Update," *Information Bulletin* 79, no. 5 (August 1979), p. 8.

[17]Larry Sabato, *Goodbye to Goodtime Charlie: The American Governor Transformed, 1950–75* (Lexington, MA: Lexington Books, 1978).

from six to twenty-three, however, probably complementing the shift from two-year to four-year terms.[18]

Gubernatorial appointment powers were strengthened somewhat during the period as the number of state elective officials declined. In 1955, a total of 385 state agencies were headed by 709 elected officials. By 1980, however, the number of agencies with elective administrators had been reduced to 338 and the number of elective officials had dropped to 592. Only three states created new agencies with elective heads while twenty-six reduced the number. At the same time, the number of states with seven or more agencies headed by elective officials (plus the lieutenant governor) declined slightly, although three-fourths of the states still elect administrative heads for three or more agencies. These figures tell only part of the story, however. A number of agencies are headed by officials appointed by the legislature or by boards, or are headed by independent commissions. Gubernatorial control and coordination is thereby hampered. Most states maintain at least ten such bodies, and some have many more.[19]

Little change occurred in gubernatorial budgeting and veto powers, principally because procedures in these areas long have conformed to recommendations. As for preparation and submission of the budget, this important facet of gubernatorial control of administration is vested in the governor in all but three states. In regard to the veto, all governors except the governor of North Carolina have authority to disapprove measures enacted by the state legislature, and forty-three exercise the item veto. Eleven states allow the governor to reduce expenditure items as well as to disallow them.[20]

States have responded positively to recommendations for higher gubernatorial compensation in order to broaden the field of candidates, discourage dishonesty, and attract administrators with expensive skills who might be deterred by limits on gubernatorial pay. In current dollars, the median salary rose from $16,180 in 1955 to $50,000 in 1980, a growth of 209 percent.[21] Inflation took its toll, however, and in constant dollars the increase amounted to only 1.03 percent. These figures do not include houses, airplanes, pensions, health and life insurance, and other fringe benefits.

Assessment of adequate staffing of the governors' offices, long recommended by those interested in strengthening state government, is complicated by differences in state population sizes and variations in the roles performed by governors. In addition, it is easy for staff to be drawn from other state agencies, which continue to compensate them, yet be assigned to the governor's office. A comparison of twenty-four states for 1949–51 and 1980 shows a substantial

---

[18]*Book of the States, 1956–57,* (Chicago: Council of State Governments, 1956); and *Book of the States, 1980–81.*

[19]Ibid.

[20]*Book of the States, 1980–81.*

[21]Ibid.

growth in gubernatorial assistance. Staffs during the earlier period ranged from three to forty-three while in 1980 the range was from six to eighty-three (New York was not included in 1980.) Almost half of the governors had staffs of twenty-five or more in 1980.[22] Although these figures do not differentiate between clerical and professional staff, it can be assumed that a portion of the increase in total staffs is in the professional category.

Overall, governors have grown in authority over the years and are better equipped to carry out their responsibilities. Nevertheless, the vigor that many associate with today's American governor is not reflected in the discussion above. Observers point to the new initiatives undertaken in many states to solve the problems they face. Governors are becoming more assertive. They speak out on intergovernmental issues and influence a wider range of opinion. Recent accounts of the activities of the National Governors' Association leave little doubt on this point.[23] Based on his study of governors, Larry Sabato noted: "The American governor has clearly been transformed in recent years."[24] Parris N. Glendening comments, "Today's governors reflect a new mode. They are both the generators and the beneficiaries of improved public attitudes toward the states."[25]

EXECUTIVE BRANCH ORGANIZATION

Those seeking to position the blame for urban difficulties during the 1960s placed it partially at the door of inadequate state executive branch organization. The Committee for Economic Development, for example, cited "innumerable deficiencies in the organization and management of state government" as at least partially responsible for "the failure of states in coming to grips with the fundamental economic and social issues within their province."[26] The states responded to this type of criticism and during the period from 1965 to 1979, twenty-two states undertook comprehensive reorganization of their executive branches. In addition, virtually all of the other states reorganized one or more departments

[22]Figures for the 1949–51 from Coleman S. Ransone, Jr., *The Office of Governor in the United States* (University, AL: University of Alabama Press, 1956), p. 314. Figures for 1980 from *Book of the States, 1980–81*.

[23]See, for example, David S. Broder, "Nation's Governors Will Be Heard," *New Haven Register*, 26 August 1980.

[24]Larry Sabato, "Governors' New Office Careers: A New Breed Emerges," *State Government* 52 (Summer 1979): 95.

[25]Parris N. Glendening, "The Public Perception of State Government and Governors," *State Government* 53 (1980): 119.

[26]Council for Economic Development, *Modernizing State Government* (New York: 1967), p. 14.

during these years.[27] Moreover, at least ten states gave their governors authority similar to the President's, to submit reorganization proposals to the legislature. Most of the reorganization efforts were based on the principles enunciated long ago by A. E. Buck: concentration of authority and responsibility; departmentalization or functional integration; abolition or elimination of boards for purely administrative work; coordination of staff services; independent audit; and recognition of a governor's cabinet.[28]

Attempts to concentrate authority and responsibility were directed principally at reducing the number of elected executive branch officials and making agency heads responsible to the governor. Twenty-four states trimmed the number of elected executive branch officials between 1964 and 1978. At the same time, eleven states opted to elect more officials than previously. These aggregate figures cloak the transformation, however. Reductions often involved the elimination of numerous elective posts, while increases usually were limited to one or two.

As for departmentalization or function integration, Council of State Governments' data on state government organization for 1950 and 1979 show a reduction in the number of separate agencies and a high degree of departmentalization. The impact of these developments is diluted, however, because heads of one or more units in a department may be subject to appointment from outside the agency. Most consolidations have been in environmental protection, transportation, and human services.[29]

The results vary as to the elimination of boards for purely administrative purposes. States discarded a number of boards, consolidated others, and reduced the number of ex officio boards. Nevertheless, all states continue to use administrative boards or commissions.

Although Buck recommended the coordination of staff services under departments of finance or administration, questions remain as to whether states should aggregate all of their centralized accounting, budgeting, purchasing, and personnel functions under one department. Whatever the verdict, forty-two states had established departments of finance or administration by 1978, although few of these included all the staff functions. A clear trend toward the creation of

[27]Compiled from George A. Bell, "State Administrative Organization Activities, 1974–75," *Book of the States, 1976–77 (Lexington, KY: Council of State Governments, 1976)*, pp. 105–113 *Reorganizing the States* (Lexington, KY: Council of State Governments, 1972), pp. 4–9; Robert deVoursney, "State Executive Branch Activities," *Book of the States, 1980–81*, p. 168; and James L. Garnett, *Reorganizing State Government: The Executive Branch* (Boulder, CO: Westview Press, 1980), p. 4.

[28]A. E. Buck, *The Reorganization of State Government in the United States* (New York: Columbia University Press, 1938), p. 14. Disagreement prevails as to what standards *should* be used.

[29]Council of State Governments, *Integrating and Coordinating State Environmental Programs* (Lexington, KY: 1975); *Human Services Integration: State Functions in Integration* (1974), and *State Government News* (January 1980).

general service agencies that aggregate such functions as communications, construction, insurance protection, and purchasing, can be observed. Seventeen states had provided for such agencies by 1974, and in other states these activities were consolidated under a department of administration.[30]

The desirability of selecting an auditor independent of the governor to audit the administration's books would appear to be self-evident. Nonetheless, this has not been the practice in all the states. As late as 1964, governors appointed auditing officials in eight states. Moreover, auditors were elected in many states, a practice that does not necessarily produce the most competent auditor. The recommended method is legislative selection, and there has been a rapid move in this direction. In 1964, only fifteen state legislatures designated the auditor. By 1979, at least two-thirds of the state legislatures selected auditing officials, although the legislative-chosen official sometimes shared the function with elected auditors. Only one state, Indiana, appeared to have an auditor appointed by the governor.[31]

A major aim of the reorganization movement was to establish governors' cabinets in the states. This institutionalizes the model employed at the national level for coordinating and directing the activities of the executive branch. Creation of state cabinets is complicated, however, because unlike the national arrangement, state government department heads are not necessarily chosen by the governor. Consequently, coordination through the cabinet is more difficult. Nevertheless, governors long have held occasional cabinet meetings. All but one of the states undertaking comprehensive reorganization of its executive branch between 1965 and 1979 provided for a cabinet system, and by 1979, a total of thirty-six had been established. It is rare, however, to find a state where the cabinet has any real authority. The meetings are useful, nonetheless, for identifying priorities and in developing new ideas for executive branch operations.[32]

Kenneth J. Meier noted a number of other impacts of reorganization including a shift in organizational purpose from the traditional emphasis on agriculture, highways, corrections, and the like, to increased emphasis on social programs, environmental protection, energy, economic development, and all modes of transportation. He also found more agencies devoted to "citizen responsiveness," such as minority rights, women's affairs, consumer protection, and handling consumer complaints.[33]

Although the effectiveness of state reorganization is difficult to assess, the 1978 American State Administrators Survey, conducted by Deil S. Wright and

[30]Bell, p. 112.

[31]*Book of the States, 1964–65* (Lexington, KY: Council of State Governments, 1964); *Book of the States, 1980–81*, pp. 208–12.

[32]*Book of the States, 1980–81*, p. 181; Judith Nicholson, "State Administrative Organization Activities, 1976–77," *Book of the States, 1978–79*, p. 107.

[33]Kennedy J. Meier, "Executive Reorganization of Government: Impact on Employment and Expenditures," *American Journal of Political Science* 24 (August 1980): 396–411.

Ted. F. Hebert, sheds some light on this issue. In response to a query as to whether the recent reorganizations in their states had affected their agencies, 55 percent of the respondents said "yes" while 24 percent replied "no." When the 757 officials who responded affirmatively to this question were asked: "Did the reorganization increase agency efficiency or productivity?" 57 percent responded "yes" and 37 percent answered "no." In thirty-three states a majority of those responding to the question indicated that the last major reorganization had increased efficiency. Respondents were divided, however, as to whether reorganization had increased executive control over the agency, with 42 percent believing it had while 54 percent thought that it had not. For the most part, the administrators rated the overall effects of the last major reorganization in their states favorably.[34] Although a 1978 survey of governors by Thad L. Beyle for the National Governors' Association did not ask the same questions, it did reveal that governors thought more reorganization was needed.[35] In the aggregate, states enhanced their executive branches structurally, if Buck's indicators are proper measures.

PERSONNEL SYSTEMS AND THE BUREAUCRACIES

Despite the attacks now being made on the merit systems for the employment, promotion, and retention of personnel,[36] such arrangements long have been recommended for state personnel. Most states adopted them with reluctance, however, and in many states a federal grant-in-aid requirement was necessary to produce change. As a result of the 1939 Amendments to the Social Security Act, all states now have merit systems for some employees. Despite a long period of foot dragging in regard to state personnel management, it became an important state priority during the late 1970s. More than half the states established study commissions charged with reviewing personnel practices and making changes. Twenty-one states revised civil service laws, and thirteen states completely or substantially altered their personnel systems.[37] According to the U.S. Office of Personnel Management, at least thirty-five states now have comprehensive merit system coverage and other states have limited coverage.[38] States

[34]American State Administrators Project, Institute for Research in the Social Sciences, University of North Carolina, Chapel Hill, 1978.

[35]Thad H. Beyle, "State Reorganization Activities Survey," National Governors Association, 1978.

[36]Some of this has come from those concerned with possible bias in the examinations used for selection and its effect on minorities. In other instances, critics have focused on bureaucratic unresponsiveness and the difficulties of removing incompetent personnel.

[37]David R. Cooke and Evan B. Hammond, "Civil Service Reform," *Book of the States, 1980–81*, p. 242.

[38]U.S. Office of Personnel Management, *1979 Annual Statistical Report on State and Local Personnel Systems* (Washington, DC: June 1980), p. 43.

followed the national example of placing restrictions on partisan activities by state employees as well. All states now have "Little Hatch Acts," some of which are more restrictive than the federal law. Financial disclosure provisions also have spread to many state bureaucracies.

Although not necessarily related to improvements in state personnel systems, state employees today are more representative and professional than once was the case. At least this is true of top administrators according to American State Administrators' Project surveys for 1964 and 1978. There was a rise from 2 percent to 8 percent in the number of women holding top posts. Ethnic representation grew by the same amount, with black administrators increasing from 1 percent to 2 percent, Orientals from 1 percent to 4 percent, and American Indians from 0.1 percent to 1 percent. As reflected in education, career patterns, and professional affiliations, there is also greater professionalism in state personnel. A total of 73 percent of the administrators had studied at the graduate level and 58 percent reported holding graduate degrees. Administrators also are younger, enter the service at an earlier age, are more likely to move from state to state but usually advanced from within their agencies, and are actively involved (98 percent) in professional organizations.[39]

Federal grant-in-aid administrators perceive better personnel performance at the state level. These officials overwhelmingly rated state personnel higher on a number of indicators in a 1975 survey than they had in 1964. Several times fewer officials in 1975 rated the states low for inadequate salaries, poor training programs, overly stringent merit requirements, and the lack of a merit system. In an overall rating, federal grant administrators, on a scale of 1 to 5 (with 1 as highest), ranked state grant recipients as follows: 1—24 percent; 2—28 percent; 3—30 percent; 4—12 percent, and 5—7 percent.[40]

No doubt, in the aggregate, state personnel administration has profited from the many changes made in recent years. Nevertheless, this is one aspect of state government that probably needs the most attention, particularly in the areas of compensation and positive personnel mangement that produce highly motivated and competent employees.

THE JUDICIARY

Probably in no other area has the old gray mare gotten as many nutrients added to her body as in connection with the courts. Certainly the judiciary needed attention. State courts handle 96 percent of all the cases tried in the United

---

[39]F. Ted Hebert and Deil S. Wright, "State Administrators: How Representative? How Professional?" *State Government* 55 (1982).

[40]Advisory Commission on Intergovernmental Relations, *Intergovernmental Grant System as Seen by Local, State, and Federal Officials* (Washington, DC: U.S. Government Printing Office, 1977), p. 191.

States, and the increasing proclivity for Americans to go to court had imposed an unbearable burden of cases in some instances. In recent years, states have made major progress in complying with the generally accepted recommendations related to: reogranization into a unified, simplified court system; establishment of a state administrative office for the courts; selection of judges on a merit basis; creation of machinery for the discipline and removal of unfit judges; mandatory judicial retirement at age seventy; requirements that judges be licensed to practice law; requirements that judges serve full time; and full state assumption of court costs.[41]

Although there is disagreement as to exactly what constitutes a unified court system, evidence reveals that thirty-four states had achieved at least a moderate degree of unification by 1978.[42] Centralized management was furthered when all states established professional court administrative offices under the direction of the chief justice or the supreme court,[43] and thirty-two gave exclusive authority to make rules to their highest courts.[44] On the other hand, relatively few have adopted centralized budgeting, an idea first formally put forward in 1972.[45] Twenty-two provide full funding for the court system and others increased the proportion of the expenses the state bears.[46]

Improvement in the quality of judges received attention as well. The number of states that fail to require legal training for judges of supreme and intermediate courts was halved between 1955 and 1979, from sixteen to eight, and these eight probably select lawyers as a matter of practice. More important has been the move to merit selection of judges. Although election is still the most popular method of choosing judges, fourteen states have adopted merit (or Missouri) plans under which all major court judges are appointed by the governor from a list submitted by a judicial selection committee that he or she appoints. After a specified period, the appointee must stand for reelection unopposed. A majority vote is necessary to continue her or him in office. Merit plans for the selection of some judges are used by nineteen states, and others incorporate some features of the plan.[47]

[41]Advisory Commission on Intergovernmental Relations, *State–Local Relations in the Criminal Justice System* (Washington, DC: 1970), chap. 2.

[42]Larry Berkson and Susan B. Carbon, *Court Unification: History, Politics and Implementation* (Washington, DC: U.S. Department of Justice, Institute of Law Enforcement and Criminal Justice, 1978), p. 46.

[43]*Book of the States, 1980–81*, p. 164; Jag C. Uppal, Director, Secretariat Services, National Center for State Courts, Williamsburg, Va., by letter to the author, March 5, 1981.

[44]Berkson and Carbon, p. 11. See also, Jeffrey Parness and Chirs Korbakes, *A Study of the Procedural Rule-Making Power in the United States (Chicago: American Judicature Society, 1973)*.

[45]Berkson and Carbon, p. 13, citing Carl Baar, *Separate but Subservient: Court Budgeting in the United States* (Lexington, MA: Heath, 1975), p. 13.

[46]Harry O. Larson, et al., *State Funding of Court Systems: An Initial Examination* (Washington, DC: American University Bar Institute Criminal Courts and Technical Assistance Project, 1979).

[47]*Book of the States, 1980–81*, pp. 156–57.

To provide effective procedures for getting rid of corrupt, incompetent, or senile judges or dealing with those who engage in misconduct, states have added judicial disciplinary and removal commissions and boards of mental and physicial disability to the apparatus used in the past. Since first used in California in 1960, disability and review commissions have spread to forty other states.[48] Moreover, thirty-seven states either mandate retirement at a certain age, usually seventy, or stipulate that judges sitting past that age forfeit retirement benefits.[49]

Overall, progress in reforming state courts has been remarkable. In addition to the changes noted above, there have been advancements in administrative and technological measures for speedy trials, expediting cases, training for judges and court personnel, public participation to make courts more accountable, and in other ways. According to one authority, "the quality of justice, as well as the expeditious handling of an increasing caseload, has improved in state courts."[50]

STATE FINANCES

A major question in regard to the states' abilities to assume greater responsibility for federal programs is whether or not they can provide the necessary financial resources as federal aid continues to decline.[51] The question is complicated by uncertainty as to just what the total devolution will include and by the lack of adequate measures of financial capacity except in relative terms. Using a variety of measures, economists can determine capacity on a relative basis but not on an absolute one because the latter depends on a state government's willingness to tax its citizens at a higher rate. The issue as to whether or not a state wants to undertake the full-funding of the welfare programs proposed to be turned over to the states then becomes a political as well as an economic one.

Although the question of state fiscal capacity cannot be answered in specific terms, an examination of what has been happening in the area of state financial systems might be in order. In the first place, based on per capita income, the gap among the states as to their financial resources has narrowed since early in the century. Secondly, state spending has slowed, and in terms of constant dollars declined, as a result of states' own retrenchment and federal cutbacks beginning under the Carter Administration. Federal aid in constant dollars crested in 1978 and began to fall off the next year. Fiscal year 1982 was the first time in more

[48]Ibid., pp. 158–63.

[49]Timothy Pyne, *Judicial Retirement Plans* (Chicago: American Judicature Society, 1980), pp. 4–5.

[50]Jag C. Uppal, "The State of the Judiciary," *Book of the States, 1980–81*, p. 143.

[51]Advisory Commission on Intergovernmental Relations, *Significant Features of Fiscal Federalism, 1980–81 Edition* (Washington, DC: U.S. Government Printing Office, 1981), pp. 93–199, for profiles on individual states' finances.

than twenty years, however, that federal fiscal assistance dropped in terms of current dollars. It fell 3.8 percent. The peak of state spending antedated both the Reagan Administration and the move toward tax and spending limitations inspired by California's Proposition 13, adopted in 1978. In constant dollars, spending from the states' own funds dropped from a high of $283 per capita in 1976 to an estimated $259 in 1981.[52]

Thirdly, many states have modified their revenue systems significantly to make them more diverse, equitable, and accountable. Forty states adopted individual income taxes to supplement the heavy reliance on sales and excise taxes. Three others have imposed limited individual income taxes. Moreover, forty-five states now add to their revenue diversity with corporate income levies. They rely less heavily on the property tax.

Equity considerations, aimed at shielding low-income individuals, are now features of more state tax systems. One or more of the following measures operates in most states: (1) food exemptions from the sales tax; (2) income tax credits; and (3) state financed "circuit-breakers" exempting low-income individuals from the property tax. Both equity and accountability are stronger in the eight states that also indexed their income taxes to deal with the problem of inflation creep in incomes and in the nine that adopted full-disclosure laws.[53] The latter require local authorities to publish the need for additional revenues subject to a recision of the assessment rise if they do not. In general, these modifications have produced higher quality revenue systems.

Although states ordinarily cannot operate at a deficit, they have incurred substantial indebtedness over the years through the issuance of bonds. State debt as a percentage of the gross national product declined in the last decade and now stands at 8.2 percent as compared to 8.1 percent in 1964. Nevertheless, interest payments are taking an increasingly larger share of state and local general revenue. Interest payments rose from 2.9 percent of own-source revenue in 1971 to 4 percent in 1980.[54]

Despite better revenue systems, states are experiencing financial difficulties. According to one report, they are in the "worst fiscal condition in 40 years."[55] Faced with an economy they cannot control, high interest rates, growing debt payments, rising unemployment that increases need for assistance, reductions in federal grant-in-aid funds, and uncertainty about new obligations under the President's New Federalism, all but a few fortunate states have fiscal worries. In some states these are aggravated by tax and/or spending limits that circumscribe

[52]Ibid., p. 10, and ACIR staff calculations.

[53]Ibid., p. 54.

[54]Ibid., p. 76.

[55]Steven D. Gold, Karen M. Benker, and George E. Peterson, "State Budget Actions in 1982," reporting on a survey by the National Conference on State Legislatures and the Urban Institute. Summary (mimeographed). See their "State Tax Increases: R_x for Ailing Budgets?," *State Legislatures* (July/August 1982).

fiscal discretion. There are exceptions, of course, highlighted by Alaska's program to give money back to its citizens.

The economy is at the crux of the state's fiscal difficulties. Its depressed condition in 1982 caused losses in sales and income tax receipts—the pillars of state revenues—as well as from motor fuel taxes. Since the states cannot regulate the economy, they have been forced to deal with these shortages by increasing taxes, cutting services, employing user fees, postponing expenditures for maintenance and capital services, and resorting to other measures to balance their budgets. Most are working hard to hold the line. Whether state governments can afford to finance their share of the New Federalism probably depends primarily on factors outside their control—particularly the economy.

BLOCK GRANT ADMINISTRATION

As for state capability to administer the new block grants, state performance involves numerous tasks[56] to which states are accustomed through a long history of grant administration dating back to the Land Act of 1796 allocating land for support of the public schools. Block grants are a relatively new mechanism for distributing federal assistance, emerging first in 1966 in the Partnership for Health program. States were prominent in its administration as well as in later blocks such as Safe Streets and the Comprehensive Employment and Training Act (CETA) programs. Those states that participate in the Appalachian Regional Commission have had additional experience at administering what are essentially block grants. One must conclude some federal satisfaction with their performance since several new blocks were included in the Omnibus Budget and Reconciliation Act of 1981, and more are proposed under the New Federalism. Moreover, the General Accounting Office reported recently that, in general, states had performed creditably in administering block grants.[57]

CONCLUSION

On the whole, states have upgraded almost every aspect of their governmental capabilities, although improvements can still be made. Perhaps equally important, they have demonstrated a willingness to change, to shake off some of the hobbles of the past and to try something new. Although change is not always beneficial,

[56]Ronald Kraatz and Maxine Shields list 61 state tasks specified in block grant legislation, 38 of which involve certification of state performance, in their paper, ''Federal Roles Under Block Grants,'' prepared for the U.S. Department of Health and Human Resources Intergovernmental Program, 1982. Appendix B.

[57]U.S. Comptroller General, *Early Observations on Block Grant Implementation*, GAO/GGD-82-79 (Washington, DC: U.S. General Accounting Office, August 24, 1982), p. 1.

the willingness to undertake it when necessary is a factor to be considered in determining the capacity of state governments to adjust to new responsibilities. Decisions, then, as to whether or not states should be entrusted with new duties ought to take into account that, while all cannot be considered thoroughbreds, they can hardly be regarded as nags.

LOCAL GOVERNMENTS
Federalism's Workhorses

The 80,000 units of local government across the country traditionally have been, and still are, the primary providers of services to the public. Local governments lead in the expenditure of funds for domestic purposes and employ the greatest number of people to carry out these goals. The flip side of the coin from the direct provision of services is, however, financing them. Thus, while local governments are by far the leaders in terms of actually expending funds and employing people, their sources of revenue—especially intergovernmental revenue—have changed dramatically.

Specifically, a look at the pattern of functional and financial assignments reveals that:

> In 1983, the national/state/local sharing of direct domestic expenditures, after intergovernmental transfers, was 34/26/41 percent. In 1977, it was 30/27/43 percent.
>
> In 1982, local governments continued to employ more than half the public sector's civilian workforce. In 1982, the proportion was 18 percent national, 23.5 percent state, and 58.5 percent local. In 1977, it was 20.9/21.7/57.4 percent.

Abstract of Albert Richter's *State and Local Roles in the Federal System* (Washington, DC: U.S. Government Printing Office, 1982), written by Stephanie Becker. Tables revised by Robert J. Dilger. Abstract originally appeared in *In-Brief: State and Local Roles in the Federal System* (Washington, DC: U.S. Government Printing Office, 1981), pp. 11–21. Reprinted with the permission of the U.S. Advisory Commission on Intergovernmental Relations.

In terms of financing governmental activity (domestic expenditures only), the most dramatic shifts over the past twenty years have occurred in the increasing reliance of local governments on intergovernmental revenues. Since the mid-1970s, intergovernmental revenues have comprised between 71 and 80 percent of local own-source revenues. In 1960, intergovernmental revenues comprised only 44 percent of local own-source revenues.

As the flow of funds and the responsibility for spending indicates, local governments are still federalism's workhorses but are financially less independent than they were just a few decades ago. Financial dependency has had other implications because intergovernmental revenues rarely come "string free."

TABLE 7–1   National and State Aid to Local Governments, Selected Years 1955–1982 (in millions of dollars)

	National Aid (direct)			State Aid	
YEAR	AMOUNT	% OF OWN SOURCE REVENUES	AMOUNT		% OF OWN SOURCE REVENUES
1982	20,919	12.8%	95,044		58.2%
1980	21,136	16.3	81,289		62.5
1978	19,393	17.5	64,661		58.4
1970	2,605	5.1	26,920		52.4
1965	1,155	3.6	14,014		43.3
1960	592	2.6	9,522		41.6
1955	368	2.5	5,987		40.6

Source: Advisory Commission on Intergovernmental Relations, *Significant Features of Fiscal Federalism, 1982–83 Edition* (Washington, DC: U.S. Government Printing Office, 1984), p. 121.

TABLE 7–2   Number of Local Units of Government, by Type 1972–1977–1982

TYPE	1972	1977	1982	% CHANGE 1972–1982
Counties	3,044	3,042	3,041	*
Municipalities	18,517	18,862	19,076	+3.0%
Townships	16,991	16,822	16,734	−1.6
School Districts	15,781	15,174	14,851	−5.9
Special Districts	23,885	25,962	28,588	+19.1
Total	78,218	79,862	82,341	+5.3

* less than .05%

Source: U.S. Bureau of the Census, Census of Governments, *Governmental Organization* (Washington, DC: U.S. Government Printing Office, 1983), p. vi.

FIVE TYPES OF LOCAL GOVERNMENT

The traditional pattern of American local government consisted of municipalities, serving concentrations of populations within well-defined territorial limits, and counties, basically providing state services at the local level in both urban and rural areas. For reasons which are many and complex, the differences among the units of general purpose local governments have gradually blurred, particularly between the city and the county. The municipal share of local government expenditures has declined slightly over the past 10–15 years, while those of the county and special district have risen. Special districts, which frequently do not have the territorial or debt limitations that constrict cities or counties, have been, and remain, an increasingly popular means of providing special services.

Municipalities

Of all the types of local government, municipalities have been historically, and still are the leading providers of services to the public. In 1982, they collectively accounted for 31.7 percent of all local expenditures and led in spending for highways, police, fire protection, sewerage, other sanitation, parks and recreation, housing, urban renewal, air transport facilities, parking facilities, and libraries. The cities' position has been somewhat weakened in recent years, however, primarily because community needs have all too often outstripped fiscal resources, and a mismatch occurs.

Certainly not all of America's 19,076 municipal governments are beset by a mismatch of sufficient proportions to be called an "urban crisis," but the number is sufficiently high to have excited a response among political decision-makers at all three levels of government. A brief glimpse at how municipalities developed suffices to explain how and why this mismatch continues to occur so often.

For a long time, municipalities met the problems of population and economic growth simply by expanding their area through annexations of adjacent unincorporated territory. This was how many of today's largest cities achieved their present size in the late nineteenth and early twentieth centuries. Early, free, and easy annexation did not last long, however, as settlements adjacent to cities incorporated to defend themselves against absorption by the neighboring city, and state legislatures, in response to pleas of the residents of unincorporated areas threatened with annexation, made it more difficult for cities to absorb unincorporated fringe territory through such requirements as concurrent majorities in the annexing city and territory to be annexed in a referendum on the issue.

At the same time that cities were seeing their geographic dimension constricted, they were faced with restrictions on their fiscal, functional, and structural powers. In 1868, Judge John F. Dillon enunciated his famous rule that a municipal corporation can exercise only those powers that are granted specifically, those that can be fairly implied in or are incident to those expressly granted, and those essential to the municipality's purposes. For some time, ''Dillon's Rule'' effectively throttled municipal efforts to expand their powers without specific legislative authorization, until the movement for constitutional home rule scored its first success in Missouri in 1875.

Even this effort fell short of its advocates' hopes, however, as the courts continued to apply the principles of the Dillon Rule. Thus, constitutions might authorize localities to frame and adopt charters, but, again, the extent of the powers that the locality could assume thereby was limited to what the legislature specifically authorized and to the court's interpretation of that authorization. In practically all cases, moreover, legislative authorization did not extend to allowing local jurisdictions to adopt nonproperty taxes and in many cases it served to limit the amount of property taxes they could levy.

County Reform

A considerable part of the effort to alleviate the servicing–financing mismatch problems of cities involved increased reliance on two other types of local government: the county and special district. Counties, of course, generally cover considerably more area than municipalities, and usually overlie municipalities. In some instances, also, as in the case of single-county metropolitan areas, their boundaries include enough territory to enable the county government to deal adequately with regional problems that spill over municipal boundaries, such as transportation and environmental protection. The counties' basic problem is that they originated as geographic subdivisions of the state for the purpose of providing state services at the local level. Congruent with that ministerial role, they typically were neither given a broad array of functions, particularly of an urban character, nor the kind of modern governmental structure required to perform such functions. The emergence of the urban county evidences progress in overcoming many of these handicaps. Fully effective urban counties strive to match their geographic adequacy with functional, fiscal, and structural competence, so that they in effect can provide the type of services that cities provide within a more restricted territory.

The record of county reform over the past few decades is laudable. For example, by 1980:

> Twenty-nine states had granted counties some type of home rule authority, compared to twenty-five in the early 1970s. Yet, many of these states place so many restrictions on implementing this authority that local discretion is weak or nonexistent. In nineteen states, the home rule authority includes the power to adopt a charter but, currently, only seventy-five counties out of 3,042 nationwide have adopted one.

TABLE 7–3   Significant Governmental Reforms at the Substate Level, 1945–80

17 successful city–county consolidations, 1947–80, including
  Anaconda/Deer Lodge County, MT (1977)
  Anchorage/Greater Anchorage Area Borough, AK (1975)
  Lexington/Fayette County, KY (1974)
  Suffolk/Nansemond County, VA (1972)
  Columbus/Muscogee, GA (1970)
  Indianapolis/Marion County, IN (1969)
  Carson City/Ormsby County, NV (1969)
  Jacksonville/Duval County, FL (1967)
  Nashville/Davidson County, TN (1962)
  Baton Rouge/East Baton Rouge Parish, LA (1947)

Dade County, FL, metropolitan federation (1957)

Minnesota's Twin Cities Metropolitan Council (1967)
  —an appointed regional council with policy responsibilities
Portland, OR, Metropolitan Service District (1978)
  —an elected regional council with policy and operating responsibilities

671 multipurpose substate regional councils (1979) with planning and coordination responsibilities

County organization and home rule authority (1979)
  21 states with county optional forms of government set forth in law
  29 states with county home rule
  75 counties with charters
  766 counties with an elected or appointed chief executive—25% of all counties compared
    with less than 3% in 1960

1,039 of 3,319 cities surveyed had transferred functions to another jurisdiction in the period
  1965–75

Source: Advisory Commission on Intergovernmental Relations staff compilations.

**TABLE 7–4   Distribution of Direct General Expenditures among Local Governments,
1972–1977–1982**

LOCAL GOVERNMENT	1972	1977	1982
Counties	21.4%	22.7%	23.4%
Municipalities	33.2	32.3	31.7
Townships	3.6	3.6	3.4
School Districts	36.5	36.0	35.4
Special Districts	5.3	5.2	6.1

Source: Advisory Commission on Intergovernmental Relations, *Significant Features of Fiscal
Federalism, 1982–83 Edition* (Washington, DC: U.S. Government Printing Office, 1984), p. 14.

Twenty-one states authorized optional forms of county government, but relatively few counties have exercised the option.

In the last two decades, the number of counties with elected chief executives has risen from eight to 253. Similarly, the number of appointed county administrators has grown from seventy-five in 1960 to 513 in 1979. Thus, the percentage of counties with the plural executive form of government dropped from 85 percent in the early 1970s to 73 percent in the late 1970s, indicating progress in this vital aspect of structural modernization.

Functionally, many counties have taken on new responsibilities, usually of an urban character, sometimes in response to federal influences, as in the case of the community development block grant.

As the above suggests, the news is not all good. Thus, while counties as a group have made significant strides as a local unit of urban government, not all states have bestowed adequate authority upon them. Even where they have, most counties have failed to take proper advantage of the authority. Moreover, most counties generally are limited fiscally by dependence on inflexible sources of revenue, mainly the property tax.

Special Districts

Just as the county offered a way to deal with problems that exceeded the authority and territorial scope of municipalities, so did the special district, but generally for single functions and on a limited/targeted territorial basis. Unlike many municipalities, special districts were not strapped by debt and tax limits, could resort to service or user charges for financing, and often had a broader tax base. Limits on some powers of municipalities led to the establishment of special districts.

In fact, of the five types of local units (counties, municipalities, townships, school districts, and special districts), special districts showed the most pronounced increase in number in the ten-year priod, rising from 23,885 in 1972 to 28,588 in 1982—a jump of 19%.

Towns and Townships

While counties have, in many states, assumed greater relative importance in performing local functions, and municipalities continue to dominate in the provision of services, what can be said about towns and townships in the federal system? The towns of the New England states and to a large extent in the five other "strong township" states (Michigan, New Jersey, New York, Pennsylvania, and Wisconsin) are in a different position from that of the rural townships of the nine midwestern states. Many are urban and industrial and frequently are similar to municipalities in functional scope. The rural township, on the other hand, were in a state of serious decline for thirty years and were even eliminated in two states, Washington and Iowa. The advent of General Revenue Sharing in 1972, studies show, appears to have had the greatest influence in reversing their downward slide, enabling them to take on new activities.

School Districts

Although school districts are special districts within the strict meaning of the term, they are counted separately because of their near universality and their importance, both fiscally and in terms of personnel employed. In fiscal year 1982–1983, they accounted for 35.4 percent of all local direct general expenditures. . . . The number of independent school districts across the country continues to decline, mainly through consolidation in rural areas.

School districts can exert significant indirect influence on budgetary decisions at the local level, because they rely heavily on the same source of revenue, the property tax, as general purpose units. Intergovernmental competition for these resources may be critical in decisions on whether a function should be assumed, expanded, contracted, or dropped, by one or more local units.

The continually changing nature of the five types of local government indicates their adaptability to changing conditions. The rise of the urban county and of special districts, in particular, are most directly attributable to the mismatch between resources and needs in municipal governments. In addition, city–county consolidation, annexation, functional transfers, and interlocal agreements all played roles of varying importance over the past twenty years.

LOCAL STRUCTURAL REFORM

Annexation

While no longer as useful a tool for cities as when they were not hemmed in by incorporated areas, annexation is still the most commmon structural modification and basic method of expanding a municipality's servicing and financing reach. Except for certain cities, though, it has not been a practical device for achieving areawide provision of services that benefit from areawide administration and financing. For example:

> From 1970 through 1977, over 48,000 annexations occurred, adding nearly 7,000 square miles and 2.5 million people to cities over 2,500 in population. But most annexations were small—the average land area was one-seventh of a square mile and the average population fifty-two people.

> In the 1970s, medium-sized cities annexed more frequently and were more likely to produce significant territorial expansion and population increases than cities of other sizes.

While most annexations have occurred in the north central region, annexation has had the greatest impact on the south and southwest in terms of population and area added.

The effect of annexation on central and suburban cities declined in the 1970s, in that the average land area and population acquired per annexation in the 1970s was less than the 1960s.

While annexation usually produces small incremental changes in city boundaries and population acquired, those cities (such as Houston and Oklahoma City) with significant annexations in land and population have been able to achieve better control over problems normally associated with benefit and cost spillovers such as environmental protection.

City–County Consolidations

Recent procedural adjustments and structural modifications such as annexation have afforded some help in dealing with servicing and financing problems at the local level, but their essential ad hoc, piecemeal character falls short of what many consider the need for fundamental adjustments of local government area and power. Special districts, despite their pragmatic appeal and appropriate uses, threaten to erode the important coordinative role of general purpose governments. Realizing the shortcomings of these approaches, reformers sometimes have focused on new organizational forms. The record shows, however, that these forms have been infrequently presented to state legislatures or local voters for approval, and in even rarer instances have they been adopted.

The most popular major reorganization approach is the consolidated city–county. Twenty-four now exist with seventeen having been formed since 1945. The number of referenda on consolidations has increased in each decade, but the percentage of successes has declined so that the 1970s produced the same number—seven—as the 1960s. Moreover, half the consolidations since 1968 have been in nonmetropolitan areas. Only one city over 250,000 population has ever succeeded in consolidating with its overlying county (Indianapolis) and that was through action of the state legislature.

City–county consolidation could be a particularly valuable form of reorganization in single-county metropolitan areas. Modernized county governments would effectively serve as regional governments in the 135 metropolitan areas where a single county serves all or most of the region's population. This was clearly the case in the Anchorage/Greater Anchorage Borough, AK, consolidation which was accomplished in 1975. When metropolitan areas encompass more than one county, local government consolidation to solve regional problems would probably be too difficult. Metropolitanwide regional bodies, like the Metropolitan Council of the Twin Cities in Minnesota and the Metropolitan Service District in Portland, OR, are sometimes created to meet multicounty needs.

Procedural Approaches

In part because of the difficulty in making structural changes, procedural methods such as intergovernmental service agreements, intergovernmental transfers of functions, and the use of extraterritorial powers have been common.

Intergovernmental service agreements—voluntary agreements by two or more local governments to cooperate in provision of a service—were used by more than 60 percent of local governments in the early 1970s. Today they remain a popular method for responding to problems arising from the mismatch between jurisdictional boundaries and service needs. As of 1976, forty-three states had some type of general law authorizing such agreements—one more than in 1972 and twenty-nine more than in 1957. Jails and detention homes, police training, street lighting, refuse collection, libraries, solid waste disposal, water supply and crime laboratory services are the most common services subject to agreements.

During the 1965–75 period, nearly one-third of a sample of cities over 25,000 population transferred functions to another jurisdiction, with larger, central cities being more likely to transfer.[1] Counties received 56 percent of the functions transferred, followed by special districts with 19 percent, and states with 14 percent. Overall, during the time period studied, over 1,700 functional transfers occurred.

Extraterritorial powers—the exercise of cities' authority outside their boundaries—are used less than intergovernmental service agreements or transfers of functions as means of adjusting area and power. In 1977, thirty-five states authorized at least some of their cities to regulate outside their limits. Yet, less than half the states authorized extraterritorial planning, zoning, and subdivision regulation—the powers that would have the most influence in dealing with fringe growth problems.

---

[1]Advisory Commission on Intergovernmental Relations, *Pragmatic Federalism: The Reassignment of Functional Responsibility* (Washington, DC: U.S. Government Printing Office, 1976).

John Shannon

8

FEDERAL AND STATE–LOCAL
SPENDERS GO
THEIR SEPARATE WAYS

The 1981–1983 period stands out for its big revenue shortfalls and the most severe economic downturn since the Great Depression, which cut federal, state, and local receipts and forced painful fiscal responses at all levels of government. With expenditure cutbacks unable to make up for the falloff in tax revenue, several states were forced to balance their budgets by increasing their sales or income taxes or both—actions that had become almost unthinkable since the 1978 tax revolt that was marked by the passage of Proposition 13. The national government also reacted with some belt tightening and limited tax hikes, but recourse to massive deficit financing constituted Washington's primary response to the revenue declines caused by the deep recession.

A MAJOR CHANGE

The 1981–83 period also provided decisive evidence that the contours of our intergovernmental landscape are being changed by a significant new trend—expenditure acceleration at the federal level and expenditure deceleration at the

Revised version, originally appeared in *Intergovernmental Perspective* 8, no. 4 (Winter 1983): 23–29. Reprinted with the permission of the U.S Advisory Commission on Intergovernmental Relations. Original article was co-authored by Susannah E. Calkins.

state–local level. For the fifth year in a row, state–local per capita expenditures (including federal aid and adjusted for inflation) declined slowly. During this same 1978–83 period, federal expenditures in per capita deflated dollars (exclusive of aid to states and localities) kept rising at an almost unprecedented peacetime rate.

This growing gap between federal and state–local expenditures contrasts boldly with earlier experience (see Fig. 8–1). From the end of the Korean War to the 1978 tax revolt, state–local spending consistently grew at a faster rate than did federal expenditures. In fact, by the early 1970s, it appeared to be only a matter of time before state–local spenders would overtake the federal government—by the mid 1980s at the latest.

Starting in 1978 and continuing through 1983, the intergovernmental spending patterns have changed radically (see Fig. 8–2). Seared by the memory of the taxpayers' revolt, state and local spenders have dropped back in the expenditure race leaving the federal government to set for itself the fastest spending pace since the Korean War.

This article examines the causes of this significant new trend—the growing divergence in federal and state–local spending patterns since Proposition 13.

THE GREAT STATE–LOCAL SLOWDOWN

The Three Rs

What caused the great slowdown in state–local outlays after 1978? For the first time since the end of World War II, it became much easier for most state and locally elected officials to say ''no'' rather than ''yes'' to proposals calling for true expenditure increases because of the restraint dictated by the three Rs—revolt of the taxpayers, reduced federal aid flow, and recessionary pressures on state and local governments that foresaw little prospect for major federal aid increases.

These three fiscal shocks came in fairly rapid succession and powerfully strengthened the backbones of elected officials in most state and local jurisdictions.

Revolt of the Taxpayers (1978–80)

The taxpayers' revolt not only imposed many tax and expenditure limitations but it also sent a powerful message to state and local policymakers, most of whom escaped highly restrictive fiscal limitations. The message was clear: If you want to avoid Proposition 13-type restrictions, make sure that the increase in public spending does not exceed the growth of the private economy.

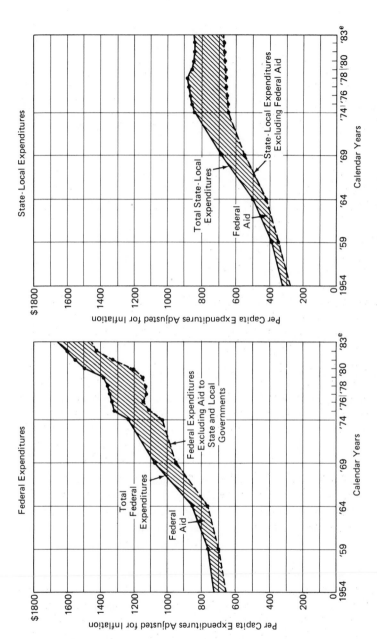

Figure 8–1   After the Tax Revolt—Federal and State–Local Spenders Go Their Separate Ways

e—estimated

[1]Inflation adjustment by GNP Implicit Price Deflator: 1972 = 100

Source: Advisory Commission on Intergovernmental Relations computations based on U.S. Department of Commerce National Income and Product Accounts.

171

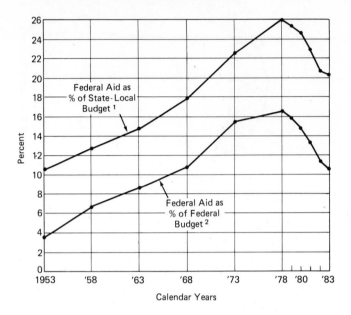

Figure 8–2   The Rise and Decline of Federal Aid

e—estimated
[1] Federal aid as a percentage of state–local expenditures after transfers.
[2] Federal aid as a percentage of federal expenditures from own funds.
Source: Advisory Commission on Intergovernmental Relations, *Significant Features of Fiscal Federalism, 1982–83 Edition* (Washington, DC: U.S. Government Printing Office, 1984), p. 10.

The fiscal braking effect of the tax revolt is clearly evident when state–local expenditure behavior is analyzed on a "before and after" basis. During the long and for the most part affluent period that started with the end of the Korean War and that ended with Proposition 13, state and local spenders chalked up a hefty 4.5 percent average annual increase in per capita expenditures (when adjusted for inflation). Between 1978 and 1983, real expenditures actually decreased 1 percent. Although a few energy-rich states—for example, Alaska and Wyoming—still kept their feet on the accelerator, most of the fifty state–local systems applied the expenditure brakes.

The same braking effect has taken place on the state–local employment front. In the pre-Proposition 13 era, states and localities averaged about a 3 percent annual increase in public employment adjusted for population. After the tax revolt (1978–83), state and local governments reversed that trend, annually decreasing employment by about 1 percent.

Reductions in Federal Aid Flows (1979–84)

Almost immediately after the taxpayers' revolt in California, state and local authorities received a second major jolt. Federal aid programs—the fastest growing items in state–local budgets prior to 1978—became a fiscal drag.

Federal aid to states and localities began to decline during the second half of the Carter Administration due both to the end of the countercyclical aid programs and to the growing federal budget squeeze. This squeeze on federal aid was greatly intensified in 1981 when Congress approved the Reagan Administration's plan to raise defense outlays sharply while simultaneously granting major tax cuts. Fearful that the resultant increase in the deficit would once again release strong inflationary forces, Congress had no alternative but to trim back low priority items in general and federal aid programs in particular.

When adjusted for inflation, the reductions in federal aid flows have not been offset by equivalent increases in state and local fiscal effort. In the past, the proliferation of federal categorical aid programs with their "matching" provisions whetted state–local tastes for various public goods and services and accelerated state–local tax effort. In the post-Proposition 13 era, federal aid cutbacks and capped block grants combined to have the opposite effect—dampening the demand for public sector goods while removing a powerful external pressure for higher state and local taxes.

Recession—No Bailout

Just when it appeared that states and localities had taken their worst lumps at the hands of the tax revolters and federal aid cutters, they received their third big jolt, the major recession that began in 1981.

The 1981–83 recession will be seared into the memory of state and local officials because of its severity, its large revenue shortfalls and its "fend for yourself" intergovernmental scenario. This third feature is especially noteworthy because it represents a sharp departure from earlier intergovernmental practices.

Over the years, state and local authorities have become accustomed to having the federal cavalry, albeit somewhat belatedly, come charging over the hill to break the recessionary siege with aid from Washington. Many officials keenly remember the Economic Stimulus Program of 1977–78 when the federal government authorized $16 billion in anti-recession grants to states and local governments.

Now states and localities see their alternatives limited to painful belt tightening and tax increases. The latest boxscore (Table 8–1) lists 126 state tax increases during the 1981–83 period, a remarkable feat in this post-Proposition 13 era.

TABLE 8–1   State Tax Increases on Households, 1981–1983

STATE AND REGION	GAS AND MOTOR FUEL	ALCOHOLIC BEVERAGES	CIGARETTES	GENERAL SALES	INDIVIDUAL INCOME
Number of States	36	25	20	23	22
New England					
Connecticut	X	X			
Maine	X	X	X		X
Massachusetts	X		X		X
New Hampshire	X	X			
Rhode Island	X	X	X		X
Vermont	X	X	X	X	X
Mideast					
Delaware	X				
Maryland	X				
New Jersey			X	X	X
New York		X	X		
Pennsylvania	X				X
Great Lakes					
Illinois	X			X	X
Indiana	X	X		X	X
Michigan			X		X
Ohio	X	X		X	X
Wisconsin	X	X	X	X	X
Plains					
Iowa	X		X	X	
Kansas	X	X	X		X
Minnesota	X	X		X	X
Missouri			X	X	
Nebraska	X	X	X	X	X
North Dakota	X	X	X	X	X
South Dakota	X	X	X		
Southeast					
Alabama	X				X
Arkansas			X	X	
Florida		X		X	
Georgia					
Kentucky	X				X
Louisiana					X
Mississippi		X		X	X
North Carolina	X			X	
South Carolina	X	X			
Tennessee	X	X			

TABLE 8–1 Continued

STATE AND REGION	GAS AND MOTOR FUEL	ALCOHOLIC BEVERAGES	CIGARETTES	GENERAL SALES	INDIVIDUAL INCOME
Virginia		X			
West Virginia	X	X		X	X
Southwest					
Arizona	X			X	
New Mexico	X	X		X	X
Oklahoma	X				
Texas					
Rocky Mountain					
Colorado	X		X	X	X
Idaho	X			X	
Montana	X		X		
Utah	X	X	X	X	
Wyoming					
Far West					
California	X				
Nevada	X	X		X	
Oregon	X		X		
Washington	X	X	X	X	
Alaska		X			
Hawaii					

Source: Advisory Commission on Intergovernmental Relations staff compilation based on Commerce Clearing House, *State Tax Reporter* (various state volumes), 15 January 1983; and National Conference of State Legislatures, Legislative Finance Paper, *State Budget Actions in 1983*, September 1983, Denver, CO.

Great State–Local Slowdown—
The Bedrock Causes

In retrospect, the three fiscal shocks that made it easier for officials of state and local governments to say "no" to program expansions were, in turn, largely the product of more fundamental economic, demographic, and fiscal changes. When the economic pie is growing, the public demonstrates a far greater willingness to support tax increases for program expansions than it does when times are bad. Demographics and the resulting need for government services also play an important role in deciding whether the public will support higher taxes to help the cause of education. When public school enrollment was growing steadily, the school lobby could muster powerful political support for those state and local officials who voted for higher taxes. Since the middle 1970s, declining school enrollments have prompted far more demands for expenditure cutbacks than for tax increases. Finally, the change in federal expenditure priorities constitutes the third fundamental explanation for growing austerity at the state–local level. As federal policymakers turned their attention to enhancing our national defense capabilities, there was both a decline in federal aid flows and a sharp drop in Washington's stimulative influence on state–local expenditures.

THE GREAT SPEEDUP IN FEDERAL EXPENDITURES

While state–local expenditures began their downward path after the passage of Proposition 13, federal expenditures turned sharply upward—rising in constant dollars from $1,146 per capita in 1978 to an estimated $1,475 in 1983, an increase of 29 percent. The increase in federal spending is attributable to the three "Ds"—deficit financing, defense, and demographics (shorthand for the heightened demand for social security and Medicare benefits).

Deficit Financing

Just as the tax revolt sharply influenced the behavior of state and local officials, deficit financing goes a long way in explaining why federal spending continued to rise in the post-Proposition 13 era. Unlike state and local officials disciplined by balanced budget requirements, federal policymakers could finesse revenue shortfalls through the simple expedient of borrowing money. Thus, deficit financing enabled federal officials to avoid making the painful choice between cutting federal expenditures or raising taxes or both.

If political realities make it hard to balance the budget in good times, acceptance of the Keynesian countercyclical doctrine has made it downright un-American to balance the budget in bad times. Conservative political leaders strongly object to major tax increases during a recession on the grounds that it is a bad economic policy. By the same token, liberal political leaders oppose major cuts in domestic programs as being both inhumane and withdrawing a necessary stimulus to economic recovery.

Although deficit financing has rendered yeoman service on the revenue side of the budget by papering over tax shortfalls, it has become a very expensive item on the expenditure side of the federal budget. After adjusting for inflation, the per capita outlay in constant dollars for interest payments on the public debt has shot up from $72 in 1969 to an estimated $190 for the 1983 calendar year. This significant increase in interest costs is due both to high interest rates and to the rapid growth in the size of the accumulated federal debt, which recently crossed the $1.5 trillion mark.

Defense and Demographics

The next two "Ds"—defense and demographics—stand out as driving forces accelerating federal spending at an unprecedented peacetime rate. Without strong braking action, the federal expenditure curve will continue to rise, probably at an even faster rate than between 1978 and 1982.

Demographics are now working against the national government because it has assumed primary responsibility for income support and medical care of an aging population. An ever-increasing number of federal beneficiaries (social security, civil service and military retirement, and Medicare), expanded benefits, and indexed cost-of-living adjustments have combined to create a fiscal triple-whammy that is driving expenditures up sharply. These entitlement programs account for the bulk of the increase in domestic federal spending.

Although substantial, the increase in actual outlays to date for federal defense programs do not reflect the full cost of our national defense buildup because we are still in the R&D phase for some of the major and most expensive weapons systems. Thus, as the buildup continues, further increases in defense spending can be expected unless a weapons "stretch-out" policy is adopted.

A FISCAL PROGNOSIS

What will happen to federal and state–local spending over the next few years? I offer two fearless forecasts: first, barring a major conflict or a serious recession, total federal spending should stop growing at a faster rate than the economy, due both to a slowdown in the defense buildup and to a freeze or a cutback in federal domestic spending. Second, there is likely to be very little in the way of real growth at the state–local level despite the concern about our "decaying" physical infrastructure and the need to strengthen our shcools.

State–Local Spending Trends

Let us look at the state–local prospects first. To a casual observer, the many state tax increases adopted in the 1981–83 period might suggest that the tax revolt is over. However, a closer look at the evidence suggests a different interpretation—a major state tax increase in the post-Proposition 13 era is more likely to signal fiscal desperation than to indicate that the big spenders are once again in office. A state government now extracts a major tax transfusion from its citizenry only when it is clearly apparent that the state is suffering a severe fiscal hemorrhage—a large and unanticipated revenue shortfall due to economic recession. In many cases, these recent state tax increases are scheduled to self-destruct in six months to a year, clear evidence that the memory of the tax revolt and public opposition to government expansion still shape state legislative be-havior.

Further evidence that the tax revolt is not dead is to be found in the fact that eight states were considering changes in their existing tax and expenditure lids in 1984 and five states will be considering new limits. The message is clear—do not let public sector spending grow at a consistently faster rate than the growth of the economy.[1]

Rainy Day Psychology

A second reason for believing that state and local policymakers are not about to embark on a new spending spree can be traced to the widespread state fear of another major recession and the belief that when it comes there will probably be no federal bailout. Although a rapidly rising economic tide is now carrying up most of the state revenue ships, we have yet to see a commensurate rise on the state–local expenditure front. Why? Because most states are still replenishing their badly depleted cash balances. Keenly aware of these fiscal realities, twenty-one states in the last few years have set up revenue stabilization ("rainy day") funds.[2]

Economic Development Concerns

Keen concern for "economic development" stands out as the third reason for believing that most state tax policymakers will pursue fairly conservative fiscal policies over the next several years. In this case, economic development is one of those nice fuzzy terms to gloss over bitter interstate competition for investors' dollars. In fact, I cannot recall a time in the last thirty years when state leaders evinced greater interest than they do now about the need to attract and to hold business investment.

The last two major recessions and the rise of the footloose multinational and multistate firms have caused state leaders to become acutely sensitive to the need to create "a favorable business climate." Although this concern for economic development has been used to justify larger appropriations for physical infrastructure and, in some cases education, more often than not it has prompted state officials to pursue conservative tax policies. For example, we recently witnessed the astounding spectacle in Indiana where all the top state officials publicly pledged to repeal the worldwide unitary method of tax accounting in return for a promise from a Japanese firm to build a $15 million plant in Terre Haute.

[1] Karen M. Benker, and Daphne A. Kenyon, "Fiscal Discipline: Lessons from the State Experience," paper given before the National Tax Association—Tax Institute of America, Arlington, Virginia, May 22, 1984. To be published in the Spring 1984 issue of the *National Tax Journal*.

[2] See Advisory Commission on Intergovernmental Relations, *Significant Features of Fiscal Federalism, 1982–83 Edition* (Washington, DC: U.S. Government Printing Office, 1984), pp. 94–95.

TABLE 8–2   Federal Expenditures (% of GNP)

CALENDAR YEAR	DEFENSE	DOMESTIC	INTEREST
1954	11.2%	6.5%	1.3%
1959	9.3	8.0	1.3
1964	7.7	9.6	1.3
1969	8.1	10.5	1.3
1974	5.4	14.1	1.4
1979	4.6	14.7	1.8
1983[e]	6.1	16.1	2.9

[e] = estimated

Source: Advisory Commission on Intergovernmental Relations staff computations.

Federal Spending Prospects

Any discussion of where we may be headed on the federal spending front must first concentrate on federal domestic programs because they have constituted the driving growth force over the last three decades.

There are two reasons for believing that federal domestic spending may actually shrink in real terms over the next few years. First, federal policymakers have lost, one by one, the four expenditure boosters that have enabled them to expand domestic programs at virtually no political risk during the last three decades.

The Income Tax Booster.   Until recently federal officials could sit back and allow inflation and economic growth to push taxpayers automatically into higher tax brackets. As a result, millions of middle-class taxpayers were pushed up into tax brackets that until recently had been the province of only the truly wealthy.

This bracket creep has contributed greatly to the growing public discontent with the federal income tax. It led to the decision of the Congress to index the income tax starting in 1985—an action that will take the inflationary wind out of the federal income tax sails.

Domestic Transfer Booster.   After the end of the Korean War, federal officials were able to shift vast sums from defense to domestic programs. This great change in expenditure priorities at no political risk provided the federal government with a fiscal advantage possessed by no state or locality.

Since the Soviet invasion of Afghanistan in 1978 it has been necessary to reverse this process. As a result, federal policymakers are now forced to pull resources away from domestic programs to help finance the Pentagon's growing requirements.

The Social Security Booster.   With virtually no political risk, Congress repeatedly raised social security tax rates during the 1960s and 1970s to finance broadened program coverage. These repeated social security tax hikes met with little public opposition because most of the public viewed them as higher insurance premiums needed to pay for better protection.

Easy votes in the Congress to raise social security tax rates are a thing of the past. In fact, the 1983 social security tax hike was justified on the grounds that it was needed to "save" the system, not to expand it. This same 1983 legislation actually trimmed some of the social security benefits—an action that would have been considered unthinkable a few years earlier.

The Deficit Finance Booster.   Public acceptance of deficit financing provided federal officials with their fourth expenditure booster—they could cover revenue shortfalls by borrowing, thereby avoiding the political pain associated with tax hikes or expenditure cutbacks. In twenty-three of the last twenty-four years the national government spent more than it collected; these deficits total about $1.5 trillion. As illustrated in Fig. 8–3, the deficit problem has been growing progressively worse over the last two decades.

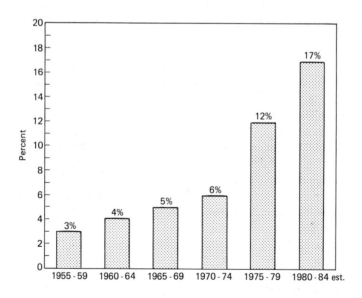

Figure 8–3 Federal Budget Deficit as a Percent of Total Federal Expenditures

Source: U.S. Office of Management and Budget, *The Federal Budget for 1984,* Table 24, and ACIR staff computations.

Quantitative differences can have qualitative effects. The enormous size of the federal deficit has now become the nation's number one economic worry. As a result, federal policymakers are about to lose their fourth and last expenditure booster.

The imperative need to resolve the deficit crisis stands out as the second reason for believing that most federal domestic expenditures will soon be placed on the fiscal austerity chopping block. The enormity of the federal deficit problem can be illustrated by a stunning intergovernmental comparison. *The federal budget deficit for the fiscal year 1983 was $24 billion greater than the total tax collections of all fifty state governments combined.*

The Great Compromise?

It is becoming increasingly clear that the growing political demand to cut federal deficits will soon force Washington into the Great Deficit Reduction Compromise. As their price for agreeing to a deficit reduction plan, the liberals will probably succeed in slowing down the growth in defense expenditures and in enacting a federal tax increase. In return for their support for deficit reduction, the conservatives will demand and probably get two far-reaching concessions:

an across-the-board expenditure freeze or cut for most domestic programs and

the enactment of a balanced budget amendment with some type of expenditure or tax lid attached.

In pushing their demand for a balanced budget, the conservatives have a powerful weapon—the state shotgun behind the congressional door. Thirty-two of the required thirty-four states have made application to the Congress for a limited constitutional convention to draft a balanced federal budget amendment. Congressional conservatives can also count on a populist, grassroots fiscal discipline movement to help carry them over the top.

DE FACTO NEW FEDERALISM

The great changes that have swept across the United States since 1978 have produced a *de facto new federalism*. This new order is not the nice, neat, and orderly "sorting out" process that political scientists and reformers yearn for. Nor has it evolved along the tax turnback and program swap lines advocated by the Reagan Administration. Rather, new federalism (which actually started in the latter half of the Carter Administration) is a slow federal retreat along the entire federal aid front—action dictated both by growing fiscal stringency and conservative political ideology. Nevertheless, *de facto new federalism* clearly represents a "sorting out" of sorts—relatively less federal financing is going into state and local programs and relatively more federal financing is going into strictly national programs—defense, social security, and Medicare, and paying the interest on a $1.5 trillion U.S. debt.

New Federalism vs. Old Federalism

The new fiscally austere federalism can best be understood by comparing it to affluent old federalism, which began at the end of the Korean War and ended in 1978—the year of the Russian invasion of Afghanistan and the California taxpayer revolt.

> Old federalism was characterized by steadily increasing state–local dependence on federal aid as the nation increasingly looked to Washington to set the domestic agenda. New federalism is marked by steadily decreasing state–local reliance on federal aid dollars as the country increasingly looks first to the localities and then to the states to handle domestic issues.
>
> Old federalism was intrusive in character—a steadily growing number of federal aid "strings" and conditions were designed to alter state and local budgetary priorities and to race state and local fiscal engines. New federalism is becoming increasingly extrusive in character—the federal government is pulling aid funds and tax resources from state and local governments to strengthen the financing of its own national programs.
>
> Old federalism represented a continuous but unplanned advance of the National Government into areas that had heretofore been the exclusive province of state and local governments. New federalism represents a continuous but unplanned retreat from federal positions staked out during the "Great Society" era.
>
> Old federalism flourished in a political environment that resolved the political and fiscal doubts in favor of social equity concerns, domestic public sector growth, and defense contraction. *De facto new federalism* operates in a political climate that resolves the doubts in favor of economic development, defense expansion, and domestic public sector containment.

SUMMARY

Future historians of our intergovernmental system may well point to 1978 as the watershed year—the Soviet invasion of Afghanistan, the taxpayers' revolt in California, and the beginning of *de facto new federalism*.

The emergence of this more austere brand of federalism can be traced to sharp breaks in two significant trends. The first was the great slowdown in state–local spending. From the end of the Korean War until 1978, state and local spending grew at a faster clip than did the economy; after 1978, state and local spending has tended to lag the growth of the economy. What caused this remarkable change in fiscal behavior? The quick answer, state and local spenders were disciplined by the three R's—revolt of the taxpayers, recession, and reduced federal aid flows.

The second trend break can be described as an intergovernmental "sorting out" of sorts. From the end of the Korean War until 1978 there was the steady but unplanned advance of the National Government into areas that had heretofore been viewed as the domain of state and local officials; since 1978 there has been a halting and unplanned retreat of the National Government along the entire federal aid front.

What caused this federal aid reversal? Again, the quick answer—federal policymakers have lost, one by one, their easy money options that in the past permitted them to continuously and painlessly expand their operations on the domestic front. Thus federal aid to states and localities—the most dispensable segment of the federal budget—became the first sector where the badly overcommitted feds pulled back.

What will the future bring? Even now, two trends are clear—first, an increasing share of the federal budget will continue to be earmarked for programs that are the sole responsibility of the National Government—defense, social security and Medicare, and interest on the debt. Second, state and local officials will continue to operate in a bracing "do it yourself" fiscal environment for the foreseeable future.

part three

FEDERALISM
IN THE 1980s

When Ronald Reagan became President in 1981, he vowed in his Inaugural Address to:

> . . . curb the size and influence of the Federal establishment and to demand recognition of the distinction between the powers granted to the Federal Government and those reserved to the States or the people. All of us need to be reminded that the Federal Government did not create the States; the States created the Federal Government.[1]

At that time, the national government was spending $91.4 billion on 533 categorical grants, five block grants, and one general revenue sharing program. Of that total, 79 percent ($72.5 billion) went to categorical grants, 11 percent ($10.3 billion) went to block grants, and 10 percent ($8.6 billion) went to general revenue sharing and several other general purpose grants.[2]

In the spring of 1981, President Reagan asked Congress to consolidate eighty-five categorical grants into seven new block grants and to reduce funding for these programs by 25 percent. The President argued that the funding reduction would be fully offset by administrative savings realized by the reduction of ''red

---

[1] *Weekly Compilation of Presidential Documents*, 17, no. 4 (26 January 1981): 2.

[2] U.S. Office of Management and Budget, *Special Analyses: Budget of the United States Government, FY 1985* (Washington, DC: U.S. Government Printing Office, 1984), pp. H-18, H-19.

tape'' associated with the categorical grants. He also indicated that state and local administrators were more sensitive to state and local needs than national administrators and would be able to run the programs more efficiently and effectively under the block grant approach. At the same time, he also proposed large funding reductions for several intergovernmental programs and the termination of many smaller project categorical programs.

Although the President was unable to secure all the changes that he wanted in intergovernmental grants-in-aid, nine new block grants were created that consolidated seventy-seven existing categorical programs and expanded two existing block grants. Four of the new block grants are in health, three in social services, and one each in education and community development. Moreover, the total number of intergovernmental grants was reduced from 539 in 1981 to 441 in 1982.

Despite the reduction in the number of categorical grants and the increased number of block grants, categorical grants still account for approximately 80 percent and block grants approximately 13 percent of total national intergovernmental expenditures. This is largely a result of increased expenditures for several large categorical programs, especially for the *Medicaid* and highway construction programs.

Not content with his victories in 1981, in his 1982 State of the Union Address President Reagan proposed to further reform the intergovernmental grants-in-aid system. The President announced a bold ''sorting-out'' of governmental responsibilities. Three readings examine the President's proposal and document the political and economic obstacles that prevented its adoption. The first reading presents the portion of President Reagan's 1982 State of the Union Address that deals with his New Federalism proposal. In reading the President's speech, note his justification for the proposal and try to determine if he built any political concessions into it. The second reading examines the political maneuvering surrounding the President's proposal. Note the position each of the poltical actors involved took and try to figure out why they took that position (that is, what did they have to gain or lose by supporting or opposing the proposal). In addition, try to figure out why they were or were not willing to compromise. The third reading examines fiscal disparities among the states and suggests that some states are better able than others to finance domestic programs. Should fiscal disparity among the states be a factor influencing the allocation of governmental functions? In addition, why do you think liberals tend to view fiscal capacity as important but conservatives do not?

Finally, the fourth reading examines the growing influence of the national taxing system on intergovernmental program areas. It suggests that tax policy is just as important as spending policy in determining the nature of intergovernmental relations in the 1980s, especially for intergovernmental programs of interest to the nation's cities. Do you think that national tax policy should be used to achieve policy objectives or should it be used just to raise revenues?

Ronald Reagan

9

1982 STATE OF THE UNION
ADDRESS
New Federalism

. . . Now that the essentials of [our economic] program are in place, our next major undertaking must be a program, just as bold, just as innovative, to make government again accountable to the people, to make our system of federalism work again.

Our citizens feel they have lost control of even the most basic decisions made about the essential services of government, such as schools, welfare, roads, and even garbage collection. They are right.

A maze of interlocking jurisdictions and levels of government confronts average citizens in trying to solve even the simplest of problems. They do not know where to turn for answers, who to hold accountable, who to praise, who to blame, who to vote for or against.

The main reason for this is the overpowering growth of Federal grants-in-aid programs during the past few decades.

In 1960, the Federal Government had 132 categorical grant programs, costing $7 billion. When I took office, there were approximately 500, costing nearly $100 billion—13 programs for energy conservation, 36 for pollution

Weekly Compilation of Presidential Documents 18, no. 4 (1 February 1982): 79, 80. Excerpt from President Reagan's 1982 State of the Union Address.

control, 66 for social services, 90 for education. And here, in the Congress, it takes at least 166 committees just to try to keep track of them.

You know and I know that neither the President nor the Congress can properly oversee this jungle of grants-in-aid; indeed, the growth of these grants has led to a distortion in the vital functions of government. As one Democratic Governor put it recently: The national government should be worrying about "arms controls, not potholes."

The growth in these Federal programs has, in the words of one inter-governmental commission, made the Federal Government "more pervasive, more intrusive, more unmanageable, more ineffective, more costly, and above all more unaccountable."

Let us solve this problem with a single bold stroke—the return of some $47 billion in Federal programs to state and local government, together with the means to finance them and a transition period of nearly ten years to avoid unnecessary disruption.

I will shortly send the Congress a message describing this program. I want to emphasize, however, that its full details will have been worked out only after close consultation with congressional, State, and local officials.

Starting in fiscal 1984, the Federal Government will assume full responsibility for the cost of the rapidly growing Medicaid program to go along with its existing responsibility for Medicare. As part of a financially equal swap, the States will simultaneously take full responsibility for aid to familes with dependent children and food stamps.

This will make welfare less costly and more responsive to genuine need because it will be designed and administered closer to the grassroots and the people it serves.

In 1984, the Federal Government will apply the full proceeds from certain excise taxes to a grassroots trust fund that will belong, in fair shares, to the fifty States. The total amount flowing into this fund will be $28 billion a year.

Over the next four years, the States can use this money in either of two ways. If they want to continue receiving Federal grants in such areas as transportation, education and social services, they can use their trust fund money to pay for the grants or, to the extent they choose to forgo the Federal grant programs, they can use their trust fund money on their own, for those or other purposes. There will be a mandatory passthrough of part of these funds to local governments.

By 1988, the States will be in complete control of over forty Federal grant programs. The trust fund will start to phase out, eventually to disappear, and the excise taxes will be turned over to the States. They can then preserve, lower or raise taxes on their own and fund and manage these programs as they see fit.

In a single stroke, we will be accomplishing a realignment that will end cumbersome administration and spiraling costs at the Federal level while we insure these programs will be more responsive to both the people they are meant to help and the people who pay for them. . . .

Timothy J. Conlan and David B. Walker

10

REAGAN'S NEW FEDERALISM
Design, Debate,
and Discord

In 1980, a new President set out to reduce the growing federal role in domestic affairs. Substantial progress toward this goal was made in 1981 as Congress and the President cut levels of federal aid, enacted nine new block grants, and launched a comprehensive program of deregulation. As 1982 began, it looked as though this transformation would continue. The President made a bold new initiative for sorting-out governmental responsibilities the centerpiece of his domestic program. Several new block grants were also proposed, and dramatic changes in urban policy were anticipated. But the response to these initiatives in 1982 differed sharply from that of 1981. Protracted negotiations between state, local and national officials on specific sorting-out legislation failed to produce agreement, and the future of the federalism initiative lay in doubt by year's end. . . .

This article will examine these and other significant intergovernmental events of 1982, summarizing the President's "New Federalism" proposals and reviewing the political reactions to them. Overall, two themes seemed to characterize the politics of federalism in 1982. First, the troubled state of the economy and fiscal pressures at every level of government tended to overshadow federalism concerns and undermine the capacity of many actors in the system to take a long-range view of intergovernmental reforms. Second, signs of "politics as

Originally appeared in *Intergovernmental Perspective* 8, no. 4 (Winter 1983): 6–22. Reprinted with the permission of the U.S. Advisory Commission on Intergovernmental Relations.

usual'' began to surface with increasing regularity as the year progressed and Congressional resistance to federal aid reforms and spending cuts mounted. For all their political difficulties and lingering uncertainties, however, the President's federalism proposals succeeded in one important respect; they placed federalism issues high on the nation's policy agenda and they sparked a nationwide dialogue on how our federal system should—and does—operate.

THE NEW FEDERALISM INITIATIVE: PROPOSALS, REACTIONS AND NEGOTIATIONS

In his 1982 State of the Union address, President Reagan condemned the existing ''maze of interlocking jurisdictions and levels of government'' and the ''jungle of grants-in-aid.'' He proposed restructuring the intergovernmental system in a ''single bold stroke.'' Although the general outlines of his federalism plan are now familiar to many, a review of the proposal and the reactions to it may help place New Federalism in perspective and indicate possible future directions.

The Initial Proposal

Although the President left many of the details open for discussion with state and local government officials, his initial federalism plan had two basic elements. First, he proposed a $20 billion ''swap'' in which the federal government would return to states full responsibility for funding Aid to Families with Dependent Children (AFDC) and food stamps in return for federal assumption of state contributions to Medicaid. Second, the President proposed a temporary $28 billion trust fund or ''super revenue sharing'' program to replace approximately forty federal programs ''turned back'' in the fields of education, health, social services, community development and transportation. Revenues for this fund would come from proceeds of the federal windfall profits tax on oil and from federal excise taxes on gasoline, tobacco, alcohol, and telephones. Initially, each state would have the choice of retaining specific programs in categorical form or accepting equivalent unrestricted monies from the trust fund. After four years, however, both the trust fund and the federal taxes supporting it would begin phasing out, leaving states the option of replacing federal taxes with some of their own to continue the terminated programs or allowing the programs to cease entirely. (For more details on the proposal, see Table 10–1 and Table 10–2.)

Reactions to the Federalism Initiative

Reactions to the federalism initiative varied widely. Many governors and state legislators welcomed the concept of sorting-out functions, an approach they had previously endorsed. . . . They spent much of the year negotiating with the

TABLE 10–1   Major Features of President Reagan's Initial Federalism Proposal

I. SWAP COMPONENT	PROVISIONS
A. Government Roles	
Medicaid	Federalize
Food Stamps	Full State Assumption
AFDC	Full State Assumption
B. Assurances for	Maintenance of state effort 1984–87 for
Medicaid or Public Assistance	public assistance; Medicaid provisions
Beneficiaries	to be determined.
II. TURNBACK COMPONENT	
A. Governmental Roles	Turnback over 40 federal grant programs to states.[1]
B. Resource Return for States[2]	
1. Transition Period (1984–91)	Trust Fund
Dollar Amount	$28 billion
Full Protection	1984–87
Partial Protection	1988–91: excise phase-out occurs
Trust Fund Growth	None
2. Post-Transition Period	
Amount and Method[3]	$11 billion via excise repeal
Federal–State Balance as of 1988	For the states, a loss more likely than a gain[4]
Distribution	By excise tax bases
3. Assurances for Local Governments, Other Former Grantees	Two part pass-through requirement 1984–87; 100% for former direct federal–local grants; 15% for former non-ed. federal–state grants. No provision for other former grantees.

[1]Counted as of FY 1982.
[2]States also would obtain fiscal relief via federalization of Medicaid. Distribution of this relief depends both on amounts states would have spent on Medicaid and changes in federal spending on Medicaid.
[3]Neither the phase-out of the oil windfall profits tax nor reduced federal budgets implying lower federal taxes are counted as resource returns to the states.
[4]Beyond 1988, a gain for the states becomes possible, assuming that Medicaid costs lifted from the states would show greater growth than the cost of meeting responsibilities turned back.

Source: Advisory Commission on Intergovernmental Relations staff.

Administration on a mutually acceptable proposal. Reactions from other quarters generally were less supportive. Many local government officials expressed concern about diminished federal aid and the severing of direct federal ties. Considerable controversy also focused on proposed reductions in the federal role in public assistance. Looming over all responses were the shadows of a lengthening recession.

TABLE 10–2   Illustrative List of Programs for Turnback to the States under Reagan's Federalism Initiative

PROGRAMS BY CATEGORY	ESTIMATED FY 1982 EXPENDITURE[1]	PROGRAMS BY CATEGORY	ESTIMATED FY 1982 EXPENDITURE[1]
Education and Training	$ 4.4 billion	**Transportation**	$ 8.5 billion
Vocational Rehabilitation		Grants-in-Aid for Airports	
Vocational and Adult Education		Highways	
State Block Grants (ECIA Ch. 2)		Primary	
CETA		Rural	
WIN		Urban	
Income Assistance	$ 1.9 billion	Bridge	
Low Income Home Energy Assistance		Construction Safety	
Social, Health, and Nutrition		Other	
Services	$ 8.7 billion	Interstate Transfer	
Child Nutrition		Appalachian Highways	
Child Welfare		Urban Mass Transit	
Adoption Assistance		Construction	
Foster Care		Operating	
Runaway Youth		**Community Development and**	
Child Abuse		**Facilities**	$ 6.3 billion
Social Services Block Grant		Water and Sewer	
Legal Services		Grants	
Community Services Block Grant		Loans	
Prevention Block Grant		Community Facilities Loans	
Alcohol, Drug Abuse, and Mental Health		Community Development Block Grant	
Block Grant		Urban Development Action Grants	
Primary Care Block Grant		Waste Water Treatment Grants	
Maternal and Child Health Block Grant		**Revenue Sharing**	$ 4.6 billion
Primary Care Research and Development		General Revenue Sharing	
Black Lung Clinics			
Migrant Health Clinics		**Grand Totals**	
Family Planning		Programs	43
Women, Infants, and Children (WIC)		Estimated expenditures,	
OSHA State Grants		FY 1982	$34.4 billion

[1]Budget authority.

Source: Advisory Commission on Intergovernmental Relations staff compilation, based on Congressional Budget Office data and the White House, "Fact Sheet, Federalism Initiative," Press Release, 27 January 1982, Appendix A.

Responses from the States.   Most state officials—Republicans and Democrats alike—applauded the thrust of the President's proposal but questioned specific provisions of the plan. Vermont Governor Richard Snelling, then Chairman of the National Governors' Association (NGA), said the President "deserves enormous praise for putting the subject on the table,"[1] and Governor Bruce

[1]"Two State Leaders Respond to Reagan's Plan," *State Government News* (March 1982), p. 14.

Babbitt of Arizona called the proposal "elegant and imaginative."[2] Both governors raised a series of critical questions about appropriate federal–state roles, however. New York Governor Hugh Carey was less positive, calling the proposal "hastily conceived and poorly designed."[3]

The Administration was sensitive to these concerns and actively negotiated with governors and state legislators on a compromise proposal. These discussions produced some modifications in the initiative, but no consensus was reached by year's end.

Much of the controversy over the President's proposal focused on its public assistance provisions. Giving states full responsibility for food stamps and Aid to Families with Dependent Children (AFDC) was a long standing goal of the President. In a 1975 speech, he declared that: "If there is one area of social policy that should be at the most local level of government possible, it is welfare. It should not be nationalized—it should be localized."[4] Seven years later, in his State of the Union address, he reiterated this position, arguing that full state responsibility for AFDC and food stamps "will make welfare less costly and more responsive to genuine need because it will be designed and administered closer to the grassroots and the people it serves."

To counter state opposition to a smaller federal role in welfare, Administration officials argued that the federalism initiative made a major concession to the states by offering to assume the full costs of Medicaid. This move would benefit states, they said, because Medicaid costs were rising much faster than AFDC expenses. Moreover, because Medicaid serves large numbers of elderly persons, they argued that the move would also benefit program users by consolidating federal responsibility for programs aiding senior citizens.

State officials strongly supported nationalizing Medicaid, but they opposed picking up the full costs of AFDC and food stamps. In keeping with their earlier position, they maintained that all income maintenance programs should be funded by the national government. . . . State officials also noted that some form of national public assistance program had been advanced by recent Presidents of both parties, including Nixon, Ford, and Carter. Finally, they questioned the rationale for dividing responsibilities for AFDC and medical assistance to the poor. According to Wisconsin State Representative Tom Loftus, this would mean that "you would be an American when you are poor and sick, but a Texan when you're just poor."[5] States especially were concerned about federal termination

---

[2]Governor Bruce Babbitt, "His Plan Deserves a Chance," *The Washington Post*, 28 January 1982, p. A25.

[3]Governor Hugh Carey, " 'New Federalism' Yes, but Reagan's Proposal Needs Major Revision," *New York Times*, 14 March 1982, p. E23.

[4]Ronald Reagan, "Conservative Blueprint for the 1970's," reprinted in *Congressional Record*, 121, 94th Cong.., 1st Sess., 1975: 31186.

[5]Quoted in David Broder. "White House Is Warned on Its Federalism Plans," *The Washington Post*, 29 July 1982. p. A10.

of the food stamp program because of its unique role in narrowing disparities among state welfare benefit levels.

Dire economic conditions and resulting state budget problems only magnified the fiscal aspects of the New Federalism for concerned state officials. Even some potential supporters feared the proposal may have come "at the worst possible time." "We may all be so anemic by the end of the year that the states won't be able to function as partners," said Governor Scott Matheson of Utah.[6]

Although the President described his initiative as a financially equal swap, many state officials feared that it would cost them more money in the long run, at a time when growing fiscal problems left less and less room to accommodate additional expenses. The Administration had correctly anticipated such resistance and had worked hard to minimize financial winners and losers among the states under its proposal.

For example, the cost to some states of assuming the total burden of food stamps and AFDC would outweigh their savings from national assumption of total Medicaid costs. Other states, however, would gain from this exchange. These disparities were to be evened out by contributions from the federalism trust fund. States gaining from the welfare–Medicaid swap would have their trust fund allocations reduced by that amount. Loser states would receive additional allotments from the fund equal to their losses. The Administration claimed that, eventually, states would gain slightly from the federalism initiative because Medicaid costs were projected to rise faster than those assumed by the states.

Despite these assurances, the fiscal consequences of the plan remained unclear because Administration estimates of the costs states would bear if they took on AFDC and food stamps assumed that these programs would be scaled back as the Administration proposed in its FY 1983 budget. Without those program changes, the Congressional Budget Office estimated that states as a whole would initially pay more to assume public assistance programs than they would save from federalizing Medicaid. States also raised questions about the Medicaid portion of the swap. Currently, Medicaid benefits vary enormously from state to state. A single national program would presumably have more uniform benefit levels—higher than low benefit states but lower than high benefit states. Some states in the latter category would probably feel compelled to continue supplementing federal Medicaid payments, thereby reducing the fiscal dividend of the swap in such states.

Finally, state officials raised questions about the trust fund portion of the initiative. Governor Carey questioned its adequacy, maintaining the programs suggested for inclusion into the trust fund would total $37 billion by 1984, not $28 billion as proposed.[7] Moreover, both the trust fund and the federal excise

---

[6]Quoted in William Schmidt, "Three Western Governors Seem to Be Potential Allies of 'New Federalism,' " *New York Times*, 18 February 1982, p. A1.

[7]Governor Hugh Carey, " 'New Federalism' Yes," p. E23.

taxes supporting it were to begin phasing out in FY 1988. Although states would have the option of levying these taxes themselves, the distribution of "tax room" would not be uniform throughout the country. Per capita revenues from cigarette excise taxes would be much smaller in Utah than in neighboring Nevada, for example, and only a fraction of states would have access to the sources of the windfall profits tax on oil. For these reasons, the National Governors' Association and the National Conference of State Legislatures (NCSL) argued for a financing scheme that would use general revenues rather than specific federal taxes and would include some degree of equalization among states with differing needs and taxing capacities.

Other Reactions and Concerns.   State officials were not alone in questioning the federalism initiative. Although public opinion polls showed considerable support for the New Federalism concept,[8] the plan encountered a barrage of criticism from members of Congress, local governments, affected interest groups, and the press. As with state officials, the bulk of the controversy focused on the "swap" elements of the plan.

Immediately on its announcement in the State of the Union address, the plan was criticized in newspaper editorials. The *New York Times* likened the plan to "turning back the clock." Although it acknowledged the need for some sorting-out of functions, it questioned: "[w]here is the logic in Federalizing one poverty program but turning back others? Do poor people get equally sick in different places but not equally hungry?"[9] *The Washington Post* called the proposal "an alarming retreat" from Washington's responsibilities for basic income maintenance and concluded that "poor people are sure to be worse off under it."[10]

To no one's surprise, many advocates of social programs felt threatened by the plan. The AFL-CIO charged the new federalism initiative would "cripple facilities and services on which all Americans depend and jeopardize the health and welfare of millions of the poor."[11] "The worst thing you can do," according to Andrew Mott of the Coalition on Block Grants and Human Needs, is to decentralize "responsibilities you know will be neglected because of lack of political will."[12]

---

[8]For example, one review of opinion surveys on the new federalism concluded that it "fit the public's image of the respective roles of the federal and state governments." Government Research Corporation, *Opinion Outlook Briefing Paper*, 12 February 1982, p. 6.

[9]"The New Old Deal," *New York Times*, 28 Janaury, 1982, p. A27.

[10]"A Great Swap Masks a Great Danger," *The Washington Post*, 27 January 1982, p. A20.

[11]American Federation of Labor and Congress of Industrial Organizations, "Statement Submitted for the Record," in U.S., Congress, Senate, Committee on Governmental Affairs. *President's Federalism Initiative, Hearings*, 97th Cong., 2d Sess., 1982, p. 482.

[12]Quoted in Neal Peirce, "The States Can Do It, but Is There the Will?" *National Journal*, 27 February 1982, p. 377.

Local officials were also wary. Many local governments were deeply suspicious of turning major program responsibilities over to the states, thereby severing their direct funding link to Washington. "The pass-through [issue] is the No. 1 problem" with the President's plan, said one urban representative.[13] A state legislator from New York observed that county governments in his state "are clearly afraid of being bankrupted in the name of the new federalism."[14]

All of these opposing views were fully represented in Congress, where one observer reported that "long knives are out," ready to kill the initiative.[15] Even some strong Congressional supporters of the sorting-out concept were troubled by specific features of the President's proposal. Senator David Durenberger, Chairman of the Senate Intergovernmental Relations Subcommittee, openly questioned the programmatic logic of the swap initiative, even after the Administration agreed in June to retain food stamps at the federal level: "I am not happy with the outcome. . . . What sense does it make to have Social Security, Medicare, Medicaid, Food Stamps and housing assistance all at the federal level and leave dependent children with the states?"[16] In addition to supporting full federal responsibility for basic income maintenance programs, the Senator proposed allocating trust fund revenues on an equalizing basis. "It is time for the federal government to recognize a responsibility for equalizing the fiscal capacity of places," he observed.[17]

The most serious obstacle to the federalism initiative may have been worsening economic and budgetary conditions, however. Many Congressmen dismissed the proposal as a diversion from more pressing economic problems or perceived it as a backdoor means of cutting social programs. Within days of the President's address, a Congressional newsletter reported the federalism plan was "sinking into a sea of economic problems of greater importance."[18] A few months later, the *New York Times* reported the proposal had "become entangled in the [budget] stalemate."[19] "Budgetary problems are taking more and more of Congress' attention, and elections are coming on," agreed one Administration adviser.[20] With the fate of the economy affecting almost every federal, state and

---

[13]Quoted in Rochelle Stanfield, "A Neatly Wrapped Package with Explosives Inside." *National Journal*, 27 February 1982, p. 360.

[14]Richard Brodsky, quoted in Howell Raines, "President Seeking Counties' Support," *New York Times*, 14 July 1982, p. A21.

[15]Richard Cohen, "Meanwhile, in Congress, the Long Knives Are Out." *National Journal*, 27 February 1982, p. 381.

[16]Quoted in Broder, "White House Is Warned," p. A10.

[17]Quoted in David Broder and Herbert Denton, "Reagan's Aides Push Program Swap," *The Washington Post*, 29 January 1982, p. A4.

[18]*Congressional Insight*, 29 January 1982, p. 1.

[19]Robert Pear, "Prospects for the 'New Federalism' Plan," *New York Times*, 5 May 1982, p. B11.

[20]Quoted in ibid.

local official and distorting fiscal estimates on which the federalism plan was based, the plan's timing became a hurdle in itself.

Negotiations on Federalism

From the beginning, the President described the details of his federalism initiative as tentative and subject to consultation with state and local officials. Subsequent strong disagreements aroused by the initiative heightened the need to present a united front before Congress, and the Administration launched a series of negotiations with the Governors' Association and the Conference of State Legislatures to formulate a joint legislative proposal.

Prior to the start of these meetings in March 1982, the governors attempted to refine their position on sorting-out while making some concessions to the President's position. They dropped their bid for the immediate nationalization of all income maintenance programs, suggesting instead that consideration of changes in AFDC and food stamps be deferred. They announced support for the creation of a federalism trust fund and a willingness to negotiate over the President's list of programs for termination. They also emphasized their support for federal assumption of Medicaid costs. But the governors' position differed with the President's in several respects. Because they removed AFDC and food stamps from the plan, their proposal was more limited in scope and contained a much smaller trust fund component. They also urged that trust fund allocations be made on the basis of state fiscal capacity.

Despite substantial areas of agreement, the positions of the states and the Administration were sufficiently distant that the talks between them were arduous, protracted and ultimately unsuccessful. Initially, the two sides had hoped to produce a specific legislative proposal by early April 1982. This target date passed, however, amidst a flurry of reports that the negotiations were in danger of collapse. Continuing talks produced some further narrowing of differences, and there were indications in July that agreement might be reached on a revised federalism plan. In a speech to the National Association of Counties, the President described the outlines of a modified proposal, containing several key concessions by the Administration:

> Food stamps would be retained at the national level rather than devolved to the states.
>
> The federal government would assume the full costs of "routine" medical care for the poor, and it would give block grants to the states to provide long-term care to the poor. This minimum level of care could be supplemented by the states.
>
> Several programs initially scheduled to be turned back to the states would be retained at the national level, including *Urban Development Action Grants*, grants for migrant health and black lung clinics, the *Women, Infants, and Children* (WIC) nutrition program, and several highway programs (including interstate and primary highways and bridge construction).

A 100 percent pass-through of trust fund monies to local governments would be assured in amounts equal to direct federal funds provided through terminated categorical grants.

Finally, the windfall profits tax was eliminated as a trust fund revenue source, replaced by an $8.8 billion contribution from general revenues.[21]

In return, several state leaders indicated a willingness to reverse their earlier position and to accept full financial responsibility for the AFDC program.[22] Encouraged, Administration officials hoped for a quick resolution of remaining differences so that a legislative proposal could be sent to Congress over the summer.

These hopes soon faded. No final agreement was reached before the Governor's Association annual meeting in August, and disappointed governors decided to develop their own federalism proposal. Gov. Snelling, the outgoing Chairman of the NGA, reported to the organization's Executive Committee that "it no longer seems prudent to pin our hopes for a new federalism on the outcome of any negotiations with the White House."[23] He laid much of the failure to reach final agreement on remaining differences over how to implement the federal takeover of Medicaid. Nevertheless, the governors agreed to continue discussions with the White House while developing their own federalism proposal.

In a letter to the President on November 19, 1982, the Executive Committee of the National Governors' Association outlined the governors' current position on federalism reform. As before, the governors would defer action on AFDC and food stamps, proposing that the federal government assume full responsibility for Medicaid in exchange for state assumption of up to eighteen existing federal grant programs. (See Table 10–3). To ease passage of this proposal, the governors suggested that Medicaid could be divided into three components: acute care for Supplemental Security Income (SSI) eligible recipients, acute care for AFDC eligible recipients, and long-term care. The national government could choose to assume any or all of these components, turning back a specific group of federal programs with each component. A revolving fund for balancing winners and losers among individual states was also proposed, but no method for dealing with fiscal disparities was indicated.

For its part, the Administration has delayed developing a legislative proposal on New Federalism . . . pending further modifications in its proposal or

[21]For details on this revised proposal, see U.S., Executive Office of the President, "Remarks at the [National Association of Counties] Annual Convention, *Weekly Compilation of Presidential Documents*, 13 July 1982, p. 899; and Timothy Schellhardt, "Reagan Revamps 'New Federalism' Plan for Welfare to Enhance Appeal to States," *Wall Street Journal*, 23 June 1982.

[22]Bill Peterson, "White House Agreement on "New Federalism." Announced by Governors," *The Washington Post*, 6 May 1982, p. A4.

[23]Governor Richard Snelling, Chairman, National Governors' Association, *"The Governors' Federalism Initiative—Report to the Executive Committee,"* unpublished statement, National Governors' Association, 8 August 1982.

TABLE 10–3   Governor's Revised Federalism Proposal: A Focus on Medicaid

FEDERAL RESPONSIBILITY	STATE RESPONSIBILITY	PROGRAM COST (billions)
Component A:		
Acute Care Medicaid Benefits for SSI eligibles ($4.1 billion)	Vocational and Rehabilitation	$ .952
	Vocational and Adult Education	.740
	State Block Grants (ECIA Ch. 2)	.537
	Small Cities Block Grant	1.020
	CSA Block Grant	.348
	Preventive Health Block Grant	.082
	ADMHA Block Grant	.432
		$4.111
Component B:		
Acute Care Medicaid Benefits for AFDC Eligibles ($5.3 billion)	Social Services Block Grant	$2.400
	Waste Water Treatment Grants	2.400
	Water and Sewer Grants	.125
	Water and Sewer Loans	.375
	Community Facilities Loans	.130
		$5.430
Component C:		
Long term care ($8.4 billion)	Turnback Option 1	
	CETA	$2.858
	Child Nutrition	3.212
	DCBG (entitlement)	2.419
		$8.489
	Turnback Option 2	
	GRS	$4.566
	Transportation Programs	
	Urban	.800
	Secondary	.400
	Bridges	.900
	Highway Safety and Safety Construction	.390
	Primary	1.500
		$8.556

Source: Governors Scott Matheson and Richard Snelling, Letter to President Reagan, 19 November 1982.

agreement with state leaders on a revised plan. Current indications suggest the President's proposal may be substantially altered, focusing almost totally on the trust fund mechanism linked to the renewal of General Revenue Sharing and the consolidation of other leading intergovernmental programs. . . .

1982: CONTINUING THE REAGAN "REVOLUTION" OR RETURN TO "POLITICS AS USUAL?"

History suggests that grand Presidential strategies for government reform are very difficult to accomplish. The bold departmental reogranization efforts of Presidents Nixon and Carter and the Nixon Administration's original ''New Federalism'' proposals met disappointment in Congress. An even more discouraging fate befell President Eisenhower's earlier attempt to return federal programs and tax sources to the states. He appointed several leading members of his cabinet and ten prominent governors to a ''Joint Federal–State Action Committee,'' instructing them to identify federal programs suitable for turn-back to states. The committee could agree on only two modest programs, however, and neither was acted on by Congress.

Seen in this light, the difficulties encountered by the President's New Federalism initiatives in 1982 were not surprising. In fact, the Administration's 1981 accomplishments in Congress were exceptional; the frustrated progress of reform and the continued pressures for new regulations and preemptions in 1982 were more characteristic of ''politics as usual.'' Other recent political developments suggest a ''return to normalcy'' as well, although continued fiscal stringency in Washington makes unlikely any return to rapidly growing federal grants and grant outlays. . . .

Robert B. Lucke

11

RICH STATES—POOR STATES
Inequalities
in our Federal System

One important consideration in moving to a more decentralized system of government as envisioned under the New Federalism is the difference between the rather extraordinary tax wealth of some states and the relatively anemic resources of others. The latest ACIR study on the tax capacity of the fifty states illustrates significant and growing disparities in their ability to raise revenue.[1] For example, Alaska has four times the capacity to finance public services as Mississippi. In the past, these differences in taxing capacity were "papered over" by an expensive federal grant system. The dramatic realignments called for in various New Federalism proposals, coupled with shrinking federal grants, have raised the issue of how federal fiscal resources should be distributed among the states.

Both the National Governor's Association (NGA) and Senator David Durenberger (MN), Chairman of the Senate Subcommittee on Intergovernmental Relations, have stressed the need to provide fiscal equalization grants to poorer states as part of reorganizing programmatic responsibilities among government levels. Senator Durenberger summed up the problem and his solution: "Large

---

Revised version, originally appeared in *Intergovernmental Perspective* 8, no. 2 (Spring 1982): 22–28. Reprinted with permission of the U.S. Advisory Commission on Intergovernmental Relations.

[1] Advisory Commission on Intergovernmental Relations, *1981 Tax Capacity of the Fifty States* (Washington DC: U.S. Government Printing Office, 1983).

disparities create wasteful tensions in a federal system. . . . [Although] complete equalization is beyond the reach of federal resources . . . some movement in that direction can and should be accomplished in the allocation of the new federalism trust fund.''[2] Others agree. Journalist Neal Peirce recently commented: ''This is an issue many of us have long wanted to see out in the open, lest wealth differentials tear at our national unity and cause immense hardships for some states and regions in the coming years.''[3]

While the targeting of trust fund allocations to the poorer states was not emphasized in the initial New Federalism proposal set forth by the President, the Administration and state and local officials are currently exploring this possibility. A compromise might find the Administration agreeing to equalization as a quid pro quo for achieving its federalism and budgetary objectives. Federalism initiatives may be more readily reconciled with tighter federal budgets in the years ahead if federal grants are targeted to those jurisdictions with the least ability to provide services from their own revenue sources.

MEASURING FISCAL DISPARITIES

Measuring differences among states in their abilities to raise revenues—or fiscal disparities—has long attracted the interest of economists, government analysts, and policymakers. Traditionally, a state's ability to raise revenue has been gauged by the per capita income of its residents. As an indicator of fiscal capacity, however, per capita income has been criticized because it does not completely account for all the sources available for state tax purposes. This shortcoming is particularly true for the energy-rich states, such as Alaska, Texas, Louisiana, and Wyoming or the tourist-rich states, such as Nevada and Hawaii, which can tap resources not strongly related to their respective state per capita incomes. Income is also an inadequate measure for farm states that have large amounts of real property and for those states that have a relatively large concentration of corporate activity. Overall, per capita income is a better measure of the economic well-being of a state's residents than of a government's ability to raise revenue. The ACIR has long been interested in developing a more comprehensive measure of fiscal capacity and recently stated its support for a measure, such as the Representative Tax System (RTS), that would provide a more accurate reflection of a state's ability to raise revenue from all sources.[4]

The Representative Tax System provides a comprehensive measure of each state's overall tax base by combining all sources of tax revenue, such as property,

[2]Dave Durenberger, ''Basic Principles for a New Federalism,'' released 2 February 1982.

[3]Neal Peirce, speech on the New Federalism before the National Center for Municipal Development, 24 March 1982.

[4]Advisory Commission on Intergovernmental Relations meeting, 29 March 1982.

income, retail sales, and minerals, into a composite index of state tax capacity. The index is calculated by estimating the amount of revenue that each state would raise if it used an identical set of tax rates. The rates used for the calculation are "representative" in the sense that they are the national average tax rates for each base. Because the same tax rates are used for every state, estimated tax yields vary only because of differences in the underlying bases.

All bases commonly subject to state and local taxation are used in the RTS measure of tax capacity. The representative tax rates are applied in every state regardless of whether a given state actually taxes a particular base. For example, Connecticut does not have an income tax, but income is included in Connecticut's tax wealth; similarly, Oregon does not have a retail sales tax, but retail sales are included in its tax capacity computation. An individual state's decision to stress one type of tax or another does not affect the measurement of its tax base and potential "tax wealth" relative to other states.

The Representative Tax System shows that states differ significantly in their abilities to raise revenues. The first two columns of Table 11–1 present the RTS measure of tax capacity in dollars per capita and as an index for 1981. Alaska ranks as the wealthiest state based on this measure—its tax capacity is $3,333 per capita and its index of 324 is 224 percentage points greater than the national average. These levels are more than four times greater than Mississippi's—$737 per capita and an index of 72. Other states high on the tax capacity scale are Wyoming (216), Nevada (148), Texas (132), and Oklahoma (127). The low capacity states are primarily found in the southeastern part of the country: Mississippi (72), Alabama (74), South Carolina (75), Tennessee (79), and Arkansas (82). In general, the western states, especially those well endowed with mineral resources, have capacities greater than those in the East.

IS THE FISCAL GAP WIDENING?

The tax capacity indices presented in Table 11–1 for 1975, 1980, and 1981 show that fiscal disparities among the states are becoming greater. One summary measure of the overall disparities among the states is the population-weighted standard deviation of the tax capacity indices. The standard deviation of the tax capacity indices measures the relative dispersion of the states around the national average. A high standard deviation indicates greater fiscal disparities than a low standard deviation. The change in fiscal disparities over time is reflected by the growth of the standard deviation of the indices from 10.4 in 1975, to 15.7 in 1980, and to 18.5 in 1981. Over the 1975–81 period, disparities increased by 85 percent. In general, the poorer states have not shown improvement since 1975, and in fact, many of the southern states, such as Alabama and South Carolina, have seen their relative capacities slip. The greatest declines between 1975 and 1981, however, occurred in the northeastern and midwestern states.

TABLE 11–1   Tax Capacity of the States—1975, 1980, and 1981

STATE	1981 TAX CAPACITY	TAX CAPACITY INDEX		
	Per Capita	1981	1980	1975
New England				
Connecticut	$1,131	110	112	110
Maine	815	79	80	84
Massachusetts	988	96	96	98
New Hampshire	982	95	97	102
Rhode Island	827	80	84	88
Vermont	824	84	84	94
Mideast				
Delaware	1,143	111	111	124
Washington, DC	1,142	111	111	117
Maryland	1,009	98	99	101
New Jersey	1,077	105	105	109
New York	916	89	90	98
Pennsylvania	931	90	93	98
Great Lakes				
Illinois	1,070	104	108	112
Indiana	932	91	92	98
Michigan	990	96	97	100
Ohio	971	94	97	103
Wisconsin	935	91	95	98
Plains				
Iowa	1,035	102	105	106
Kansas	1,125	109	109	109
Minnesota	1,030	100	102	97
Missouri	947	92	94	96
Nebraska	996	97	97	106
North Dakota	1,271	123	108	101
South Dakota	888	86	90	94
Southeast				
Alabama	766	74	76	77
Arkansas	839	82	79	78
Florida	1,040	101	100	102
Georgia	838	81	82	86
Kentucky	843	82	83	85
Louisiana	1,200	117	109	97
Mississippi	737	72	69	70
North Carolina	818	80	80	84
South Carolina	774	75	75	77
Tennessee	812	79	79	84
Virginia	969	94	95	93
West Virginia	926	90	94	89
Southwest				
Arizona	913	89	89	92
New Mexico	1,170	114	107	92
Oklahoma	1,310	127	117	98
Texas	1,359	132	124	110

TABLE 11–1   Continued

STATE	1981 TAX CAPACITY	TAX CAPACITY INDEX		
	Per Capita	1981	1980	1975
Rocky Mountain				
Colorado	1,160	113	113	106
Idaho	891	87	87	89
Montana	1,168	114	112	103
Utah	890	86	86	86
Wyoming	2,227	216	196	153
Far West				
California	1,186	115	117	110
Nevada	1,523	148	154	145
Oregon	1,019	99	103	100
Washington	1,020	99	103	98
Alaska	3,333	324	260	154
Hawaii	1,076	105	107	110
U.S. Average	1,029	100	100	100
Standard Deviation		18.5	15.7	10.4

Source: Advisory Commission on Intergovernmental Relations.

Delaware, Vermont, Nebraska, and New York experienced the largest declines. In contrast, the greatest growth in tax capacity occurred in the western states, particularly the energy-rich states of Alaska and Wyoming. Alaska's increase was not surprising due to its rapid entry into the club of large oil producing states.

The growing gap between rich and poor states is not so apparent when per capita income is used to measure capacity. For some time now, economic activity and population movements have tended to converge per capita income levels across the country. However, since the mid-70s, increased state revenues from nonincome-related sources have tended to make per capita income an even less reliable measure of tax capacity.

THE NATIONAL INTEREST IN FISCAL EQUALIZATION

Fiscal equalization as an issue arises in the debate over new federalism because of the growing fiscal disparities among states. Fiscal disparities arise because economic growth and prosperity are not shared equally across jurisdictions. Furthermore, with individual subnational units of government responsible for financing the public services they provide, disparities in capacity can result in differences in the quantity and quality of public services offered and in the tax rates necessary to provide them.

Historically, the redistribution of revenue from wealthy to poor governments has been justified on equity grounds. In 1964 the ACIR concluded that the objective of fiscal equalization is:

to achieve a national minimum level of program operations by varying the federal grant offer to the states directly in proportion to their program needs and inversely with their fiscal capacities. The objective is to enable all states to achieve the nationally defined minimum service level if they make a uniform effort to tax resources available to them.[5]

The equity rationale is primarily based on two arguments, both of which have been emphasized in the debate over school finance reform. The first argument is that some communities, by virtue of their wealth, are able to finance a much higher level of educational services than their less wealthy counterparts. Thus, fiscal disparities not only reflect current differences in the abilities of communities to support public services, but they can have lasting effects on individual citizens through the unequal educational opportunities or other services they may receive across jurisdictions. Because government services, such as education or health, contribute to the earning potential of the recipient, current disparities in the ability to finance public services can contribute to differences in individual income levels well into the future. Therefore, fiscal equalization grants are a way of providing more equal access to government services, particularly to the less privileged segments of the population residing in the poorer states.

Equity concerns also arise from the fact that taxpayers can face substantially different tax rates for a given package of services simply because of their place of residence. Because poorer jurisdictions often must levy higher tax rates than their wealthier counterparts to provide the same level of services, individuals with like incomes will pay different amounts in taxes depending on the jurisdiction in which they reside. In the classic school finance case *Serrano* v. *Priest*, the plaintiffs illustrated that poor school districts often had much higher tax rates than their wealthier counterparts, yet raised much less revenue.[6] The tax capacity indices in Table 11–1 indicate that a low capacity state like Mississippi could only raise 72 percent of the revenue of the average state, even if both imposed identical tax rates. Equity suggests that equalizing grants should be used to equalize the tax burdens or tax prices associated with like levels of public services. In the educational finance literature, this form of equalization system is commonly referred to as "district power equalization," because it equalizes the tax power of the school districts.[7] In other words, the equalizing grants are distributed to school districts in such a way that each district would have the same amount of revenue per pupil if each were to levy the same tax rate.

In addition to equalizing taxpayer burdens for comparable levels of spending, equalization grants can promote economic efficiency by inhibiting the migra-

---

[5]Advisory Commission on Intergovernmental Relations, *The Role of Equalization in Federal Grants* (Washington, DC: U.S. Government Printing Office, 1964), p. 4.

[6]*Serrano* v. *Priest*, C 3d 584 487 P 2d 1241 (1971).

[7]Robert D. Reischauer and Robert W. Hartman with assistance of Daniel J. Sullivan, *Reforming School Finance* (Washington DC: The Brookings Institution, 1973).

tion of labor and production facilities based purely on fiscal considerations. By reducing differentials in tax rates per unit-of-service across jurisdictions that arise strictly from fiscal disparities, equalization grants can offset the tendency of labor and capital to move to high capacity areas to take advantage of lower tax prices. Indeed, one of the primary arguments advanced by Senator Durenberger for equalizing grants is that "[e]conomic relocation driven by the individual desire to avoid high taxes in low capacity states contributes to an inefficient allocation of social resources."[8]

Of course, locational decisions regarding labor and investment are not only based on tax price variations, but on the real economic advantages of one area over another as well. For example, wage rates, energy prices, and transportation facilities substantially differ across jurisdictions and will have a significant effect on the locational decisions made by businesses and individuals. Care must be taken to assure that a system of equalization grants does not go beyond correcting for disparities in capacities so that real (nonfiscal) differences in regional comparative advantages can continue to influence resource flows.

THE ROLE OF GRANTS IN ACHIEVING FISCAL EQUALIZATION

The United States, unlike a number of other federal countries, does not have a program specifically designed to reduce fiscal disparities among its states. Although General Revenue Sharing (GRS) provides payments with few strings, the program is relatively small and only modestly equalizes disparities. Most fiscal assistance to state and local governments in the U.S. takes the form of categorical or block grants. To some extent, the federal intergovernmental aid system does achieve a degree of equalization by using allocation formulas that are sensitive to a state's fiscal capacity. Per capita income is used as a proxy for fiscal capacity in a number of grant programs, including GRS, Medicaid, and Aid to Families with Dependent Children (AFDC). Because the per capita income measure is used in combination with other factors, the equalization power of these programs is limited. For example, using tax effort, urban population, or programmatic expenditures in federal aid formulas partially offsets the effects of per capita income in equalizing fiscal resources.

To gauge the equalization effectiveness of current grant allocations, the amount of federal aid each state receives was added to the state's tax capacity in Table 11–2. The change in state tax capacity after the addition of these payments provides an indication of how well the grant system functions as an equalizer.

The set of indices in column 2 of Table 11–2 is based on the RTS for 1980, plus General Revenue Sharing allocations. The GRS payments had very

---

[8]Dave Durenberger, "Basic Principles for a New Federalism."

TABLE 11–2 The Impact of Grants on Fiscal Disparities

STATE	1980 Tax Capacity INDEX	1980 Tax Capacity PLUS GRS	Tax Capacity PLUS ALL GRANTS
New England			
Connecticut	112	111	106
Maine	80	81	91
Massachusetts	96	97	105
New Hampshire	97	96	96
Rhode Island	84	84	97
Vermont	84	85	111
Mideast			
Delaware	111	112	113
Washington, DC	111	112	234
Maryland	99	99	102
New Jersey	105	105	103
New York	90	91	104
Pennsylvania	93	93	94
Great Lakes			
Illinois	108	107	105
Indiana	92	92	87
Michigan	97	97	100
Ohio	97	97	92
Wisconsin	95	95	99
Plains			
Iowa	105	105	100
Kansas	109	108	103
Minnesota	102	102	100
Missouri	94	93	92
Nebraska	97	97	94
North Dakota	108	108	116
South Dakota	90	91	111
Southeast			
Alabama	76	76	84
Arkansas	79	79	86
Florida	100	100	92
Georgia	82	82	90
Kentucky	83	83	88
Louisiana	109	109	105
Mississippi	69	70	84
North Carolina	80	80	81
South Carolina	75	76	79
Tennessee	79	79	83
Virginia	95	95	92
West Virginia	94	94	102
Southwest			
Arizona	89	89	85
New Mexico	107	107	114
Oklahoma	117	116	108

TABLE 11–2 Continued

STATE	1980 Tax Capacity INDEX	1980 Tax Capacity PLUS GRS	Tax Capacity PLUS ALL GRANTS
Texas	124	123	108
Rocky Mountain			
Colorado	113	112	105
Idaho	87	88	93
Montana	112	112	125
Utah	86	86	90
Wyoming	196	194	185
Far West			
California	117	117	110
Nevada	154	153	140
Oregon	103	103	108
Washington	103	102	103
Alaska	260	258	267
Hawaii	107	107	111
U.S. Average	100	100	100
Standard Deviation	15.65	15.28	14.24

Source: Advisory Commission on Intergovernmental Relations.

little effect on the individual state indices, only reducing the standard deviation by 2.4%, from 15.65 to 15.28. Based on the RTS measure of tax capacity, it appears that the fiscal equalization aspects of the program are relatively weak. Indeed, had the GRS allotments been based on a purely per capita basis, the standard deviation (15.32) would have been virtually the same as the standard deviation calculated under current law. Although the program is designed to achieve goals other than equalization, the equalizing attributes of the existing GRS formula are equivalent to an allocation based solely on population.

The third column of Table 11–2 shows the indices of capacity after *all* federal intergovernmental transfers are accounted for, including GRS. In FY 1980 these grants totaled $90 billion, or $395 per capita.[9] The equalizing effect of all grants is indicated by a reduction in the standard deviation to 14.24, a decrease of 9 percent from the initial level. While this equalizing impact is greater than that of GRS alone, it is still less than if all grants were distributed on a per capita basis. If all intergovernmental aids were allocated solely on the basis of population, the measure of disparities would decline to 11.05, about 22 percent lower than under the existing distribution. In other words, about 22 percent greater equalization could be achieved under a per capita distribution than under the current set of allotments. Clearly, federal aid programs are designed

[9]U.S. Department of the Treasury, *Federal Aid to the States, Fiscal Year 1980* (Washington, DC: U.S. Government Printing Office, 1981).

to meet objectives other than fiscal equalization and their weak equalizing performance bears this out.

FISCAL EQUALIZATION IN OTHER FEDERAL SYSTEMS

In other countries with a federal structure, fiscal equalization has been a traditional
function of the national government. In West Germany, Australia, and Canada,
the national government provides fiscal equalization grants to lower levels of
government to compensate for the fiscal disparities that exist among them. These
equalization payments are typically unconditional and are designed to enable the
fiscally weak governments to finance adequate levels of public services.

Australia has a comprehensive system of fiscal equalization that takes into
account both the fiscal capacity of the states and the differences in the costs of
providing public services. The Australian system of equalization essentially measures "revenue need" as the difference between the revenue the recipient state
would have raised had it applied the average revenue effort of the standard states
to its revenue base and the revenue it would have generated, on the basis of the
standard revenue effort, if its per capita revenue base had been the same as the
average revenue base of the standard states. Expenditure needs are assessed by
the difference between the expenditure the recipient state would have incurred
if it had provided the same average range and quality of services as the standard
states and the expenditure it would have incurred if its per capita expenditure
had been the same as the average of the standard states. Total assessed needs
are measured by the sum of assessed revenue and expenditure needs, representing
the recipient state's shortfall in revenue-raising capacity relative to the standard
states and its additional costs to provide services comparable to those of the
standard states. The standard states in this program are the two states with the
highest fiscal capacity, thus providing a much higher standard of equalization
than that used in other federal countries.[10]

The West German system of equalization grants consists of two distinct
parts—"vertical" equalization payments from the national government to the
states, and "horizontal" equalization payments directly from the rich states to
the poor states. The vertical transfers used by West Germany are based on its
value-added tax and are allocated to each state's tax revenue to bring up the
capacities of the poorer states to 92 percent of the national average. After taking
into account the vertical transfers, the states negotiate direct transfers between
themselves that are designed to bring up the capacities of the poorer states to
nearly the average for all states.

[10]Advisory Commission on Intergovernmental Relations, *Studies in Comparative Federalism:
Australia* (Washington DC: U.S. Government Printing Office, August 1981), pp. 17–26.

The Canadian equalization program distributes grants only to those provinces having capacities below the national average; they are not provided to provinces with above average capacity. The grants are meant to equalize capacities so that each and every province can provide the average level of public services at average rates of taxation.

The Canadian system of equalization is of particular interest to the U.S. because the Canadian federal government provides fiscal equalizing transfers to the provinces based directly on the Representative Tax System measure of fiscal capacity. In FY 1979, the Canadian equalization program, as outlined in the 1977 Fiscal Arrangements Act, distributed $2.9 billion to seven provinces which together have 45 percent of Canada's population. The three other provinces received nothing under this program.

The equalization payment provided to a province equals the difference between its fiscal capacity and the national average capacity. For example, in FY 1979–80, Manitoba's Representative Tax System yield was $1,101.38 per capita and the national average yield was $1,383.60 per capita. Manitoba's equalization payment was $282.22 ($1,383.60 less $1,101.38) times its population to get a total $291.7 million grant. The payments are financed out of general federal revenues and unlike West Germany, there are no "negative aids" paid by those provinces with greater than average capacity. The provinces are brought up to the national average but the system is asymmetric because it does not reduce the capacity of the wealthy provinces.

The effectiveness of the Canadian equalization program can be appraised by how well it reduces fiscal disparities among the provinces. The FY 1979 representative tax yield or tax capacity for each of Canada's provinces is shown in Table 11–3; capacity is shown on a per capita basis, and indexed to the national mean. The indices range from a high of 232 for Alberta to a low of fifty-five for Prince Edward Island, indicating that Alberta has more than four times the revenue capacity of the poorest province. Regionally, the three western provinces (Alberta, British Columbia, and Saskatchewan) rank well above those in the East. Although the most populous province, Ontario, ranks above average on the nonmineral resource sources of revenue, its relative disadvantage on the natural resource base pulls its overall index below the average. The Maritime provinces (Newfoundland, New Brunswick, Novia Scotia, and Prince Edward Island) are the weakest fiscally.

In 1979, the standard deviation computed prior to the inclusion of equalization payments was 42.3. The average yield of the RTS was $1,691 per capita, with a standard deviation of $716. The third column in Table 11–3 shows the capacity indices after equalization payments have been added to each province's capacity. After equalization payments are counted, all provinces, except Ontario, have capacities closer to the mean. Because the wealthy provinces are not required to finance payments directly to the less prosperous jurisdictions, equality is not

TABLE 11–3   Canadian Representative Tax System Yields, FY 1979

PROVINCE	CAPACITY PER CAPITA	INDEX*	INDEX AFTER EQUALIZATION UNDER CURRENT LAW
Alberta	$3,931.62	232	217
British Columbia	1,948.66	115	107
Manitoba	1,306.56	77	88
Newfoundland	971.03	57	85
New Brunswick	1,058.32	63	85
Nova Scotia	1,090.06	64	85
Ontario	1,573.19	93	87
Prince Edward Island	930.07	55	84
Quebec	1,335.81	79	87
Saskatchewan	1,739.23	103	98
Average	1,691.47	100	100
Standard Deviation: (population-weighted)	715.66	42.31	35.80

*Index is percent of national per capita average.

Source: Federal–Provincial Relations Division, Department of Finance, Government of Canada, *Provincial Fiscal Equalization, Fiscal Calculation, 1978–79*, Printout, 7 April 1981.

achieved. However, with the exceptions of Alberta and British Columbia, all provinces fall within a 15 point range from 84 percent to 98 percent of the national average after accounting for equalization grants. Disparities are significantly lessened with the standard deviation dropping to 35.8, a 15.4 percent reduction. The equalization program is especially important to the Maritime provinces whose capacity index, taken as a group, is increased from 61.5 to 84.5, a rise of 37.3 percent. Because Ontario has been excluded from the equalization program, although technically qualifying, its capacity falls from 93.0 to 86.7 after equalization.

U.S. FISCAL EQUALIZATION, CANADIAN STYLE

As part of the ACIR staff's analysis of New Federalism issues, a simulation has been conducted to analyze the implications of adopting a Canadian-type equalization program in the United States. In conjunction with a decentralization of programmatic responsibilities, an equalization program might improve the flexibility of state and local governments and temper the impact of cuts on the governmental entities with the least capacity to raise their own revenues. The 1980 RTS provides an opportunity to assess the equalizing impacts of such an approach.

Although the U.S. and Canadian federal systems have many similarities and face common problems, important differences do exist. One difference is that the disparities between the American states are not as great as those between the Canadian provinces. The 1980 standard deviation of the tax capacity measure prior to the inclusion of any grants in the U.S. is 15.65—only 37 percent of the comparable Canadian measure. Even after the Canadian equalization payments are taken into account, the U.S. standard deviation is still just 44 percent of the Canadian index. This result is a little surprising; because Canada is composed of ten provinces rather than fifty states, one might expect that disparities among the provinces would tend to average-out because of their large size.

The relative disadvantage of the poorer states is not as severe as that of their counterparts in Canada. Four provinces (Newfoundland, Prince Edward Island, Nova Scotia, and New Brunswick) rank well below the poorest of the states. Combined, these provinces have a capacity index of 61.54—8.9 percent less than Mississippi's index. These poorer provinces account for about 9.5 percent of Canada's population. After equalization, however, the poorest provinces all rank as high (or higher) than the low tax capacity American states if all domestic aids are included.

The results of a simulation based on the Representative Tax System under the Canadian approach are presented in Table 11–4. The equalization program would only provide aids to the twenty-eight states whose capacity is below the national norm. New York ($1.6 billion), North Carolina ($1.1 billion), and Alabama ($0.9 billion) would receive the largest equalization grants. In general, the states in the southeast region would benefit most from such a program. As a group, these states would receive more than half the total funds appropriated for equalization. By using this approach, the overall cost of such a program in FY 1980 would have been about $12.2 billion or about 14 percent of all federal aid provided to state and local governments in that year.

The impact on disparities from a Canadian-type program would be quite substantial. The indices in Table 11–4 are based on the 1980 RTS measure of tax capacity, including the simulated equalization payments while excluding all other federal aids. Because negative aids are not assessed, many states are below the average capacity after the equalization grants, although none falls below its initial capacity level.[11] The reduction in the standard deviation from 15.65 to 10.54, a decrease of 33 percent, indicates that disparities would be reduced by about one-third. In contrast to the existing aid structure, the reduction in disparities would be significantly greater under the Canadian-style program (33 percent versus 9 percent). Simply put, the $12.2 billion program could buy 3.75 times more fiscal equalization than that achieved currently by the entire $90 billion

[11]The initial capacity per capita equals $948.73; after equalization the average capacity equals $1,002.59. Because states are only equalized up to $948.73, their resulting index is 95 [948.73/1002.59] and not 100. The difference ($53.86) is solely due to the added equalization payments.

TABLE 11–4   Equalization Grants Based on the Representative Tax System

STATE	FISCAL EQUALIZATION GRANT ($000)	TAX CAPACITY PER CAPITA AFTER EQUALIZATION	TAX CAPACITY INDEX AFTER EQUALIZATION	PERCENTAGE CHANGE IN TAX CAPACITY INDEX AFTER EQUALIZATION
New England				
Connecticut	$ —0—	$1,058	106	-5.4%
Maine	213,716	949	95	+ 18.2
Massachusetts	207,877	949	95	- 1.6
New Hampshire	30,631	949	95	- 1.9
Rhode Island	146,220	949	95	+ 13.0
Vermont	75,533	949	95	+ 12.0
Mideast				
Delaware	—0—	1,057	105	- 5.4
Washington, DC	—0—	1,051	105	- 5.4
Maryland	32,635	949	95	- 4.6
New Jersey	—0—	997	99	- 5.4
New York	1,645,786	949	95	+ 5.0
Pennsylvania	833,849	949	95	+ 2.2
Great Lakes				
Illinois	—0—	1,021	102	- 5.4
Indiana	406,063	949	95	+ 2.6
Michigan	267,137	949	95	- 2.4
Ohio	327,846	949	95	- 2.3
Wisconsin	236,197	949	95	- 0.1
Plains				
Iowa	—0—	998	100	- 5.4
Kansas	—0—	1,032	103	- 5.4
Minnesota	—0—	969	97	- 5.4
Missouri	299,855	949	95	+ 1.1
Nebraska	47,838	949	95	- 2.2
North Dakota	—0—	1,028	103	- 5.4
South Dakota	64,524	949	95	+ 4.9
Southeast				
Alabama	899,318	949	95	+ 25.0
Arkansas	456,384	949	95	+ 19.8
Georgia	934,767	949	95	+ 15.4
Florida	—0—	949	95	- 5.4
Kentucky	592,947	949	95	+ 14.1
Louisiana	—0—	1,036	103	- 5.4
Mississippi	735,150	949	95	+ 36.5
North Carolina	1,144,568	949	95	+ 19.0
South Carolina	734,679	949	95	+ 25.8
Tennessee	917,520	949	95	+ 19.8
Virginia	266,192	949	95	- 0.1
West Virginia	117,156	949	95	+ 1.0
Southwest				
Arizona	292,676	949	95	+ 6.7

TABLE 11–4   Continued

STATE	FISCAL EQUALIZATION GRANT ($000)	TAX CAPACITY PER CAPITA AFTER EQUALIZATION	TAX CAPACITY INDEX AFTER EQUALIZATION	PERCENTAGE CHANGE IN TAX CAPACITY INDEX AFTER EQUALIZATION
New Mexico	—0—	1,016	101	- 5.4
Oklahoma	—0—	1,108	111	- 5.4
Texas	—0—	1,173	117	- 5.4
Rocky Mountain				
Colorado	—0—	1,068	107	- 5.4
Idaho	112,335	949	95	+ 8.2
Montana	—0—	1,067	106	- 5.4
Utah	194,843	949	95	+10.1
Wyoming	—0—	1,862	186	- 5.4
Far West				
California	—0—	1,110	111	- 5.4
Nevada	—0—	1,465	146	- 5.4
Oregon	—0—	979	98	- 5.4
Washington	—0—	976	97	- 5.4
Alaska	—0—	2,463	246	- 5.4
Hawaii	—0—	1,011	101	- 5.4
U.S. Total	12,234,256	1,003	100	0.0
Standard Deviation:	—	106	10.54	—

Source: Advisory Commission on Intergovernmental Relations.

aid system. While the high capacity states of Alaska (246), Wyoming (186) and Nevada (146) would remain well above the rest of the states, their advantage would be reduced. The remaining states would all fall within a 24-point span.

TOWARD A NEW FEDERALISM

The Reagan Administration's proposals to restructure our federal system have sparked a serious debate over the viability of the intergovernmental grant system. Despite—or perhaps because of—the dramatic increase in federal aid to state and local governments over the last two decades, little attention has been paid to differences in the ability of state and local governments to raise their own revenues. ACIR's recent research shows that disparities among states in their revenue raising capacitites are increasing and that the current federal grant-in-aid system only modestly equalizes these differences. Now, as a major restructuring of programmatic responsiblities is being considered, it is timely to ask whether more attention should be directed to assisting the fiscally weakest states.

Frank Shafroth

12

TAXING QUESTIONS
FOR CITIES

The 1980's have posed significant new issues for cities in intergovernmental relations. With the advent of the Reagan administration, the era of increasing direct federal assistance has come to a halt. Although Congress, the states, and the cities all rejected the concept of "New Federalism," the role of the federal government as a partner with state and local governments has been altered. What were once intergovernmental and national concerns have become local problems and responsibilities. Privatization has come to mean eliminating any governmental role—at any level—rather than developing incentives for government to work together with the private sector to meet the void left behind by a lesser federal role.

Now that the nation is into the second Reagan term, it is important to examine what has happened in order to anticipate what might happen. It has been an extraordinary period. More tax bills have been enacted than at any similar period in American history; federal deficits have accumulated to a greater total than that of all previous administrations combined; yet, the administration is proposing to embark upon a stormy sea of deficits and tax reform. How these issues are presented and acted upon will determine the course of the intergovernmental system in years to come.

Portions excerpted from "President, Lawmakers Reject Early Actions on Tax Reform," *Nation's Cities Weekly*, December 10, 1984. Reprinted with permission of *Nation's Cities Weekly*, official publication of the National League of Cities.

FEDERAL TAX REFORM PROPOSAL

Even before the Treasury Department's detailed explanation of its tax reform proposals hit the capital's bestseller list in December of 1984, the proposal had become an orphan.[1] The White House made explicit statements that the massive federal tax reform proposal submitted by Secretary of the Treasury Donald Regan *was not* an administration proposal. Not only did the proposal receive a tepid reception at the White House, but it was also demoted from a top priority by the president. The White House indicated that an overhaul of the tax system should be considered only after major deficit reductions were achieved.

In Congress, any possibility of early action in 1985 on tax reform affecting cities had already been dispelled. The House and Senate leaders indicated—as did the National League of Cities at its annual meeting in November of 1984—that tax reform should only be considered as part of an effort to reduce the federal deficit. Both the House Ways and Means Committee Chairman Dan Rostenkowski (D-Ill.) and Senate Majority Leader Robert Dole (R-Kan.) specifically linked tax reform to overall efforts to reduce the nation's deficit. Moreover, any hope of early consideration of tax reform was dashed by Senate Finance Committee Chairman Bob Packwood (R-Ore.). Packwood, who strongly supports many of the tax expenditures which provide incentives for certain kinds of private sector investments, but which would be repealed by the Treasury proposal, announced that his committee would hold hearings on the President's tax reform proposal in the spring and summer of 1985. Because an off-year August recess by Congress traditionally marks the official opening of the following year's House and Senate campaigns, most observers interpret Packwood's statement to preclude any serious Congressional action in 1985.

TAX REFORM AND CITIES

As the 99th Congress and the Reagan administration consider the sixth major federal tax bill in five years, municipal officials will watch the process with more than usual apprehension. Not only are city officials concerned about the impact of proposed changes on their respective cities, but there is growing apprehension that instead of major tax reform, the administration and Congress will use the Treasury proposal as a menu or "hit list" to cut tax expenditures.[2] For the nation's cities, the stakes are enormous. Overall tax reform would have a far different impact on cities than selected "loophole" closings. Failure to

---

[1]Secretary Regan proposed to lower federal marginal tax rates and to significantly broaden the tax base by taxing items that were exempt from taxation. His proposal was revenue neutral, meaning it did not raise any more revenue after the base broadening than before.

[2]Tax expenditures are simnilar to spending programs, instead of providing funds to support a particular activity the national government "spends" tax dollars by not collecting them.

consider tax reform or changes as part of the deficit reduction process would mean greater and greater losses of revenue to the federal Treasury. Reduced revenues, due to the reduced federal tax base, force even greater pressures to eliminate all direct federal assistance programs to cities.

Taxes and Urban Issues

City leaders, in increasing numbers, are realizing that the federal Treasury and Internal Revenue Service have come to dominate federal urban policy, virtually preempting other federal cabinet agencies. Similarly, in the Congress, the Senate Finance and House Ways and Means Committee have inadvertently become the preeminent urban policy makers in the fields of housing, economic development, transportation, energy, employment, health, income security, infrastructure, and municipal fiscal stability (see Table 12–1).

HOW HAS THIS EVOLUTION HAPPENED?

In the past few years, the enormous federal deficit, seeming to stretch out forever, has led the administration and Congress to reduce or freeze virtually all assistance programs to cities. Thus, housing, community and economic development, and wastewater sewage treatment grant programs have been cut substantially. Federal assistance for low income housing construction has been virtually eliminated. Other programs, such as General Revenue Sharing (GRS), have been frozen at 1976 nominal levels. Measured in real dollars, GRS payments made to cities in 1984 are worth less than 50 percent of the amounts received in 1976. The actions of the admininstration in seeking deep cuts in domestic programs, and the Congressional process of authorizations, budget resolutions, and appropriations mean that every direct assistance program to cities is under intense scrutiny and must overcome at least four obstacles (President's budget, first Congressional budget resolution, authorization action, and appropriations).

With these reductions in both nominal and real dollars, there is less and less of a policy making role for cabinet agencies and Congressional authorizing committees. For instance, when the administration proposes to eliminate all funding for an agency such as the Economic Development Administration (EDA), the U.S. Commerce Department gives up much of its ability to direct federal municipal economic development policy. Likewise, as Congress has agreed to severe reductions in an agency such as EDA, relevant Congressional authorizing committees (Senate Environment and Public Works, House Public Works and Transportation) have a relatively reduced role in setting municipal economic development policy. The fewer the dollars available to assist economic development in cities, the greater the reduction of the role of these committees.

TABLE 12–1 Tax Evolution on Key Urban Issues

DIRECT ASSISTANCE (IN MILLIONS)			TAX EXPENDITURES (IN MILLIONS)	
I. Economic Development[1]				
1979	$ 2,377		$ 585	
1984	$ 1,173	(−51%)	$ 2,155	(+268%)
II. Housing[2]				
1979	$30,334		$28,300	
1984	$13,564	(−55%)	$71,310	(+152%)
III. Jobs[3]				
1979	$11,694		$ 15	
1984	$ 3,583	(−69%)	$ 1,015	(+6667%)
IV. Pollution Control[4]				
1979	$ 5,415		$ 415	
1984	$ 2,825	(−48%)	$ 1,330	(+220%)
V. Fiscal Assistance[5]				
1979	$ 7,150		$16,300	
1984	$ 4,574	(−36%)	$31,630	(+94%)
VI. Energy[6]				
1979	$ 450		$ 825	
1984	$ 490	(+9%)	$ 1,395	(+41%)

[1]This includes the National Development Bank, EDA, Local Public Works, Rural Development and Business Assistance for direct, the revenue loss associated with the issuance of small issue industrial development bonds for the tax expenditure side.
[2]This includes a) direct: public, subsidized, rural, rehabilitation, and credit programs and b) tax: housing bonds, mortgage interest deductions, property tax deducations, expensing, depreciation, deferral of capital gains and carryover, and rehabilitation and historic tax credits.
[3]This includes a) direct: CETA, and Employment and Training Assistance and b) tax-targeted jobs credit.
[4]This includes a) direct: wastewater construction grants and hazardous waste assistance and b) tax: pollution control bonds.
[5]This includes a) direct: General Revenue Sharing and targeted fiscal assistance and b) tax: exclusion of interest on G. O. bonds and the deductibility of state and local taxes, except on owner-occupied homes.
[6]This includes a) direct: energy conservation, schools and hospital programs, weatherization, b) tax: energy facility bids, residential energy credits, and alternative energy credits.

In contrast, provisions in the internal revenue code which provide incentives for certain kinds of investment undergo little scrutiny. They are immune to policy considerations from the appropriate federal agencies and Congressional committees. They are immune to the Congressional budget process.

Except in rare instances, tax incentives or federal tax expenditures become indexed entitlement programs. That is, once a provision creating a certain kind of tax incentive is inserted in the code—for instance, the mortgage interest deduction—the value of the revenue loss to the federal treasury is not subject to any policy review by HUD or the House or Senate Housing Subcommittees. The value is not subject to concurrent budget resolutions, nor is it subject to the congressional appropriations process. Moreover, because it is built into the tax system, it is a value which grows significantly faster than inflation.

In both the federal and Congressional budget process, direct spending programs are segregated from tax revenues. Thus, when the federal government makes its annual budget review in preparation for the submission of the president's budget, the housing and commerce portion of the budget provides review only of the Housing and Urban Development (HUD) and Farmer's Home Administration direct assistance programs. That portion of the budget does not include the myriad of provisions in the tax code to benefit housing, such as single–family mortgage revenue bonds, multi–family rental housing bonds, accelerated depreciation, rehabilitation tax credits, mortgage interest deductions, capital gains deferrals for principal homes, etc. Similarly, when the House and Senate budget committees consider the housing function, they review only those direct spending and, in some cases, credit programs under the jurisdiction of the respective House and Senate housing subcommittees. Neither the Housing subcommittees, Budget committees, nor Appropriations committees have any jurisdictional review over the tax-related housing expenditures.

The federal Treasury and Congress' tax writing committees—originally charged with revenue raising responsibilities—have evolved with much greater power than any other entities. These powers are jealously protected. They adhere to the Biblical prescription: It is better to give than receive.

WHAT DOES IT MEAN?

Heretofore, those entering the tax arena have predominantly been sophisticated tax attorneys and wealthy investors. Indeed, tax incentives are successful only if an individual finds that a tax benefit has greater advantages than a non-tax motivated investment, and that the investor has enough surplus disposable income to make such an investment. Cities have not consciously sought to use the tax code in the past for major urban programs. They have, for the most part, treated the internal revenue code as more complex than the evolution of modern mathematical theory written in Greek.

City officials have assumed that the selling of federal urban policy is the job of HUD and the House and Senate Banking and Urban Policy Committees. They have assumed that when federal housing policy is determined annually, all federal elements are thrown into a large mixing bowl out of which is fashioned a carefully crafted public policy. Yet, the opposite is increasingly the case. Every year, a smaller and smaller percentage of federal housing program elements go into the mixing bowl. Every year a significantly greater percentage of federal housing expenditures are withheld from the mixing bowl. It is not unlike trying to bake a cake without sugar, flour, milk, or eggs. The salt and vanilla do not go very far. Consider an example. The U.S. Treasury has estimated that in 1984, federal housing tax expenditures for the mortgage interest deduction for vacation homes equalled $1.2 billion. Yet, there is no evidence that anyone at HUD reviewed the expenditure and recommended that part of the federal housing policy should allocate $1.2 billion of assistance to Americans who could afford vacation homes. Similarly, no committee in Congress held hearings to determine if—at a time when cities are faced with a growing problem of housing the homeless—it was appropriate to provide these families with assistance for a second home. Moreover, this is assistance that has grown annually in every year without any committee review when the current administration and Congress have said time and time again that the federal government must take drastic action to reduce federal assistance for housing.

As the role of direct assistance and policy making has declined, the role of tax policy and its impact on cities has become proportionately greater. This is a pattern, moreover, which is unlikely to change. David Stockman, President Reagan's Budget Director, agrees that federal deficits are not going to simply melt away in the face of a growing economy. As a result, there will be more intense pressure to make major reductions in domestic spending. Indeed, with the largest non–means entitlement program held harmless, the Pentagon seeking increases, interest payments on the federal debt increasing at a rapid rate (estimated at $165 billion for FY'85), and the president pledged not to increase taxes, to make even a partial reduction of the nation's deficits would require domestic program cuts at least twice as large as Congress enacted in 1981. By attempting to further reduce the federal government's role in direct spending, without any change in the tax revenue it collects, the tax system becomes the dominant factor in shaping not only intergovernmental relations, but the shape of cities in the future.

part four

IMPLEMENTATION PROBLEMS AND THE FUTURE OF INTERGOVERNMENTAL RELATIONS

Although government spending is well over a trillion dollars a year on programs designed to protect and improve American life, Americans have become increasingly skeptical and even cynical about governmental performance. Many people believe that the national government, in particular, wastes money, is run by big "special" interests, cannot be trusted to do what is right, and is run by people who do not know what they are doing.[1]

During the past decade, many political scientists have begun to explore the implementation process—the actual carrying out, or administration, of policy—as one of the possible causes of the public's growing dissatisfaction with governmental performance. Adopting a policy designed to eradicate urban blight, for example, even if the policy could work, does not necessarily mean that urban blight will be eradicated if that program is poorly administered because of program design flaws or administrative incompetence.

Implementation of intergovernmental programs is particularly difficult because the programs involve multiple sets of administrators who operate in a highly charged political environment. Often, intergovernmental implementation is a political struggle because many laws are purposefully written in vague terms

---

[1]Richard Harwood, ed., *The Pursuit of the Presidency, 1980* (New York: Berkeley Books, 1980), p. 8.

in order to promote consensus within the legislative body. Vague legislation invites, and sometimes forces, administrators to interpret the law's intent. Because administrators possess varying political ideologies and concerns, conflicting interpretations of legislative intent often arise, causing confusion and delays in the implementation process. As a result, the time needed to implement many intergovernmental programs is often measured in years, not weeks or months.

The following readings are designed to introduce you to some of the major implementation concerns involving intergovernmental programs. The first reading examines the many administrative conditions—otherwise known as red tape—that state and local administrators must face, even in programs supposedly devoid of many conditions. It argues that these administrative conditions not only hinder program implementation by promoting program complexity, costs, and delays, but also raise serious accountability questions. You should be able to differentiate the various kinds of administrative conditions that are being discussed and understand why they were established. Do you think the national government should continue to use direct orders, crosscutting requirements, crossover sanctions, and partial preemptions? The second reading indicates that national bureaucrats are regularly and unjustly held responsible for programs that they do not run. It suggests that much of the growing dissatisfaction with governmental performance results from the "curious way" the national government "manages" its programs. As you read it, try to determine who or what is really at fault: Is it the implementation process, Congress, the President, or us? The third reading examines the political dynamics involved in the creation of allocation formulas for intergovernmental grants. It argues that there is often a fundamental disagreement over the objective definition of programmatic need and that this causes the distribution of intergovernmental grants to be skewed by political considerations, thereby frustrating the implementation process even before it has begun. Be certain that you understand the difference between grantsmanship and formulamanship, the vertical and horizontal views of the grants-in-aid system, and the various allocational principles employed in grants.

This part, and the book, concludes with two readings chosen from the work of two of America's leading intergovernmental scholars, Thomas Anton and Daniel Elazar. Both authors are responding to the U.S. Advisory Commission Intergovernmental Relations multivolume report, *The Federal Role in the Federal System*, which indicated that intergovernmental relations had become seriously overloaded by 1980. The report recommended a number of major reforms, including a redistribution of governmental functions, with the national government assuming responsibility for most income maintenance programs and the states and localities assuming responsibility for most of the other governmental activities. Anton examines the operation of the contemporary intergovernmental system and argues that while it does suffer from many problems, it is basically sound and responsible for many impressive achievements. Moreover, he argues that state and local governments still play an important role in governing the nation. For these and other reasons, he opposes ACIR's recommendations. Elazar, on the other hand, argues that the national government has preempted many state and local functions and has fundamentally altered the American federal system in an almost vulgar way. To restore constitutional "good sense," he also rejects ACIR's functional redistribution of responsiblities and provides six specific recommendations of his own. Who do you think is right—ACIR, Anton, or Elazar?

David R. Beam

13

WASHINGTON'S REGULATION
OF STATES
AND LOCALITIES
Origins and Issues

During most of this past decade, the major issues of intergovernmental relations revolved almost exclusively around the difficulties of managing the burgeoning system of categorical grants-in-aid. Fragmentation was the rallying cry; consolidation, under the banner of "New Federalism," was the most trumpeted response. Presidents Nixon and Ford in particular—but even their Democratic successor, Jimmy Carter—urged policy devolution through block grants as a way to reduce federal red tape and excessive national control. Despite their efforts, however, many of these same problems still remain, with some 200 new aid programs established since 1969.

All of this is, of course, well known. What is less widely recognized is that this period also was characterized by a second intergovernmental trend: the growth of new forms of intergovernmental regulation. This movement was in precisely the opposite direction—toward Washington, rather than away. While there was an effort to reduce federal leverage as exercised through the "carrot" of narrow-purpose categorical grants, there was a substantial increase in the use of the tougher and more intrusive federal regulatory "stick." Thus, the decade

Originally appeared in *Intergovernmental Perspective* 7, no. 3 (Summer 1981): 8–18. Reprinted with permission of the U.S. Advisory Commission on Intergovernmental Relations.

of the 1970s left two quite different, even contradictory, legacies. Overall, federal control did not decline. From the state and local vantage point, what one hand gave, the other took away.

REGULATION OLD AND NEW

Federal regulation, in itself, is nothing new. The national government has regulated important aspects of the behavior of business firms since the formation of the Interstate Commerce Commission in 1887. Especially during the New Deal, federal controls—typically administered by other similarly constituted independent commissions—were extended over the conditions of entry and prices charged in a variety of other fields. Examples include the Federal Trade Commission (1914), the Federal Power Commission (1930), the Federal Communications Commission (1934), the Securities and Exchange Commission (1934), the Federal Maritime Commission (1936), and the Civil Aeronautics Board (1938).

More recently, federal controls have been instituted over the nonmarket behavior of business firms as well. Among the major "new social regulatory agencies" are the Equal Employment Opportunity Commission (1964), the Environmental Protection Agency (1970), the Occupational Safety and Health Administration (1970), and the Consumer Product Safety Commission (1972).[1]

Furthermore, although most federal regulation traditionally was directed at the private sector, state and local governments have long been faced with certain kinds of constraints:

> First, they are bound by the Fourteenth Amendment to respect the rights of individuals to "due process of law" and "equal protection of the laws." Many of the major legal struggles of federalism over the past half-century have involved the extension of individual rights under the Constitution to states and localities, with the Supreme Court serving as the ultimate arbiter.
>
> Secondly, state and local governments bind themselves to certain kinds of federal regulations when they accept federal grants-in-aid. Here as elsewhere, there is no free lunch. Federal grants universally have program conditions or "strings" attached: planning requirements, administrative procedures, auditing standards, and so forth.

Although both of these regulatory forms have expanded in recent decades, the fundamental principles involved are old hat.

What is quite new, and a sharp departure from traditional practices, is the growth of a host of federal regulatory programs *aimed at* or *implemented by* state and local governments. Beginning in the mid-1960s, and more notably

---

[1]David B. Frohmayer, "Regulatory Reform: A Slogan in Search of Substance," *American Bar Association Journal* 66 (July 1980): 871–72; see also William Lilley, III and James C. Miller, III "The New 'Social Regulator'," *The Public Interest* 47 (Spring 1977): 49–61.

during the 1970s, the federal regulatory presence has spilled over from the traditional economic sphere to include the nation's states, cities, counties, school districts, colleges, and other public jurisdictions. What was quite unthinkable (and seemingly politically impossible) a few decades ago has both been thought of and come to pass.

Many of the most important of these regulatory statutes are listed in Table 13–1. Much, though not all, of the "new social regulation" falls into this intergovernmental category. Though certain programs remain wholly national responsibilities, the states and localities have been conscripted into the battles against pollution and for civil rights. In some areas, they have been charged with regulating the conduct of private business firms. In others, they have been obliged to remedy perceived shortcomings of their own.

An examination of this table will demonstrate the substantial growth of intergovernmental regulation, especially during the early 1970s. Although the initial forays occurred earlier, eighteen of these thirty regulatory statues—including nearly all of the most far-reaching ones—were adopted during 1969–75, when the "New Federalism" also was at its height. Though few stressed it at that time, this period saw a dramatic shift in the character of intergovernmental relations. Just as the mid 1960s were marked by an "explosion" of categorical grants-in-aid, the past decade was characterized by the proliferation of major new regulatory programs.

Other evidence in support of this conclusion is provided by the findings of a recent ACIR study, *The Federal Role in the Federal System: The Dynamics of Growth*. Case studies profiling the development of national policy in the fields of elementary and secondary education, higher education, and environmental protection, in particular, noted a dramatic increase in regulatory initiatives. Federal pollution policy, for example, turned from research (inaugurated in the late 1940s) to construction grants (beginning in the 1950s and expanded in the 1960s) to mandatory national standards in the 1970s. Intergovernmental tensions rose simultaneously. . . . Similar trends were noted in the other fields studied.

Thus, the character of American federalism has been substantially altered over the past decade. Although in prior years, the problems of intergovernmental relations revolved almost exclusively around federal aid—*whether* it should be provided and, if so, *how*—these regulatory programs present new issues which can no longer be ignored. Indeed, as Mel Dubnick and Alan Gitelson have commented,

> Our federal system has evolved through a number of stages, each given appropriate labels by analysis. If we were to label the current trend, perhaps it should be best described as *regulatory federalism*.[2]

---

[2]Mel Dubnick and Alan Gitelson, "Intergovernmental Relations and Regulatory Policy," paper presented at a Symposium on Regulatory Policy, Houston, TX, 19–20 November 1979, p. 30.

TABLE 13–1   Major Statutes of Intergovernmental Regulation, 1960–80

1964	Civil Rights Act (Title VI)
1965	Highway Beautification Act Water Quality Act
1967	Wholesome Meat Act
1968	Civil Rights Act (Title VIII) Architectural Barriers Act Wholesome Poultry Products Act
1969	National Environmental Policy Act
1970	Occupational Safety and Health Act Clean Air Amendments
1972	Federal Water Pollution Control Act Amendments Equal Employment Opportunity Act Education Act Amendments (Title IX) Coastal Zone Management Act
1973	Flood Disaster Protection Act Rehabilitation Act (Section 504) Endangered Species Act
1974	Safe Drinking Water Act Hazardous Materials Transportation Act National Health Planning and Resources Development Act Emergency Highway Energy Conservation Act Family Educational Rights and Privacy Act Fair Labor Standards Act Amendment
1975	Education for All Handicapped Children Act Age Discrimination Act
1976	Resource Conservation and Recovery Act
1977	Surface Mining Control and Reclamation Act
1978	National Energy Conservation Policy Act Public Utility Regulatory Policy Act Natural Gas Policy Act

Source: Advisory Commission on Intergovernmental Relations.

THE NEW KIT OF TECHNIQUES

An element of *compulsion* is one key feature of the new intergovernmental regulation that distinguishes it from the usual grant-in-aid conditions. The requirements traditionally attached to assistance programs may be viewed as part of a contractual agreement between two independent, coequal levels of government. Cooperation is sometimes said to be the motivating force. In contrast, the policies which the new intergovernmental regulation imposes on state and local governments are more nearly mandatory. They cannot be avoided, without incurring some federal sanction, by the simple expedient of refusing to participate in a single federal assistance program. In one way or another, compliance has been made difficult to avoid.

A variety of legal and fiscal techniques has been employed by the national government to encourage acceptance of its regulatory standards. Four major strategies—direct orders, crosscutting requirements, crossover sanctions, and partial preemption—are described below.

Direct Orders

In a few instances, federal regulation of state and local government takes the form of direct legal orders that must be complied with under the threat of civil or criminal penalties. For example, the *Equal Employment Opportunity Act of 1972* bars job discrimination by state and local governments on the basis of race, color, religion, sex, and national origin. This statute extended to state and local governments the requirements imposed on private employers since 1964.

For the most part, however, Washington has exempted governments from many of the kinds of direct regulatory statutes that apply to businesses and individuals. Thus, although state governments may administer the *Occupational Safety and Health Act,* they (and local governments) are exempt from its provisions in their capacity as employers. Politics often has dictated this course, but there also are some Constitutional restrictions on the ability of Congress to regulate directly. The wage and hour requirements imposed by the 1974 amendments to the *Fair Labor Standards Act* were overturned by the Supreme Court in *National League of Cities* v. *Usery* (1976).[3] The Court's ruling held that the law interfered with the "integral functions" of state and local governments, and thus threatened their "independent existence."

Much more commonly, then, Washington has utilized other regulatory techniques to work its will. These may be distinguished by their breadth of application and the nature of the sanctions which back them up.

Crosscutting Requirements

First, and most widely recognized, are the cross cutting or generally applicable requirements imposed on grants across the board to further various national social and economic policies. One of the first and most important of these requirements was the non-discrimination provision included in the Title VI of the *Civil Rights Act of 1964,* which stipulated that

> No person in the United States shall on the ground of race, color, or national origin, be excluded from participation in, be denied the benefits of, or be subjected to discrimination under any program receiving federal financial assistance.

[3]*National League of Cities* v. *Usery*, 426 U.S. 833, 1976. The Usery case was overturned on February 19, 1985 in *Garcia* v. *San Antonio.*

Since 1964, crosscutting requirements have been enacted for the protection of other disadvantaged groups (the handicapped, elderly, and—in education programs—women). The same approach was utilized in the environmental impact statement process created in 1969, and for many other environmental purposes, and has also been extended into such fields as historic preservation, animal welfare, and relocation assistance. A total of some thirty-six across-the-board requirements dealing with various socioeconomic issues, as well as an additional twenty-three administrative and fiscal policy requirements, were identified in a recent OMB inventory.[4] Of the former group, the largest number involve some aspect of environmental protection (16) and nondiscrimination (9). Two-thirds of the fifty-nine requirements were adopted since 1969.

Crosscutting requirements have a pervasive impact because they apply "horizontally" to all or most federal agencies and their assistance programs. In contrast, two other new forms of intergovernmental regulation are directed at only a single function, department, or program. These are sometimes referred to as "vertical" mandates.[5]

Crossover Sanctions

One approach relies upon the power of the purse. It imposes federal fiscal sanctions in one program area or activity to influence state and local policy in another. The distinguishing feature here is that a failure to comply with the requirements of one program can result in a reduction or termination of funds from another separately authorized program. The penalty then "crosses over."

The history of federal efforts to secure the removal of billboards from along the nation's major highways illustrates the use of the traditional financial "carrot" along with this new financial "stick"[6] Beginning in 1958, the federal government offered a small bonus in the form of additional highway funds to states that agreed to regulate billboard advertising along new interstate highways. By 1965, however, only half of the states had taken advantage of this offer—not enough to suit the Johnson White House.

A dramatic change occurred with the adoption of the *Highway Beautification Act of 1965*. The bonus system was dropped, and Congress substituted the threat of withholding 10 percent of a state's highway construction funds if it did not comply with newly expanded federal billboard control requirements. Despite the bitter opposition of the outdoor advertising industry, thirty-two states had

---

[4]Office of Management and Budget; *Managing Federal Assistance in the 1980s, Working Papers*, Volume 1 (Washington, DC: U.S. Government Printing Office, 1980).

[5]Catherine H. Lovell, et. al., *Federal and State Mandating on Local Governments: An Exploration of Issues and Impacts* (Riverside, CA: Graduate School of Administration, University of California–Riverside, 1979), p. 35.

[6]Roger A. Cunningham, "Billboard Control under the Highway Beautification Act of 1965," *Michigan Law Review*, 71 (July 1973): 1295–1374.

enacted billboard control laws by 1970, though only eighteen of these were judged to be in full compliance. Nearly all of the rest fell quickly into line when Congress made appropriations to compensate partially for the cost of removing nonconforming signs, and the Federal Highway Administrator stepped up his pressure on them.

A similar strategy has been employed since in a number of other programs. In the wake of the OPEC oil embargo, federal officials urged the states to lower their speed limits, and the Senate adopted a resolution to that effect. Twenty-nine states responded to this effort at "moral suasion." But these pleas were quickly replaced by a more authoritative measure: the *Emergency Highway Energy Conservation Act of 1974* prohibited the Secretary of Transportation from approving any highway construction projects in states having a speed limit in excess of 55 mph. All fifty states responded within two months.

Partial Preemption

These fiscal sanctions, as well as the crosscutting requirements, are both tied directly to the grant-in-aid system. Federal power in these cases derives from the Constitutional authority to spend for the general welfare. A final innovative technique has another basis entirely. It rests upon the authority of the federal government to preempt certain state and local activities under the Supremacy Clause and the Commerce power.

This is preemption with a twist, however. Unlike traditional preemption statutes, preemption in these cases is only *partial*. While federal laws establish basic policies, administrative responsibility may be delegated to the states or localities, provided that they meet certain nationally determined standards.

James B. Croy offers the *Water Quality Act of 1965* as an initial example of this strategy, which he terms the "if–then, if–then" approach. The statute was the first to establish a national policy for controlling pollution. While the law allowed each state one year to set standards for its own interstate waters, the Secretary of Health, Education, and Welfare was authorized to enforce federal standards in any state which failed to do so. That is, in Croy's words,

> if a state does issue regulations acceptable to the U.S., *then* a federal agency or department will do so, and if the state does not adopt and enforce these regulations, *then* the federal level of government will assume jurisdiction over that area.[7]

This same technique—which others have called the "substitution approach" to federalism[8] —has since been extended to a variety of other areas. For example,

---

[7]James B. Croy, "Federal Supersession: The Road to Domination," *State Government* 48 (Winter 1975): 34. Emphasis added.

[8]Frank J. Thompson, *Health Policy and the Bureaucracy: Politics and Administration* (Cambridge, MA: MIT Press, 1981), p. 240.

the OSHA law asserts national control over workplace health and safety but permits states to operate their own programs if their standards are "at least as effective"as the federal ones.

The most far-reaching application, however, is in the *Clean Air Act of 1970*. This path-breaking environmental statute set national air quality standards throughout the nation, but requires that the states devise effective plans for their implementation and enforcement. The compass is great: EPA can, for example, require that states change their own transportation policies (perhaps by giving additional support to mass transit), or that they regulate private individuals (as in establishing emission-control requirements and inspection programs for automobiles). . . .[9]

These four techniques—direct legal order, crosscutting requirements, crossover sanctions, and partial preemption—are the major new statutory tools in the federal government's kit for intergovernmental regulation. Separately and together, they pose important new problems of policy, law, administration, and finance.

ISSUES AND IMPACTS

Especially in the past two years, the growing federal regulatory presence has become a major source of concern of intergovernmental policymakers. State and local officials, in particular, have sounded the alarm against costly federal mandates and unreasonable federal intervention into local affairs. Even erstwhile liberals have objected to the fiscal strains and policy controls imposed on hard-pressed cities and states, while conservatives—who had always warned that federal controls would follow federal dollars—seem to have been proven right.

A *New York Times* editorial, "Fighting Federal Mandates," observed that

> Local governments are feeling put upon by Washington. Each new day seems to bring some new directive from Congress, the courts, or the bureaucrats: cities must make public buildings accessible to the handicapped, states must extend unemployment compensation to municipal and county workers, and on and on. The mandates are piling up so fast that liberal governors and mayors are enrolling in a cause once pressed only by arch-conservatives.[10]

Mayors and county officials—responding to the double-whammy of federal as well as state mandates[11]—have been especially vocal, and the major research

[9]Congressional Budget Office, *Federal Constraints on State and Local Government Actions* (Washington, DC: U.S. Government Printing Office, 1979), p. 7.

[10]"Fighting Federal Mandates," *New York Times*, 16 August 1980, p. 20.

[11]Advisory Commission on Intergovernmental Relations, *State Mandating of Local Expenditures* (Washington, D.C.: U.S. Government Printing Office, 1978).

studies to date all have examined the impact of federal regulations on the nation's cities and counties. . . . City officials responding to a recent survey identified federal wastewater treatment, environmental impact, handicapped access, and safe drinking water regulations as especially burdensome and most urgently in need of modification (See Table 13–2). Reforms also were called for in a great variety of other areas.[12] That county officials share these perspectives is suggested by the fact that the National Association of Counties selected "Controlling Mandates" as the theme for its 1981 annual conference. A joint statement issued last November by the executive committees of the National Governors' Association and the National Conference of State Legislatures pushed for the enactment of fiscal note procedures as a first step in controlling federal mandates, and also contended that

> if a situation is of such compelling national concern as to prompt enactment of a federal program to respond to it, the federal government should normally fund that program.[13]

National officials, too, have been disturbed by the rising tide of regulatory efforts. Joseph A. Califano, an HEW Secretary during the Carter years, recalls that "Our big trouble wasn't with the old Great Society programs. It was with the explosion of regulation from the 1970s."[14] And the view of many in the Reagan Administration has been aptly summarized by Murray L. Weidenbaum, the chairman of the Council of Economic Advisers and a noted expert in the regulatory field. "In the past decade," Weidenbaum has written,

> we have seen a boom in social regulation with devastating consequences for the federal system. The federal government, through many of its regulatory actions, has reduced the autonomy of state and local governments and centralized the responsibility for many important programs. This loss of autonomy has weakened the states and reduced their independence, while the centralization of responsibilities better handled at the state and local levels has limited the effectiveness of the federal government.[15]

Seven Problems

Although particular problems vary from program to program, critics have leveled at least seven frequent charges against federal intergovernmental regula-

---

[12]Clint Page, "NLC Surveys Members on Federal Rules," *Nation's Cities Weekly*, 6 April 1981, p. 1.

[13]"Statement on Federalism Reform Adopted by the Executive Committees of the National Conference of State Legislatures and the National Governors' Association," *State Legislatures*, February 1981, p. 7.

[14]Suzanne Garment, "Califano's Memoir: Washington before the 1980 Flood," *The Wall Street Journal*, 29 May 1981, p. 24.

[15]Murray L. Weidenbaum, "Let States Decide How to Muffle Garbage Trucks," *Washington Star*, 6 May 1981, p. A14.

TABLE 13–2   **How City Officials View U.S. Regulatory Programs**
Question: **How important is it that the Administration act to alleviate the burdens caused by present federal regulations or requirements on the following subjects?"**

	PERCENT SAYING URGENT OR IMPORTANT
Wastewater Treatment	86%
Environmental Impact Review	80%
Accessibility for the Handicapped	77%
Safe Drinking Water	74%
Air Pollution Control	70%
Occupational Safety and Health	68%
Prevailing Wages	68%
Nondiscrimination or Affirmative Action	64%
Public Education for Special Groups	58%
Flood Disaster Protection	56%
Historic Preservation	56%
Uniform Relocation Assistance	49%

Source: Based upon Clint Page, "NLC Surveys Members on Federal Rules," *Nations's Cities Weekly*, 6 April 1981, p. 10.

tions singly and as a whole. The new mandates, they believe, are too often *expensive, inflexible, inefficient, inconsistent, intrusive, ineffective,* and *unaccountable.* Each of these interrelated concerns is illustrated, with a single example, in the discussion below.

Cost.   Given the fiscal pinch caused by an unstable economy, the federal aid slowdown, and taxpayer revolts, it is not surprising that the costs imposed by federal mandates have been a major, perhaps even preeminent, concern. Simply put, state and local government officials object to footing part of—or, in some cases, most of—the bill for someone else's program. What Washington wants done, many believe, Washington also should be willing to pay for.

Accurate information on the total cost of implementing federal mandates nationwide simply is not available. However, of the five major programs examined in an Urban Institute report, the *1977 Clean Water Act* imposed by far the largest fiscal costs on seven cities and counties studied.[16] This act, which supplemented and modified the far-reaching *Water Pollution Control Act Amendments of 1972,* requires the development and implementation of wastewater treatment management plans which meet pollution discharge standards set by

[16]Thomas Muller and Michael Fix, "The Impact of Selected Federal Actions on Municipal Outlays," in U.S. Congress. Joint Economic Committee, *Special Study on Economic Change*, Vol. 5. *Government Regulation: Achieving Social and Economic Balance*, 96th Cong., 2nd Sess., 8 December 1980, p. 327.

the Environmental Protection Agency for 1983. While the act also authorized a very large construction grant program covering 75 to 85% of construction and conversion costs, the balance is borne by local (and, in some instances, state) governments. No aid is provided for operating and maintenance expenses.

According to the Urban Institute report, the cost of meeting these requirements ranged from zero in Burlington, VT—where a new plant already was under construction to meet state standards—to $51.8 million in capital outlays, plus an additional $10.4 million in operating expenses, in Newark, NJ. Here, as in many other states, a portion of this cost is borne by the state government. However, local outlays totalled $62.54 per capita for capital improvements and $31.42 per capita for operating expenses.[17]

As this example shows, the costs of implementing federal regulatory programs can vary widely from place to place. But nationwide, according to EPA estimates, cities will have to spend nearly $120 billion to build additional wastewater treatment plants to comply with the *1983 Clean Water Act* standards.[18] Even then, it is not certain that the objectives of the program will be realized. GAO audits have concluded that, as a result of design and operating deficiencies, many of the plants built so far are unable to meet national performance standards. These failures, according to the GAO, "may represent the potential waste of tens of millions of dollars in federal, state, and local moneys.[19]

Inflexibility.   Closely following cost as a concern of state and local officials are problems of inflexibility in federal regulatory programs. Washington, they believe, has neglected the old adage, "there's more than one way to skin a cat." Instead, federal officials too often have prescribed rigid policies and performance standards, regardless of the varying circumstances in which they are to be applied.

Perhaps no area better illustrates state and local concerns about federal inflexibility than the bilingual education regulations proposed by the Carter Adminstration and withdrawn by the Reagan Administration early in 1981. Although Washington has encouraged bilingual education with federal aid for over a decade, a strong regulatory role dates from the 1974 decision of the Supreme Court in *Lau* v. *Nichols*. Responding to a complaint of some Chinese-American parents in San Francisco, the Court held that the *Civil Rights Act of 1964* prohibited school districts from taking a "sink or swim" approach to the education of non-English speaking students.

The Court instructed HEW to develop appropriate regulations, but specified no particular approach. Indeed, the decision states that, "Teaching English to

[17]Ibid., p. 335.

[18]U.S. Environmental Protection Agency, *1980 Needs Survey: Cost Estimates for Construction of Publicly Owned Wastewater Treatment Facilities* (Washington, DC: U.S. Government Printing Office, 1971), p. 4.

[19]Comptroller General of the United States, *Costly Wastewater Treatment Plants Fail to Perform As Expected* (Washington, DC: U.S. General Accounting Office, 1980).

the student of Chinese ancestry is one choice. Giving instruction to this group in Chinese is another. There may be others.'' However, the regulations drafted by the Department of Education required that students with limited proficiency in English be offered subject-matter courses in their native language wherever there were twenty-five or more students in two consecutive grades. Alternative approaches, including ''English as a Second Language'' (ESL) instruction, were generally precluded. A failure to conform to national standards could result in a cutoff of education aid.

The proposed regulations were greeted with vociferous opposition from many state, local, and education groups. Many of these critics supported the use of bilingual education in certain areas—for example, in innercity or southwestern school districts with large Spanish-speaking populations. And cost was not the major issue, because most schools already provided special instruction for their non-English speaking students.[20] What was objectionable was the federal stipulation of a particular instructional technique, to the exclusion of others, in areas where it might well be inappropriate. Where, they asked, can a city find qualified subject matter teachers fluent in Vietnamese or Ilokano (a language of the Phillippines)?[21] Why should Fairfax County, VA, not be allowed to continue its program of special instruction in English for its students of more than 50 different foreign language backgrounds?

To many state and local officials, there was no satisfactory answer. A statement prepared by the National Governors' Association, the National Conference of State Legislatures, the Council of Chief State School Officers, and the National Association of State Boards of Education charged that ''a national prescription of a single approach to instruction to the exclusion of other alternative methods is educationally without merit and would be a disservice to many children who can benefit more from other methods of instruction.''[22]

Inefficiency.   Efficiency is a matter of bang for the buck. To be ''efficient'' in economic terms, the benefits from a program should exceed its costs. Furthermore, the efficiency criterion dictates that a choice between two or more equally effective means should be decided in favor of the least expensive one.

Too often, critics believe, Washington has ignored these obvious prescriptions. The benefits of regulations have been poorly specified, while the likely costs to be imposed have sometimes been wholly ignored. Federal officials have locked onto very costly techniques or standards as the one-and-only way to meet national goals, even when more economical approaches were available.

---

[20]Rochelle L. Stanfield, ''Are the Federal Bilingual Rules a Foot in the Schoolhouse Door,'' *National Journal*, 18 October 1980, p. 1736.

[21]Ibid., p. 1739.

[22]State-Based Groups Urge Congressional Hearings on Bilingual Education Rules,'' *Governor's Bulletin*, 31 November 1980.

Perhaps no regulatory policy has come under as much criticism on efficiency grounds as the Department of Transportation's regulations written to carry out Section 504 of the *Rehabilitation Act*. This crosscutting requirement, intended to bar discrimination against the handicapped, has been interpreted by DOT to require full access to existing transit systems, while prohibiting the use of much cheaper and more flexible paratransit alternatives.

This decision was a costly one and was greeted with protests from transit officials around the nation. Chicago's hardpressed Regional Transit Authority claimed that retrofitting its system would cost more than all the capital invested in it since 1890, while the shaky New York Metropolitan Transportation Authority spoke of the dangers of bankruptcy.[23] An independent study by the Congressional Budget Office also has warned of inefficiency. It noted that the rules

> require transit systems to equip buses with lifts for wheelchairs, to install elevators in many underground and aboveground rail stations, and to modify rail cars to accommodate the wheelchairs. While the program would be very expensive—$6.8 billion over the next thirty years—relatively few handicapped persons would benefit from it.[24]

The CBO study estimated that the cost of providing full wheelchair access to mass transportation would average about $38 per trip.[25] It indicated that alternative approaches—such as special taxi service or helping the severely disabled to purchase and equip their own cars—could serve many more handicapped persons at lower cost.

Inconsistency.   The problem of inconsistency is a special curse of the crosscutting requirements. While most of these stem from a single statutory enactment, the requirements are interpreted and enforced by each grant-awarding agency, usually with some guidance from a designated "lead agency." As a result, there may be significant differences in the manner in which federal requirements are applied in particular programs. An OMB study noted:

> In too many cases, a single generally applicable requirement has been implemented differently for several assistance programs. The result is that a recipient of several agencies may receive inconsistent or conflicting instructions for meeting a single requirement. . . .[26]

---

[23]Timothy B. Clark, "Regulation Gone Amok: How Many Billions for Wheelchair Transit?" *Regulation* (March/April 1980), p. 49.

[24]Congressional Budget Office, *Urban Transportation or Handicapped Persons: Alternative Federal Approaches* (Washington, DC: U.S. Government Printing Office, 1979), p. xi.

[25]Ibid., p. xii.

[26]Office of Management and Budget, "Proposed Circular on Managing Generally Applicable Requirements for Assistance Programs," *Federal Register*, 7 November 1980, p. 74416.

Questions of policy and administrative coordination have been an important issue in the drive to eliminate discrimination against blacks, ethnic minorities, the elderly, women, and the handicapped. Individual agencies have followed different patterns in the interpretation of such across-the-board requirements as Title VI of the *Civil Rights Act* and Section 504 of the *Rehabilitation Act*. Furthermore, in addition to the series of nine crosscutting requirements in this field, separate civil rights protections have been written into many particular programs, including General Revenue Sharing and the *Housing and Community Development Act*. As a consequence, state and local officials have been faced with a confusing array of sometimes conflicting goals, standards, procedures, and timetables. . . .

Intrusiveness. It is one thing, of course, for the national government to tell state and local governments *what* they must do. That, very often, has been objectionable enough. But it is yet another thing to tell them not only what they must do but exactly *how* they should do it. Many intergovernmental regulatory programs do in fact carry with them rather detailed organizational and procedural standards. At times, state and local officials believe, Washington has intruded into areas that, by tradition and even the Constitution, are their own business.

The *National Health Planning and Resources Development Act of 1974* (P.L. 93-641) is a case in point. This act both created a new health planning and regulatory network at the state and local levels and prescribed, in great detail, that network's structure and functions. Born out of Washington's concern with the inflationary impact of rising health care costs, P.L. 93-641 required in each state the designation of a State Health Planning and Development Agency (SHPDA), the delineation of local health service areas, and the formation in each area of a consumer-and-provider controlled Health Systems Agency (HSA).

Most importantly, every state also was required to enact certificate-of-need (CON) legislation meeting minimum federal standards. These CON programs set up a review process whereby the SHPDA must approve all major capital development projects undertaken by health care facilities. Moreover, states were empowered to periodically review the "apropriateness" of institutional health services. The HSAs are authorized to review and approve or disapprove a variety of federal health funds coming into their areas.

This highly prescriptive and extremely detailed statute also was backed by an unusually harsh fiscal sanction. A state's failure to comply jeopardizes its entitlement, not just to the planning funds made available under the act, but to a variety of programs for public health services, community mental health, and alcohol abuse as well. For these reasons, attorney Thomas J. Madden has declared that "the *Health Planning Act* intrudes upon state and local operations to a greater degree than almost any other grant program."[27]

[27]Thomas J. Madden, "The Law of Federal Grants," in Advisory Commission on Intergovernmental Relations, *Awakening the Slumbering Giant: Intergovernmental Relations and Federal Grant Law*, (Washington, DC: U.S. Government Printing Office, 1980), p. 17.

State and local opposition to some provisions of the *Health Planning Act* resulted in a series of political and legal confrontations, including arguments that the law is unconstitutional. The State of North Carolina protested that it was being forced to regulate the actions of private health care institutions—contrary to its own state constitution—or forego participation in some forty-two federal assistance programs. This, it believed, represented unlawful coercion and was a violation of basic states' rights protected by the Tenth Amendment. Similarly, Montgomery County, MD, challenged the provisions that allow local HSA's to make decisions which cannot be overruled by local county governments.

Neither case was successful, however. In *North Carolina* v. *Califano* (1978), the U.S. Supreme Court upheld the act as a valid exercise of the spending power, and a U.S. District Court reached the same conclusion in *Montgomery County, Maryland* v. *Califano* (1979). Both regarded the law as essentially a "cooperative venture" between governments, offering inducements for state action, but not coercing it.

Ineffective.   As the foregoing suggests, state and local officials have raised a variety of objections to the federal regulations which have been imposed upon them. But another sort of concern has been voiced chiefly by others. These critics doubt that the mounting paperwork and red tape, the mandated expenditures, and the federal intrusions into local decision making have reaped commensurate benefits in the quality of human life.

Many policy analysts—particularly, many economists—believe that regulatory programs have been rather ineffective in achieving social and environmental objectives, and argue that alternative implementation strategies might prove more successful.[28] Members of the intended beneficiary groups, on the other hand, frequently protest that Washington has failed to follow through adequately on the committments enshrined in law. For different reasons, both sets of critics argue that in practice, intergovernmental regulatory programs have not worked very well.

The Occupational Safety and Health Act (OSHA) would be high on many people's list as an example of an ineffective regulatory program. Launched with high hopes—one sponsor expected a 50% reduction in job-related accidents by 1980—OSHA has instead become a symbol of bureaucratic red tape and bumbling. Its thousands of detailed regulations and standards have in fact done little to improve working conditions. . . .[29]

Unaccountability.   A final problem posed by intergovernmental regulation relates to the democratic process itself. "Who is responsible?" is the basic question. "Not me" often is the official reply.

---

[28]Charles L. Schultz, *The Public Use of Private Interest* (Washington, DC: Brookings Institution, 1977).

[29]Richard Zeckhauser and Albert Nichols, "The Occupational Safety and Health Administration—An Overview," in U.S. Congress, Senate, *Study on Federal Regulation: Appendix to Volume VI: Framework for Regulation*, 95th Cong., 2nd Sess., December 1978, p. 165.

To many critics, regulatory policies seem to bring out the worst in both federal legislators and bureaucrats. It is too easy for them to consider only the broad objectives of a program and ignore operational realities. It is simpler to frame standards to fit the few worst cases, but neglect the impact upon other jurisdictions. And it is tempting to forget about the costs of achieving national goals when the money being spent must be raised by a lower level of government, rather than Washington itself.

Furthermore, the complex chain of events from enactment, to administrative interpretation, to adjudication, through final implementation at the state and local level (or both) diffuses policy responsibility. In one too-common scenario, Congressmen blame bureaucrats for overzealous interpretations of legislative intent; bureaucrats blame Congress for either overspecificity or a lack of adequate guidance; state and local officials charge that their hands are tied by national requirements, and Washington points a finger at them for improper performance. Everyone, as often as not, blames the courts, while judges reply that they were only reading the law.

The problems of accountability in regulatory programs are aptly illustrated by the *Clean Air Act*. The joint federal–state system employed to establish and enforce air quality standards means that most voters find it difficult to know whom to blame for unpopular or unsuccessful policies. In this and similar programs, according to Joseph F. Zimmerman,

> the relationship between the levels of government has become so complex and intertwined. . . that the average citizen is unable to comprehend the system or to determine who is responsible for failure to achieve goals. The lack of citizen understanding and the failure of the system to achieve Congressionally mandated goals suggests that consideration should be given to the relative advantages of alternative methods of achieving national goals.[30]

Reauthorization of the 185-page *Clean Air* legislation promises to be "as complicated as rewriting part of the Talmud" since "major policies are hidden in small phrases, subordinate clauses and fine print. . . "[31] Because of the intricacy of the issues involved, it is likely that neither the nation's citizens nor most of its legislators will play an effective role in the deliberations:

> "It's the kind of thing where a Congressman is going to say to the staff guy, 'Just tell me how to vote,' and the third-level bureaucrat is the one who's going to get the pressure because the agency administrator will have to take his word for it."

[30]Joseph F. Zimmerman, "Frustrating National Policy: Partial Federal Preemption," in Hanus, ed., p. 98.

[31]Johanne Omang, "The Clean Air Act: Straightening Out a Regulatory Maze," *The Washington Post*, 22 February 1981, p. A28.

said a former Senate staff worker. Only the few who care very much will be involved in the decisions.[32]

CONCLUSION

The substantial growth of intergovernmental regulations during the 1970s has brought to the fore a whole new set of complex, difficult, and controversial policy issues. As this review shows, state and local officials object to mandated federal costs and protest the inflexibility, inefficiency, inconsistency, and intrusiveness of new forms of federal regulation. Other critics wonder if the new regulatory programs are very effective in accomplishing their objectives, and whether national policies accurately reflect the views and preferences of the voting public and its elected representatives.

Because of this development, the battle to strengthen American federalism must now be fought on two fronts simultaneously. Grant consolidation cannot fully accomplish its objective of devolution unless the burden of intergovernmental regulation is reduced simultaneously. Recent and projected declines in the level of federal aid make reforms aimed at increased efficiency and flexibility in meeting federal, state, and local priorities all the more urgent. . . .

[32]Ibid.

Lester M. Salamon

14

RISE OF THIRD PARTY GOVERNMENT

The *Post's* recent series . . .on federal research contracting deals with a single, if revealing, part of a larger transformation that has taken place in the federal enterprise. This transformation involves a fundamental change in the way the federal government carries out its business, a change that has been under way for more than a generation but that is still only dimly perceived.

The heart of this change is a shift from direct to indirect or "third-party" government, from an arrangement in which the federal government ran its own programs to one in which it relies primarily on others—states, cities, special districts, banks, nonprofit corporations, hospitals, manufacturers and others—to carry out its purposes instead.

To be sure, press accounts still speak of this or that "federal program." But those who work in the federal bureaucracy know that these are merely euphemisms behind which lies a cruel reality in which federal officials are regularly held responsible for programs they do not really run.

Few federal bureaucrats have been the object of more derision, for example, than those responsible for the "the federal welfare program." In point of fact,

Revised version, originally appeared in *The Washington Post*, 29 June 1980, page C7. Reprinted with the permission of *The Washington Post*.

however, no such entity exists. This "federal" program is really fifty, or 3,000, different programs run by state and local officials who use federal funds but who have the discretion to make their own decision about who is eligible for assistance, over what period of time, under what conditions and at what level of benefits. . . .

In area after area, the same pattern holds. Indeed, third-party government now dominates the federal domestic-program landscape, though this has yet to be fully appreciated, let alone carefully analyzed and assessed.

What is involved here is not simply the contracting out of well-defined functions or the purchase of specified goods and services from outside suppliers. The distinctive feature of "third-party government" is that what is being delegated and shared is a far more basic governmental function—the exercise of discretion over the spending of federal funds and the use of public authority.

The central reality of most federal programs today is that the lion's share of discretionary authority is vested not in federal officials, but in one or another of a wide array of nonfederal implementers.

The classic vehicle for this third-party government is the grant-in-aid, through which federal resources are put at the disposal of state and local officials to assist them in carrying out a federal goal.

From its meager beginnings in the nineteenth century, the grant-in-aid device has mushroomed into a massive system of intergovernmental action. More than 400 separate grant-in-aid programs are now on the books, providing aid for everything from emergency medical services to the construction of interstate highways. Since 1955 alone, grant-in-aid funding has grown thirty fold, more than twice as fast as the budget as a whole. Since 1980, almost half of all federal grants-in-aid outlays for domestic purposes, aside from Social Security and other direct payments to individuals, have gone out in the form of grants-in-aid to nonfederal government or quasi-governmental entities.

But grants-in-aid have now been joined by a host of other ingenious devices for sharing federal authority with nonfederal actors—credit insurance, loan guarantees, tax incentives, regulations and new forms of contracting and procurement. Here as well, federal officials retain responsibility but are required to surrender much of the operational authority.

In loan guarantee programs, for example, the key decisions are made by private bankers, who process the loan applications and extend the credit that the federal government then guarantees. In the procurement of major military systems, the federal government increasingly depends on contractors not just to provide specified pieces of equipment, but to conceive and design whole weapons systems of enormous complexity.

Since they do not show up in federal budget totals, many of these latter forms of third-party government have gone largely unnoticed. Yet their scale is tremendous. In fiscal year 1983, for example, the federal government assumed over $138 billion in new loan or loan guarantee commitments and provided over

$200 billion in special tax incentives, and exacted regulatory costs exceeding $60 billion—in all a hidden budget in excess of $400 billion.

This curious pattern of third-party government is a natural byproduct of political pressures and of the love–hate relationship Americans have long had with the federal government.

The grant-in-aid device came of age during the New Deal as a political response to the conservative argument that New Deal programs violated states' rights. Since then, cutting key user groups into a piece of the action has been a standard prerequisite for gaining their support for federal undertakings. The third-party approach has also been dictated by federal personnel ceilings and budget pressures, which have clamped a lid on federal employment despite often dramatic expansions of federal programs and responsibilities.

The advantages of this approach, moreover, have been substantial. Through it, the federal government has been able to tap the talents and resources of a wide assortment of different institutions and sectors, to adapt national programs to local circumstances and to limit the growth of the federal bureaucracy. Thanks to the emergence of a third-party government over the past 30 years, it has been possible to hold the federal work force to a growth rate of only 50 percent, while the federal budget increased in real terms by 300 percent and the number of federal programs increased thirty or forty fold.

But these advantages are purchased at significant cost, for third-party government brings with it immense problems of management, major impediments to coordination, and profound issues of accountability arising from the fact that those who now exercise federal authority are not responsible to the Congress that authorizes the programs.

Whether these problems can be overcome remains to be seen. The first step, however, is to educate the nation about how the federal enterprise actually operates. While exposès that poke fun at the madcap behavior that sometimes results from this brave new world of third-party government can help, there is a danger that the resulting bemusement or cynicism will deflect attention from the underlying cause and add to the problem rather than to the cure.

For, if the argument here is correct, much of the problem results not from the malfeasance or incompetence of federal bureaucrats, but from the curious way we have required them to operate. No amount of preachment about better management or tighter controls can afford to overlook this central fact.

Robert Jay Dilger

15

GRANTSMANSHIP, FORMULAMANSHIP, AND OTHER ALLOCATIONAL PRINCIPLES
Wastewater Treatment Grants

In order to study the intergovernmental grant system in an orderly manner, researchers have identified three grant mechanisms (categorical, block and general revenue sharing) which are differentiated according to the range of activities eligible for funding and the degree of federal versus state/local control over administration of the program. Of the three grant types, categorical grants can only be used for a specific stipulated activity and provide the greatest degree of federal control over the use of the funds; block grants offer recipients a number of eligible activities to choose from and tend to carry fewer administrative restrictions than categorical grants, and general revenue sharing provides recipients the widest scope of permitted activities and the least federally mandated administrative restrictions.[1]

It is usually not very difficult to guess which of the grant types a particular individual considers best, provided one knows whether or not the individual believes state and local officials can be trusted to spend federal money wisely.[2]

Originally appeared in the *Journal of Urban Affairs* 5, no. 4 (Fall 1983): 269–86. Reprinted with permission.

[1] Advisory Commission on Intergovernmental Relations, *Categorical Grants: Their Role and Design* (Washington, DC: U.S. Government Printing Office, 1978), pp. 5–9.

[2] Daniel J. Elazar, "The New Federalism: Can the States Be Trusted?" *The Public Interest* (Spring 1974), pp. 89–102.

Liberals tend not to trust state and local officials (primarily due to past experience on racial and environmental questions), while conservatives do trust state and local officials (or at least distrust them less than federal officials). Wisdom, of course, is a relative term employed here and by practitioners generally as referring to which actor is more likely to allocate more resources in my or my friends' direction. Many clientele interest groups, for example, view grant consolidation as a threat to their program and actively lobby to retain their program's individual identity and budget. These groups (many of them oriented towards programs helping the poor and minorities) worry that state and local officials (many of whom are white and viewed as being oriented towards programs helping more prosperous constituencies) would prove to be less sympathetic to their interests than federal bureaucrats. Federal bureaucrats, of course, oppose any dilution of their control over project categorical grant expenditures. Given the large amount of money involved, . . . it is not surprising that conservatives Richard Nixon and Ronald Reagan made the question of grant type a central part of their respective domestic programs. Both argued for greater reliance on state and local governments by providing greater recipient choice through grant consolidation, reducing federally mandated *red tape* through regulatory reform, and eliminating federal bureaucratic control over allocation decisions by using allotment formulas.

Although political scientists seem to disagree as much as politicians as to which grant type is best, they have contributed to the argument by indicating that some block grants have created red tape jungles of their own.[3] And while the debate raged over which grant type was best, the growth of intergovernmental regulations have added federal requirements and red tape to general revenue sharing as well as block grants.[4]

The argument over which of the three grants is best has primarily been waged in terms of the grant's effect upon the vertical relationship between the federal and subnational governments rather than the grant's effect upon the horizontal relationship among subnational governments. This is largely due to the readily identifiable differences among the grant mechanisms on the vertical relationship. One of the most damaging arguments against the project-categorical grant approach, however, is that project grants allocate their funds among subnational governments according to grantsmanship rather than need. Larger cities with larger budgets and more skilled grant seeking staffs clearly enjoy an advantage over smaller communities or those less adept at the art when it comes to the project grant application process.[5] Since most block grant and all general revenue sharing funds are allocated by formula, they are freed of the grantsmanship defect and may be preferred over project grants on equity grounds.

[3] Advisory Commission on Intergovernmental Relations, *Categorical Grants*, p. 40.

[4] David Beam, "Washington's Regulation of States and Localities, Origins and Issues," *Intergovernmental Perspective* (Summer 1981), pp. 8–18.

[5] Deil S. Wright, *Understanding Intergovernmental Relations* (North Scituate, MA: Duxbury Press, 1978), pp. 77–84

It is at this point that the argument over which grant mechanism is best either ends (formula-based grants being victorious) or the concern over the trustfulness of state and local officials surfaces. What is not questioned is whether the formulas used to allocate some categorical, most block and all general revenue sharing funds are inherently biased by means other than grantsmanship. This article will examine how political forces shape the creation of allocation formulas. It will be argued that while formula based grants are immune from the defects of grantsmanship, they are subject to formulamanship—the creation of formulas utilizing political fair share instead of program need as the major allocational principle.[6]

FOUR ALLOCATIONAL PRINCIPLES

There are four general allocational principles employed in grants-in-aid formulas: fair share (or political equity); the need for services based on objective criteria of need; the actual level of services or cost; and fiscal capacity (or financial need).[7] Each approach maximizes certain values: fairness, need, effort, and equalization. Liberals advocate the use of program need and fiscal capacity in allotment formulas because they equalize (by redistributing wealth among communities) what liberals view as an unacceptable imbalance in the needs and resources among subnational governments. Conservatives, on the other hand, want to identify and reward community self-determination, are less concerned with equalization as a goal, and, therefore, prefer to reward community effort by employing the cost criterion in allotment formulas.[8]

Given these ideological differences, the creation of allotment formulas are, as one would expect, a highly politicized matter. What is surprising is that none of the three allocational principles advocated by conservatives and liberals are used in allotment formulas as much as the fair share principle. The most common factor of need employed in formulas in 1975, for example, was population.[9] Population tends to equalize benefits among recipient governments because every congressional district is guaranteed a share of the funds regardless of recipient need, cost, or fiscal capacity. It has been argued that the formulas for general revenue sharing and most block grants rely heavily upon population as a criterion of need because these programs support a broad range of services that no single measure of need can reflect adequately.[10] Many formula-based categorical grants,

---

[6]I would like to thank Christopher Leman for suggesting the use of the term formulamanship.

[7]Advisory Commission on Intergovernmental Relations, *Categorical Grants*, p. 199.

[8]Samuel Beer, "The Adoption of General Revenue Sharing: A Case Study in Public Sector Politics," *Public Policy* 24 (Spring 1976): 132–49.

[9]Advisory Commission on Intergovernmental Relations, *Categorical Grants*, p. 101.

[10]Ibid.

however, also employ population as a major factor in their allocation formulas, suggesting that it is not the range of services, but the politics of the formula creation process which accounts for the use of the fair share principle. Another device, particularly popular in the Senate, for insuring a *fair share* distribution is to guarantee each state a minimum entitlement. Sixty percent of all formulas in 1975 had a minimum entitlement.

In order to determine if political fair share was still being employed as a major factor in formulas, I examined the formulas of the six largest grant-in-aid programs using formulas in fiscal 1980: Highway Research, Planning and Construction ($8.4 billion); Comprehensive Employment and Training ($8.2 billion); General Revenue Sharing ($6.8 billion); Wastewater Treatment Construction Grants ($3.6 billion); Community Development Block Grants ($2.7 billion); and Grants for Educationally Deprived Children ($2.6 billion). Collectively, these six programs accounted for over $32 billion, more than one-third of the total for all intergovernment grant funding and approximately one half of formula-based grant funding in fiscal 1980. Four of these six programs used population as a criterion of need: Highway Research, Planning and Construction; General Revenue Sharing; Wastewater Treatment Construction Grants; and Community Development Block Grants. Four of the six used either minimum or maximum allocations or hold harmless clauses (which guarantee recipients a given percentage of its previous allotment after a formula change) in order to more broadly distribute their funds: Comprehensive Employment and Training, General Revenue Sharing, Wastewater Treatment Construction Grants, and Grants for Educationally Deprived Children. Obviously, the political fair share principle is not only still widely employed in allotment formulas but is used in the largest intergovernmental programs as well.

In order to determine why the fair share principle is used as much as it is, the Wastewater Treatment Construction Grants program was selected for intensive study. This particular program was chosen because: (1) it is one of the largest formula grants programs; (2) the program was, conveniently, working its way through congress as I began this project; and, most importantly (3) the program is a formula-based categorical grant. Studies of the formulas of general revenue sharing[11] and Community Development Block Grants[12] had established that formulas of programs supporting multiple services were subject to political compromise and the fair share principle. Samuel Beer (1976) argued that party atrophy weakened the ability of ideologues to adopt either the liberal or conservative allocational principles without compromise. The argument could still be made, however, that the fair share principle was employed because no single measure of need could adequately reflect a multi-service program's objectives.

---

[11] Samuel Beer, "The Adoption of General Revenue Sharing," pp. 127–95.

[12] Robert Jay Dilger, *The Sunbelt/Snowbelt Controversy: The War over Federal Funds* (New York: New York University Press, 1982).

Wastewater Treatment Construction Grants, however, are used for a single service. Theoretically, a single, objective measure of program need can be determined for this program. The fact that the political fair share principle was a major factor in its formula suggested that a study of the congressional reconsideration of this program's formula could provide a greater understanding of why the political fair share principle dominates intergovernmental allotment formulas.

WASTEWATER TREATMENT CONSTRUCTION GRANTS

The national water pollution control effort emerged with the adoption of the Water Pollution Control Act of 1956. The Act authorized $50 million a year for ten years to assist localities in the construction of treatment plants and interceptor sewers (large diameter pipes designed to carry wastewater from large geographic areas to the plant). At first, only small communities participated in the program because grants were limited to 30 percent of the project cost or $250,000, whichever was less.[13] In 1966, the Clean Water Restoration Act opened the program to cities of all sizes by removing the dollar ceiling increasing the federal share of project cost to 40 percent and increasing program authorization to $3.5 billion during fiscal years 1967–1971.

In 1972, the federal role in water pollution control was dramatically increased by the Federal Water Pollution Control Act Amendments. The Amendments set as a national goal the elimination of all pollution from America's waters by 1985, authorized $18 billion for fiscal years 1973–75, increased the federal share of project cost to 75 percent, and expanded funding eligibility from construction of the treatment plant and interceptor sewers to include collectors (small diameter pipes which carry wastewater to the main interceptor pipelines), sewer rehabilitation, correction of infiltration/inflow (leaky pipes), combined sewer overflow problems (prevalent in older cities in the East which have systems that mix storm water with wastewater, causing temporary system overloads), and certain land acquisition costs. Funding was also made available for facility planning (step 1 grant), design and specifications (step 2 grant), as well as actual construction (step 3 grant).[14]

Under the 1972 Amendments, a minimum water quality standard for treatment plant discharges into fresh water, referred to a secondary standard, was established by the Environmental Protection Agency. Municipalities were given until mid-1977 to meet the standard. Non-compliance was punishable by fines

---

[13]Henry Eschwege, statement before the Senate Committee on Environment and Public Works, in *Municipal Wastewater Treatment Grants Program* (Washington, DC: U.S. Government Printing Office, 1981), p. 152.

[14]John Hernandez, statement before the Senate Committee on Environment and Public Works, in *Municipal Wastewater Treatment Grants Program* (Washington, DC: U.S. Government Printing Office, 1981) pp. 4, 5.

and/or imprisonment. However, in implementing the law it became clear that the original deadline was not going to be met because municipal treatment needs had been underestimated, inflation was escalating construction costs, and President Nixon's unexpected impoundment of $9 billion of the program's funds caused unanticipated delays.[15]

Recognizing these problems, the Clean Water Act of 1977 extended the deadline for meeting the secondary treatment requirement until July 1, 1983, and increased authorization levels to $4.5 billion in fiscal year 1978 and $5 billion per year for fiscal years 1979–82. This made the wastewater treatment construction program the nation's second largest non-defense public works program (second only to highway construction). At the same time, the reliability of the Environmental Protection Agency's technique in determining program cost was brought into question.

The Environmental Protection Agency determines program cost in its biennial Needs Survey which represents the EPA's definition of program need. The Needs Survey is developed in cooperation with the states and includes cost estimates for treating current wastewater flows and anticipated flows in the year 2000. The EPA hires a contractor who reviews all planning documents produced by the states and then estimates cost for each eligible category of need for each wastewater facility in the state. These estimates of cost are then forwarded to the states for comment. States naturally have an incentive to inflate their statements of need because more need means more federal dollars. Of the 210,000 estimates of need examined in 1980 only 57,000 were found to be valid by the EPA. Of these 57,000 need estimates, the actual cost estimate in the Needs Survey was reached by negotiation between the contractor and state officials.[16]

Because the EPA's contractor and state officials often disagreed over the need for services as well as the cost of those services, none of the political actors in this case had a clean, unambiguous definition of need against which they could compare any proposed need formula. Not only was the EPA's decision on cost subject to state appeal, there were over 150,000 rejected estimates of need which the states insisted were valid indications of program need. Lacking an objective definition of either program need or cost, many political actors viewed the program not only in terms of clean water and effective sewage treatment, but as a program of general fiscal support. This, in turn, led political actors to ask how much of the program's funds were going to their state relative to other states—leading to formulamanship.

Lacking an objective definition of program need, liberals could have fought for inclusion of the fiscal capacity principle in this program's allotment formula. This did not occur because waterways tend to be most polluted in manufacturing regions and in communities experiencing rapid growth. Since both of these

[15]Ibid., pp. 45, 46.
[16]Ibid., pp. 115, 116.

community types are as apt to be relatively high income areas as not, the fiscal capacity principle would not have redistributed wealth in a manner consistent with program need and was not advocated by any of the political actors in this case.

THE 1977 FORMULA

As there was no nationally defensible criteria of program need, the House and Senate adopted different allotment formulas in 1977 which reflected the two institutions' differing political characteristics. The House allotment formula was a political compromise which included the fair share, needs, and cost principles: 25 percent on population, 25 percent on partial needs (only secondary treatment, more stringent treatment and new interceptors eligible for funding), and 50 percent on the Needs Survey. The Senate adopted two formulas: 100 percent on 1975 population figures and 100 percent on the 1976 Needs Survey minus new collectors, each state receiving the higher allotment prorated so that total funding did not exceed 100 percent. Also each state was guaranteed 0.5 percent of the funds (to attract votes from Senators representing small population states).

The final conference committee agreement reconciled the difference in the bills' formulas by looking at a series of computer printouts and agreeing on how much each state would get. While the 1976 Needs Survey and population figures produced the initial bargaining positions, neither factor had a direct relationship to the agreed upon state-by-state distribution of funds. There was, in fact, no needs formula created for this program. Every state received a straight percentage of the funds. For several states the conference committee's allotment exceeded both the House and Senate approved allotments, while for other states the conference committee's allotment fell short of both the House and Senate approved allotments. There was no identifiable pattern except that House conferees agreed to the Senate request that every state be provided at least 0.5 percent of the funds.

1981: THE REAGAN PROPOSAL

Despite the awarding of nearly 17,000 design, planning, and construction grants, the effects of the 3,200 sewage treatment plants currently in operation, and the expenditure of nearly \$33 billion during fiscal years 1973–81, critics of the program indicate that there is little data to support the contention that the nation's waterways have been made significantly cleaner. They are especially critical of the secondary treatment requirement for discharges into fresh water, regardless of the effect such treatment has on water quality. It is their contention that many locations only marginally improve the quality of the receiving water at a huge cost to the taxpayer. They also charge that the plants are politically attractive *pork barrel*, but do not justify their expense given the lack of evidence concerning their impact on the nation's waterways. Others argue that the construction of these plants has hastened urban sprawl. Still others are shocked at the Environmental Protection Agency's projection in its 1980 Needs Survey that the cost of those plants eligible for construction grants could top $120 billion through the year 2000 (Table 15–1, Col. I, p. 256). Because the grants cover 75 percent of cost, the potential cost to the federal government was estimated at $90 billion (see Table 15–1, Column II). As a consequence of current economic conditions and a $1 trillion federal deficit, critics urged a scaling back of the program.

Given the expense and controversy surrounding the sewage treatment plant construction program, his pledge (subsequently withdrawn) to balance the budget by fiscal 1984, and lacking empathy for the environmental movement, President Reagan announced a major overhaul of the program on March 10, 1981. He asked for (and received) a rescission of $1.7 billion in remaining fiscal 1980 and 1981 grant funds. He also indicated in March that he would seek $2.4 billion for fiscal 1982 sewage treatment plant construction (instead of $5 billion) and he would veto even that amount if the federal government's estimated future obligation of $90 billion was not reduced to $23 billion (see Table 15–1, Column III). In order to achieve these savings Reagan proposed eliminating funding for reserve capacity beyond 1980 population levels (termed backlog or accumulated needs) to replace or repair existing pipelines, and to store overflow. Only secondary, or more stringent treatment plants (those going beyond the secondary requirement) targeted into urban areas where expenditures would serve the greatest water quality benefit per dollar expended, and new interceptor sewers would be funded.[17] Also, the allotment figures per state would be based solely on remaining grant needs as determined by the 1980 Needs Survey (no minimum state guarantee and only backlog needs represented).

Table 15–2, Col. II (p. 258), indicates the state-by-state allotment pattern under the Reagan proposal. Table 15–2, Col. I indicates what the state-by-state allotment pattern would have been if funding were reduced from $5 billion to $2.4 billion as Reagan requested but project eligibility and the 1980 allotment formula were retained. Because the President promised to veto any legislation authorizing more than $2.4 billion, Column I was used by most political actors as a base for comparison. Under the President's proposal, thirty-three states (twenty-three in the South and West) would have lost money. Most of these *loser* states are from the South and West because they hold a disproportionate share of reserve capacity needs (no longer eligible for funding under the Reagan proposal) due to their projected population growth. California, for example, would have lost $67.8 million and Texas $47.8 million under the President's proposal. Table 15–2, Column III illustrates how radically Reagan's proposals would have altered the state-by-state allotment of funds. Five states would have

[17]Kathy Koch, "Senate Is Starting Reform of U.S. Construction Grants for Sewage Treatment Plants," Congressional Quarterly, *Weekly Report* (13 June 1981), p. 1044.

had their allotments increased by over 50 percent (Alaska, Massachusetts, New Jersey, Rhode Island, and Wisconsin), while eleven states would have had their allotments decreased by greater than 50 percent. Montana, North Dakota, and the District of Columbia, no longer protected by the Senate's minimum, would have lost nearly all of their federal sewage dollars. An EPA official commented that the Reagan allotment formula was "courageous" in that it attempted to target funds to states with "real" need but did not stand a chance because of political realities. Too many people benefited from the existing formula to adopt such a radical revision.

FORMULAMANSHIP IN THE SENATE

One would think that a Senator from a growing population state of the South or West would have been the first to challenge the Reagan allotment formula but that was not the case. The challenge came from Senator John Chafee, R-RI, chairman of the Senate Subcommittee on Environmental Pollution. Chafee's bill (S.1274) accepted the President's restrictions on grant eligibility, but reauthorized the program at $2.4 billion per year for four years (to enable recipients to plan their capital budgets). An additional $200 million per year was provided to help communities (such as Providence, Rhode Island, in Chafee's home state) to correct combined sewer overflow into marine bays and estuaries. Also, the federal share of eligible construction cost was to be reduced to 65 percent in fiscal 1982–84 for all projects except those awarded step 3 grants prior to December 31, 1981. In fiscal 1985, the federal share would be reduced to 55 percent (to encourage localities to be more cost conscious and to decrease anticipated federal exposure).[18] Finally, Chafee's bill revised the President's proposed allotment formula by including in the formula combined sewer overflow needs in fiscal 1982 and 1983 (increasing the Northeast–Midwest's share of funds) and guaranteeing every state 0.5 percent of funds (benefiting small population states). Beginning in fiscal 1984, funds would be allotted among the states according to relative effect of publicly owned treatment works on water quality in each state.

The state-by-state allotment of funds under Chafee's proposal is presented in Table 15–3, Col. II (p. 260). From a pork barrel standpoint, Chafee's proposal did not stand a better chance than Reagan's original proposal. Only seventeen states (most in the Northeast) and the District of Columbia stood to receive more funds in fiscal 1982 if the Chafee proposal were adopted and the current allotment distribution was dropped. This left thirty-three *loser* states (sixty-six votes in the Senate).

[18]The Senate termed potential federal cost *exposure*. The House termed potential federal cost *obligation*.

TABLE 15–1   State by State Needs (in millions of dollars)

STATE	EPA NEEDS SURVEY 1980	FEDERAL SHARE 1980 NEEDS SURVEY	FEDERAL SHARE REAGAN'S PROPOSAL
Alabama	903	677	178
Alaska	507	380	186
Arizona	606	454	113
Arkansas	496	372	110
California	6,773	5,080	1,725
Colorado	1,006	754	70
Connecticut	1,734	1,300	360
Delaware	499	374	56
D.C.	442	331	6
Florida	4,907	3,680	793
Georgia	1,679	1,259	266
Hawaii	818	614	204
Idaho	509	382	99
Illinois	4,529	3,397	1,034
Indiana	4,027	3,020	330
Iowa	1,259	944	380
Kansas	1,134	850	249
Kentucky	2,459	1,844	295
Louisiana	1,148	861	223
Maine	1,524	1,143	209
Maryland	3,031	2,273	494
Massachusetts	4,719	3,539	1,026
Michigan	4,953	3,715	1,201
Minnesota	1,563	1,172	488
Mississippi	844	633	226
Missouri	2,752	2,064	817
Montana	252	189	24
Nebraska	362	272	104
Nevada	242	182	57
New Hampshire	1,295	971	299
New Jersey	6,466	4,850	1,231
New Mexico	194	146	46
New York	18,331	13,748	3,109
North Carolina	1,740	1,305	442
North Dakota	86	64	10
Ohio	6,373	4,780	937
Oklahoma	624	468	104
Oregon	1,252	939	146
Pennsylvania	7,785	5,839	966
Rhode Island	979	734	213
South Carolina	871	653	315
South Dakota	252	189	53
Tennessee	1,854	1,391	368
Texas	4,392	3,699	531
Utah	400	300	174
Vermont	445	334	92
Virginia	1,960	1,477	573

TABLE 15–1   Continued

STATE	EPA NEEDS SURVEY 1980	FEDERAL SHARE 1980 NEEDS SURVEY	FEDERAL SHARE REAGAN'S PROPOSAL
Washington	3,125	2,344	460
West Virginia	1,866	1,399	338
Wisconsin	2,271	1,703	919
Wyoming	150	113	26
Territories	1,488	1,135	489
TOTAL	119,896	89,924	22,945

Source: *Congressional Record* 127, no. 154 (27 October 1981), pp. 7765, 7766.

The Senate Subcommittee on Environmental Pollution was chaired by Chafee but dominated by Senators from the West.[19] As one would expect, the subcommittee was not going to adopt Chafee's allotment formula without major revisions. Senators George Mitchell (D-Maine) and Slade Gorton (R-Washington), ranking Republican on the Subcommittee, advocated the addition of various hold harmless clauses to Chafee's formula in order to gain the support of Senators from the South and West. A 90 percent hold harmless provision guarantees each state no less than 90 percent of what it would have received if the old formula had been retained. Under a 90 percent hold harmless provision, only twenty-five states (instead of thirty-three) would receive less funds in fiscal 1982 than would have been the case if the current distribution were retained (see Table 15–3, Column III). While northeastern states would still benefit from Chafee's formula, the hold harmless provision would increase the southern and western share of funds relative to the northeastern states. Florida, for example, would receive only $36 million under Chafee's formula (see Table 15–3) but would receive $81.7 million under a 90 percent hold harmless clause. New York, on the other hand, would get $393.8 million under Chafee's formula but only $266.8 million under a 90 percent hold harmless clause. The effects of two other hold harmless provisions which were seriously considered during subcommittee markup are presented on Table 15–3, Columns IV and V. Both would narrow the allotment differences between the regions relative to Chafee's formula.

The bipartisan desire to employ hold harmless clauses obviously had nothing to do with targeting Wastewater Treatment funds to states with either greatest need or demonstrated effort in the construction of wastewater treatment facilities. This move was based on the political necessity of employing the fair share principle in order to attract votes necessary for the program to be adopted. Senate committee members recognized that, without an objective standard of need or program cost, ideologues identified their political interests as getting as many dollars for their state as possible.

[19]Subcommittee on Environmental Pollution members: Chafee (R-RI), Simpson (R-WY), Symms (R-ID), Gorton (R-WA), Mitchell (D-ME), Hart (D-CO), and Moynihan (D-NY).

TABLE 15–2   State by State Allotments (in millions of dollars)

STATE	FUNDING AT $2.4 BILLION	FUNDING UNDER REAGAN'S PROPOSAL	CHANGE UNDER REAGAN'S PROPOSAL
Alabama	30.4	18.7	-38.5%
Alaska	11.8	19.5	+65.2%
Arizona	18.4	11.3	-38.6%
Arkansas	17.8	11.5	-35.4%
California	188.2	120.4	-36.0%
Colorado	21.7	7.3	-66.4%
Connecticut	26.4	37.6	+42.4%
Delaware	11.8	5.9	-50.0%
D.C.	11.8	.6	-94.9%
Florida	90.8	82.9	- 8.7%
Georgia	46.0	27.7	-40.0%
Hawaii	18.8	21.3	+13.3%
Idaho	11.8	10.3	-12.7%
Illinois	112.9	108.1	- 4.2%
Indiana	65.5	34.5	-47.3%
Iowa	30.7	39.7	+29.3%
Kansas	20.8	25.0	+20.2%
Kentucky	34.6	30.9	-10.7%
Louisiana	29.9	23.3	-22.1%
Maine	17.7	21.9	+23.7%
Maryland	65.7	61.6	- 6.3%
Massachusetts	69.9	107.3	+53.5%
Michigan	97.8	125.5	+28.3%
Minnesota	44.2	51.0	+15.4%
Mississippi	22.9	23.7	+ 3.5%
Missouri	59.1	35.4	-40.1%
Montana	11.8	2.3	-80.5%
Nebraska	13.0	10.3	-20.8%
Nevada	11.8	5.9	-50.0%
New Hampshire	20.9	31.3	+49.7%
New Jersey	84.5	128.7	+52.3%
New Mexico	11.8	4.9	-58.5%
New York	251.4	325.2	+29.4%
North Carolina	46.9	46.2	- 1.5%
North Dakota	11.8	1.0	-91.5%
Ohio	153.0	98.0	-35.9%
Oklahoma	22.0	10.3	-53.2%
Oregon	30.7	15.3	-50.2%
Pennsylvania	103.2	101.1	- 2.0%
Rhode Island	12.4	22.3	+79.8%
South Carolina	27.8	14.0	-49.7%
South Dakota	11.8	5.5	-53.4%
Tennessee	36.7	32.4	-11.7%
Texas	103.3	55.5	-46.3%
Utah	11.8	15.5	+31.4%
Vermont	11.8	9.7	-17.8%
Virginia	46.4	60.0	+29.3%

TABLE 15–2 Continued

STATE	FUNDING AT $2.4 BILLION	FUNDING UNDER REAGAN'S PROPOSAL	CHANGE UNDER REAGAN'S PROPOSAL
Washington	41.9	48.2	+15.09%
West Virginia	42.4	35.3	-16.8%
Wisconsin	46.2	96.1	+108.0%
Wyoming	11.8	2.8	-76.3%
Territories	35.6	49.8	+39.9%
TOTAL	2,400.0	2,400.0	

Source: U.S. Congress, House Public Works Committee, "State by State Allotment."

On July 15, 1981, the Senate subcommittee adopted a compromise bill which provided for an allocation of funds for four years. In the first three years, fiscal 1982–84, the funds would be allotted according to Chafee's formula, but with a descending hold harmless provision of 90, 85 and 80 percent of the EPA's 1980 Need Survey. In 1985, funds would be allotted among the states according to the impact of publicly owned treatment works on water quality. No state would receive less than 0.5 percent of the funds. The point is that there was no objectively defensible criterion of need. Each Senator tried to get as much as possible for his state but within the restraint of having to produce an allotment formula acceptable to the Senate as a whole.

During committee markup, southern and western Senators successfully deleted the inclusion of combined sewer overflow needs (an earlier issue) from the allotment formula. They also successfully introduced amendments to continue funding for some already approved collector and reserve treatment projects that both Chafee's and the President's proposal would have terminated. As a result, the Senate Environment and Public Works Committee's bill (now designated S. 1716) was less similar to the Reagan proposal, but still quite close. The allotment formula used the same grant eligibility criteria as the Reagan proposal, but had the descending hold harmless feature and also guaranteed each state 0.5 percent of funding (Table 15–4 p. 262). The Senate's bill accepted Reagan's limitation of eligibility to secondary treatment, more stringent treatment and new interceptors. It also accepted the President's proposal to eliminate reserve capacity in the calculation of needs. As a result, the Senate bill reduced anticipated federal exposure to approximately $30 billion, only $7 billion over the figure sought by the President.

FORMULAMANSHIP IN THE HOUSE

As the 1981 Senate markup progressed the House Public Works and Transportation Committee's Subcommittee on Water Resources, chaired by Robert Roe, (D-New Jersey) also examined the President's proposal. Unlike their Senate

TABLE 15–3   Based on $2.4 Billion Total Appropriation (in millions of dollars)

STATE	FY 77–81 FORMULA	S. 1274 AS INTRODUCED	90% HELD HARMLESS	85% HELD HARMLESS	80% HELD HARMLESS
Alabama	$ 30.4	$ 11.5	$ 27.4	$ 25.8	$ 24.3
Alaska	11.8	11.5	16.0	16.9	17.5
Arizona	18.4	11.5	16.5	15.6	14.7
Arkansas	17.8	11.5	16.0	15.1	14.2
California	188.2	95.6	169.4	160.0	161.7
Colorado	21.7	11.5	19.6	18.5	17.4
Connecticut	26.2	38.5	30.9	32.7	33.7
Delaware	11.8	11.5	12.0	12.0	12.0
D.C.	11.8	14.5	12.0	12.0	12.0
Florida	90.8	36.0	81.7	77.2	74.3
Georgia	46.0	23.0	41.4	39.1	36.8
Hawaii	18.8	11.5	17.5	18.5	19.1
Idaho	11.8	11.5	12.0	12.0	12.0
Illinois	112.9	122.2	110.6	104.5	98.3
Indiana	65.5	114.0	59.0	55.7	52.4
Iowa	30.7	27.1	32.6	34.5	35.6
Kansas	20.8	21.5	21.4	22.6	23.3
Kentucky	34.6	41.2	31.1	29.4	27.7
Louisiana	29.9	11.5	26.9	25.4	23.9
Maine	17.7	41.8	18.0	19.0	19.6
Maryland	65.7	25.0	59.2	55.9	52.6
Massachusetts	69.9	116.8	88.1	93.2	96.2
Michigan	97.8	117.2	103.1	109.1	112.6
Minnesota	44.2	32.9	41.8	44.3	45.7
Mississippi	22.9	11.5	20.6	20.6	21.2
Missouri	59.1	64.4	70.1	74.2	76.6
Montana	11.8	11.5	12.0	12.0	12.0
Nebraska	13.0	11.5	12.0	12.0	12.0
Nevada	11.8	11.5	12.0	12.0	12.0
New Hampshire	20.9	27.8	25.7	27.2	28.0
New Jersey	84.5	150.8	105.6	111.8	115.4
New Mexico	11.8	11.5	12.0	12.0	12.0
New York	251.4	393.8	266.8	282.4	291.5
North Carolina	46.9	20.1	42.2	40.1	41.4
North Dakota	11.8	11.5	12.0	12.0	12.0
Ohio	153.0	145.1	137.7	130.1	122.4
Oklahoma	22.0	11.5	19.8	18.7	17.6
Oregon	30.7	15.8	27.6	26.1	24.6
Pennsylvania	103.2	192.6	92.9	87.7	90.6
Rhode Island	12.4	22.1	18.3	19.3	20.0
South Carolina	27.8	11.5	25.1	23.7	22.3
South Dakota	11.8	11.5	12.0	12.0	12.0
Tennessee	36.7	24.2	33.0	33.3	34.4
Texas	103.3	24.7	93.0	87.8	82.6
Utah	11.8	11.5	12.8	13.5	13.9
Vermont	11.8	11.6	12.0	12.0	12.0
Virginia	46.4	40.8	49.2	52.1	53.7

TABLE 15–3 Continued

STATE	FY 77–81 FORMULA	S. 1274 AS INTRODUCED	90% HELD HARMLESS	85% HELD HARMLESS	80% HELD HARMLESS
Washington	41.9	49.5	39.6	41.9	43.2
West Virginia	42.4	42.6	38.1	36.0	33.9
Wisconsin	46.2	54.6	78.8	83.4	86.1
Wyoming	11.8	11.5	12.0	12.0	12.0
Territories	35.6	22.8	43.4	45.4	46.7

Source: United States Senate, Committee on Environment and Public Works

counterparts, the House subcommittee decided not to work towards a multi-year bill. Instead, they decided to work on a one-year reauthorization because it would provide less controversy than a multi-year bill (anyone who is upset can appeal for redress the following year) and, given the rescission of 1981 funds and the fact that thirty states had exhausted all of their federal sewage treatment dollars, most members of the House subcommittee wanted to put off a formula fight so that a bill could be adopted and the flow of federal funds to the states resumed. Robert Edgar (D-Pennsylvania) a liberal member of the subcommittee and chairman of the Northeast–Midwest Congressional Coalition (one of the prime instigators of formula fights in the House), explained why the subcommittee did not fight over the formula and opted to retain the existing formula without revision:

> The 1977 allotment formula was like throwing mud against the wall and scrapping it off to see what was left. It didn't make any sense. Everyone recognized that it was put together in a haphazard way. But we need time to develop the reforms the Administration requested. Once we make up our minds on grant eligibility then we can crank it (the allotment formula) into the computers, get the GAO (General Accounting Office) to help and hopefully produce a formula that makes sense, one that reflects needs. But before the conference the question was really whether or not we were going to get a bill out of committee. The best way to insure that was to avoid a formula fight.[20]

Two other factors help to explain the absence of a formula fight in the House. First, most state and local officials preferred the current allocation formula to the uncertainties of a formula fight.[21] Also, there was a real sense of camaraderie between Roe and the subcommittee's ranking Republican, John Hammerschmidt (R-Arkansas). The President's proposed allotment formula promised to cut southern aid in general, and Arkansas' aid by 35 percent. According to Bill Van den Broek, Assistant Counsel for Water Resources with the House Public Works Committee:

[20]Interview with Robert Edgar, 10 December 1981, Washington, DC.

[21]Interview with Henry Longest, Director of Water Operations-E.P.A., 11 December 1981, Washington, DC.

TABLE 15–4   State Allotment Formula (in millions of dollars)

STATE	FY 1982	FY 1983	FY 1984
Alabama	27.3	25.8	24.3
Alaska	15.9	16.9	17.4
Arizona	16.5	15.6	14.6
Arkansas	16.0	15.1	14.2
California	169.3	159.9	161.7
Colorado	19.5	18.4	17.4
Connecticut	30.8	32.6	33.7
Delaware	12.0	12.0	12.0
D.C.	12.0	12.0	12.0
Florida	81.7	77.1	74.3
Georgia	41.3	39.0	36.7
Hawaii	17.5	18.5	19.1
Idaho	12.0	12.0	12.0
Illinois	110.6	104.5	98.3
Indiana	58.9	55.6	52.4
Iowa	32.5	34.4	35.5
Kansas	21.3	22.6	23.3
Kentucky	31.1	29.4	27.6
Louisiana	26.9	25.4	23.9
Maine	17.9	19.0	19.6
Maryland	59.1	55.8	52.6
Massachusetts	88.0	93.1	96.2
Michigan	103.0	109.0	112.6
Minnesota	171.4	44.2	45.7
Mississippi	20.5	20.5	21.2
Missouri	70.0	74.1	76.5
Montana	12.0	12.0	12.0
Nebraska	12.0	12.0	12.0
Nevada	12.0	12.0	12.0
New Hampshire	25.6	27.1	28.0
New Jersey	105.6	111.8	115.4
New Mexico	12.0	12.0	12.0
New York	266.8	282.3	291.5
North Carolina	42.2	40.1	41.2
North Dakota	12.0	12.0	12.0
Ohio	137.7	130.0	122.4
Oklahoma	19.7	18.6	17.5
Oregon	27.6	26.1	24.5
Pennsylvania	92.9	87.7	90.5
Rhode Island	18.2	19.3	19.9
South Carolina	25.0	23.6	22.2
South Dakota	12.0	12.0	12.0
Tennessee	32.9	33.3	34.4
Texas	92.9	87.7	82.6
Utah	12.7	13.5	13.9
Vermont	12.0	12.0	12.0
Virginia	49.2	52.0	53.7
Washington	39.5	41.8	43.2

TABLE 15–4 Continued

STATE	FY 1982	FY 1983	FY 1984
West Virginia	38.1	36.0	33.9
Wisconsin	78.8	83.4	86.1
Wyoming	12.0	12.0	12.0
Territories	43.3	45.4	46.7
TOTAL	2,400.0	2,400.0	2,400.0

Source: *Congressional Record* 127, no. 154 (27 October 1981), pp. 12248, 12249.

You can't put together a bill from this subcommittee that goes against the interests of the ranking minority member. There is a good bipartisan relationship within the subcommittee. In fact, this committee is a bastion of logrolling. We have sunbelt members on this committee who are important and Representative Hammerschmidt is one of them.[22]

The House retained the 1977 percentage distribution figures (see Table 15–3, Column I) and markup debate centered on the President's proposed cutback on grant eligibility. In order to provide cities an opportunity to adjust to a scaling back of the program, Roe submitted a bill (H.R. 4503) which *grandfathered* eligibility criteria for all ongoing projects. It even allowed each state's governor to use up to 30 percent of his state's funds on categories of treatment works which would become ineligible for federal funding. In order to attract southern and western support Roe's bill authorized full (twenty-year) reserve capacity needs but Roe successfully amended his own bill during committee markup (voice vote) to limit full reserve capacity to already approved step II (design) and step III (construction) grants. Step I (planning) grants would be limited to only ten years to reserve capacity. Although the amendment hurt the South and West, southern and western committee members recognized that the Senate had completely eliminated reserve capacity and were happy to see some reserve capacity in the bill. Finally, an amendment introduced by Buddy Roemer (D-Louisiana) to extend grant eligibility to infiltration/inflow needs (leaky pipes) was agreed to in committee. Despite these additions, the amended bill (approved by House Public Works Committee on September 30, 1981) would have cut anticipated federal obligation to $55 billion. However, this amount was still $32 billion more than the President's proposal and $25 billion more than the Senate's bill.[23] On October 19, 1981, President Reagan announced his opposition to the House bill. The full House, nevertheless, approved the bill, 382–18, on October 27, 1981, the same day the Senate approved its bill.

[22]Interview with William Van der Brock, 10 December 1981, Washington, DC.

[23]Kathy Koch, "House Committee Approves Sewer Grant Bill," Congressional Quarterly, *Weekly Report* (30 Octobert 1981), p. 1910.

FORMULAMANSHIP IN THE CONFERENCE

The Conference Committee members began their deliberations on November 12, 1981, with the cloud of a potential presidential veto hanging over their heads. When the conference ended on December 10, 1981, the final bill (H.R. 4503) gave the President approximately 90 percent of the reforms he sought. The bill (agreed to by the House and Senate on December 16, 1981) authorized $2.4 billion for four years for treatment works and an additional $200 million for each of fiscal 1983–85 to correct combined sewer overflows into marine bays (as in the Senate's bill). It agreed to use the House allotment formula for fiscal 1982 and an average of the House formula and the Senate formula for fiscal 1982 (80 percent held harmless) for fiscal 1983–85 allotments (see Table 15–5). The conference report also agreed to *grandfather* all grant eligibility criteria until 1984. After 1984 only secondary treatment, more stringent treatment, correction of infiltration/inflow and new interceptor sewers would be eligible for funding. The federal percentage share of costs would remain at 75 percent until 1984 and be reduced to 55 percent after that (with some exceptions). It retained existing reserve capacity rules (twenty years) until October 1, 1984. After that, no grant can be made for reserve treatment capacity in excess of population needs existing as of the date the step III grant was awarded and in no event for needs in excess of these as of October 1, 1990.[24] Each state was also allowed to spend up to 20 percent of its allotment on categories that become ineligible after 1984.

The point is that the process of putting together formula grants is one of political accommodation—of constructing formulas and eligibility criteria that: (1) benefit your district as much as possible; yet (2) can still pass. In this sense the politics of formula grants apparently follows the pattern of distributive policies, where long range policy goals often become lost in the heat of political negotiations and ideological considerations are, at least in part, muted.[25]

CONCLUSION

In the Wastewater Treatment Construction Grants program the EPA attempted, through its Needs Survey, to provide Congress and the President an assessment of cost based upon the program's compliance criteria (the secondary treatment standard). The disagreement over the contractor's findings precluded a consensus on both the need for services and cost of services allocational principles. This fundamental disagreement over an objective criteria of need was to be expected

---

[24]Kathy Koch, "Congress Clears Sewer Grant Legislation," Congressional Quarterly, *Weekly Report* (19 December 1981), p. 2527.

[25]Theodore Lowi, "American Business, Public Policy, Case-Studies, and Political Theory," *World Politics* 16 (July 1964): 677–715; and Randall Ripley and Grace Franklin, *Congress, the Bureaucracy, and Public Policy*, rev. ed. (Homewood, IL: The Dorsey Press, 1980).

TABLE 15–5   Who Got What (in millions of dollars)

STATE	FY 1982	FY 83–85	STATE	FY 1982	FY 83–85
Alabama	30.4	27.3	Nevada	11.8	11.9
Alaska	11.8	14.6	New Hampshire	20.9	24.4
Arizona	18.4	16.5	New Jersey	84.5	99.9
Arkansas	17.8	16.0	New Mexico	11.8	11.9
California	188.2	174.9	New York	251.4	271.4
Colorado	21.7	19.5	North Carolina	46.9	44.1
Connecticut	26.2	29.9	North Dakota	11.8	11.9
Delaware	11.8	11.9	Ohio	153.0	137.7
D.C.	11.8	11.9	Oklahoma	22.0	19.7
Florida	90.8	82.5	Oregon	30.7	27.6
Georgia	46.0	41.3	Pennsylvania	103.2	96.9
Hawaii	18.8	18.9	Rhode Island	12.4	16.2
Idaho	11.8	11.9	South Carolina	27.8	25.0
Illinois	112.9	110.6	South Dakota	11.8	11.9
Indiana	65.5	58.9	Tennessee	36.7	35.5
Iowa	30.7	33.1	Texas	103.3	92.9
Kansas	20.8	22.0	Utah	11.8	12.9
Kentucky	34.6	31.1	Vermont	11.8	11.9
Louisiana	29.9	26.9	Virginia	46.4	50.0
Maine	17.7	18.7	Washington	41.9	42.5
Maryland	65.7	59.1	West Virginia	42.4	33.3
Massachusetts	69.9	83.0	Wisconcon	46.2	66.1
Michigan	97.8	105.2	Wyoming	11.8	11.9
Minnesota	44.2	32.9			
Mississippi	22.9	22.0	Territories	35.6	41.1
Missouri	59.1	67.8			
Montana	11.8	11.9	TOTAL	2,400.0	2,400.0
Nebraska	13.0	12.5			

Source: U.S. Congress, House, *Municipal Wastewater Treatment Construction Grant Amendments of 1981,* H. Rept. 97-408 to Accompany, H.R. 4503, 97th Cong., 1st Sess., 1981, pp. 6, 7.

in a formula-based block grant program, or in general revenue sharing, because of the multitude of services available but was somewhat surprising in a formula-based categorical grant program. Because categorical grants are used for a specific stipulated activity, the opportunity for deriving an objective criteria of need is theoretically present. In reality, however, it is apparent that the Wastewater Treatment Construction Grants program is hardly unique in its inability to target funds according to objective need. The problem is not politicians engaging in formulamanship but the difficulty in arriving at a consensus on objective need. Grants under Title I of the Elementary and Secondary Education Act, for example, are intended to assist students suffering from "education deprivation." There is no objective criteria of need for educational deprivation.[26] There are, however,

[26]Advisory Commission on Intergovernmental Relations, *Categorical Grants*, p. 210.

a number of subjective criteria of need for educational deprivation—leading into formulamanship.

It would be easy to condemn the formulamanship process for its inability to target funds to areas of greatest need but in the absence of a consensus or an objective definition of need it cannot be argued that the Wastewater Treatment Construction Grant's formula is illogical. It is as logical as it can be in a republican form of government. While one is left wondering whether all those low population states really deserve .5 percent of the funds, at least the program is in operation and meeting the needs of thousands of localities throughout the United States. While inefficient in an economic sense, formulamanship does provide a benefit in that all sectors receive some benefits. Similarly, the Quebec problem in Canada, for example, stems, at least in part, from a perceived notion that various sectors and provinces are being advantaged at the expense of other sectors and provinces.

Could this program have targeted funds *better* if it were a project-categorical grant instead of a formula-categorical grant? Given the disagreement over program need and cost there would always be someone claiming that any allocational pattern was illogical or unfair. The effects of grantsmanship would also have to be considered before one took a position on which mechanism—project or formula—was better at targeting to *real* need. The major issue is that neither mechanism—project nor formula—can be judged superior to inferior in targeting terms in the absence of objective criteria of need.

While we now know that formula grants are not necessarily any better than project grants at targeting to need, the answer to the question which grants mechanism is best remains evasive. Some people will conclude that, given the inability of project and formula grants to target funds according to an objective standard, the best course to follow is to let state and local officials allocate program funds through general revenue sharing or block grants because state and local officials are physically closer to the problems and, therefore, more likely to recognize the most efficient means of responding to local needs. There is evidence, however, which suggests that state and local officials are just as susceptible to allocating funds according to the political fair share criteria as are federal officials.[27] Also, so long as the federal government retains its fiscal superiority over the states, the argument can be made that someone at the federal level will have to determine how much each state and locality is going to receive. Because criteria of need are inherently subjective, formulamanhip is going to be present no matter who makes the allocational decision, be it on the state level or the federal level.

There may be some who would cry "a plague on all your houses" and demand that governments at all levels get out of program service and "let the

[27]Donald Kettl, "Can the Cities Be Trusted?" *Political Science Quarterly* 94 (Fall 1978): 437–51.

market do it.'' This argument ignores all the good reasons why governments become involved in providing program service in the first place: superior fiscal capacity, national objectives, spillover effects, political and fiscal equalization.[28] While government actors may be less than perfect in targeting to need, the market ignores many needs altogether.

[28]Advisory Commission on Intergovernmental Relations, *An Agenda for American Federalism: Restoring Confidence and Competence* (Washington, DC: U.S. Government Printing Office, 1981), pp. 33–100.

Thomas J. Anton

16

DECAY AND RECONSTRUCTION IN THE STUDY OF AMERICAN INTERGOVERNMENTAL RELATIONS

Academic perspectives on the state of the American polity tend to be dominated by the prevailing political mood of the day. Twenty years ago, before we had seriously attempted to engage intractable social problems such as poverty, structural unemployment, and environmental pollution, political science was largely a celebration of America's "pluralist democracy," in which no organized interest or group was left out of the political process. Today, having learned how difficult it can be to make headway against such problems when buffeted by inflation, recession, and political stealth at the highest levels of government, our prevailing mood seems much more sober. The participation of citizens in the political process that we prized so highly two decades ago now seems somehow excessive, organized not by any general sense of the public interest but by the narrow programmatic desires of single-issue constituencies. The pride in governmental responsiveness that was apparent in studies of public sector program development has given way to unhappiness about the size of government and its increasingly costly undertakings. Our earlier confidence in the capacity of our governmental systems to solve problems has dissolved into widespread doubt about the desira-

Originally appeared in *Publius: The Journal of Federalism* 15 (Winter 1985). Copyright by CSF Associates. Reprinted with permission.

bility of any governmental action. Despite good intentions and often lavish public spending, our governmental systems seem to have become worse rather than better.

Nowhere is this sense of institutional decay more evident than in recent analyses of American intergovernmental relations. Stimulated by complaints from state and local officials over the confusion, delay, and red tape caused by new federal assistance programs, and nourished by academic or official studies of program "failure," a deep sense of malaise over the condition of our inter-governmental systems has become widespread among both politicians and analysts. . . . Fortunately, the expansion of government that has excited criticism of intergovernmental relationships has also stimulated an outpouring of analyses of those relationships. It is thus possible to develop empirical evidence to assess ideas that form the core of the theory of intergovernmental decay that is now so fashionable. Five central assertions structure that theory:

1. *Government Size*—Critics assert that the federal government is too large and has grown too fast, particularly in grants to state and local governments. We can ask what growth rates have been and what the relative balance between state and federal sectors has become since the 1950s.

2. *Accountability*—Critics believe that government growth and the proliferation of grant programs have created a system so complex that citizens can neither understand who is responsible for what nor hold officials responsible for their actions. We can review evidence showing more or less complexity and ask how such evidence affects conclusions about accountability.

3. *Programmatic Control*—Critics allege that massive federal grants have both stimu-lated state and local governments to undertake programs they would not have attempted without federal assistance and prevented state and local governments from actions they would have taken absent federal pressure. We can ask whether the many recent studies of federal assistance programs support, challenge, or modify this "usurpation" hypothesis.

4. *Capacity*—Critics believe that federal grants have reduced the capacity of state and local governments to function effectively by encouraging administrative frag-mentation and financial dependence on federal aid. We can ask what evidence exists for either assertion.

5. *Achievement*—Critics believe that most, if not all, federal grant programs have failed to achieve their objectives or have produced harmful unanticipated conse-quences. We can ask how such judgments are made and what kind of evidence is used to support them.

THE THEORY OF INTERGOVERNMENTAL DECAY: AN EMPIRICAL ASSESSMENT

Growth.   Increases in government revenues and expenditures occur both because the costs of existing activities increase over time and because govern-ments undertake new programs. American governments have clearly spent more and done more than ever before in the past three decades. If we compare public sector revenues and expenditures to GNP for the period 1950–1980, for example, we discover that the national product increased more than six-fold and that total public sector activity increased from roughly a quarter of GNP in 1950 to well over a third of GNP in 1980. . . . These increments, together with the associated increase in public sector payroll costs from 6.4 to 9.6 percent of GNP, make it clear that all governments have been growing, relatively as well as absolutely. Although media attention has focused on the large amounts raised and spent by the national government, the really striking *rates* of growth have occurred in the state–local sector, where both revenues and expenditures as a share of the national product more than doubled between 1950 and 1980. Recent growth in American governmental activities therefore appears to have been led by state and local rather than federal officials.

This conclusion is strongly reinforced when we examine the distribution of public sector employment and compare that distribution to either the national population or the civilian labor force. . . . Federal government employees as a percent of total public sector employees declined from 33.1 percent in 1950 to only 17.9 percent in 1979. Between 1955 and 1979 fewer than 500,000 employees were added by the federal government—indeed, federal employment actually *declined* by some 130,000 workers from 1970 to 1979. During the same 1955–1979 period, however, more than 8 million new employees went to work for state and local governments. Nearly 3.7 million people (up from 1.5 million in 1955) now work for state governments, while more than 9.4 million (up from 3.8 million in 1955) work for the cities, counties, townships, and school districts that comprise American local government. From the 1950s through the 1970s state and local governments were the major growth industries, with federal employment in a state of comparative decline. . . .

Accountability.   At one level, the proposition that federal grant proliferation has complicated government beyond the ability of citizens to either understand or control seems indisputable. The flowering of new grant programs that began with President Johnson's administration and continued under Presidents Nixon, Ford, Carter, and Reagan has given the national government hundreds of responsibilities in areas previously thought to be beyond its concerns. It is doubtful that many public officials, let alone citizens, have a clear understanding of what these programs are or what they do, despite OMB's provision of the massive *Catalog of Federal Domestic Assistance,* with its 1,000 or so separate programs, and efforts of agencies such as the U.S. Advisory Commission on Intergovernmental Relations to disseminate information about federal program activities. To the extent that the accountability of public officials is based on knowledge of their program activities, it seems clear that accountability has been made more difficult by growth in federal grant programs.

At another level however, the arguments that flow from this increment in complexity seem vastly overdrawn. When we identify the programs that contribute to the $90 billion in intergovernmental grants distributed in 1980, it turns out that more than half of the dollars distributed were provided by only six programs, and more than 70 percent of all grant funds came from only ten programs: Medicaid, Highway Planning and Construction, Rural Electrification, Aid to Families with Dependent Children (AFDC), General Revenue Sharing (GRS), Comprehensive Employment Training Act (CETA), Tennessee Valley Authority (TVA), EPA Wastewater Treatment, Community Development Block Grants (CDBG), and Social Services' Title XX. A great deal is known about all of these programs, largely because congressional oversight has been intense and scholarly attention voluminous. Since these programs have also been modified repeatedly—indeed, CETA no longer exists—it would be difficult to argue that political accountability has not been exercised. Adding another ten programs increases the dollar fraction to 90 percent, and includes activities such as Urban Mass Transit (UMTA), and Head Start that are similarly well known and modified repeatedly.

The case for increased confusion and decreased accountability thus turns on the existence of programs that are large in number but small in dollars. On examination, these turn out to be dominated by grants for various forms of medical research, awarded to hospitals or universities, and grants to schools for special educational programs. Of the 162 grant programs operating in Detroit in fiscal 1981, for example, sixty-nine were health research grants and another twenty-nine were for special educational programs. None of these were large enough to be included in the largest twelve programs in Detroit, which together accounted for nearly two-thirds of the $533 million in federal assistance available to the city in that year. The large number of small medical and educational grants may be confusing to analysts, but confusion has not been an issue locally. Meanwhile, the largest dozen programs are carefully monitored by federal, as well as state and local, officials. . . .

Usurpation.   Most analysts agree that federal aid "stimulates" a higher level of state–local spending than would have occurred without federal funds, although the stimulation effect varies with the type of aid and with the passage of time.[1] To what extent, then, is the recent expansion of state and local governments attributable to federal grants? That federal aid has caused some new

---

[1]Edward M. Gramlich, "The Effect of Federal Grants on State–Local Expenditures: A Review of the Econometric Literature," in Stanley J. Bowers, ed., *Proceedings of the 62nd Annual Conference on Taxation, National Tax Association* (Columbus, OH: National Tax Association, 1970); and Edward M. Gramlich and Harvey Galper, "State and Local Fiscal Behavior and Federal Grant Policy," in Arthur M. Okum and George L. Perry, eds., *Brookings Papers on Economic Activity* (1973), pp. 15–58.

activities to be undertaken by states and cities seems undeniable. One way to see this relationship is to borrow a phrase from a study done by Robert Yin and his associates: "counterpart bureaucracy." They argue that certain federal aid programs induce local governments to create new organizations ". . . in direct response to the initiation (or cessation) of the relevant federal program."[2] These "counterpart bureaucracies" maintain close relationships with appropriate federal agencies, are typically supported by "soft" (that is, federal) money, and work to coordinate local participation in some federal program. Although these authors have in mind primarily more recent counterpart organizations such as CETA consortia or CSA agencies, they also recognize that the counterpart pattern has a much longer history. Local public housing authorities were required by the 1937 public housing legislation; local urban renewal authorities were stimulated by housing acts of 1949 and 1954; all but a handful of today's local and state planning agencies came into existence (and until recently were supported) through Section 701 of the 1954 *Housing Act,* and so on. In addition, more than a thousand regional and metropolitan agencies—from councils of governments to metropolitan transit authorities—have been stimulated by federal legislation in areas such as environmental protection, transportation, and health. It is therefore clear that federal programs have had a very important impact on state–local government structure, the actors who become involved in the determination of program and budgetary priorities, and thus the processes of state and local politics.

It is far less clear that the activities stimulated by federal assistance have represented federal, rather than state or local, program priorities. For one thing, federal program priorities are seldom very clear: Congressional coalitions strong enough to pass programs are far easier to build if goals remain vague rather than precise.[3]

For another, most (two-thirds) grants are distributed according to some formula, usually one that includes population among its terms, which discourages strict application of program performance criteria in fund distribution.[4] Block grants, which generally contain loose definitions of multiple-purposes designed to maximize state and local discretion, not only discourage strict performance criteria but render the use of such criteria virtually impossible. Significantly, both formula-based and block grants expanded much more rapidly during the

[2]Robert K. Yin, et al., *Federal Aid and Urban Economic Development: A Local Perspective* (Santa Monica, CA: The Rand Corporation, 1979), pp. vi–26.

[3]Phillip Monypenny, "Federal Grants-in-Aid to State Governments: A Political Analysis," *National Tax Journal* 13, no. 1 (March 1960): 1–16; and Thomas Anton, "Federal Assistance Programs: The Politics of System Transformation," in Douglas E. Ashford, ed., *National Resources and Urban Policy* (New York: Methuen, 1980).

[4]Danuta Emery, et al., "Distributing Federal Funds: The Use of Statistical Data," in *Statistical Reporter* 81, no. 3 (December 1980): 73–90; and Helen Ingram, "Policy Implementation through Bargaining: The Case of Federal Grants-in-Aid," *Public Policy* 25, no. 4 (Fall 1977): 499–520.

1970s than did the more tightly constrained category of project grants.[5] Recent dramatic increases in federal grants to state and local governments, in short, have been accompanied by the growing utilization of program instruments that reduce federal programmatic constraints.

Quite apart from issues of federal program design, however, the existing maze of state and local revenue and expenditure account structures, often pegged to fiscal years different from the federal fiscal year period, make it extraordinarily difficult for the federal government (or anyone else!) to monitor federal program dollars as they move between governments and within governments across account entities. The federal government has neither maintained an information system capable of producing such information nor employed a sufficiently large and well-financed (to say nothing of politically supported) core of program auditors able to accurately report the uses of federal funds.[6]

Thus, as Carl Stenberg noted recently, " . . . much activity under federal programs actually escapes review or scrutiny. The General Accounting Office, for example, recently released a study of seventy-three grant recipients that revealed that 80 percent of their federal funds were not audited by grantor agencies."[7] State and local governments clearly have been more free to decide how to spend federal dollars than many recent critics of federal usurpation appear to believe. . . .

Capacity.   Multiplication of grant programs, granting agencies, and regulations have led some writers to wonder whether federal fragmentation has been exported to lower units, causing a loss in political and/or management capacity. While such assertions clearly are impossible to evaluate comprehensively, given the number of units involved and the ambiguity of the notion of "capacity," it is generally true that larger and wealthier units are likely to have larger numbers of better–trained and better–paid employees, operating more service programs than are available in smaller and poorer units. To the extent that these characteristics indicate "capacity," then federal assistance does not appear to be harmful, since these are also the units that generally receive higher amounts of federal assistance, from a larger number of federal programs. It is also possible to suggest that fragmentation in federal policymaking need not imply fragmentation in implementation. In welfare, for example, programs such as food stamps,

[5]Thomas J. Anton, "Toward a Human Assistance Budget: Structure and Change in the Distribution of Federal Expenditures, 1971–1980," (unpublished manuscript, Institute for Public Policy Studies, The University of Michigan, Ann Arbor, Michigan, June 1983).

[6]Thomas J. Anton, "Federal Assistance Programs: The Politics of System Transformation," in Douglas E. Ashford, ed. *National Resources and Urban Policy* (New York: Methuen, 1980).

[7]Carl W. Stenburg, "Federalism in Transition: 1959–1979," in *Conference on the Future of Federalism: Report and Papers* (Washington, DC: Advisory Commission on Intergovernmental Relations, 1980), p. 37.

AFDC and Supplemental Security Insurance (SSI) appear to be developed by separate policy systems in Washington, having little regard for program interactions.[8] State implementing agencies, on the other hand, often coordinate their uses of these programs in order to secure advantages to themselves. For example, many states attempted to shift persons from the AFDC program to the SSI programs prior to 1974, in order to minimize state and maximize federal costs.[9] Similarly, many states have routinely encouraged welfare clients to participate in the Food Stamps program, which is federally funded, rather than AFDC, which is partially funded by states.[10] These kinds of actions may or may not represent "good" policy, but they clearly demonstrate state ability to coordinate program administration when financial interest is at stake. . . .

Achievement.   Consideration of how federal grant dollars are actually used in local and state environments challenges stereotypical images of federal program failure. Evidence of program ineffectiveness is commonplace, but much of it takes the form of contrasts between statements of program goals and reports of the use made of particular awards. The difficulty with such evidence—apart from the ease with which vaguely expressed goals can be used for political purposes—is that local officials tend to think in terms of projects, rather than individual awards, and tend to use multiple awards from any reasonable source to support ongoing projects to completion. To evaluate an individual award properly, therefore, an individual grant should be placed within a project context. As Yin suggests, "An award-oriented research design, which typifies most federal evaluation studies, is likely to produce misleading results because it will probably fail to capture the dynamics at the most aggregate level.[11] If so, judgments about program inadequacy may reflect conceptual inadequacy on the part of evaluators more than program failure.

Nowhere is this conceptual inadequacy more clear than in the treatment of time in program evaluation. Programs are often evaluated without any consideration of the time period within which one might expect an "impact" to be felt, yet the passage of time is a crucial consideration in the formulation of judgment.[12] In 1967 Martin Anderson published a blistering critique of federal urban renewal programs, then a decade old (*The Federal Bulldozer*).[13] The

---

[8]Richard A. Hoefer, "The Rise of Entitlements: 1971–1980," (unpublished manuscript, Institute for Public Policy Studies, The University of Michigan, Ann Arbor, Michigan, 1983).

[9]*Congressional Quarterly*, 12 June 1976.

[10]National Academy of Sciences, *Family Assistance and Poverty: An Assessment of Statistical Needs* (Washington, DC: National Academy of Sciences, 1983).

[11]Robert K. Yin, et al., *Federal Aid and Urban Economic Development*, pp. vii–12.

[12]Lester M. Salamon, "Follow-up, Letdowns, and Sleepers: The Time Dimension in Policy Evaluation," in Charles O. Jones and Robert Thomas, eds., *Public Policy Making in a Federal System* (Beverly Hills, CA: Sage Publishers, Inc., 1976), pp. 257–84.

[13]Martin Anderson, *The Federal Bulldozer* (New York: McGraw-Hill, 1967).

programs were shown to have destroyed more housing units than they replaced, to have become programs of ''black removal'' in many places, to have distributed federal subsidies to persons and groups with little or no need for subsidy, and to have done little to check the continuing decay of central cities. It is fair to say, I think, that these intensely critical images dominated public perceptions of urban renewal programs from that time until the programs were replaced by CDBG in 1974.

A later paper by Haywood T. Sanders, however, challenges these largely negative images.[14] Observing urban renewal for its entire history, 1949–1974, Sanders finds the imbalance between housing units destroyed and units replaced is far smaller than had been suggested, that 40.2 percent of the 98,000 acres of land acquired under the program were devoted to new housing as of December 1974, that while 57.9 percent of *families* displaced by urban renewal were black or other minority, 55.5 percent of the *individuals* displaced were white, and that ''. . . of the new housing units actually underway or completed from 1950 to 1972, almost 55 percent are specifically designed for low- and moderate-income families, using both federal and state subsidy programs.''[15] Sanders documents extraordinary variety in local renewal programs and shows that federal imposition of tighter constraints in 1967 actually increased local participation in the program.[16] Land clearance and redevelopment took a great deal more time in some cities than in others, and Sanders offers harsh judgments about program quality and consequences in such cities. Other cities did far better, on the other hand, allowing Sanders to discuss the conditions under which more or less success was achieved. Sanders clearly presents a more balanced perspective, made possible largely because of his use of a more appropriate time-frame for analysis. . . .

TOWARD CONCEPTUAL RECONSTRUCTION

Although the above evidence challenges the theory of intergovernmental decay, it should now be clear that the major defect of that theory is not empirical but conceptual. The principal focus of the theory, in fact, is not intergovernmental relationships but national government programs. Judgments about those programs are derived from vague or wholly unspecified criteria rather than empirical evidence of program performance. To the extent that criteria of evaluation are made clear, they appear to rest on a belief that federal, state and local governments were assigned distinctively different functional responsibilities by the *U.S. Constitution* and that these assignments recently have been undermined by national

---

[14]Haywood T. Sanders, ''Block Grants and Federal Bucks,'' (unpublished manuscript, Institute of Government and Public Affairs, University of Illinois, Urbana, Illinois, 1980).

[15]Ibid., p. 7.

[16]Ibid., p. 31.

government programs that intrude into state and local areas of responsibility. Whether such a machine-like system of governance was intended by the authors of the *Constitution,* few scholars accept the metaphor of the machine as a useful guide to understanding interactions among American governments. Instead, as Martin Landau pointed out some years ago, "We are, most of us, Darwinians these days," by which he meant that most of us accept a biological metaphor, conceiving of government. . . " 'as if' it were a 'living' organism which 'grows and evolves' in relation to an external environment. . . ."[17] From this point of view, of course, the idea of a fixed division of governmental responsibilities makes little sense. Since decay theorists nonetheless place great emphasis on the recent "loss" of previously fixed assignments, it seems worthwhile to consider why biology rather than mechanics structures so much of our analytical thinking.

There is, first of all, the historical record. At least since the work of Grodzins and Elazar it has been clear that sharing of responsibility among national, state and local governments is the typical American governmental pattern—and has been typical for most functions since the beginning of the republic.[18] Two decades later, a similar assessment seems reasonable: government is doing much more today than it did in 1962, providing more occasions for federal–state–local interactions, but without clearly fixed boundaries defining separate responsibilities. The national government has indeed become involved in local fire protection or sewerage systems, but local governments in Vermont and California have become involved in issues of foreign and military policy as well. Anyone searching for clarity or mechanical precision would be frustrated by such developments, but they can be interpreted to represent the growth and adaptation characteristic of biological organisms.

Quite apart from an historical record of growth and change rather than stability and repetition, the notion that there exists some "principle" or "principles" according to which "national" and "local" functions might be distinguished seems fundamentally mistaken. Decay theorists appear to believe that such principles should structure the federal system, but Rufus Davis long ago demonstrated that distinctions between "national" and "local" are entirely subjective, as are similar distinctions between "common" and "particular," "important" and "unimportant," and so on.[19] Depending on the interests or purposes of politicians, *any* governmental activity can be designated as either national or

---

[17]Martin Landau, *Baker* v. *Carr* and the Ghost of Federalism," in Charles F. Cnudde and Deane E. Neubauer, eds., *Empirical Democratic Theory* (Chicago: Markham Pub. Co., 1969).

[18]Morton Grodzins, "The Federal System," in *The Report of the President's Commission on National Goals, Goals for America* (Englewood Cliffs, NJ: Prentice-Hall, 1960), pp. 265–82; Daniel Elazar, *The American Partnership: Intergovernmental Co-operation in the Nineteenth Century United States* (Chicago: The University of Chicago Press, 1962); and Daniel Elazar, *American Federalism: A View From the States*, 2nd ed. (New York: Thomas Y. Crowell, 1972).

[19]Rufus Davis, "The 'Federal Principle' Reconsidered," in Aaron Wildavsky, ed., *American Federalism in Perspective* (Boston: Little, Brown, 1967).

local in significance, and a designation made at one point in time can be altered at some other point in time. It follows that a "federal" constitution can be no more and no less than. . . a political bargain, struck by political bargainers. . . .[20]

A governmental system characterized by continuous growth or other adjustment to changing circumstances, with no clear or fixed allocation of functional responsibilities among governments, clearly is difficult to describe, let alone understand. Part of the difficulty is that many of the words we use suggest hierarchy: "subordinate" or "lower-level" or "inferior" are common modifiers of state and local governments. Since most of these units can raise their own taxes, choose their own political and administrative officers, and initiate proposals for public action, the hierarchy model seems descriptively inappropriate and analytically confusing. Elazar has suggested recently that it would be more useful to think of American governance as a "matrix" of influence or, as he puts it, ". . . a noncentralized political system in which the powers were not allocated by 'levels' but divided among different arenas—federal, state, and local."[21] Elazar uses the term "noncentralized" self-consciously, in order to make clear that the American system is not a *de*centralized system, or one that at some point had been centralized.

This formulation seems to have several advantages. To begin with, it recognizes what recent empirical work has clearly demonstrated, namely, that state and local governments are organizational systems that behave according to their own patterns of interest, incentive, and constraint. Such a formulation can accommodate variety without denying that structure can exist within variety. Second, this view avoids the largely artificial, "top-down" view of influence that flows from hierarchical images and permits analysis of the far more complicated reciprocal processes that characterize American intergovernmental behavior. Third, by recognizing that federal, state, and local jurisdictional designations represent arenas for joint action rather than separate levels of responsibility, this perspective encourages a better understanding of the political sources of intergovernmental activity. . . .

Consider what we can now say about the structure of American intergovernmental relations. If . . . organizations are best understood as coalitions of power, based on interest, then the organizations we know as state and local governments are appropriately viewed as coalitions. Since environmental conditions differ considerably from one area to another, the interests represented in these coalitions will also differ, giving rise to the frequently observed variety in programs offered by these organizations. . . .

. It is exceedingly important to understand that, within this structure, *each governmental unit constitutes an interest that is part of the political environment*

[20]Ibid., p. 9.

[21]Daniel J. Elazar, "American Federalism Today: Practice versus Principle," in Robert B. Hawkins, Jr., ed., *American Federalism: A New Partnership for the Republic* (San Francisco: Institute for Contemporary Studies, 1982), p. 40.

of other governments. In addition to the organizational maintenance and programmatic purpose goals that are common to all organizations, therefore, American governments all engage in political representation of organizational and constituency interests. This, I take it, is partly what Elazar has in mind when he writes that American governments are "forced" to interact. From a local unit point of view, the state and federal governments provide much of the revenue and all of the regulations that constrain their activities, while other local governments pursue interests or provide resources that often require sustained attention. From a state point of view, legal and financial responsibility for local government actions combine with localized legislative representation to determine much of state policy, while the administration of programs partially funded by the national government make national agencies daily participants in state action. From a national point of view, localized representation in Congress and the locally specialized interests of national administrative agencies (i.e., HUD to serve northeastern cities, Interior to service the joint federal–state interests in western states, Defense to interact largely with southern and coastal regions) give much of national policy its traditionally localized configuration. Shared responsibilities, in short, guarantee that many governments will have an "interest" in any given program and that those interests will be represented in political coalitions. Politically, intergovernmental relationships are themselves part of the "structure." . . .

CONCLUSION: UNDERSTANDING FAILURE
AND RATIONALIZING SUCCESS

Most of the empirical work I have reviewed here has been self-consciously "objective" rather than normative, designed to illuminate how systems work rather than argue for reform. Nevertheless, if my reading of these works is as realistic as it is optimistic, they should have given us some basis for evaluating intergovernmental patterns and judging proposals for reform. The theory of intergovernmental decay seems to me to be wide of the mark, but that is hardly to say that our intergovernmental systems cannot be improved. What, then, do empirical analyses tell us about problems in our systems or prospects for reform?

One major problem that emerges repeatedly is a continuing inability of the organs of the national government to either define or to agree on *national* interests in the design of domestic policy programs. The ambiguity of goals that Monypenny's analysis suggests is inherent in grant programs facilitates "spreading" federal dollars around to a large number of jurisdictions or individuals, who are then relatively free to use the funds according to their own interests, but a national interest in the spreading of program dollars is often difficult to enforce. Agency efforts to enforce national definitions of purpose are often thwarted by Congressional intervention. Or, success in constraining state and local uses of federal dollars—as in the 1978 CETA amendments—leads to a loss of program support. *The result is not too much federal control but too little:* whatever national purposes remain in final legislative language fall victim to the multiple uses that can be made of national dollars once they leave Washington. This may well serve the interests of state and local governments, which shift many of their financial burdens to a larger national tax base, but it is not at all clear that identifiable national interests are served by such practices.

A second apparent difficulty is the continued pre-eminence of organizational maintenance goals among dominant coalitions. Since survival is likely to be the first rule of all organizational units that provide jobs, salaries and career opportunities, the relegation of goal achievement and representation obligations to second and third place in hierarchies of purpose should not be surprising. In systems so thoroughly intergovernmental as the American system, however, an emphasis on organizational maintenance creates serious problems. Programmatically it is manifested in a variety of "turf protection" strategies designed to protect existing organizational relationships against any form of change: outside funds or personnel are integrated into existing streams of authority where possible in order to control them; if integration is not possible, outside resources are often isolated in separate units or separate financial accounts that can easily be eliminated if there is any change in the level of outside support. These strategies reinforce distinctions between "our" resources and programs and "their" resources and programs that often delay or defeat the achievement of intergovernmental program purposes.

Politically, the emphasis on maintenance values takes the form of policies that are proposed to solve one unit's problems without taking into account the interests of other units certain to be affected by the policies. This is a common occurrence during budget cycles, when governments often raise taxes or reduce expenditures *for their operations* with neither advance warning nor prior consultation with other units affected by such proposals. Such "failures of communication" are sources of much frustration, though they are also sources of dynamism, since they force affected units to scramble to adjust to unanticipated events. Perhaps the best recent example of this behavior pattern is President Reagan's proposals for a New Federalism. Although the President's new block grants and budget reductions forced state and local governments to adjust their policies in a variety of ways, major portions of the president's plan have not been implemented, in part, because little prior consultation with governors and mayors appears to have taken place in drafting the plan. Defined as a national rather than a joint national-state-local program, the president's imaginative reforms developed only weak constituency support.

Whether "reform" becomes more probable in the years ahead thus depends on the willingness of governmental actors to recognize the reality of organizational interests other than their own and the legitimacy of actions designed to express those interests. Recent scholarship has made clear that the expression of governmental interest is not always synonymous with governmental selfishness and that the frustration of inaction is not always impossible to overcome. For those who advocate reform, this scholarship has much to offer. For those who practice scholarship, the search for a more precise understanding of the conditions under which positive intergovernmental outcomes are produced remains an exciting and unending challenge.

Daniel J. Elazar

17

IS THE FEDERAL SYSTEM
STILL THERE?

. . . As long as there was a persuasive and unchallenged sense of the Constitutional division of powers between federal and state governments, of Constitutional limits on federal action, and of the federal role as supportive rather than domineering—as long as the relatively powerful federal government in all its branches had to be somewhat apologetic about getting involved in any particular function, it was possible for Washington to work with the states and localities on a partnership basis. Somewhere along the line, however—perhaps with the death of the dualistic doctrine—the sense that the federal government was Constitutionally limited essentially disappeared. In great part this was a result of decisions of the U.S. Supreme Court, of its becoming too active a partisan and abdicating its umpire role, as this report suggests.[1] But, beyond that, it was also an abdication on the part of the executive and legislative branches of the federal government, who refused to accept their role as interpreters of the Constitution. Instead, they

---

Originally appeared in *Hearings on the Federal Role* (Washington, DC: U.S. Government Printing Office, 1980). Reprinted with permission of the U.S. Advisory Commission on Intergovernmental Relations.

[1]Dr. Elazar is referring to the U.S. Advisory Commission on Intergovernmental Relations, multivolume report, *The Federal Role in the Federal System* (Washington, DC: U.S. Government Printing Office, 1980).

demonstrated a willingness to reflect any interest that could move them, leaving it entirely to the Court to determine questions of Constitutionality.

The natural history of this change is easily traced. In the 1950s the federal government became actively involved in a supportive role in virtually every field of governmental endeavor, other than the most utterly local. The 1960s witnessed a shift in that involvement—from supporting state and local initiatives to taking the initiative and requiring the states and localities to conform to federally established directions. This led, in turn, in the early 1970s to increasing federal preemption of state and local powers, and in the mid-1970s to the notion that the federal government was the policymaker by right, while the states and localities were merely convenient administrative arms to be subjected to all kinds of federal regulations, whether authorized by Congress or not. Even governors came to believe that the states could not initiate programs on their own but had to wait for, or seek, Washington's lead.

By the end of the decade, we had reached the point at which the states increasingly were being excluded by federal preemption from fields that until relatively recently were considered their exclusive prerogative. In recent years Congress has acted with no restraint and the Court with virtually none, despite the efforts of some justices to revive the idea that there are indeed Constitutional questions to be faced.

There were those of us who raised the issues contained in the report at the beginning of the decade, but our words apparently fell on the deaf ears of a Congress whose members no longer seem to know or care what federalism is all about. This occurred despite the fact that every President since Lyndon Baines Johnson has paid obeisance to the federal principle and has claimed to stand four square on the side of a healthy and vital federal system in all its parts. Our warning then, which I would suggest is even more correct now, is that what the Presidents were advocating was decentralization, not federalism.

Once upon a time we had a Constitutional sharing of powers in which each partner was given due respect—"full faith and credit" in a real sense—by every other partner and in which the federal government, as the strongest partner (if only because it has always had an easier time raising revenues, and since 1862, the exclusive power to print money), was prepared to exercise self-restraint in dealing with the states. More recently we have moved to a system whereby it is taken as axiomatic that the federal government shall initiate policies and programs, shall determine their character, shall delegate their administration to the states and localities according to terms that it alone determines, and shall provide for whatever intervention on the part of its administrative agencies as it deems necessary to secure compliance with those terms.

Elsewhere I have suggested that the proper model of a federal system is a matrix of governments serving larger and smaller arenas, with the federal government as the framing institution serving the largest arena, but with no greater legitimacy outside the spheres of its principal responsibility than the other governments serving smaller arenas in the spheres of their principal responsibility. It is most emphatically not a power pyramid consisting of higher and lower levels, with the federal government presumably on top and the states and localities tiered below it (and the people presumably underneath the entire structure). The operative ideology today begins with the pyramid model and leads to the effort to substitute decentralization for federalism. Even our language reflects it. The American people have drawn the right conclusions—coming to look upon all government as simply a pyramid weighted down upon them; one to be milked for whatever a person or group can get; the lesser of evils or the path of least resistance since there is no way to get it off our backs.

Not only has the Constitutional theory of federalism been replaced by a half-baked theory of decentralization, but it is a vulgar and, at times, vicious theory as well. What it has meant is that Presidents and Congresses have done exactly what common sense would have suggested they would do: namely, used decentralization in an effort to keep the political "goods" for themselves and pass the tough problems on to the states and localities. President Nixon even articulated this approach, indicating that he would keep those responsibilities that brought his Presidency credit but pass on the other ones, the difficult ones, to the Governors and Mayors. Subsequent Presidents and Congresses have done the same thing without saying so.

Witness the sorry spectacle of summer 1979, during the height of the gasoline shortage when the President tried to force the governors to establish and enforce unpopular control mechanisms, and the governors refused to accept the political liability of doing so. The President self-righteously proclaimed his devotion to federalism in order to "stick" the governors with this unenviable task, while the governors self-righteously evoked the idea of federal responsibility to pass the buck back to Washington.

During the year 1979, this trend reached a new high. Indeed, in the first few weeks of 1980 alone we have seen the advancement or enactment of legislation substituting national for state standards for highway truck weight—most assuredly not for the benefit of the highways so much as for the benefit of the truckers; expanding the federal "right" to intervene in the management of state institutions, presumably to protect the rights of U.S. citizens incarcerated within them; providing for federal override of state legislation and local ordinances in certain energy-related matters; and requiring each state to establish a commission to study ways to improve state and local government operations as a condition of receiving its share of federal revenue sharing.

This latter represents another effort in a growing series of attempts to influence the very structure of state and local governments—not merely their functions but touching matters that were sacrosanct even in the heyday of New Deal interventionism. The list of similar examples is growing longer all the time.

Moreover, the state and local response to all this seems to be merely acquiescent. Thus, the National Governors' Association (NGA) *Governors' Bul-*

letin of February 29, 1980, reporting on the NGA winter meeting, reports that the Governors indicated their willingness to accept the Carter Administration proposal requiring states to establish commissions to encourage structural change, "but only if such commissions did not hamstring the states with unreasonable and unnecessary controls." The most they could do is criticize the Administration's draft proposal, which authorizes the Secretary of the Treasury to intervene in, and approve state procedures and decisions, and the requirement that the commissions be dominated by representatives of the localities.

The governors were on the defensive in almost every respect. They had to publicly oppose federal efforts to circumvent substantive provisions of state water law and urged that the President, not the Administrator of the Environmental Protection Agency, have the authority over laws issued by governors to facilitate the use of coal. And so it went. The plaintive cry of the governors to be included as partners at a time when all knowledgeable observers agree that most states are functioning as well as, if not better than, the federal government itself reflects the present state of affairs all too clearly.

If all of this centralization had led to the desired improvements, perhaps even those of us who are committed federalists—who believe that the federal system is one of the fundamental bulwarks of liberty, which for us remains a principal goal of the American experiment—might be prepared to pay the price. Alas, the true record is now emerging.

Again, looking only at the most immediate examples, *The New York Times* of March 8, 1980, includes an article on the increase in traffic deaths in 1979 which quotes Howard L. Anderson, the recently retired Federal Highway Administration associate administrator for safety: "Much of our present highway design criteria is [sic] based on what is now an obsolete design vehicle. . . concrete median barriers which safely redirect the two-ton and larger vehicles have shown a disturbing tendency to cause the sub-compact car to roll over."[2] Those of us who were witness to the defacing of miles and miles of highway with ugly concrete barriers, destroying green median strips, at untold cost, because the federal government required that change if the states were to continue to receive highway funds, are now faced with the spectacle of those barriers serving as killers rather than the safety purposes for which they were presumably designed. It is important to recollect that those barriers were being erected during the mid-1970s—after the energy crisis of 1973–74, and precisely when the country was being pushed by other federal agencies (quite properly, if not sufficiently) to shift to smaller cars.

Similarly, *The New York Times* has printed a series of articles on the untoward consequences of deinstitutionalization, another major federal effort, revealing case after case of people wandering the streets or being left to shift

---

[2]Robert E. Tomasson, "Traffic Deaths Up in 1979; Small Cars Held a Factor," *New York Times*, 8 March 1980, p. 6.

for themselves without proper care. Two colleagues at the University of Southern California, Arthur J. Naperstek and David E. Biegel, have written as follows:

> Federal mental health planners envisioned the flowering of a network of support services to care for deinstitutionalized patients at the community level through the stimulus of federal seed money. But 1,300 of the 2,000 community mental health centers projected for 1980 have failed to materialize and many that did have failed to service this chronically ill population. Deinstitutionalization, an ostensibly humane treatment program, has degenerated into a tragic crisis. Public scrutiny of the situation needs to begin now.
>
> Planners, without real consultation, assumed that strong communities would accept the chronically ill. When few welcomed large numbers of these troubled people, patients were steered to transitional neighborhoods that would not put up a fuss, but the strong community support factor essential for successful aftercare was absent. The result was that city streets became wards of mental hospitals, and it was out of the snakepits and into the gutter for victims of the deinstitutionalization policy.[3]

In more than a few cases, those deinstitutionalized include people who have committed violent criminal acts. But even if that is merely random, we are left with the sadness of the nonviolent suffering from a process that never took into consideration the fact that, given the human condition, perfection was not obtainable either inside or outside of institutions.

The list of federally generated mistakes grows longer and longer every day. One can forgive all the well-meaning people who are involved for making those mistakes. None of us are immune from the laws of overly high hopes and unanticipated consequences. One cannot forgive them, however, for arrogating to themselves and the federal government a presumed omniscience that they did not have at the expense of the federal system.

So here we have it—a federal government unrestrained in all three branches, one in which the Constitutional issues are never raised and are considered irrelevant by those who presumably have taken an oath to "preserve, protect, and defend the Constitution." Where does that leave us? If we are to accept Alexander Hamilton's minimalist definition of a federal polity in *Federalist No. 9:*

> Simply. . . an assemblage of societies or an association of two or more states into one state. The extent, modifications, and objects of the federal authority, are mere matters of discretion. So long as the separate organization of the members be not abolished; so long as it exists, by a constitutional necessity, for local purposes; though it should be in perfect subordination

---

[3]David E. Biegel and Arthur J. Naparstek, "The Care Wasn't There," *New York Times*, 26 January 1980, p. 21.

> to the general authority of the union, it would still be, in fact and in theory, an association of states, or a confederacy. . . .

then we can be content that we still have a federal system. If, however, we modify that definition with Madison's in *Federalist No. 14,* which describes what the framers expected the American federal system to be:

> The general government is not to be charged with the whole power of making and administering laws. Its jurisdiction is limited to certain enumerated objects, which concern all the members of the republic, but which are not to be attained by the separate provisions of any. The subordinate governments extend their care to all those other objects which can be separately provided for, but retain their due authority and activity. . .

then we have much to worry about indeed.

We have long since encroached on the Madisonian definition, which if one notes carefully, limits national intervention to those objects that concern all the members of the Republic but which are not to be obtained by the separate provisions of any. (Education, for example, concerns all the members of the Republic, but was held by the founding fathers to be separately attainable by each state—yea, each locality—acting separately.) The fact is that we are now even encroaching on the Hamiltonian definition by indirect means, with federally mandated commissions to implement the latest federally supported fads in governmental structural reform, which are likely to become the concrete barriers and deinstitutionalization programs of tomorrow, and federal executive overrides of legitimate state laws to expedite this project or that.

I like to think of myself as a perennial optimist and am even on record as such. In that spirit, I would suggest that if this great federal republic has not lost its way, then at the very least we are in the position of Daniel Boone who, when asked if he had ever been lost in the woods, retorted, "Nope, but once I was bewildered for three days." We have been bewildered for longer than that. We are so bewildered that with all their importance, specific palliatives will no longer save the federal system. Only a clear restoring of a sense of Constitutionalism and Constitutional priorities can possibly do so. . . .

The most important point to be made is that the old palliatives will not work. Nor will transferring welfare, health insurance, and social insurance programs to exclusive federal control with the concomitant expansion of a bureaucracy already too big at specific points, even if its total size is no greater than it was thirty years ago. From the perspective of federalism, that will only provide further reason for turning public attention to Washington. Even the case for transfer still rests on unproven assumptions. Moreover, in today's climate, such a transfer will simply strengthen the centralizing tendencies. . . by knocking out the last prop maintaining a semblance of the old federalism—namely, the idea that domestic social functions are primarily the province of the states, and if no longer theirs exclusively, are at least intergovernmental.

The real problem is clear. It is not a question of structures, nor of procedures, but of people—people in government who in certain respects are too activist, too eager to do more; people in and out of government who have too many vested interests; and people everywhere who are too unrestrained in their demands. It is the problem of people who have lost their public-mindedness, who may no longer even see themselves as part of an American public, not to speak of state publics or civil communities. . . .

Our problem today is precisely that every citizen believes he or she is sovereign to do what he or she wishes. How did this come about? There is no single cause, but no doubt the diminution of local loyalties has played its role. The American people is a people precisely because it is compounded of the several state and local publics. John Dewey, who in so many respects was a precursor of contemporary notions, noted this well in his now neglected classic, *The Public and Its Problems*. When that compounding was lost, we became too diffuse as a people, which is now leading us to become a nonpeople. . . Only a restoration of Constitutional good sense can save the situation. Nothing less will do.

In that connection, my recommendations are:

1. Undertake a major political education campaign to advance the understanding of Constitutional federalism. Such a campaign should be directed principally toward those involved in public life who hold or will hold public office, will be employed in the public service, or will be active in the various public institutions and organizations of American civil society. These are the people who are most involved in the consideration of public issues and whose opinions (not in the sense of polling but in the original sense of opining) have been crucial in bringing the old system to its present state. They will be equally crucial in making any changes in the future. Thus, public education in this case is not a television blitz prepared by the Advertising Council to sell a candidate or a slogan, but a process of opinion formation that does not attempt to suggest a doctrine of federalism so much as to revive a sense of the place of federalism in the American political tradition, to help increase the public-mindedness necessary to make that tradition and the system linked with it work toward the achievement of its proper ends.

2. Write or rewrite federal legislation to restore the possibility of a more state-centered political party system. . . .

    It is possible, and may even be desirable to foster responsible state political parties. That is where they have worked best in the United States, precisely because they are part of a larger federal framework that acts as a countervailing force to the centralizing tendencies already noted in the report. Given such state parties, the iron law of oligarchy would tend to work along with them. Responsible state parties can achieve the goals that advocates of responsible parties seek to promote in the realm of policy formulation and the citizen involvement. Responsible national parties will defeat the purposes toward which every other recommendation is directed.

So, too, would more federal funding of campaigns. Indeed, there should be less. We are rapidly becoming aware of how the present federal laws providing for the financing of Presidential campaigns discourage party organizations and the activity of individuals, and encourage the power of single-interest political action committees (not to speak of the problems they have created with regard to the length and rigidity of the Presidential races themselves). Short of abandoning any federal oversight over public funds, there is little that can be done about this under present conditions except to make the regulations even more complex and thus entangle Presidential campaigns in the same thicket that ensnares the administration of programs in the federal system.

3. Restrict the scope of the conditions attached to federal grants-in-aid. Here I refer particularly to those general provisions attached to all grants-in-aid that have nothing directly to do with the implementation of programs but which utilize the grant mechanism to advance other goals. These other goals may indeed be laudable. I tend to identify with virtually every one myself, but there is a time and a place for everything. The grant system is a convenient but inappropriate mechanism for advancing those purposes, given the other purposes that it abuses in the process.

4. Cull federal grant programs and drop those that do not deal with any substantial federal question or are explicitly directed toward the institutions of state and local government. Here, Madison's definition of a proper federal role becomes very important. Together with some of the concrete recommendations presented in this report regarding program size, it is possible to fashion a basis for doing just that.

5. It would be counterproductive to make any current intergovernmental domestic programs into wholly national ones. On the contrary, for any national health insurance program that emerges out of Congress, efforts should be made to vest primary responsibility in the states, with appropriate federal funding. This is done in Canada, which has one of the most successful national health programs in the world. Past experience has shown that any effort to separate functions by governmental plane is more likely to lead to greater decentralization. All the evidence indicates that it is easier to transfer functions to the federal government than to return them to the states. . . .

6. All three branches of government, but particularly the U.S. Supreme Court, must be encouraged to reassume their responsibilities as interpreters of the Constitution from a federalist perspective. Although it is possible to narrow broad interpretations developed over the past generation or two (and this should be encouraged) in other ways, we cannot go back to earlier times. It seems unlikely that dual federalism in the nineteenth century style could become even a predominant theory, much less a predominant form of practice, which it was not then either. Thus, it is necessary to develop new doctrines or expand old ones.

I would suggest two: First, following Madison's definition from *Federalist No. 14*, we can once again begin to ask of a particular piece of legislation, regulation, requirement, or procedure whether a substantial federal question is involved. Thus, in the right way—one that recognizes the inevitability and logic of intergovernmental sharing in a dynamic civil society located in an increasingly complex environment— new limits can be established with regard to the expansion of federal powers, and real Constitutional barriers can be developed once again.

Second, I also would suggest the development of a new doctrine based upon a new interpretation of the principle of full faith and credit. This principle, which is included in the Constitution with regard to interstate relations, also could become very important with regard to federal–state and even federal–state–local relations. If the federal government serving the larger arena would, as a matter of Constitutional comity, extend full faith and credit to the actions of the state and local governments, serving the smaller arenas, the problem of federal encroachment would be reduced substantially.

This idea of full faith and credit is something on the order of the principle of *bundesfreundlichkeit*, which the German federal constitutional court has developed into a constitutional doctrine to foster better intergovernmental relations. It is the kind of comity based upon constitutional obligation that prevents overly narrow, self-serving interpretations of constitutional matters by the parties involved. It is another way in which to demonstrate Chief Justice John Marshall's great dictum that, "it is a Constitution we are expounding." Just as that means broad powers of interpretation to keep the Constitution from becoming too narrow a contract, so too should it mean broad willingness to be considerate of one's partners in the federal system.

INDEX

National Industrial Recovery Act of 1933, New Deal, 51–53
National Institute of Municipal Law Officers, 67
National Labor Relations Act of 1935, 54
   legality, 55, 132
National League of Cities, public interest group, 21
   Nation's Cities Weekly, 216n
   tax reform position, 217
National League of Cities versus *Usery*, minimum wage, 59, 60, 231
   national regulations, 65, 231
   overturned, 60n, 231n
National minimum wage, upheld, 56
   applied to states and localities, 59, 60, 231
National Municipal League, 144
National Republican Party, 117, 118
National Recovery Administration, New Deal, 51–53
Nationalist interpretation, v. states' rights, 7, 8
Necessary and proper clause, xvi
   description, 31–33
   McCulloch decision, 35, 36
   unitary federalism, 7
Needs Survey, wastewater treatment, 252, 253, 264
Neubauer, Deane E., 276n
New Deal (*see also* Grants-in-aid)
   grants, 14, 29
   discussion, 50–57, 72–74
   turning point, 130–133
   coalition, 132
   legacy, 137
New Federalism (*see* Grants-in-aid)
New Jersey plan, constitutional convention, 31
New Partnership, Carter's proposals, 81, 82
New York Times, libel rules, 68
   deinstitutionalization, 284, 285
   national regulations, 234
   Reagan's swap, 195, 196
   traffic deaths, 284
New York Times versus *Sullivan*, libel, 68
Nichols, Albert, 241n
Nixon, Richard M., (*see also* Grants-in-aid)
   advocates decentralization, 283
   Aid to Families With Dependent Children proposal, 193, 248
   impounds wastewater treatment funds, 252
   New Federalism, 22, 23, 78–80, 87, 102
North Carolina versus *Califano*, national regulations, 61, 241
Northeast–Midwest Congressional Coalition, grant formulas, 261
Northwest Ordinance of 1787, 9

Occupational Safety and Health Act, 231, 241
Occupational Safety and Health Administration, 228, 234
Office of Management and Budget, Circular A-85, 78
   Circular A-95, 23, 80
Ogden, Aaron, Gibbons v. Ogden, 38
Oklahoma versus *Schweiker*, Medicaid, 63
Okum, Arthur M., 271n
Oleomargerine, interstate commerce, 45, 46
Omang, Johanne, 242n, 243n
Omnibus Crime Control and Safe Streets Act, 22, 158

Omnibus Budget Reconciliation Act of 1981, 83, 87, 105, 107, 158
"One man, one vote" principle, 64
Oppenheimer, Bruce, 97n
Orfield, Gary, congressional initiatives, 97
Ornstein, Norman, 99n, 106n
Ostrogorski, Moisel, 124n, 125n
Overmeyer, Allan, 96n

Packwood, Robert, tax reform proposal, 217
Page, Clint, 235n
Palley, Marian Lief, 25n
Parness, Jeffrey, 155n
Partial preemption, legality, 58, 59
   discussion, 233, 234
Partnership for Health Act, 22, 102, 158
Patterson, James T., 130n, 131n
Patterson, Samuel, 97n
Pear Robert, 196n
Peeters, Donovan, 147n
Peirce, Neal, 195n
   fiscal capacity, 201
Peltason, J. W., 5n, 6n
Pennhurst State School and Hospital versus *Haldeman*, national regulations, 64
Per capita income, fiscal capacity measure, 202, 203
Perkins, Carl, special revenue sharing, 103
Perry, George L., 271n
Peterson, George E., 157n
Peterson, William, 198n
Picket fence federalism, description, 21, 22
Pierce, Franklin, vetoes funds for the insane, 119, 120
Plessy versus *Ferguson*, civil rights, 65
Political parties, congressional elections, 95, 96, 106
   decentralization theory, 106, 137
   historical development, pre-1828, 112–116
      early 1900s, 127–133
      1800s, 116–127
      1940s and 1950s, 133–135
      post-1960, 106, 107, 135–137
   strong state parties advocated, 287
Polsby, Nelson W., 96n, 125n
Populist Party, 126–128
Pottker, Janice, 101n
Pound, William, 148n
Post, C. Gordon, 120n
Presidential initiatives (*see also* Grants-in-aid)
   Roosevelt to Reagan, 73–86
Presidential Task Force on Regulatory Relief, 28, 83–85
Price, David, 97n
Price, H. Douglas, 125n
Progressives, 12, 13, 44–48
Pressman, Jeffrey L., xxii
Public interest groups, listed, 20
Public Utilities Holding Act of 1935, 54
Public Works Administration, New Deal, 51
Public Works Employment Act of 1976, 99
Pure Food and Drug Act, 46
Pyne, Timothy, 156n

Quebec, Canada, formula allocations, 266